fri 19th Dec

sun 21st Dec

mon 22nd Dec

tues 23rd Dec

DAVID
KIMCHE

GW01192032

Produced for the Politics Association

Studio 16, 1-Mex Business Park,
Hamilton Road, Manchester M13 0PD

Series Editor Duncan Watts

Other titles in this series;

Introducing International Politics
Peter M Jones

Introducing The European Union
Duncan Watts

Introducing Concept and Doctrines in British Politics
Ian Adam and Bill Jones

NB   The views expressed by the writers in this series are personal ones.
They do not necessarily represent those of the Politics Association.

Sheffield Hallam University Press
Learning Centre
City Campus
Pond Street
Sheffield S1 1WB

First published 1997

Designed and typeset by Design Studio, Learning Centre, Sheffield Hallam University

©2003   ISBN 0 086339 6577

 *Sheffield Hallam University*

COMPARATIVE GOVERNMENT

Alan Davies

About the Author

Alan Davies is the Principal Examiner for Edexcel Politics Route D (International Politics). A graduate of the London School of Economics he gained a Distinction in the MSc in Politics and Public Administration at Birkbeck College. He is the Principal of Wentworth Tutorial College in Hendon, London and has taught Comparative Government for the last 20 years.

Acknowledgements

I am much indebted to the various people who have helped with the writing of this book, the errors are of course all mine. Firstly, Duncan Watts the editor of the series who has been extremely patient and understanding throughout and everyone at SHU Press and Sheffield Hallam, especially Monica Moseley for being so efficient. Secondly everyone at Edexcel. Thirdly, the various embassies, The Guardian and the political parties who allowed use of the pictures included. Fourthly, Richard Ball Publishing who published some of this material in a different form several years ago and have allowed it to be reproduced here. Fifthly, the staff and students at Wentworth Tutorial College especially the college administrator Karen Nedas and her assistant Sandy Spencer, my Head of Department Jody Newman, Manuel Guimaraes and the Politics class of 2003, another vintage year.

Last, but not least, I want to thank my wife Diane and our three sons, William, Joshua and Harry for putting up with an all too often absent husband and father. I would like to dedicate this book to them with much love although I suspect that they would rather read 'Harry Potter'. I hope the same is not true of everyone who reads this book.

Preface

What follows is an attempt to discuss some of the main features of the British and American political systems. It ought to be of use to anyone studying Comparative Government and Politics at either A level, whatever the exam board, or undergraduate level.

The book begins with a discussion of some of the key concepts in politics such as democracy, the state, totalitarianism and so on. We then look at constitutions and in particular the constitutions of the UK and the USA. Chapters 3, 4 and 5 look at the three branches of government; the legislature, the executive and the judiciary.

Chapters 6, 7 and 8 are concerned with the 'mobilisation of bias' and look at the role of pressure groups, parties and the media. In Chapter 9 we consider electoral systems before ending with a look at the relationships between the central government and the various local and regional authorities. Recommendations for further reading are to be found at the end of the book.

Contents

Chapter 1
Democracy

What follows is an attempt to discuss some of the main features of the British and American political systems.

Because the book is most concerned with two liberal democracies it addresses the key concepts employed in such systems, such as representation, sovereignty, democracy and pluralism. In order to contrast Western notions of politics with the supposed totalitarian regimes of the Communist world, it is necessary to consider concepts and institutions drawn from such models. It is important to avoid simplistic notions and dichotomies such as democracy versus totalitarianism. Similarly whilst the UK and the USA are both examples of liberal democratic regimes, there are so many differences that it makes little sense to see them as paradigms of a particular pluralist approach. It is also necessary to put the British and American political systems into an historical context. Before we can do any of this though, we need to explore some basic political concepts such as the state, democracy and power.

The State

The state, in Max Weber's often quoted definition, is an institution which claims a monopoly of legitimate force over a given territorial area. The

1

term nation refers to a group of people who share a similar cultural outlook and are often bound by ties of language, religion and ethnicity. We talk of nation-states whereby the cultural formation (which is the nation) has found political expression in a state of its own, based on self determination. The concept of the nation state only entered political theory in the 16th century. According to Weber, nation states have three characteristics: a territory, a population, and a government. Palestine as of 2003 clearly does not comprise a state because although there is a Palestinian nation which, despite the Palestinian Diaspora lives largely in the territory claimed by the Palestinian government, there is no sovereign Palestinian authority able to exercise a monopoly of the legitimate use of force within that territory.

Sovereignty is the right to the exclusive regulation of the legitimate use of physical force within a given area, in other words supreme authority. It was first described by Jean Bodin writing in the late 16th century about the power of the 'New Monarchies' which had established the trappings of the modern state. This gave rise to concerns as to whether the sovereign power, what Hobbes called Leviathan, could be resisted by its own subjects and whether it was bound by its own laws. Hobbes claimed that the alternative to subjection to the Sovereign power is the jungle, where life is 'nasty, brutish and short'. However, in response to the violation of natural law and natural rights by the sovereign other theorists developed ideas of civil disobedience. The idea of limited government, by which the sovereign is limited by law, began to emerge.

In the 17th century, following the English Civil War and the Glorious Revolution the contract theorist John Locke argued that there are advantages in accepting the restraints of civil society in order to preserve life, liberty and property. This led on to an emphasis on liberties, separation of powers and restraints on government. This is the origin of what we call liberalism with its concern for the sovereignty of the individual. The individual needs the **protection of the state**, property needs to be protected, contracts need to be upheld, but the individual also needs **protection against the state** which is potentially tyrannical. This view was particularly prevalent in the English speaking world.

In the 19th century the Prussian theorist Hegel argued that: "The nation state is the highest form of social organisation .. People must therefore work in a united way for the benefit of the state." This is a very different conception of the state to that of classical liberalism which favoured a very limited degree of state intervention. C20th Liberals such as Popper saw Hegel as one of the antecedents of totalitarian thought.

Even within the liberal democracies there are important differences over attitudes towards the state. David Marquand argues that the UK and the USA have a more negative attitude towards the state than for example Germany, France and Japan which he characterises as **developmental states**. An important reason for the divergence is that in the Anglo-American cases industrialisation took place largely without state direction but on the more corporatist continent the state took a more active role for reasons of national security and power.

Totalitarianism

The most statist of the ideologies which have arisen since the French Revolution was Fascism and its German variant Nazism. The Italian theorist Gentile argued that Italian Fascism was totalitarian because it embraced and synthesised all sectors of Italian society. However historians of totalitarianism such as Arendt have claimed that Italian Fascism was in practice autocratic rather than totalitarian because there were always centres of autonomy in particular the Church and the Monarchy. Arendt believed that the most totalitarian of the European political systems was the USSR under Stalin. Engels had said that the state always served the interests of the dominant class, under Communism there would be no classes therefore the state would wither away. In fact the state became all encompassing under Stalinism. Arblaster argues that totalitarianism is an ideological notion developed during the Cold War by liberal theorists such as Arendt, Popper, Brzezinski and Talmon as a way of conflating Nazism and Communism and 'proving' the superiority of open, liberal societies. The Cold War ended by 1991 with 'victory' for the West. It is because Communism is on the retreat all over the world that Fukuyama talks of **the end of history** as liberal capitalism faces no global challengers.

3

Power

Power is a very difficult concept to define clearly. According to Max Weber, power is: "the chance of a man or a number of men to realise their own will in a communal action, even against the resistance of others who are participating in that action."

In its most basic form, the exercise of power depends on being able to use force. Often the threat rather than the actual use of force is enough. Weber distinguished power from authority. In most situations one person obeys another not because they are frightened but because they accept the right of that person to give instructions. Authority is legitimate or morally justifiable power. According to Rousseau 'the strongest is never strong enough unless he can turn power into consent, might into obligation'.

In the context of the authority of the state, Weber distinguished three 'ideal types' of authority: traditional as with a Monarch and hereditary peers, charismatic exemplified by Hitler, Gandhi, Martin Luther King and Nelson Mandela and legal rational authority such as either an elected MP or an appointed bureaucrat possess.

Charismatic leaders, Gandhi and King

The Marxist View of Power

According to Marxists, such as Westergaard and Resler, capitalist society is run by and for capitalists. Whatever the formal democratic trappings, power in Britain and America is concentrated in the hands of a capitalist elite and the state serves the interests of the 'bourgeoisie', the ruling class..

Bachrach and Baratz saw power as the ability to set the agenda: "limiting the scope of the political process to public consideration of only those issues which are comparatively innocuous to the powerful". In the 1950s, the American radical, C Wright Mills, argued that American politics was actually dominated by a pro-capitalist 'Power Elite'. It did not really matter whether a Democratic or Republican administration was in power in Washington because they both served the interests of 'big business'. The same could be said of other supposedly pluralist systems. Thus the fact that the French Socialists were in power from 1981 to 1995 made little difference to French society because radicalism was constrained by the demands of the French elites.The 'New Labour' government of Blair accept the capitalist order and reject redistributive policies, indeed Britain is now a more unequal society after 6 years of Labour Government.

Ralph Miliband an instrumental Marxist analysed the extent to which a ruling class directly controls capitalist states such as Britain. Most High Court Judges, Mandarins, Cabinet Ministers and Army Commanders were educated at one of the leading public schools followed by Oxbridge. Structuralist Marxists such as Althusser argue that it does not matter what the class background of state officials is, under capitalism the state will always serve the interest of big business. Poulantzas agrees that the state has relative autonomy from capital which allows it to appear neutral. Capital is itself divided into fractions and the state is able to reconcile their different interests. However ultimately the state does serve big business as became clear when capital experienced a crisis after the 1970s and the state began to erode welfare.

Pluralists believe that the state under capitalism is neutral so that when a party wins office in an election it is able to take power whereas Marxists

5

believe that capitalist democracy is simply a sham helping to obscure the true reality that power is exercised by a ruling class.

Ultimately arguments between pluralists and Marxists are not resolved empirically because the two sides are using different notions of power.

Ideology

Ideology is an over-worked word; it has merely become a label to be tied to doctrines which we dislike, a synonym for 'doctrinaire' and 'dogmatic'. Yet all coherent political doctrines are ideological, a set of logically integrated general ideas that can be used to interpret and evaluate political, social and economic issues. According to the Italian Marxist Gramsci 'Ideologies create the terrain on which men move, acquire consciousness of their position, and struggle'. Marx argued that ideological beliefs reflected the particular interests and aspirations of hostile social classes. Ideology was subservient to the interests of the ruling groups which presided over the dissemination of social knowledge.

The dominant ideology operated through deception, it provided false pictures of a harmonious political order. All human thought, ideas and theories (consciousness) were determined by material factors (social circumstances). The economic structure of society determined all its other aspects - social relations, political forms, law, morality, knowledge. According to Marx, capitalism fosters two antagonistic classes, the bourgeoisie and the proletariat. Capitalist ideology may 'resolve' class conflict by emphasising the common interests and harmony between the classes, bourgeoisie and proletariat, or the organic nature of society but cannot alter the real antagonism between the interests of those classes.

Democracy

The simplest and most common distinction between systems of government is that of democracy versus dictatorship. Dahl argues that democracy is a political system in which the opportunity to participate in decisions is widely shared among all adult citizens. A dictatorship is a political system in which the opportunity to participate in decisions is restricted to a few. China appears to conform to the latter description because there is an increasing degree of economic freedom but alongside an almost complete absence of political rights whilst Russia, whatever the flaws in the system, appears closer to the former.

In 19th century Britain democracy was a term of abuse, used to describe rule by the uneducated, dangerous, 'mob'. Victorian politicians pointed to America and Australia as evidence of the undesirability of majority rule yet today it is almost always used in a positive sense and if an institution such as the European Union or a state such as, arguably, the UK, suffers from a **democratic deficit** then this as seen as detrimental.

Nations define democracy in different ways. The Soviet Union and the former Communist nations of Eastern Europe appeared to Western eyes to be closed, totalitarian societies. However their constitutions proclaimed them to be 'people's democracies'. The Soviet Constitution of 1977 contained commitments to the classic democratic rights and liberties of the individual including freedom of speech and freedom of belief and it also enshrined (enshrined) equal rights for women. Supporters argued that Communist democracy was superior to Western bourgeois democracy which claims to guarantee political equality but tolerates chronic economic inequality which Marxists think is incompatible with 'true democracy'.

Over 2,000 years ago Aristotle distinguished types of government according to the number entitled to govern and in whose interests they governed.

		Rulers rule in the interests of	
		All	**Themselves**
The number of	One	Monarchy	Tyranny
citizens	Few	Aristocracy	Oligarchy
entitled	Many	Polity	Democracy
to rule is			

Aristotle thus saw dangers in democracy but he also believed it to be the least bad of the three self interested arrangements.

Tony Benn argues that citizens should ask the following questions of those with power over them; what powers have you got? who gave them to you? in whose interests do you use them? and how do we get rid of you? Abraham Lincoln gave perhaps the most succinct, favourable definition of democracy as 'government of the people, for the people and by the people'. It was not until 1920, and the 19th Amendment guaranteeing women the vote, that reality in the USA conformed to Lincoln's rhetoric. For a century after Lincoln's Emancipation Proclamation of 1863, Negroes in the 'Deep South' were deprived of their most basic civil rights by a variety of subterfuges such as the grandfather clause, the whites only primary, and, when these were ruled unconstitutional in 1944, by sheer intimidation. It was not until 1965 and the Voting Rights Act that the democratic process was extended to southern blacks.

Britain had overtaken America in the evolution towards universal adult suffrage. British adults had full democratic rights by 1928. These were extended in 1969 to include 18 year-olds. The voting age in America was also lowered to 18 by the 26th Amendment of 1971.

Direct Democracy

Liberal democracies at least give their citizens the right to choose their rulers, in that sense they are democratic, there is government by consent. Yet the right to a secret ballot, essential though it is, does not of itself constitute democracy. Rousseau argued that the surrender of individual rights was not made to the sovereign power but to the whole of society. The **social contract** is between all people who agree to forgo their natural freedom by constituting an organised state which is to act for all its members. Rousseau made the point that a four or five yearly vote in a ballot to elect representatives to the legislature did not amount to democracy; what he favoured was direct democracy where the people made all the decisions themselves.

This was what the ancient Greeks had meant by democracy, except that they excluded slaves and Greek women. A form of direct democracy still exists in the Swiss Cantons, which employ referendums as a way of deciding policy, although again it is notable that until recently women could not vote in national elections in Switzerland. The small New England townships still try to decide important local issues through mass meetings. It is what Perot and Peter Mandelson have argued for, by-passing discredited political elites and allowing the people to make decisions directly via computers or interactive TVs.

Whether direct democracy is appropriate to nation states with millions of electors trying to decide immensely complicated policy issues such as the type of nuclear reactor to build or which kind of exchange rate regime is preferable is very debatable. Referendums have been used more frequently in the UK in recent years but only on constitutional issues such as devolution.

Democratic Centralism

Marx and Engels believed that historical materialism involved an inevitable sequence, feudalism, through capitalism, industrial capitalism followed by a revolution which would institute the dictatorship of the proletariat before giving way to Communism, the highest stage, in which there would be no classes and therefore no need for a state which would therefore wither away. Liberals such as Popper and Gellner believe the problem with Marxism is that it does not accept that its central tenets, historical materialism, have been falsified.

Lenin's seminal 'What is to be done?' written in 1902 gave his rationale for achieving Communism in a country which had not yet experienced an industrial revolution. In the absence of a sizeable proletariat a **vanguard party** would lead the workers to revolution. The party had to be based on an almost military discipline known as **democratic centralism**. 'The organisation must consist chiefly of people professionally engaged in revolutionary activity.'

The architects of the Soviet state, Lenin and Stalin

Developmental Democracy

When between the 1940s and the 1960s the European colonies in Asia and Africa were 'given' their independence they generally established western-style democratic systems. Few of the newly independent nations maintained a pluralist, liberal regime, many, such as Sudan, Pakistan, Egypt, Ghana, Nigeria and Indonesia became one-party states, what McPherson calls developmental democracies, or were taken over by military juntas. Very occasionally the military restored democracy. In Ghana Jerry Rawlings seized power in a coup but then put himself forward for election and won.

Democracy did survive in India, the world's largest democracy. The Indian National Congress Party has been in power for most of the time since independence in 1947. Eurocentric approaches to democracy also ignore Japan where since the Second World War a liberal democratic regime has presided over an economic miracle. Japan is, or at least was, a good example of a **dominant one party system** in that the same party, the Liberal Democrats, controlled the government from 1955 to 1993. This led to corruption and scandal. However a dominant one party system is a world away from a one party state and anyway external reasons accounted for Japan's political system, in particular the Cold War and the influence of America. Japan's politics had much in common with India. Both were run for most of the past 50 years by a single party whose dominance stifled the growth of viable alternatives thereby depriving the voters of any real choice and allowing the ruling parties to grow fat on corruption and pork barrel politics. The defeat of the ruling Liberal Democrats in Japan in 1993 started a still unfinished process of democratisation.

The evolution towards democracy in Western Europe took a long time and it did not prevent European nations from embracing Imperialism, Fascism and Communism along the way, therefore the idea that only Europeans are capable of sustaining democracy is nonsense.

Pluralism

Even among western-style liberal democracies, such as Germany, France, the USA and Britain, there are major differences in the degree to which openness and pluralism characterise the political system. France is a highly centralised nation, a legacy of the revolution and the Napoleonic era. Education in France, for example, is rigidly controlled from the centre. Germany is a federal state, a legacy of the pre-1871 era when there was no such thing as a German nation. Federalism survived until 1933, when it was destroyed by Hitler. However, it was re-born in the 1949 constitution which guarantees certain rights to the Lander. The UK is a unitary state; power became more centralised in the 1980s and 1990s but devolution has now been introduced.

The USA remains the best example of a federal system although even here the way that federalism has developed in the 20th century bears little resemblance to what the Founding Fathers envisaged. Politics has been to a large extent 'nationalised' in America since the New Deal of the 1930s. Germany has a different form of Federalism. There is a great deal of subsidiarity and intergovernmentalism; the Lander employs most of the bureaucrats, and the Federal Government is relatively small. Canada is another Federal state and here regional autonomy is so great that Quebec actually had a referendum on its constitutional future.

Despite their difference over central-local government relationships, all these states are regarded as liberal democracies because they guarantee fundamental freedoms such as religious toleration, fair and free elections, press freedom, the right to form pressure groups, to demonstrate, to strike, in short the right to dissent. None of these freedoms are absolute. For example, in Germany, there are restrictions on 'extremist' parties such as the neo-Nazis and the Communists.

The alleged defects of the electoral system render British democracy less than perfect. In the British election of 1950 turn out was 84%, by 2001 it was down to 59%. In some of the poorest inner city areas it was much lower, in West Newcastle in 1992 it was just 20%. One in five young people are not on the register, neither are 24% of Afro-Caribbean's and 15% of Asians. Membership of all parties is falling and ageing, almost 75% of Liberal Democrat members are above 46. Yet a study by Parry and Moyser 'Political Participation and Democracy in Britain' (1991) found that a more educated citizenry given more political information by the media was becoming more involved politically particularly in environmental issues. Low turn out in 2001 was a major problem. The opposite extremes were Winchester with 72.4% and Liverpool Riverside with 34.1%. Over 13 million people voted in the final stages of Big Brother, more than for any party in 2001. Amongst 18-24 year olds turnout was only 38%, among voters over 64 it was 79%. A study by the Hansard Society show that young people were not apathetic rather they felt alienated from the political system because they felt ill informed. Hain has argued for compulsory voting as in Australia.

The Electoral Commission was established in 2000 to register political parties, oversee a new transparent regime for donations, to control election spending and to oversee and review the conduct of elections and referendums. New limits have been set for party spending on campaigns, Reforms to registration and voting procedures and experiments with postal and electronic voting etc are to be introduced to facilitate wider registration and participation in voting. Homeless people and other excluded groups are given an effective right to vote. It is clearly too early

The Welfare State

By the time of the First World War, the role of the state had expanded enormously, as it began to provide more services, so it had to levy higher taxes. Two forces lay behind this challenge. Firstly, the extension of the franchise to working-class males, secondly, the rise of socialist movements throughout Europe. The logic of the interventionist state was that the richest people in society ought to pay more to help the poorest. Even the USA had introduced a progressive income tax by 1913. America lagged behind Europe in the provision of welfare; old age pensions, for instance, were not introduced in the USA until 1935, over 25 years after Britain and 50 years after Germany.

However, it was the Second World War, the 'People's War', that transformed the role of the State. In Britain, the acceptance of Keynesian economic policy was enshrined in the 1944 White Paper on Employment Policy whereby governments accepted as one of their prime responsibilities, "the maintenance of a high and stable level of employment". In the United States, the Employment Act of 1946, although watered down by the Republicans in Congress, accepted a similar commitment to full employment and created the Economic Advisory Council to help the President monitor the state of the economy.

The long post-war boom of 1948-1973 seemed to vindicate the Keynesian orthodoxy. Keynesianism was one of the two pillars of the post-war consensus, the other was the concept of the welfare state. Those such as Frederick von Hayek who opposed 'welfare statism' because it was 'The Road to Serfdom' were in a very small minority.

By the 1960s, most advanced industrial nations had created some form of welfare state although the degree of state provision varied widely. The Scandinavian countries led the field, the USA lagged behind. However, even the USA, after a 20-year struggle, introduced schemes such as Medicare, Medicaid and the Food Stamp Programme.

Apart from material inequalities, a more serious charge against liberal democracies would be that there is still great inequality in political power and influence. Most people have no easy access to the news media or to the high officials in the government. British society is renowned for its elitism.

Marxists argue that the owners of wealth have made some limited concessions to non-owners so as to preserve their relative positions. The right to vote, the right to social security and the right to a free national health service were given to the working people as a 'sop', so as to ensure that dissatisfaction over economic inequalities did not erupt into serious social unrest or revolution. Citizenship is a disguise which masks continuing inequalities of wealth and power.

The Welfare State in Crisis

As the optimism of the boom decades, the 1950s and 1960s gave way to the 'new depression' in the 1970s, 1980s and 1990s, so the welfare states which were created in the 'age of affluence' have come in for criticism. Within the liberal democracies, there are disputes as to what direction the welfare state ought to take with even independent minded Labour MPs such as Frank Field beginning to think the unthinkable about targeting welfare. Field was briefly a Junior Minister working on restructuring the Welfare State.

In the USA traditional Democrats favour the extension of state welfare whereas the Republicans and 'New Democrats' want to trim back welfare. In 1992 Clinton pledged to 'end welfare as we have known it'. However when reform came in August 1996 it was a Republican inspired measure. Aid for Dependent Children was terminated by Clinton in 1996 with the Personal Responsibility and Work Opportunity Reconciliation Act. An individual can only receive welfare for 5 years during their entire adult lifetime. Within 2 years of receiving welfare claimants must work. This was a major move way from *welfare towards workfare*. Clinton reluctantly signed it, despite Democrat opposition, because an election was looming. Clinton did manage to defend Medicare, which is more popular, from a similar attack.

It is not only in Britain and the USA that the post-war consensus has been challenged. The New Right philosophy has had a big impact throughout the liberal democracies. In West Germany, the Social Democrats, in power from 1969 to 1982, gave way to Kohl's Conservative government. In Australia the Labour government led initially by Bob Hawke and then Paul Keating introduced measures which many would regard as right-wing and reaped an electoral reward until 1996 when the unpopularity of Keating saw Labour defeated.

The success of this approach did not mean a return to the 19th century or even inter-war conception of the proper role of the state. There has been a great deal of 'privatisation' in the UK and 'de-regulation' in the USA but neither has gone as far as the 'New Right' desire. In Britain the degree of public support for institutions such as the NHS places limits on the extent to which public expenditure can be cut. In fact public spending has gone up, in real terms, in both Britain and the USA since the 1980s. In the USA this resulted in a budget deficit of over $200 billion dollars a year by 1993. Although governments have changed their approach to economic management and the provision of welfare, there is no easy way of reducing the role of the state in 20th century democracies.

Left-wing critics argue that the New Right substitute a consumerist model of citizenship for the real thing as with Major's Citizens Charters. According to Democratic Audit 'poverty and inequality run deeper in the UK than in any comparable European country, with nearly a quarter of the population living below the official poverty line (60% of median income), this includes one third of all children.' The Blair government have promised to eradicate child poverty within a few years. New Labour emphasise welfare to work as opposed to old Labour who believed in cradle to grave welfare. Their stress is on full employability through education and training rather then the traditional left wing goal of full employment.

Social Divisions in Britain

In order to understand politics it is necessary not just to consider the structure of government but also the nature of the society. Finer argued decades ago that whereas some European states are divided by religion, or language the UK is divided by class. In the USA race, religion and region are said to be the dominant cleavages. There is an ethnic dimension to British politics but the number of non-whites is tiny in comparison with

17

the USA. The total non-white population of the UK is probably less than 4 million, about 7% of the total.

The 1964 election had seen Tory candidates in East London and the Midlands play the race card. In 1968 Enoch Powell gave the notorious 'rivers of blood speech' and in 1978 when still Opposition leader Thatcher had made her infamous comments about British people feeling 'swamped' by immigrants. One result of all this is that black voters consistently support Labour. Shamit Saggar points out that in the 1987 election 72% of black voters (that is Afro-Caribbean as well as Asian) backed Labour and that this was in line with all elections since 1974 despite the aggressive 1983 Tory campaign featuring a picture of a smart young black man over the slogan 'Labour says he's black, we say he's British'.

Afro-Caribbean voters appear more solidly pro-Labour than Asians, in 1987 86% of the former group and 67% of the latter supported Labour, partly confirming the much heralded mushrooming of Asian support for the Tories. However the 1992 election saw Labour continue to be the beneficiary of votes from both groups. A report from the Commission for Racial Equality showed that 29% of ABC1 ethnic minority voters supported the Tories whilst for white ABC1s the figure was 41%. The 1997 and 2001 elections confirmed this picture. 76% of blacks and 69% of Asian voters supported Labour in 2001, whilst the Conservatives got just 9% and 11% respectively. This would suggest that black support for Labour is based on more than just class but obviously this is a very difficult issue to be precise about.

Religion has not been a serious political issue on mainland Britain since the turn of the century, in Northern Ireland it is *the* key issue. The Church of England was formerly described as the 'Tory party at prayer' but those days are long since over. It was often said that Catholics were more likely to vote Labour but that is because they were more likely to be working class. Hindus and Moslems are more likely to vote Labour but then presumably that has nothing to do with religion in just the same way as the Jewish community's preference for the Tories is because of the British Jewish community's socio-economic status rather than any doctrinal affiliation.

There is a regional divide in Britain and it probably became more pronounced after 1979 as the Conservatives became the party of *England*, as opposed to *Britain*, in particular South East England. Labour is the party of the Celtic fringe, the North of England and the inner cities. At the 1992 election the Tories won 209 out of 261 seats in the South of England, 57 out of 100 in the Midlands but just 53 out of 161 in the North. Labour won 107 of the Northern seats. At the 1997 election the Conservatives did not win a single seat in Scotland or Wales and in effect became the party of the English countryside. In 2001 they won one seat in Scotland. Thus there is a North-South divide, even so it is too small a country for sectionalism on the scale of the USA. Hence Finer's conclusion that the cleavage that really counts in Britain is class.

America is often portrayed as a society free of class division in which the only thing that counts about someone is how hard they work, not who their father was - achievement, rather than ascription, is the source of status. This is meant to help account for the lack of a European style Socialist movement and the acceptance by the American worker of the virtues of capitalism. The British Trade Unions and the old Labour Party supposedly never really accepted the need for the profit motive.

According to historians such as Martin Weiner there has always been and is still an anti-commercial snobbery about the British elite. Both sides of the political divide, Labour and Tory, unions and managers, blame the outdated class system for many of the ills afflicting British industry causing her relative economic decline.

One of the problems with the whole debate about class is that the terms are very vague and need to be clarified. Clearly class is dependent on more than income differentials, it implies something about lifestyle, home ownership, attitudes towards education and work, the degree of job security and so on.

Class lines have supposedly blurred in industrial, or post-industrial societies and theorists such as Gorz have bid 'farewell to the working class'. Not everyone agrees with post-modernist or post-industrial ideas about the decline of class allegiance and the rise of new social divisions. Commentators such as Gordon Marshall stress that Britain remains a society structured by social class and talk of a classless society is pure rhetoric. There is still a wealthy elite and there is still a poverty problem, indeed the number of poor people is growing. In a country where the distribution of wealth and income is left to market forces, as in the case of the UK and the USA in the last two decades, greater inequalities are found.

The policy of cutting taxes for individuals and corporations in order to generate a high level of economic growth, the fruits of which would *trickle down* to the poor, has not achieved its aim. The opposite has happened, income inequality has been deliberately widened. Between 1979 and 1988 the take-home pay of the top 10% non-manual employees rose by 41% while, for the bottom 10% of manual workers, the increase was 1.7%. **Half of all the tax and benefits changes of 1979-97 ended up in the pockets of the richest tenth of the population.**

It is the case that nearly two-thirds of households now own their own home. Together with the enormous boost that privatisation has given to share ownership - from 6% of the population in 1984 to 20% in 1988 - this was the basis of Thatcher's claim to have built a 'people's capitalism'. In 1981, the bottom 50% owned just 6% of all marketable wealth, by 1985 this had increased to 7% - so much for a property and share-owning democracy. When it comes to wealth which confers economic power, rather than simply more security, the same people appear to be in the driving seat. The proportion of those in higher' education who went to public school has stuck at 25%. The proportion for Oxbridge is 50% and yet only 7% of all children attend private schools.

The whole basis of class division in the industrialised nations is in a state of flux as economic change breaks up old class patterns. All over the industrialised world the older, heavy industries such as coal, shipbuilding, the iron and steel industries and heavy engineering where the majority of manual workers were employed, are in decline. The new jobs are being created in the service sector but they tend to be non-manual jobs often lacking in skill content and very vulnerable to mechanisation. Often they are done by part-time women workers who are difficult to enrol in unions, they form a peripheral labour market.

Social Divisions in the USA

The debate about political correctness has opened up some very raw wounds about what constitutes 'Americanness'. Liberals such as Schlesinger are concerned to avoid a fragmentation, a ghettoisation of American society. The successful assimilation of refugees from Vietnam and Kampuchea is evidence that the American 'melting pot' still exists. So well, in fact, have the recent Asian immigrants adapted that they are excelling at the most prestigious universities and 'WASPs' are being exhorted to work harder and learn from these refugees from Communism. Immigrants have often been disappointed with what they found, but that impulse to search for a more tolerant society has had an abiding impact on American life.

It would be very naive to imagine that everyone in the USA really is politically equal or that all pressure groups have equal access to the levers of power. Barely half of those entitled to do so bother to vote in Presidential elections. There are clearly an enormous number of people who feel alienated from the political system. Studies show that the non-voters tend to be young, poor, ill educated, Black or Hispanic. They are non-voters not because they are happy with the system but because they feel excluded from it. They form part of a disturbingly large and growing underclass which lives in the ghettos of the conurbations such as New York, Chicago and Los Angeles and periodically erupts in riots. They live in grinding poverty alongside, but not part of, the opulent affluence of one of the richest nations in the world.

Neither the Republicans nor the Democrats (Jesse Jackson excepted) seem able to entice such people into the political mainstream. The fear of course is that unless such groups have access to the political system then they will resort to non-democratic methods such as rioting. The middle class in contrast is articulate and well organised. They form pressure groups to fight for the causes they believe in and the politicians take notice because such people have the resources to make their voices heard.

It is obvious that America is a very unequal society; wealth and income are not even as evenly distributed as in Britain. As the American economist Felix Rohatyn stresses the US taxation system is less progressive than throughout Europe. The capitalist ethos demands that there must be incentives, otherwise no one will bother to work hard. It presupposes *equality of opportunity*, but not *equality of outcome* because that requires too much state control. Private provision, of for example health care and education, is assumed to be superior to state provision. This explains the lack of a national health service in America; individuals (except for the old and the very poor) have to provide for the possibility of illness through private insurance.

America is a more meritocratic society; it never had a feudal system and the essence of the 'American Dream' is that anyone can make it to the top provided they have talent and work hard. The legend of 'log cabin to White House' still has a powerful impact on American culture. Many Presidents, especially Richard Nixon, have emphasised, perhaps exaggerated, their lowly origins.

According to surveys, the majority of Americans regard themselves as middle class. However, the recession of the post-1973 era has made people very fearful over job security with even the middle class afraid of downsizing. Marxists such as Harry Braverman argue that a middle class, non-manual worker is just as much part of the labour force as the more traditional 'old working class' of skilled men. This is the 'proletarianisation thesis'. Thus bank clerks need the protection of a trade union just as much as carpenters; both are at the 'mercy' of capitalist forces. According to this analysis, the 'contradictions of capitalism' will bring about a crisis similar to that in the 1930s and all of the rhetoric about the end of the 'class war' will be exposed as hollow. America is just as class ridden as Britain, only Americans do not realise it.

There has been much talk in recent years about 'declining social capital' in the USA. Robert Putnam in a very influential book, 'Bowling Alone', argues that there is a decline in participation across the spectrum from churches to unions to voting to team sports. However others such as Ronald Inglehart claim that the US is now a 'post-material society' in which people are increasingly concerned by issues such as the environment, sexual behaviour and lifestyle choice. Even Putnam accepts that after September 11th 'we Americans have surprised ourselves in our solidarity'. The British commentator Jonathon Freedland is impressed by the participatory nature of American democracy at local level and contrasts it with the overly deferential political culture of the UK. On the other hand the USA has a vast prison population. The Democratic Audit points out that the UK has the highest imprisonment rate in the EU after Portugal with severe overcrowding, insanitary conditions and curtailed rehabilitation programmes as a consequence.

Race and Ethnicity in the USA

Social scientists see the term race as a social construction, they prefer the term ethnicity. The term black has gone from being a term of abuse to a term of pride as in 'black is beautiful'. Jackson has argued that the term African-American is better because 'to be African-American is to have cultural identity, to look at your place on the map and the globe'.

Richard Polenberg's book 'One Nation Divisible; Class, Race and Ethnicity in the United States since 1938', emphasises the interrelated nature of issues of class and colour in America. There is a long running debate among sociologists over the nature of the black experience. Put simply, are the majority of American Negroes so disadvantaged because they are poor or because they are black? The answer has crucial implications for race relations, the creation of a black middle class and the relationship between the black community and other ethnic minorities such as the Hispanics.

America is perhaps a special case because of the legacy of slavery and segregation, but actually rather similar questions about the relationship between class and race are pertinent to Britain where members of the ethnic minorities are among the poorest people in British society. The Labour Party assumes that it is the natural home for the less privileged whatever their colour. However, increasingly the Conservatives and the Liberals are trying to challenge this by arguing that they too speak for the ethnic minorities.

Slavery had been abolished in the USA in 1865 and the blacks were supposedly given constitutional rights by the 13th, 14th and Amendments ratified in the late 1860s. However White Southerners had introduced **De Jure Segregation** which, despite the 14h Amendment, the Supreme Court upheld as constitutional in the case of Plessy vs. Ferguson (1896). In practice, the only people who could vote in the South were the whites. Starting in the 1950s, the Civil Rights Movement led by Martin Luther King, pressed for southern blacks to be given real equality. There was some progress, e.g. in Brown vs. Board of Education 1954 the Supreme Court overturned the Plessy judgement and ruled that segregation was unconstitutional.

In the summer of 1963, responding to pressure from King, JFK introduced a Civil Rights Bill. LBJ got Congress to pass the bill which became the Civil Rights Act 1964. He won a landslide victory in his own right in November 1964 and the Democrats won sweeping victories in Congress. He then persuaded the 89th Congress (1965-7) to pass a whole series of measures known collectively as the Great Society reforms. The Voting Rights Act of 1965 meant that southern blacks were finally enfranchised. LBJ persuaded Congress that the alternative to reform was even greater discord.

By the mid-1960s the non-violent protest movement of Martin Luther King and the NAACP had given way to Stokely Carmichael ("this nation from top to bottom is racist") and the Black Panthers. In 1963 there was trouble in Harlem; in 1965 in Watts, a ghetto in Los Angeles, 34 were killed and over 1,000 inured in a riot causing $40 million worth of damage; and in 1967 in Detroit 43 were killed and in Newark 26 died. It was a spontaneous outburst of anger from the "underclass" and revealingly (apart from a riot in Atlanta) it occurred not in the "racist" South but in the supposedly integrated North.

Whereas the South had practised "de jure" segregation backed up by law, the North and West had practised "de facto" segregation based on unequal job opportunities and segregated housing. It was less obvious but more hypocritical. Young, urban blacks rebelled against it, just at the very time that Johnson was doing more for blacks than anyone since Lincoln. Johnson responded by appointing the Kerner Commission which in its report blamed "white racism'. Kerner commented 'our nation is moving towards two separate societies, one white, one black - separate and unequal'.

The Nixon administration introduced quotas but by the 1970s the Right was very strongly opposed to them. The Reagan administration had been very influenced by New Right thinkers such as Nathan Glazer and Irving Kristol who opposed what they saw as the liberal consensus on civil rights led by the NAACP, the Leadership Conference on Civil Rights, the National Urban League and the ACLU. They supported the right of Christians to preserve their private schools even where they did not have any significant numbers of ethnic minority students. The composition of the Civil Rights Commission was shifted to the right. Congress overturned Reagan's veto in spring 1988 and passed the Civil Rights Restoration Act to strengthen the scope for Federal government regulation of institutions which discriminated and to overcome the Grove City v Bell judgement of 1984.

Bush had voted against the Civil Rights Act of 1964 although later he appeared to change his mind. He vetoed the Civil Rights Act in October 1990 which attempted to reverse the Supreme Court decision in Wards Cove in 1989. Griggs v Duke Power Company of 1971 had outlawed tests which seemed to benefit whites more than blacks unless they were essential to a company's survival but the Cove case reversed this. Bush signed the Civil Rights and Women's Equity in Employment Act in October 1991 and this overturns Wards but it remains to be seen how the courts will interpret it. Bush had only one African-American in his cabinet, the Health Secretary Louis Sullivan. Three days into the LA Riots Bush called a conference of black leaders in the White House but it all seemed too little, too late after years of neglect and Clinton blamed the riots on 12 years of Republican rule.

The Position of Blacks in the USA Today

35 years after the murder of King the progress that has been made is extraordinary. De jure segregation is a thing of the past but blacks **have not caught up** at all and the majority of America's 31 million blacks remain underprivileged and in many cases alienated. Race obsesses America, look at the Rodney King trial when four Los Angeles policemen who had beaten a black driver 56 times after stopping him for speeding were acquitted leading to a riot in LA in April 1992.

The Thomas nomination, the O.J. Simpson acquittal, the 'million man march' on Washington, the controversy created by affirmative action, the debates about a politically correct education and the arguments of the 'Bell Curve' all show the centrality of racial politics. In November 1991 a former leader of the Klan, David Dukes, won 55% of the white vote in the Louisiana Gubernatorial election. He was defeated but only through the back vote. Colin Powell, now the Secretary of State, argued that both Dukes and Louis Farakhan, the black separatist, are unrepresentative; most people on both sides of the racial divide want harmony not conflict.

Every indicator of economic well being whether it be unemployment rates or poverty rates shows blacks doing far worse than whites. Black family income is 60% that of whites compared with 65% in 1970. Blacks are much more likely to be victims of violent crimes than whites, they form 12.8 % of the American population but 40% of those on death row. Black men have a 1 in 4 chance of going to prison during their lifetime compared to 1 in 6 for Hispanics and 1 in 23 for white men. America's black population exhibits far higher rates of coronary and lung disease, alcohol and drug dependency and they account for one third of AIDS cases. Black children do less well at school even though black college entrance levels are rising. The average black boy is more likely to go to prison than college. About two thirds of black children are born out of wedlock. National unemployment in 1994 was about 7% but among blacks it was over 14%. 1.46 million black men of a total black male voting population of 10.4 million have lost their right to vote due to a felony conviction. This may have had a big impact on the Florida election result in 2000.

There is a black middle class and the gulf between it and the rest of the black community is growing, literally, as black suburbanisation occurs. It is these blacks who have benefited from affirmative action. However blacks are much less likely than whites to be granted a mortgage and only 424,000 out of the 17.5 million US businesses were owned by blacks in 1992. In 1990 about 13.5% of the total population lived below the poverty line, for blacks the figure was 31.9% . The African-American sociologist Julius Wilson argues that these people are the 'truly disadvantaged'. In the South about 20% of the population is black but only about 3 % of its congressmen are. The Congressional Black Caucus has grown in importance although

Reagan never once held a meeting with it during his 8 years as President. The blacks are so central to the Democrat coalition that when they stayed at home in November 1994, in protest at Clinton's failure to tackle the problems blacks face, then the Democrats were routed. Where blacks did turn out to vote as in the Virginia Senate race, then the Republican, in that case Oliver North, lost. The black vote was crucial to Clinton's re-election in 1996 and the mid-term elections of 1998.

The blacks remain the most reliable element of the 'Democrat Coalition'; in the 2000 election, 90% of black voters supported Gore. Jesse Jackson and other black leaders believe that the Democrats have taken black support for granted and Jackson's strategy is to make the party more aware of the needs of the ethnic minorities, hence the talk of a separate party, a 'Rainbow Coalition'. Jackson knows he has no chance of winning the Democratic nomination and there are many on the left who want him to demonstrate that there is a radical alternative to the 'pragmatic liberalism' of the Democratic Leadership Council.

However he is extremely unlikely to break from the Democrats because he knows a third party would be marginal and have less impact than he had fighting from within in 1988.

Ethnic and Religious Minorities

The Jews and Catholics were attracted to the Democrats because they regarded the Republicans as the party of WASPs - White Anglo Saxon Protestants. In 1960, the Democrat John Kennedy became the first Catholic President of the USA. Many of the ethnic minorities, such as the Poles, the Italians and the Irish, are predominantly Catholic. Figures such as ex-Governor Cuomo of New York typify the urban, ethnic appeal of the Democratic party. Similarly, the Democrat candidate in 1988, Governor Michael Dukakis of Massachusetts, appealed to Americans of Greek extraction.

The three big 'I's in American politics - Israel, Ireland and Italy - demonstrate the continuing importance of ethnic issues. It is often argued that the Jewish lobby has a disproportionate amount of power and that this enables them to direct American foreign policy. Certainly the lobby is always held up as an example of a successful pressure group, for example it targets political critics of Israel by giving PAC money to their opponents. It is seen as an example of a wealthy group which is able to buy political access, thereby safeguarding Israel's interests. Indeed the war on Iraq has been blamed on the Jewish pro-Israel clique within the Bush Administration.

However, it could be argued that the reason why American administrations since 1948 backed Israel is little to do with A.I.P.A.C. (American Israel Public Affairs Committee) - it was because of the Cold War. The US needed an ally in a sensitive region: Israel filled that role. If true, this would help explain why America under Bush-Baker took a tougher line with Israel once the Cold War was over. The refusal to extend loan guarantees and the pressuring of Israel over the Peace Process may indicate that the days when AIPAC was pushing at an open door are over. Islamic fundamentalism could be said to have replaced communism as the new threat. It is extremely difficult to prove either case and this is a good illustration of why the whole pluralist-elite theorist debate is so complex. The Jews continue to favour the Democrats, approximately 80% voted for Clinton in 1992 and 1996 and Gore in 2000, although Jewish support in US politics tends to have as much to do with the parties' attitudes towards Israel as with domestic concerns and both parties remain supportive of Israel.

Democrat Senators tried to block the ratification of an extradition treaty with Britain in case it offended Irish American voters and Democrat leaders including Clinton have been very welcoming to Sinn Fein leader Gerry Adams, Clinton was the most pro-Irish Nationalist President we have known and played a crucial role in the Northern Ireland Agreement of April 1998.

The Hispanics or Latinos amounted to 11.8% of the population in 2000 compared to African-Americans 12.8%. Hispanics, generally one of the poorer sections of American society, look to the Democrats as 'their' party. This however does not apply to the Cuban refugees of recent years who are virulently anti-Communist and tend to be pro-Republican. The Black Congressional Caucus argue that the black community, which outnumbers the Jewish community by about seven to one, ought to be able to wield the kind of influence over US foreign policy that the Jewish lobby has long wielded. The defeat of Reagan over the sanctions issue in 1986 is one of the few, the very few, occasions where US foreign policy has been pushed in a particular direction by pressure from the black community.

The Religious Right

The Founding Fathers aimed to build a 'wall' between Church and State so that religious persecution would be avoided. This is no abstract notion, it is constantly being tested in cases brought before the Supreme Court; for example the failed attempt by Christian fundamentalists to forbid the teaching of 'Darwinism'. The US is a much more religious society than the UK and this is reflected in the political system. Bush is a born again Christian but even Clinton held prayer meetings with the Reverend Jessee Jackson after the Lewinsky scandal became public. The Moral Majority founded in 1979 by Jerry Falwell campaign for a return to 'traditional' morality, they oppose abortion, favour school prayer, oppose pornography and the permissive society. They had been galvanised by opposition to Roe v Wade, feminism and the Equal Rights Amendment. They are closely associated with the 'New Right' and were big supporters of Reagan in 1980. They felt he had let them down somewhat by his failure to have Roe v Wade (1973) reversed or school prayer ruled constitutional. By 1988 the Christian Coalition led by Pat Robertson had taken the lead.

In 1992 Buchanan claimed that 'there is a religious war going on in this country for the soul of America. It is a cultural war, as critical to the kind of nation we shall be as the Cold War itself, for this war is for the soul of America and in that struggle for the soul of America Clinton and Clinton are on the other side and George Bush is on our side.' The forces of Buchanan and Pat Robertson had dictated terms to the 1992 Republican ticket with a no-exceptions anti-abortion amendment which Phyllis Schlafy described as 'total victory'. However the 'born again' right have always been rather suspicious of Bush and Dole, who they do not regard as true conservatives. The Christian Coalition under Ralph Reed backed Dole in 1996 and was even prepared to downplay the issue of abortion so as not to antagonise voters just as they were willing to let the abortion, homosexual and school prayer issues be left out of the 10 point Contract with America in case their hard line on these issues cost votes.

The abortion issue is an excellent example of pressure group activity. Whilst liberals and feminist groups such as NOW (National Organisation of Women) continue the fight for a 'woman's right to choose' and celebrate the anniversary of the Roe judgement, the anti-abortion 'Right to Life' lobby continue their struggle to have the judgement reversed They had a partial success with the Webster Judgement in 1989 but were disappointed by the failure of the Rehnquist Court to ban abortion in the Casey judgement of 1992.

The Christian Right were outraged by Clinton and in particular the Lewinsky scandal. They pushed moderate Republicans in Congress into voting for his impeachment. In the 2000 election white Protestants voted 63:34 in favour of Bush. Whereas in the past Catholics were predominantly Democrat millions are now voting Republican. In 2000 Catholics were 49:47 for Gore.

Liberal Democracy

Whilst recognising that democracy should be a fundamental human right rather than something specifically European we should not fall into the equivalent trap of assuming that liberal democracy is perfect.

One of the problems with the end of ideology debate of 40 years ago or the end of history debate of today is that in rejecting Communism and Nazism commentators sometimes endorse western liberal democracy and its associated market economy as beyond criticism. There are problems with liberal democracy which as we have seen is anyway not homogeneous and the same is true of 'capitalism'.

Theorists such as Ernest Laclau and Chantal Mouffe accept that western democracy as currently constituted is seriously flawed, in that it is elitist, patriarchal and conservative but they believe that a reinvigorated form of liberal democracy offers the best opportunity for an active citizenry and genuine government by consent.

Laclau and Mouffe believe that real politics operates outside the closed confines of Parliament and that New Social Movements such as the anti-globalisation movement demonstrate a live concern for rights and for principles. What is needed is some mechanism for 'uniting the fragments' and rejuvenating civil society. Carole Pateman has argued for a new 'sexual contract' which recognises that half the population are discriminated against by the other half.

These ideas are paralleled in the thinking of Paul Hirst who has called for 'Associative Democracy' based on the ideas of the early English pluralists such as G.D.H. Cole. David Held has demanded a cosmopolitan democracy which recognises the growing internationalisation of politics. It is fashionable to argue as David Held has done that we should bid 'Farewell to the Nation State' which is in long term decline. This is part of a supposed process of **globalisation** which means that more and more international constraints limit the autonomy of states and impinge more and more upon their sovereignty. This argument has been challenged by commentators such as Hirst who argues that the state remains the focus of political loyalty for citizens and even of economic loyalty for corporations. Certainly the concept of sovereignty is contentious and requires careful consideration.

It is probably best when considering Britain and the USA to employ the terms representative, liberal or pluralist democracy but even here there are problems because the two nations differ in their approach to important issues such as secrecy and the role of the judiciary. Russia after 1991 appears to conform more to the pluralist model, albeit a badly flawed version, than any other. China remains closer to our conception of totalitarianism whilst recognising that true totalitarianism is probably as unachievable as it is undesirable.

Democracy is a relative not an absolute concept and just because a policy has the approval of the majority, it does not necessarily make it morally right; popular support for Nazism is a good example of this. It is important not to take a 'holier than thou' stance when looking at systems very different to our own.

Chapter One

No political system is perfect. Churchill called democracy the worst system of government ever invented with the exception of all the others.

Having introduced some of the basic concepts it is now useful to look in detail at the way certain political systems are organised and it is necessary to begin with consideration of constitutions because they supposedly shape political systems.

Chapter 2
Constitutions

A constitution is effectively a set of rules regulating the relationship between the different organs of the state, between the state and the individual and between central government and the regions or localities. Constitutions can be written or unwritten although it is difficult to conceive of a constitution which would be entirely unwritten; therefore it is better to talk of codified and uncodified. Lots of questions arise as to the superiority or otherwise of codified constitutions. What is gained in terms of certainty may well be lost in terms of rigidity. A more interesting question may well be to what extent constitutions, whatever their precise form, actually determine the way political systems operate?

As the Conservative Ian Gilmour argues, formal constitutional rules actually tell us very little about how a country is governed. The Soviet Constitution of 1936 was a remarkably impressive document limiting the power of the State, guaranteeing fundamental freedoms and enshrining the rights of minorities. It was never actually operated: Stalin simply ignored it as he perpetrated some of the worst crimes against humanity in the history or the world. The Chinese Constitution of 1982, the latest in a long line of constitutions, supposedly guarantees freedoms but this did not prevent tyranny in Tiananmen Square in 1989. The Weimar constitution of 1919, a model of democracy and liberty, was in operation when Hitler came to power. This is not of course an argument against liberal constitutions. It is merely to emphasise that the way a political system operates has more to do with the attitude and **political culture** of the society than with the formalities of a document.

Constitutions are not necessarily permanent, France has had 13 since 1789. The strength of a constitution is measured not in its text or format but in the extent to which it operates successfully, with reasonable stability and continuity. The Russian Constitution of 1993 may 'establish itself', gaining legitimacy and status with the passage of time so that it becomes progressively more difficult for politicians to tamper with for partisan reasons; conversely it may not.

Like many aspects of modern politics, concern for constitutions and constitutionality was largely a product of the French revolution of 1789. The revolutionaries wished to limit the powers of the Monarch and looked to both the USA and to England for inspiration. By the early C19th as a middle class emerged all over Europe they demanded a constitution which would guarantee them a 'career open to talents' and protection against the arbitrary power of the crown.

A concern for constitutionalism was associated with liberalism, the 'dominant ideology' of the western world in Marx's phrase. As countries achieved self determination they sought to codify rights and duties. France was to experience so many upheavals between 1789 and 1958 that her constitution was rewritten time after time. There were revolutions in 1789, 1830 and 1848, the Monarchy was restored in 1815 and again in 1830. The First Republic of 1792 to 1794 gave way to a Directory leading to a military dictatorship and then Empire under Napoleon; the Second Republic lasted just four years 1848 to 1852 before giving way to the Second Empire under Louis Napoleon which lasted until defeat at the hands of Prussia in 1870 provoked the Paris Commune and the Third Republic. This lasted until defeat by the Nazis following which there was Fourth Republic from 1946 but political instability was endemic and the Fifth Republic came into existence in 1958.

De Gaulle effectively wrote the French Constitution and his party controlled the state until 1981, although it had splintered into two factions. Mitterrand (left) showed it could survive a change of party. Chirac (right) replaced him in 1995.

There were concerns that the constitution could not cope with a change of regime but it has done so twice now, 1981 when Conservatives gave way to Socialists and 1995 the other way around. It has also coped with **cohabitation**, a Socialist President working with a Conservative PM, and after 1997 President Chirac working with the Socialist PM Jospin. Thus even though the French Constitution is just over four decades old, younger than the body now known as the EU, it has a substantial degree of democratic legitimacy which the EU could be said to lack. Perhaps despite all the talk of supranationalism and globalism citizen's loyalties remain primarily national and therefore the constitution of a nation has more status than that of a non-national organisation.

Germany, created as an imperial state in 1871, experienced defeat in war and a revolution from above in 1918. This led to the Weimar Republic which succumbed to the Nazis in 1933. The Third Reich was defeated by 1945 and Germany partitioned, seemingly permanently, into the pro Western FDR and the Soviet satellite the DDR. Unification came in 1990 and with it the East Germans embraced the constitution of the FDR. The Basic Law enshrines certain principles of subsidiarity to balance the powers of the Federal Government and the Lander. Again the Constitution is relatively recent, less than half a century old but it has acquired a degree of consent which Weimar never managed to do.

Canada was governed according to the 1867 British North America Act but in 1982 the Constitution Act gave the Canadians control over their own constitution, it was as it were repatriated. At the same time the Charter of Rights and Freedoms guaranteed the standard liberal rights and gave the judges, headed by a Supreme Court of 9, the power to uphold them although the Parliament can declare an Act valid 'notwithstanding' an apparent conflict with the Charter. Those within the UK who want a codified Constitution point to the Canadian example as one to follow.

The Israeli Declaration of Independence of 1948 promised a constitution that would ensure equality and freedom for all. However Israel like the UK had a sovereign Parliament unrestrained by a Bill of Rights. Yet in 1992 the Freedom of Occupation Act and the Human Dignity and Freedom Act were passed. According to the Supreme Court Chief Justice Aaron Barak the two Acts guarantee freedom of religion and expression and the right to assemble and demonstrate and comprise a 'constitutional revolution'. They are in effect a Bill of Rights and therefore deeply disturbing to Orthodox Jews. Certainly the Religious Parties see the Court as a bastion of liberalism and wish to clip its wings.

The UK Constitution

It is the British who are unusual, perhaps unique, in that they do not have a codified constitution. Aristotle said that constitutions were a 'power map'. The British Constitution is unusual in that the map is uncodified with only part of it being written, much of it is still based on conventions. It is flexible in that the 'Crown-in-Parliament' can alter any rule as to the constitution as readily as it may alter any other part of the law because Parliament is sovereign and not subject to domestic judicial review. This **legal sovereignty** is qualified by the **political sovereignty** of the electorate. It is therefore a highly political constitution in that its provisions can be changed as part of the normal process of politics, there is no entrenchment and few formal checks and balances It is Monarchical in that the Head of State is a hereditary position but it is a constitutional Monarchy. The constitution entails both representative and responsible government in that Parliament, or rather the Commons, consists of representatives elected by the people and Ministers are responsible to Parliament, particularly the Commons, and must secure the approval of a majority of the House to continue in office and to secure support of their policies. It is unitary in that all legal power flows from one source, Parliament.

Flexibility

The British Constitution is said to be easily amended, giving a flexibility denied to the more rigid systems common elsewhere. Thus whilst it is very difficult to amend codified constitutions, the British Constitution can be amended by a simple Act of Parliament. Flexibility is a two-edged sword; it can work to the disadvantage of citizens.

In 1911, during a spy scare, the British Parliament passed the now infamous Official Secrets Act within less than 24 hours; in 1940 Parliament voted for an Emergency Powers Act which gave the government total control over people's lives: where and when they could work, what they could say and print, and so on. After the Birmingham pub bombing of 1974 the "liberal" Home Secretary, Roy Jenkins proposed the Emergency Powers Prevention of Terrorism Act. It was rushed through Parliament within days, even though it is so draconian in the extra powers it gives to the police that its continuation on the statute book has to be annually reviewed. In 2000 it was replaced by the Terrorism Act.

These Acts have restricted the freedom of the individual in the UK in a way that would not be possible in the US, because in the US the rights of individual citizens are protected by a written constitution.

When in 1975 the Wilson government held a referendum on whether Britain should remain in the EEC, again it simply needed an Act of Parliament to introduce this novel feature into the constitution. In 1920, the UK Parliament set up the Northern Ireland Parliament known as Stormont. The devolved Assemblies set up in Scotland and Wales could be abolished by a future Parliament. In 1972 it abolished Stormont and returned the nce to Direct Rule. Similarly, the abolition of the GLC in 1984; no-one able to challenge the decision as unconstitutional in the courts.

Conventions do not have the force of law and they change over time. In 1983 Thatcher departed from a 20-year-old convention by creating three hereditary peers. Labour protested in 1979 when Lord Carrington became Foreign Secretary because they felt it broke a convention that such key positions ought to be held by members of the House of Commons where they can be more easily held accountable.

Discrimination on the grounds of race and gender was outlawed in this country by statute, the Race Relations Acts and the Sex Discrimination Acts respectively, whereas in the USA it required constitutional amendments to ban racial discrimination. There was an attempt to ban discrimination on grounds of gender, the 27th, or so-called Equal Rights Amendment, but it had to be abandoned in the early 1980s because not enough states ratified it.

Conservatives such as Gilmour recognise the threat of over-powerful government but prefer other remedies such as proportional representation. 'Fixed constitutions with their guarantee of every known right provide more of an illusion of safety than safety itself'. Look at the USA before the 1960s where the record on the treatment of Southern blacks was appalling despite the Bill of Rights. The US treatment of Japanese-Americans during World War Two was unconstitutional but the Court let Franklin D Roosevelt get away with it. Gilmour quotes Justice Frankfurter; 'Judges, like other men, are too apt to be moved by the deep undercurrents of public feeling.'

Despite the much-vaunted flexibility of the constitution it could be said that the British system is stable, conservative, even rigid.

A Bill of Rights   19- 5

It is in the C21st, as the UK becomes more and more integrated into the European Union, that the real flexibility of the British Constitution is being tested and there are growing demands for a Bill of Rights similar to that found in most democracies.

Britain's Bill of Rights, dating back to 1689, stipulates relations between the Crown and Parliament. It is not a Bill of Rights in the sense in which the term is used in contemporary debate. In fact prior to 2000 there was no enumerated code of human rights, embodied via statute. Individual liberty was secured by judicial decisions determining the rights of individuals in cases brought before the courts. Under the doctrine of Parliamentary Sovereignty, Parliament could if it so wished interfere with or destroy such judge made rights.

A Bill of Rights with entrenched provisions would be beyond amendment by the ordinary legislative process. As the Times put it in 1986 a Bill of Rights "is supposed to be a fundamental statute guiding all other laws . . . if it were entrenched against parliamentary meddling, that would shatter the whole traditional doctrine of parliamentary sovereignty.'

The existence of the Human Rights Act has not fundamentally altered the fact that in Britain the right of freedom of speech and of association are determined in a negative rather than in a positive way, those rights exist except insofar as they are curtailed by the ordinary law. The right of free speech is restrained principally by the law of defamation and legislation such as the 1976 Race Relations Act. The right of assembly is restricted by legislation such as the Public Order Act of 1985 and the Criminal Justice Act of 1994. Nowhere is there a positive right, either as part of some codified constitution or as a 'free standing' Bill of Rights, to free speech or freedom of association and of assembly.

Origins and Development of the Debate

By the 1960s/1970s there was a growing body of thought asserting that Parliament was no longer a reliable body for protecting the liberties of individuals and that such protection must be provided by another means. In the 1970s pressure built up for constitutional reform, especially after the election of February 1974 saw the first minority government since the 1930s. The October 1974 election produced a wafer thin majority for the Labour Party, a government with a small plurality of votes obtaining the passage of measures without regard to their lack of support in the country. The 1974-1979 Parliament saw moves towards devolution, the first ever nation-wide referendum (on whether to stay in the EEC) as well as referendums in Scotland and Wales on devolution, worries about the trend towards corporatism, a Lib-Lab Pact, and because the government had lost its majority through by-election defeats the first defeat of a government through a vote of no confidence since 1924.

Against this novel political background the issue of constitutional reform began to be widely debated. In the Hamblyn lecture Lord Scarman argued that unless there is a Bill of Rights 'protected from repeal, amendment or suspension by the ordinary processes of a bare parliamentary majority controlled by the government of the day human rights will be at risk'. He wanted 'a new constitutional settlement that makes use of judicial rower to keep within constitutional limits the legislative sovereignty of Parliament'. A Supreme Court with power to invalidate legislation that was unconstitutional and to restrain anyone - citizen, government even Parliament itself from acting unconstitutionally.

It is significant, said Scarman, that 'the real opposition to the Bill of Rights comes from the party-controlled House of Commons. It indicates the true nature of the resistance to the judicial protection of human rights. It is fear of judicial rower to curb or review legislation.'

The Conservative Lord Hailsham demanded; "Nothing less than a written constitution for the UK, and by that I mean one which limits the powers of Parliament and provides a means of enforcing those limitations both by political and by legal means." Hailsham's call was echoed by other lawyers and in 1980 by Lord Denning in the Dimbleby lecture - 'Misuse of Power'. He recognised that Parliament is supreme but he saw the judges as the real guardians of the constitution' and felt that they 'ought to have a power of judicial review of legislation similar to that in the USA whereby a judge can set aside the statutes which are contrary to our unwritten constitution - in that they are repugnant to reason or to fundamentals.'

Few commentators feel that it would be realistic to try to get the all-embracing agreement that would be necessary to write a constitution for Britain from first principles so attention has shifted to the more limited goal of achieving a Bill of Rights.

More modest reformers advocated a Bill of Rights as an ordinary legislative measure but with provision that it is to take precedence over subsequent measures unless the latter state specifically that they override the Bill of Rights as in the Canadian 'notwithstanding' clause.

Thatcher and Civil Liberties

In 1987 Ascherson argued; 'there ought not to be any doubt now that liberties in Britain need protection. This particular government has practised an odious combination of laissez faire in the economy and society with a rapid increase in state and police power over the individual. Few democratic countries with a written constitution would have got away with the Public Order Act, the tilting of court rules against the accused or a string of laws reducing trade union rights - to name but a few recent offences.'

Left wingers such as Ascherson, Ewing and Geary argue that Thatcher 'has simply utilised to the full the scope for untrammelled power latent in the British Constitution but obscured by the hesitancy and scruples of previous consensus-based political leaders'. As Charter 88 puts it; 'A process is under way which endangers many of the freedoms we have had. Only in part deliberate, it began before 1979 and is now gathering momentum'. Professor Dworkin too argues that the problem predates Thatcher: "The erosion of liberty is not the doing of only one party or one government. Labour governments in the 1970s compromised the rights of immigrants, tried to stop publication of embarrassing political material, and tolerated an outrageous censorship and intimidation of journalists by the newspaper unions. But most of the worst examples of the attack on liberty have occurred in the last decade, and Thatcher and her government are more open in their indifference to liberty than their predecessors were.'

The supposed list of constitutional (or in some cases unconstitutional) departures in the Thatcher years is very long. Abolishing a tier of local government because it was controlled by the opposition; barring unions at GCHQ without even prior discussion, intimidating the media through attempted bans on documentaries ('Zircon', 'Real Lives at the Edge of the Union') criticism of documentaries such as 'Death on the Rock' or of news

41

reports such as Kate Adie's on the US bombing of Libya The blanket media ban on Sinn Fein, suppression of newspaper coverage of 'Spy-catcher', prosecution of Civil Servants such as Ponting and Tisdal and the introduction of a more draconian Official Secrets Act removing the 'public interest' defence, politicisation of previously apolitical posts within the Civil Service and within the Health Authorities and other QUANGOs. Cabinet government was suppressed in favour of a more Presidential approach. All appear to be evidence of an attempt to reduce pluralism and concentrate power at the centre.

Charter 88 claim that the Thatcher years saw 'Scotland governed like a province from Whitehall. More generally the government has eroded a number of important civil freedoms e.g. the universal rights to habeus corpus, to peaceful assembly, to freedom of information, to freedom of expression, to membership of a trade union, to local government, to freedom of movement, even to the birth-right itself.' The police were given new powers with PACE, public order restrictions (1985 Act), telephone tapping and the Prevention of Terrorism Act.

The Case For a Bill of Rights

300 years after the Glorious Revolution a 'left-wing' pressure group (deliberately not attached to any one party, and indeed opposed by Labour's then leadership) Charter 88, was established to campaign for a new constitutional settlement including an entrenched Bill of Rights.

The journalist Neal Ascherson, a member of Charter 88, derides 'the doctrine of parliamentary sovereignty as the curse of British politics which makes effective reform of our institutions almost impossible A Bill of Rights challenges that dogma. It suggests that there should be some authority to which even Parliament should be subordinate. In most modern countries, this is a written constitution, which is not just a sacred piece of parchment but a recognition, that the state and the legislature and its civil servants and laws are the servants of the people.'

Charter 88 propose that such a settlement would 'enshrine by means of a Bill of Rights, such civil liberties as the right to peaceful assembly, to freedom of association, to freedom from discrimination, to freedom from detention without trial, to trial by jury, to privacy and freedom of expression. Establish freedom of information and open government. Create a fair electoral system of proportional representation. Reform the upper house to establish a non-hereditary second chamber. Place the executive under the power of a democratically renewed Parliament and put all agencies of the state under the rule of law. Ensure the independence of a reformed judiciary. Provide legal remedies for all abuses of power by the state and the officials of central and local government. Guarantee an equitable distribution of power between local, regional and national government. Draw up a written constitution, anchored in the idea of universal citizenship, that incorporates these reforms.

As Paul Hirst put it - 'Charter 88 is asking for a constitutional settlement that is the norm in most countries.' Charter 88 is asking for ideas about government that were well established in the C18th and are now commonplaces of constitutional law throughout the democratic world. This conforms how pre-modern and pre-democratic British institutions are. In the British context Charter 88's constitutional settlement is little less than revolutionary.

Ewing and Geary are sceptical about the usefulness of a Bill of Rights; "like treating a heart attack with a used Band-Aid." They rejoin the Charter 88 view in their conclusion; 'liberty flows only from democracy and despite the rhetoric of liberalism there has never been a democratic culture in England.'

Some people advocate an entrenched Bill which would take precedence over Acts of Parliament, they would be invalid if they contravened the Bill of Rights. Those who advocate a Bill of Rights claim that even if it was not entrenched then Parliament would hesitate to pass measures which contravened it. Moral restraint thus makes entrenchment unnecessary, thereby avoiding crucial constitutional problems regarding Parliamentary Sovereignty. To avoid the problems of entrenchment other supporters of a Bill of Rights recommended incorporating the European Convention into British law.

The European Declaration of Human Rights and the Human Rights Act

The UK was one of the first countries to ratify the European Convention of Human Rights in November 1950. Although Britain gave early moral support to the idea of guaranteeing individual freedoms against the state it was not until 1966 that she was prepared to admit the right of individual citizens to petition the Commission on Human Rights directly. Even so there was no guarantee that a complaint which reached the European Court and was upheld would be remedied. Certain references to the Commission proved highly embarrassing for the UK which was the only signatory of the Convention not to have incorporated its principles into law or to have a Bill of Rights.

Since 1966 twice as many petitions have been lodged against Britain as against any other member, and it has lost more serious cases than any other nation. Examples include Britain's treatment of Kenyan Asians after 1968; one sensitive area which keeps producing conflicts is the question of the treatment of prisoners in Northern Ireland, their right to see a lawyer over misconduct by a prison officer; the use of torture by the security forces in Ulster (some prisoners were interrogated while up against a wall with their arms wide apart). Other judgements which have gone against Britain include; the existence of birching in the Isle of Man, caning in schools, telephone tapping, the laws on homosexuality in Northern Ireland, the legal rights of mental patients, and the unequal retirement age for men and women.

In May 1985 the Court ruled that the changes in the immigration rules introduced by the Conservative government in 1980 were unlawful because they discriminated against women. This was the 12th judgement against the UK by the Court; in contrast, only 2 cases had gone in favour.

This country's record is far worse than any of the 17 other signatories to the Convention which are comparable; the Court has ruled against them on a total of 39 occasions. In 1988 the Court ruled that the powers of the police under the Prevention of Terrorism Act violated rights and ordered Britain to change them. The Thatcher government argued that it had the right to derogate from its obligations under that Convention because

Article 15 allows a state to derogate in 'time of war or other public emergency'.

Even certain supporters of a Bill of Rights believe that the European Convention as it stands is not appropriate to British conditions. Dworkin argued; "The European Convention is not a perfect Bill of Rights for Britain. It was a compromise drafted to accommodate a variety of nations with different legal systems and traditions; it is in many ways weaker than the American Bill of Rights: and it is hedged about with vague limitations and powerful escape clauses of different sorts. The Convention does protect liberty better than it is now protected by Parliament alone. It protects freedom of speech, religion and expression, privacy and the most fundamental rights of accused criminals, and it grants in an indirect but effective way rights against discrimination.' Lord Hooson argued that the section on vagrants 'should not be introduced'. Some people argue the same thing about Article 17 regarding censorship and Article 11 regarding trade unions. Others such as Simon Lee argued that as Britain had already signed the European Convention there was little need to incorporate it into British law.

However it has been incorporated into UK law by the Labour Government and this took effect in October 2000 as the Human Rights Act. The Labour government argued that by incorporating the European Convention into British law it would save the slow and fearfully costly business of taking an appeal abroad to Strasbourg

Canada adopted a Charter of Rights and Freedoms in 1982. The courts can hold a statute inoperative but the legislature can resurrect it by re-enacting the provision with a clause stating that it applies 'notwithstanding the Charter'. In contrast New Zealand adopted a Bill of Rights in 1990 but the courts have no such power. There is simply a provision that urges the judges to adopt an interpretation of a statute consistent with the Bill of Rights. If that is impossible they must give effect to the statute.

The UK followed the New Zealand example which is why it is described as 'soft incorporation'. Judges in the higher courts have the power to declare a statute incompatible with the Human Rights Act. The government could then change the law by the fast track of an Order in Council that would simply require a resolution of both houses of Parliament.

The Democratic Audit of 2002 produced by the University of Essex argues that the Act 'has gone a long way to remedying the systematic inadequacies of civil and political rights protection identified in our first audit. The inclusion of a human rights component in the new compulsory citizenship education programme reflects an emerging rights culture in the UK'. In its view 'longstanding inadequacies in the legal accountability of ministers and public officials have been addressed through the extension of judicial review and the Human Rights Act which makes all public authorities accountable for rights violations.'

A Joint Committee on Human Rights has been set up in Parliament to examine all bills for compliance with the Human Rights Act and to review progress on the Act's objectives. However there is no independent Human Rights Commissioner.

After September 11th 2001 the Blair Government rushed through the Anti-Terrorism Crime and Security Act. Its most controversial measure is the power it gives the government to intern foreigners without trial. The government had to suspend Britain's obligations under the European human rights convention, which guarantees the right to liberty except prior to a trial and after conviction by a court. The convention allows states to avoid their obligations 'in times of war or other public emergency threatening the life of the nation'. Civil rights groups say there is little evidence of any such threat. Britain is alone among signatories in imposing any derogation in the fight against terror.

The European Court of Justice
There has been a growth in cases involving British practice before the (quite separate) court of the European Union (ECJ). It is a doctrine of both EU law and British domestic law that, on matters within the competence of the EU, Community law is superior. Hence, to the extent that the EU looms larger in political life, the significance of the European Court as a way of holding British governments to account will grow.

Arguably it is in these little understood European institutions that Britain is finding itself a system of checks and balances of the kind familiar in most other democracies. It may be that the UK will gradually be pushed towards constitutional reform simply due to the pressures on British politics brought about by membership of the EU and other supranational and intergovernmental bodies.

The Case Against a Bill of Rights

The government under Major claimed to be neutral arguing that it required all party discussions but in practice it was anti-Bill of Rights. The Labour Party was not unanimous in its opposition, support was growing for constitutional reform. Most Conservatives and most lawyers are against a Bill of Rights because they fear it would weaken the judiciary by bringing them into the political arena (as in the USA). However, even without a Bill of Rights, judges have become more willing since the 1960s to challenge the executive.

The main argument against a Bill of Rights is that it would remove from Parliament a decision making role that rightly belongs to Parliament. Political decisions must be taken by politicians who can be challenged and removed, rather than by judges. Disputes as to encroachment on fundamental rights are essentially political disputes and must be resolved politically not judicially. As Lord Lloyd puts it; 'if what we fear is 'political tyranny' then we must seek to control that by political means.' Lord McCluskey in the Reith lectures asked why should it be supposed that elderly lawyers with cautious and backward-looking habits of thought are qualified to overrule the judgements of democratically elected legislators?'

Whether based on the European Convention or not a proper Bill of Rights would stipulate rights in very broad terms and effectively bestow wide powers upon the bodies empowered to interpret it. Left-wingers such as Professor John Griffith object to the effect the courts could have on radical legislation and social and economic rights. According to the National Council for Civil Liberties; "this country's judges are drawn from a very narrow social base, they are generally conservative in their views and it is feared that a Bill of Rights will allow them to strike down progressive legislation." Is that not a good argument for broadening the base of judicial recruitment rather than an argument against a Bill of Rights?

Should judges, unelected and unaccountable be given such a central role in the preservation of liberty? Ewing and Geary suspect that the enthusiasts for a Bill of Rights pass too quickly over these difficulties, which are far more important and intractable than the technicalities of whether a Bill of Rights could be entrenched. Charter 88 say only that a new constitutional settlement would 'ensure the independence of a reformed judiciary'. Of the 3,704 judges only 15% are female, only 2.5% are from ethnic minorities - none of them at senior levels.

There is an absence of any agreement on the rights to be protected. Party disagreement underpins the desire for a Bill of Rights yet all-party support is necessary for an effective Bill of Rights, otherwise it will become a political football as one party emphasises certain rights and others differ. Certain rights may conflict with others. Civil and political rights may conflict with economic and social rights. The Bill of Rights proposed by the Institute of Economic Affairs would have prevented certain pro-Trade Union legislation passed under Labour between 1974/79; new right thinkers such as Keith Joseph would like to put limits on taxes under a Bill of Rights.

The left argue that those who favour a Bill of Rights tend to see the state in purely negative terms, regarding it as the only threat to individual liberty and freedom (except that posed by the trade unions). Freedom is defined negatively as the absence of public and legal restraints on individual action. *There is a lack of sympathy for a more positive view of the state as a collective means of extending rights to less-favoured groups and helping people to combat powerful vested interests and to secure real opportunities to live a worthwhile life.*

As Dearlove and Saunders put it; "many constitutional authorities, such as the New Right, seem to be keener on securing economic freedoms for particular individuals than they are to secure broad social freedoms for the mass of the population against the freedoms of the few."

It is perhaps because the 1980s saw no alternation of power that the decade was one of those periods when constitutional reform interested many in politics. In the 1980s and 1990s it was politicians or commentators owing loyalty to the Labour Party or the centre parties who led calls for reform. Yet, during the Labour government of the 1970s, little was done to enable either Parliament, or anyone else, to exercise real control over governmental powers.

There is in Britain a degree of government by consent, surely a litmus test of democracy. A checklist of the inadequacies of Britain's democratic arrangements is not difficult to draw up. Our upper chamber is unelected, our Head of State is chosen by virtue of inheritance rather than merit, our system of local government is rapidly becoming one of local administration of policy decided centrally. Our electoral system could be described as one of disproportionate representation and we have no codified constitution guaranteeing civil liberties.

Yet, despite this, the British clearly do enjoy a measure of democracy. Despite the absence of formal checks and balances, there are plenty of informal, uncodified constraints on those in power. In the end government cannot govern without consent.

To constitutional reformers such as Charter 88 or the Liberal Democrats the potential, or latent, problem of a dominant state became manifest in the 1980s. It could be argued that, just as Hailsham's fears in the 1970s were based on partisan motives, so the fear of Thatcherism centralising power reflected the left's discontent at being excluded from power.

Norton argues that the British constitution is based on 'dynamic pluralism'. In some ways power has been centralised, especially in regard to local government, but in other ways the central state has lost power, for example through privatisation and the fragmentation of the Civil Service. Power is shifting all the time from Parliament and the Executive to supra-national bodies such as the EU and NATO. Far from being an 'Elective Dictatorship', the British government is increasingly unable to control economic policy or defence policy.

Party Positions on the Main Constitutional Issues

Each party's position on constitutional issues, as on several others, is a combination of tactical self interest and ideology.

1. Electoral Reform

(For details see section on electoral systems)

Labour's 'traditional' position on electoral reform was that it was opposed to PR for two reasons

a)   because Labour did 'quite well' out of FPTP, from 1945 to 1979 it was in office for exactly half the time and

b)   because its ideology of democratic socialism required 'strong government' to implement.

By the mid-1990s Labour had come round, with varying degrees of enthusiasm, to a willingness to at least consider PR. By 1991 Robin Cook was claiming that 'it is no longer a question of whether Labour will commit itself to electoral reform but when and for what elections.'

This change of approach reflected two things

a)   Labour had stopped winning elections under FPTP, it had not won a general election since 1974, it had not gained even 40% of the votes since 1970. Significantly when Labour was a minority party in the 1920s and 1930s it had favoured electoral reform so in that sense the party had come full circle. Arguably prior to 1997 Labour had never done well under FPTP in that Labour had held office for just 20 years of its 97 year existence but it had been in power with a majority in double figures for just 11 of those years. Thus despite Labour's huge majority in 1997 past performance indicated that it was unlikely to win by such a margin at the next election.

b)   because Labour has shifted ideologically, towards social democracy and therefore towards the Liberals. Ashdown sat on a Cabinet Committee on constitutional reform and the Liberal Lord Jenkins chaired the Commission considering electoral reform. However the promised referendum on PR never materialised and given Labour's election victories in 1997 and 2001 the party has cooled towards PR.

The Liberals are very much in favour of PR a) because they generally do badly under FPTP as in the 1983 election when they got 25.4% of the votes but just 3.5% of the seats. In 2001 they got about 18% of the votes but less than 8% of the seats. The Liberals would benefit from PR, whichever system is adopted and b) because they fear an over-powerful executive and PR helps prevent this.

Conservatives favour FPTP despite their 1997 and 2001 defeats

a)   because they do well under it having been in power for most of the post war period and having held at least a share, usually the preponderant share of power since 1886, hence the 'dominant one party' thesis and

b)   because they favour a 'strong state' which arguably PR prevents.

The group Conservative Action on Electoral Reform (CAER) enjoyed a brief period of influence in the mid-1970s following the Tory disasters of 1974, Heath included a commitment to a Speakers Conference on the issue in the October 1974 manifesto but under Thatcher and Major the party was very hostile to PR and CAER has withered. Perhaps it will revive now.

2. A Bill of Rights

(For details see earlier)

Labour used to oppose one

a)   because they felt that it would prevent strong government and

b)   because they did not trust reactionary judges, Labour left-wingers such as Griffiths still feel the same.

Labour modernisers favoured the incorporation of the European Convention in Human Rights into UK law as the closest thing to a real Bill of Rights

a) as they are talking of a culture of pluralism and individual liberties instead of collectivism and

b) because they argue that a new breed of judges is emerging, witness the Conservative government's conflicts with the courts in the period 1979-97. However the Human Rights Act is not entrenched and already the anti-terror legislation has departed from fundamental principles of civil liberty.

The Liberals favour an entrenched declaration of rights as the best way to guarantee civil liberties and prevent elective dictatorship.

Conservatives oppose a Bill of Rights as it would

a) infringe the sovereignty of Parliament and weaken the government and

b) politicise the judges. They would point critically to the situation in the USA where the appointment of judges becomes political theatre as in the Thomas nomination. They opposed the Human Rights Act as unnecessary even though it is not an entrenched Bill of Rights.

3. Parliament

(For details see section on Parliament)

Labour favour replacing the undemocratic Lords with a partly elected but mostly appointed chamber. The Liberals want an elected chamber. The government is currently considering the options. Lord Cranbourne, the Tory party leader in the Lords tried to reach agreement with New Labour over Stage 1 and was sacked by Hague for doing so but the agreement - the Wetherhill Amendment sparing 92 hereditaries - happened anyway. The Conservatives would now like to see 80% elected.

There has been little real reform of the Commons. A Modernisation Committee exists under the Leader of the House of Commons to initiate reforms to the House's conduct of business but it is not going to affect the concentration of power in the hands of the government. The hours of work have changed; more bills are published in draft form earlier to allow better scrutiny by back benchers and bills will be carried over from one parliamentary session to the next rather than 'failing' if not completed by the end of the session. This is *modernisation not reform*. Most importantly PR has not been introduced for the Commons. The Lords remains half reformed, the Commons is unreformed.

4. Devolution

(for details see section on Local Government)

Labour is for it, witness its referendum in 1997 on devolution for Scotland and for Wales, claiming that it is the best way to prevent demands for independence from growing and thereby maintain the Union. Cynics argue that Labour's support is tactical, most of the 72 Scottish seats are Labour and that it has not really answered the West Lothian question first posed by one of its own MPs Tam Dalyell. Labour's response is to introduce devolution for the regions of England but there is no obvious support for this. The Liberals also favour devolution as a way of maintaining the Union and as part of a general attempt to introduce subsidiarity aimed at diffusing power.

The Conservatives oppose devolution arguing that it will increase taxes, referring to Labour's 'tartan tax', and bureaucracy. They also say it would lead to an independent Scotland and therefore break up the Union. However Smith accepts that it will be difficult to reverse.

5. Freedom of Information Act

(For details see sections on Judges and Open Government)

Labour is in favour of open government, Cook argues that it was the main moral to be drawn from the Scott Report. When it was last in office Labour vigorously applied the OSA but New Labour promised more open government and has passed a limited Freedom of Information Act although it will not take effect until 2005.

The Liberals are in favour arguing that knowledge is power and that citizens have a right to know what government is doing in their name as this will empower them.

The Tories are against a FOIA believing that too much openness is incompatible with good government and that the only beneficiaries would be pressure groups and the media. Major claimed to have opened up government where necessary with the publication of previously secret material and with an emphasis on information through the Citizens Charters, school's league tables and so on.

6. Local Government

(For details see section on local government)

Labour claim that it will restore powers to local authorities and has replaced the GLC by setting up an elected authority for London - the Greater London Authority - with a directly elected Mayor. However previous Labour governments have eroded the powers of local authorities, for example over education.

The Liberals favour community politics and would return power to local people as part of a wider process of subsidiarity.

The Tories claim that they took power away from Town Hall bureaucrats and made local councils more responsive to their consumers. New Right Tories wish to go further and abolish the Local Education Authorities altogether. There is nothing new about central government manipulating local government. A Conservative government under Macmillan established the GLC in 1963 for partisan reasons. Similarly, it was a Labour Secretary for the Environment, Crosland, who told local authorities 'the party is over'. Labour controlled most local councils in the past but the Conservatives have staged a recovery in recent local elections. Will Labour still be so keen on returning powers to councils if the Tories run most of them?

7. Referendums

(For details see section on elections)

A convention appears to have arisen that governments should only introduce major constitutional reforms after they have been approved in a referendum. Labour have held four such major referendums since 1997 and have promised one on the Euro at some point. They did however fail to hold the promised referendum on PR for the Commons. The Liberals support the use of referendums but the Conservatives have traditionally distrusted such devices as undermining representative democracy. However the Major government did promise a referendum on the Euro, something which Smith has subsequently ruled out.

It is left to the government's discretion whether to call a referendum and also the form of its wording, although the Political Parties, Elections and Referendums Act 2000 has introduced regulations on the conduct of referendum campaigns.

8. The European Union

The United Kingdom joined what is now called the European Union in 1973. During that time the organisation has evolved through various treaty changes and what was once a common market has become a single market with most member states embracing a single currency. The EU has always been about more than just economic integration, the Treaty of Rome of 1957 commits member states to 'ever closer union' and the EU has long had a 'social dimension' and a political agenda. Since 1973 membership of the EU has impacted upon literally every aspect of British politics from the Constitution to local government, from Parliament to pressure groups from political parties to the role of judges. Whether that impact has been beneficial or detrimental is open to debate, The only thing that can be said with any degree of certainty is that the scale of the impact has been enormous and will continue to increase whether the UK joins the single currency or not.

Those who opposed the UK joining the EU claimed that it would end the three hundred year old tradition of Parliamentary sovereignty. An outside body would be able to overrule an Act of Parliament for the first time since 1689. Although supporters of membership tended to downplay this issue the reality was that Community law was superior to the domestic law of all member states. In the early 1990s the Factortame case saw the Merchant Shipping Act of 1989 ruled invalid because it breached community law.

Those who has been concerned about sovereignty such as the Conservative MP Teddy Taylor or the Labour MP Tony Benn saw this case as vindication of their fears. However the Conservative academic Lord Norton, an advisor to Smith, stresses that Parliament remains legally sovereign because it could repeal the 1972 Act, which took the UK into the EU. Norton argues that a more important issue is the way in which British Ministers on the Council of Ministers can have their objections overruled through Qualified Majority Voting. Ironically it was the Eurosceptic Thatcher who helped remove the national veto from many areas of policy by pushing through the Single European Act of 1986. The SEA helped create a single market but it required institutional reform to enact, it also stimulated demands for a single currency, an issue that continues to divide British politicians.

Both the political executive and their civil service advisers are deeply involved in EU affairs on a daily basis. Most Ministers spend an increasing amount of time working with their European counterparts. This is perhaps most obviously true of those responsible for Agriculture, Foreign Affairs and Trade but the whole of Whitehall is involved in European matters in an on-going way. As for the Civil Servants they have to work with their European counterparts through bodies such as COREPER and to those such as Benn who are suspicious of the mandarins Brussels looks like a 'bureaucrats paradise'. Arguably it is harder and harder for Parliament to hold the executive properly accountable when more and more power is moving to the European Union. Prime Ministers such as Blair are able to enhance their authority through their role as European statesman as the European Council grows in importance but at the same time the EU acts as a check and balance on all the politicians involved including the Heads of Government.

The UK is unique among member states in not having a codified constitution or a tradition of positive rights defended by judges. Although the European Court of Human Rights is not part of the EU it has, together with the work of the European Court of Justice, inevitably had an impact on the way British judges see their role. British judges have watched European judges overrule British governments on numerous occasions and it has inevitably made British judges more willing to enter the political arena. The Blair governments constitutional reforms have also changed the way the judges operate, they now have to apply the Human Rights Act as well as act as arbiters in disputes between the national government and the devolved bodies. At the same time the UK has adopted electoral systems based on proportional representation for the devolution elections, for elections to the European Parliament and for the Greater London Authority. The old Westminster model of a sovereign Parliament, a unitary state and an electoral system that normally gave one party a majority in the Commons is undergoing great change. One of the forces promoting change is membership of the European Union, in that sense the British political system is becoming more Europeanised.

Parties and pressure groups have also been very affected by the EU. The issue of European integration has historically divided both main British parties. The issue helped split the Labour Party in 1981 and was a major factor behind the landslide defeat of the Conservatives in 1997. Hague did what Major refused to do and taken a definitive Eurosceptic stance which Smith has taken even further. That is why senior Conservatives such as Clarke, Heseltine and Hurd are not in the Shadow Cabinet, they are too pro-Europe. Hague and Smith's stance has brought clarity but at the expense of exclusion and narrowness. Blair has yet to establish his definitive line on Europe. Labour remain divided over the single currency and it is not just the left of the party which has concerns over Europe. Ken Livingstone is in favour of the Euro whilst people on the right of the party such as Austin Mitchell are antagonistic. British business pressure groups such as the CBI and the National Farmers Union have long realised the importance of the EU and have generally been supportive. It was only with the BSE affair of the 1990s that the NFU saw Europe as hostile to their interests. With the Trade Unions it was the other way around, initial hostility to what they saw as a 'capitalist club' gave way to enthusiasm once Jacques Delors began promoting a social chapter. It is no coincidence that the left grew generally warmer towards the EU from 1988 just as the Thatcherites were moving towards a more sceptical position.

Both the major parties are split on this issue and confusingly the division does not always follow a simple left-right axis. For example Benn on the left of the Labour Party is a Eurosceptic maybe even Europhobe but then so is Austen Mitchell both on the right of the Labour Party. Similarly in the Tory Party, Lawson a key figure in the New Right supported membership of ERM whereas other New Right radicals such as Portillo are very opposed to fixed currencies.

The Liberals are consistently pro-European; indeed they are the only party that is unambiguously federalist.

Blair's constitutional reforms, in particular devolution, could be said to be promoting a more pluralist political system. In that sense the UK is approaching the continental version of subsidiarity in which decisions are taken at the lowest level possible compatible with efficiency. The introduction of devolution and the reform of local government through executive Mayors does not make the UK federal in the way of say Germany but it does, or should, help avoid over centralisation. The degree to which the UK should become more integrated into the EU remains the most controversial item on the British political agenda. Very few senior politicians favour withdrawal from the EU but equally very few are prepared to commit the UK full membership of a federal Europe. In practice the impact of the EU upon British politics grows more obvious year after year and the mainstream politicians have to work out how best to manage that impact on an on-going basis.

Conclusion

By 1997 Labour had a commitment to introduce 8 bills involved with constitutional reform. Robert Harris pointed out the difficulties experienced in the past on issues such as the reform of the Lords. Adonis argued that each measure was capable of taking up enormous amounts of parliamentary time unless there were changes to Commons procedure. He also argued that there is no hope of inter-party agreement on these issues and that the best way for Labour to proceed was to go ahead with the same kind of determination that Thatcher showed over Trade Union reform.

Conservatives and some of the leadership of the Labour party (especially Prescott) are sceptical about the public's interest in, or desire for, constitutional reform. However David Marquand argues that Tony Blair was astute in upgrading the issue of constitutional arrangements.

Firstly, because with increased concern about Britain's future relations with Europe, obvious desire for some movement regarding Scotland's position within the UK, a growing awareness that relations between local government and the centre have been increasingly politicised over the past 25 years, and a declining level of satisfaction with many of the institutions which the British used to regard with pride - Parliament, the police, the legal system, the educational system - there is below the surface a constitutional debate 'waiting to be born' If Labour and the Liberal Democrats can convince the electorate that constitutional issues are not irrelevancies but are intimately linked, indeed inseparable from, the causes of Britain's economic and social problems, the party can capitalise on the underlying unease.

What then are the constitutional issues on which the parties agree? They all favour the retention of the Monarchy and a negotiated end to the conflict in Ulster. On these issues a constitutional consensus prevails.

 Is the British Constitution itself now an object of political dispute?

The US Constitution

It is vital to understand the way in which the American Constitution emerged if we are to comprehend how current American politics operates.

During the War of Independence against the British the Americans had a common enemy, a common purpose and a form of government, the Articles of Confederation. Now Britain had been defeated by her former American colonies and the Americans had to decide how to govern themselves, so 55 delegates from the 13 states met in Philadelphia to revise the articles; instead they drew up a new constitution.

One of the great American historians, Charles A. Beard, claimed that the framers were representatives of the American elite and they drafted a Constitution which would safeguard their interests. They succeeded in obtaining ratification despite the indifference or opposition of a majority of the people. Today, few, if any, historians accept the Beard thesis without qualification.

Historians such as Jack Rakove (The Beginning of National Politics, 1979) while accepting that men such as Madison, Hamilton and Mason were not radicals, point out the revolutionary nature of the system they devised. Several key principles underlay the work of the "Founding Fathers" of the American Republic. They wanted to create a Republic, in which power was to be shared between the central government and the regional authorities, and in which there was to be a Separation of Powers at both national and state level, with the entire mechanism held together by a system of checks and balances to prevent the accumulation of power and the potential for "tyranny".

The Founding Fathers based the Constitution on the work of John Locke, the 17th century English philosopher, and Baron Montesquieu, their close contemporary. Both these authors admired the British system of constitutional monarchy as opposed to the absolute monarchies prevailing in C18th century Europe. The Americans had just liberated themselves from colonial, monarchial power and they were anxious to prevent a return to tyranny in the form of an over-powerful Presidency. Hence the system of checks and balances which constrain Presidential power. However, men such as Benjamin Franklin, Alexander Hamilton and even Thomas Jefferson, the author of the Declaration of Independence and the Bill of Rights, were equally anxious to avoid "democracy". Hence their concern to limit the power of the House of Representatives by according equal power to the Senate. It was not until 1913, in response to pressure from the Progressives, that direct elections to the Senate were introduced.

The new nation was to be a Republic rather than a Monarchy. This may seem unremarkable now; however, in the 18th century, Absolute Monarchy was the norm There were other Republics in 1787, for instance Holland and Switzerland, but no other nation had a President elected by his peers (as the original Electoral College was intended to operate) and limited in his power by a codified document.

The United States was to have a Federal system in which power was dispersed and decentralised. Again, this was to go against the prevailing orthodoxy which held that power had to be centralised otherwise a nation would be weak in the face of external aggression and internal fragmentation. The individual states were proud of their newly won independence and reluctant to surrender too much power to a centralised government. The answer was a compromise; they were allowed to retain many of their jealously guarded rights but they had to pool some of their sovereignty in the form of a Federal Republic in which supremacy ultimately lay with the Federal Government in Washington. The smaller states, fearing domination by their bigger neighbours, insisted on equal representation in the Senate regardless of population. The South was allowed to count slaves as three fifths of a person thus giving them greater leverage in the House of Representatives which was based on population.

The three branches of government must be separated and no one individual ought to be allowed to serve in more than one branch at a time. The only exception to this exclusion principle was (and still is) the Vice-President, who is the formal head of the Senate but cannot take part in its debates and only votes in the event of a tie. This was significant in 2001 when the Senate was split 50:50 and Vice President Cheney used his casting vote.

This separation of legislature and executive limits the potential for patronage and has restrained the growth of a cohesive party system. It has not prevented the emergence of the President as the "Legislative Leader' but it has reduced the chances of getting a President's proposals through Congress.

The Founders introduced a system of "checks and balances" whereby each of the three branches would be able to prevent the accretion of power. Thus the President appoints the members of the executive branch, but subject to approval by the Senate; similarly, he appoints all federal judges but if the Senate feel that the nominee is unsuitable they can reject him/her.

The President was to be allowed to make treaties with other nations, but again the Senate has to ratify them before they become operative. This is far from a formality, as the battle for the passage of the North America Free

Trade Agreement (NAFTA), illustrates. Presidents can by-pass such problems by making Executive Agreements instead, but even here the Senate can demand to be informed as to the contents of such agreements. The President, as head of the armed forces, wages war but only Congress can declare it, hence the furore over the War Powers Act of 1973. The President presents his budget to Congress but they will really decide what happens to spending and taxation.

The President and the Congress are both checked and balanced by the third branch, the Supreme Court. Thus the three branches were to be jealous rivals, alert for any attempt to encroach upon their preserve. The same principle also applies at State level, where the Governor is the head of the Executive branch but needs the approval of the State Legislature for his policies to become state law, and where the State Supreme Court checks and balances the other two branches.

There are also "checks and balances" within Congress where the Senate is accorded some specific powers which are denied to the Representatives and vice versa. Often the same party controls both Houses but this does not guarantee harmony as the two are still intent on restraining each other and will often disagree. They are approximately co-equal in power, although the Senate has more authority, there is no equivalent of the Parliament Act which formalises the supremacy of the Commons. Two-thirds of both Houses need to agree to overturn a Presidential veto.

The American experiment involved more than the mechanics of government - it was also concerned with a new conception of liberty. The Declaration of Independence in 1776, written by Thomas Jefferson, is one of the most ringing expositions of human rights in history: 'We hold these truths to be self evident, that all men are created equal and are endowed by their Creator with certain inalienable rights and that among these are life, liberty and the pursuit of happiness.'

This was the truly novel, indeed revolutionary, aspect of the American Constitution, and within a generation it was to have profound implications for Europe as the French Revolution built on the ideas of the American experiment. However, the Jeffersonian conception of human dignity did not extend to the native Americans or to the slaves. It is important to recognise the limitations of the original Constitution; the Founding Fathers were, after all, representative of the prejudices of their age.

The Developing Constitution

There has always been anxiety about the Constitution. George Washington predicted for years that the 13 states would fly apart. It was felt that, in a great crisis, the Constitution would cripple Presidents with laws they would have to break and a Congress they could not direct. Bagehot predicted dissolution and anarchy. In fact, the Constitution withstood the test of the Civil War, of the great depression of the 1930s and of the political crises of the 1960s and 1970s.

Roosevelt steered the country through the depression and war

In the post-colonial world, the American system of a Federal Republic has become the model for many newly independent nations. When it was drawn up, the USA was a new nation of thirteen States, with a population of just a few million (including slaves) and a predominantly agricultural economy. Today, the USA is a superpower, both militarily and economically, with a population of nearly 280 million. Yet the Constitution is largely unchanged, at least formally. There have been just 27 amendments in those two hundred years and the philosophy underlying the Constitution, the belief in 'a government of laws not men' still pervades the American political system. However whether the rhetoric matches the reality is very debatable.

Formally, little has changed in the American system. The President is still chosen by the Electoral College, he is now limited to two full terms by the 22nd amendment of 1951. Both Houses of Congress are bigger and both are directly elected.

However, in another sense, a great deal has changed since Washington's time. The Presidency has grown enormously in power. The election of Roosevelt in the 1930s led to the active Presidency, a "Chief Legislator", proposing bills to Congress and expecting them to pass in a recognisable form. The Presidency, which was expected to be a symbolic, unifying institution, taking little part in partisan controversy had, by the 1930s, become the focus of political power. The Supreme Court had, after a bruising battle with the Roosevelt administration, "followed the election returns", and taken a more liberal stance towards Federal government intervention, so that by the 1960s the Warren Court was accused by "strict constructionists" of trying to usurp political authority. Congress itself was willing to allow Presidents, such as Truman and Johnson, a relatively free hand in the foreign policy sphere, while they concentrated on domestic issues and parochial concerns.

However, the tragedy of Vietnam changed all this and, since the War Powers Act of 1973, Congress has carefully scrutinised Presidential initiatives in external policy. Hence the "Vietnam Syndrome", a reluctance to commit US Forces abroad which even the Gulf Wars have not entirely erased. A Republican dominated Congress and a Democratic President produced deadlock in crucial domestic and foreign policy areas in the 1990s.

The Watergate affair of 1972 to 1974 and the "Irangate" affair of 1986/7 both illustrate key aspects of the American Constitution. Watergate showed that the system of checks and balances still works although it could be argued that the two year crisis weakened America for a decade. Irangate did not lead to an equivalent crisis of the system, but illegality was exposed. Contrast this with the way in which the British executive was able to control Parliament over Westland and the Scott Report and we see why British constitutional reformers look across the Atlantic with envy.

After Watergate, Presidents continue to find it a struggle to assert their authority. In the British system of parliamentary government, a Prime Minister with an overall majority is more or less assured of getting his/her Cabinet's policies approved. The US system deliberately makes it hard for the Executive to get policies through the system. This is one of the fundamental differences between parliamentary government and presidential government. Professor Rose talks of a post-modern President where the concentration is on campaigning at the expense of governing and where electoral pressures generate unrealistically high expectations that are always going to be dashed because Presidents lack the support mechanisms to achieve them. The constitution has nothing to say about political parties and yet they are a vital, unifying, link between the executive and the legislature that allows greater co-operation between the two.

Bibby points out that the separation of powers has always been a fiction. The Executive and the Legislature overlap through Iron Triangles. Only 1% of the 1,100 treaties signed by the President have been rejected. There have been over 5,600 executive Agreements, including ones as important as Yalta and Potsdam. The President has become legislative leader and the Congressional veto has been inserted into 126 statutes since 1933. Of the 302 Presidential vetoes between 1945 and 1983 only 36 were overturned and 8 of these were during the Ford administration.

Neustadt argues that the American system comprises "separate institutions sharing power'. Congress impinges on foreign policy in a way that the Founding Fathers never envisaged. Conversely Congress has only declared war five times but since 1933 there have been 165 occasions when the US used force abroad. The US fought for ten years in Vietnam without Congress ever formally declaring war. Indeed the war was extended to Cambodia without Congress even being informed. So little did Nixon and Kissinger care for the separation of powers. Presidents have always complained about Congressional interference in national security issues. Bush senior was able to get Congressional support for his actions in the Gulf, but then the consensus on this occasion was exceptional. The current President is an even stronger position - a Republican President facing a

Republican Congress and looking likely to be re-elected. Again though, much of this is due to exceptional circumstances after September 11th.

States Rights

The Constitution assumes that the States will be relatively autonomous and that the Federal government will be only concerned with defence, foreign policy, the currency and inter-state arrangements. Yet within two decades the Supreme Court under John Marshall had confirmed the supremacy of Federal laws over state laws and the process of "nationalisation" of American politics had been set in train.

The issue of States' Rights was to cause a very bloody Civil War and provide the greatest test which the Republic has ever faced, yet without the Constitution the Union would simply have dissolved. The 14th Amendment (1868) was intended to create equality before the law, yet for close on a century the Southern States practised systematic discrimination and used the euphemism of "States' Rights" to entrench racism. The point is that the Constitution had been sufficiently flexible both to allow Southern "apartheid" to continue, and later, in a different political and social climate, to dismantle it.

The huge extension in the power of the Federal Government since 1933 has weakened the concept of Federalism despite 34 years of 'New Federalism'. The States still have rights which Washington cannot take away, but the Founding Fathers would not recognise the current imbalance between Federal and State power.

Reforming the Constitution

Constitutional reformers in Britain often cite the USA as a model of an open and democratic political culture. American would-be reformers often point to Britain as an example of a successful flexible system. Five thousand amendments have been introduced into Congress, although, given the difficulties of amending the Constitution - it requires the approval of two-thirds of Congress and three-quarters of the states - most stood no chance of getting through. The most recent serious attempt was in the early 1970s with the Equal Rights Amendment which got the necessary support in Congress but secured the approval of only 35 states.

The current US reform agenda includes proposals for a six year, one term Presidency, concurrent elections for both Houses and the executive, abolition or reform of the Electoral College, a line item veto for the President, a balanced budget amendment and term limits for Congress. There have been frivolous proposals for change such as an amendment to ban flag burning.

Pressure groups which seek to block change to the Constitution only need to persuade 34 senators to oppose an amendment and that amendment fails. Thus, if there was a serious attempt to repeal the Second Amendment - the Right to Bear Arms - then the relevant pressure groups including the powerful and wealthy National Rifle Association, whose members include Bush and Reagan, would lobby Congress and presumably block the change. The opposite is true of groups which seek to promote change. There has to be a very wide consensus in favour of change for it stand a chance of success.

It could be argued that, in practice, the Supreme Court amend the Constitution through Judicial Review - or at least they bring it up to date, into line with present realities.

Conclusion

It is true that there have been periods in American history when fundamental rights have been abridged. The treatment of both native Americans and black Americans certainly was the most shameful departure from the idealism of the Declaration of Independence. It could be argued that the Patriot Act passed in the wake of September 11th also violates rights. The Act gives government greater powers to restrict civil liberties by for example computer tracking of phone calls, e-mails and bank details. The Department of Homeland Security merges 22 agencies and employs 170,000 people. The American Civil Liberties Union regard all of this as unconstitutional and it may yet be tested in the courts.

There is probably no state on Earth which has not at some period in its history been guilty of oppression, either of some of its own population or more usually foreigners. The Germans, Japanese, Italians. Israelis, Russians, British and French all have abuses of liberty of some kind to account for.

The USA has always been the very antithesis of a totalitarian state, indeed Americans have even rejected the level of state intervention which is commonplace in Western Europe and Australia. The encroaching power of the state is viewed with grave suspicion. Americans since Jefferson have boasted of their respect for liberty and civil rights. What Seymour Lipset refers to as 'American Exceptionalism', the belief, as Reagan put it, that the USA is a beacon of hope, is deeply ingrained in American culture.

Even disregarding the more fanciful notions of American Exceptionalism, it would generally be agreed that the USA is a good, perhaps the best, example of a pluralist state. It has a very open political system where power is fragmented and decentralised. Although there is enormous economic inequality everyone is, in theory at least, politically equal and there is a strong belief that government must be held accountable. Pressure groups flourish, there are very few limits on free speech and citizens can take the initiative by calling for a referendum or a 'recall' election. The success of Proposition 13 (limiting property taxes) in California in 1978, or Proposition 187 (tightening up on illegal immigrants) again in California in 1994 are just the best known examples of state-wide referendums. The American Civil Liberties Union even protect the rights of those, such as the American Nazi Party, who would deny others any rights at all.

Americans, perhaps because of the emphasis on the Bill of Rights, are more aware of their 'citizenship rights'. It is not necessary to eulogise the American political system. If there was such a temptation, then the crises of the last few decades would have restored some perspective. However, even whilst recognising its painful limitations there is arguably a more thoroughly democratic political culture in existence in America than in Britain or perhaps in the rest of Europe.

?   Compare and Contrast the Division of Powers Between Legislature, Executive and Judiciary

Introduction

In any political system, there are three functions which have to be performed: the passage of legislation, the implementation or execution of law, and the adjudication of legal disputes.

In a 'totalitarian' system such as China today, all three functions are in practice controlled by the same group of people (the Chinese Communist Party) as was also the case in the USSR before 1985. However, in liberal democracies, there is some attempt at separating the functions, the USA taking the process furthest with an almost complete separation of powers. The UK, unusually for a liberal democracy, has a very limited separation of powers. The British government is part of the legislature, but the British judges are said to be independent. Russia is a system dominated by the Executive, in a similar way to France. Whether theory really matches practice in any country is debatable.

Paragraph 2

Look at the way in which the Congress in America really is separate from the administration. Congress checks the executive and has real power, it can overturn a Presidential veto on a bill provided two thirds of Congress agree. It can, again by two thirds, help to change the constitution. Congress can reject budgets, the Senate can reject treaties, congress declares war and through the War Powers Act it can limit Presidential wars. Contrast with the limited powers of the British Parliament.

Paragraph 3

Look at the UK where there is a fusion of powers rather than a separation of powers. Government is part of the legislature and this is said to give the government enormous power. Thus there is dominant government, weak legislature. The British legislature is supposed to check the executive but arguably does so ineffectually. Contrast the House of Commons Select Committees set up in 1979, with their absence of powers with the power of the Congressional Committees. What the UK is supposed to have is Parliamentary government but there are lots of ways in which government dominates Parliament. However put into perspective by contrasting the apparent weakness of Parliament with the much weaker Russian Duma or 'talking shop' Chinese legislature.

Paragraph 4

The US judges have the power to declare acts passed by Congress "unconstitutional". The US judges ruled that Nixon had to hand over information. US judges are apparently much more political, they are the constitutional referee, or arbiter through judicial review The UK also has judges appointed by politicians, the Lord Chancellor, currently Lord Irvine, and the PM, but they are appointed for non-party reasons, that is they are appointed on merit. They are independent of political parties and do increasingly frequently rule against the government. Lord Justice Taylor criticised the Conservative governments sentencing policy. In the Tameside case in 1976 the Law Lords ruled a Labour government ultra vires. In the Matrix Churchill case in 1992 in which businessmen were accused of illegally selling arms to Iraq the judge dismissed the case causing the Major government to set up the Scott Inquiry which was later to cause them so much trouble. Contrast with the role of the judges under both the USSR and China neither of which emphasise an independent judiciary or the rule of law.

Paragraph 5

The US Constitution was written in 1787; in the 20th century the executive has become the chief legislator. The President is expected to deliver a programme of bills to the legislature. At the same time Congress has interfered in executive functions through the Congressional veto as in the War Powers Act which reduced the war waging power of the President. Now if the President wants to despatch troops he has to give Congress a written explanation as to why and if they don't agree, then they can force them back. A more accurate description of US politics comes from Professor Neustadt - "Separate Institutions Sharing Powers".

Although there are few formal checks and balances in the UK, people such as Professor Norton argue that Parliament does check the government. Certainly the Labour governments in the late 1970s, the Thatcher governments in the 1980s and the Major governments in the 1990s all been constrained by Parliament and the same is also happening under Blair.

Again emphasise this by putting the 'decline of Parliament' arguments into perspective, it remains legally sovereign.

Conclusion

In all liberal democracies in the 20th century, whatever formal arrangements exist concerning the distribution of power, there has been a shift of power to the executive. This has been particularly true of the UK because of the absence of a codified constitution. Hence the growing demands for major constitutional reform. However, experience of the USA shows that even if you have a codified constitution with clear divisions between the three branches of power, there are no guarantees that this will be adhered to. In practice, the division of power in the US today bears little resemblance to that devised in 1787.

Chapter Two

Chapter 3
Legislatures

All political systems require a body to legislate, a body to execute that legislation and a body to adjudicate disputes arising from legislation. Liberal democracies tend to separate the three functions so that the same people are not able to perform all three. The most extreme form of separation of powers is found in the USA where only the Vice President is allowed to be a member of more than one of the three branches. There are lots of countries with parliamentary forms of government. Germany has such a system so that ultimately the Chancellor is dependent on the Bundestag which, even though Germany has regular elections, can call a constructive vote of no confidence bringing about an election. Similarly India, Australia, Canada and New Zealand have forms of parliamentary democracy.

The UK is, again, unusual in that there is both a fusion of powers between the legislature and the government, the political executive, and also a limited fusion of judiciary and legislature in that the Law Lords, the highest court of appeal, are members of the upper chamber of Parliament. However even in systems with a separation of powers such as the USA the legislature is involved in the execution of legislation and the executive is involved in the legislative process. In China the legislature acts as a rubber stamp, automatically approving the Communist Party's decrees. The C20th has seen the rise of 'big government', the 'interventionist state' all over the democratic world and with it has come the apparent decline in the power of legislatures and the emergence of powerful executives employing large bureaucracies spending a high proportion of GNP. This seems to describe the changed role of the UK Parliament quite accurately. Whether all legislatures have declined in this way is debatable. It is hard to see how Congress could be described as a 'talking shop' indeed if anything Congress could be said to be too powerful. Owens and Foley argue that Congress is co-equal with the Presidency and that the two institutions genuinely share power.

Arno Lijphardt argues that 'majoritarian' systems have eight characteristics. The concentration of executive power in the hands of one party. A lack of separation between executive and legislature. A unicameral legislature, or at least one weighted towards one House. A two party system which is aligned along one set of issues, particularly economic and social policies. A first past the post electoral system. A unitary state and finally an unwritten constitution.

The British system fits these criteria better than any other liberal democracy, Israel has PR, Germany has a form of PR, Federalism and a codified constitution, Australia has Federalism and a codified constitution. Steve Ludlam argues that in the UK we should speak of executive sovereignty rather than parliamentary sovereignty

Legislatures

Australia - Bicameral; upper chamber the Senate 76 members representing the states and territories elected to 6 year terms by STV, lower chamber the House of Representatives 148 members elected to 3 year terms by AV.

China - Unicameral legislature; the National Peoples Congress - elected for five year terms by indirect election. All candidates members of the CCP, approx. 3,000 delegates, meets rarely, entrusts its business to a Standing Committee.

France - Bicameral; upper chamber the Senate, an advisory body of 321 elected for 9 year terms by indirect election with rights to examine and comment on and delay but not veto legislation approved by the lower chamber, the National Assembly, with 577 deputies elected for five year terms by party list. The PM and the Council of Ministers are responsible only to the National Assembly.

Germany - Bicameral; the upper chamber the Bundesrat or federal council made up of delegates chosen by the Lander, the lower chamber the Bundestag elected by AMS for four year terms has more power and can override a veto by the Bundesrat.

Israel - Unicameral legislature; the Knesset, 120 members elected by a party list system.

Russia - Bicameral; the Upper Chamber with 176 members is the Federation Council, the lower Chamber, the Duma with 450 members is the more powerful.

UK - The British Parliament is bicameral; technically we should speak of the Crown-in-Parliament but in reality the Monarch is a figurehead and we are entitled to concentrate attention on the two chambers, the Lords and the Commons.

USA - Bicameral; upper chamber Senate, lower chamber House of Representatives

The British Parliament

Introduction

The phrase 'Westminster Model' was used to describe the British system in the 1950s at a time when Britain's former colonies in Africa were developing their own constitutions often modelled on the 'Mother of Parliaments'. It consisted of a unitary state with a sovereign Parliament untrammelled by a codified constitution. The party which won most seats (almost always a majority) formed a government and claimed a mandate to implement its manifesto commitments. It faced on official opposition whose task was to constructively criticise the government and act as a 'government in waiting'. The model presupposed the existence of a duopoly so that a simple plurality electoral system achieved a reasonably proportionate result.

These constitutional arrangements, which had evolved over generations, were complemented by a settled political culture within a supposedly deferential society. The strong commitment to the rule of law, consensus about constitutional procedure and a high degree of public confidence in the competence and incorruptibility of government, all contributed to what now seems a rather complacent satisfaction with the British political system.

As late as the 1960s, despite problems, there was still an underlying consensus regarding the desirability of maintaining the 'Westminster Model'. Parliament, unlike Congress, was said to be legally sovereign, there were no legal limits to the power of Parliament. This is no longer the case because the European Court of Justice can overrule an Act of Parliament. In March 1989 in the Factortame case the British High Court granted an interim injunction suspending the 1988 Merchant Shipping Act. The Act was referred to the ECJ which overturned it in July 1991 on the grounds that it was in breach of Community law. As Borthwick points out increasingly British law is made by the European Union and this will become ever more true as time goes on irrespective of who is in power in the UK.

Parliament has lost authority with the public. Following evidence of sleaze under the Major Government there was a drop in public confidence in the integrity of Ministers and MPs. The Hamilton case and the Jonathon Aitken affair did much damage. Since then there has been progress in developing codes of conduct. However the first Commissioner for Parliamentary Standards, Elizabeth Filkin, was undermined by some of the very MPs to whom she was formally accountable. This exposed the limits of parliamentary self-regulation.

'Parliamentarianism' is the name given to the notion that Parliament is the central institution of political life. Marxist such as Miliband deride the Labour Party's commitment to Parliament on the grounds that 'Parliamentary Socialism' is oxymoronic; Parliament cannot serve as the vehicle for arriving at socialism because it serves the interests of the powerful and enhances the status quo. However, Labour's leadership have always been convinced that Parliamentary Socialism is possible and even Labour's left-wingers such as Bevan, Foot and Benn have been good 'House of Commons men'.

The Monarchy

The British system has evolved over the centuries with few traumatic interruptions. Cromwell instituted a Republic but the Monarchy was restored within 11 years and remains entrenched. Many democratic states retain a Monarchy, albeit a constitutional one. Lord Gilmour argued that "legitimacy, the acceptance by the governed of the political system, is far better aided by an ancient monarchy set above the political battle than by a transient president, who has gained his position through that battle. Modern societies still need myth and ritual. A monarch and his family supply it."

One hundred years ago the USA was the odd one out in having an elected Head of State; today, the UK is in a minority in still having a Monarch as Head of State. Throughout Europe, 1918 saw 'the Kings depart', although France had dispensed with hers - literally - in 1793. The continuation of Britain's Monarchy is a reflection of the evolution of the British political system over the centuries, which is itself a product of her relative immunity from the upheavals which traumatised Europe. It was the English Channel rather than the bravery of British soldiers or the brilliance of the British elite which accounts for the failure of Napoleon, the Kaiser or Hitler to occupy these islands. Had they done so presumably the Monarchy would have been abolished; unless of course it had collaborated.

With a few recourses to Europe when the immediate Royal line ran out the British Monarchy has continued for almost a thousand years. The Royal Prerogative refers to the powers which, in legal terms, are still those of the monarch in that they do not stem from Parliament. In the process of time, the power of Parliament and of the Government within Parliament became supreme over the monarch, and most of the powers of the monarch have gradually been transferred by convention to ministers, and particularly the Prime Minister. Thus the Queen acts on the 'advice' of Her ministers and is sheltered from party political controversy. According to Dicey, the prerogative is "the residue of discretionary or arbitrary authority, which at any given time is legally left in the hands of the Crown." Some of the more important of the Royal Prerogatives include the appointment of the Prime Minister, the appointment of ministers and the dissolution of Parliament. Tony Benn argues that the Royal Prerogative gives enormous power not to the Monarch but to the Prime Minister. In the USA, the Executive can only despatch troops subject to Congressional approval; either Congress declares war or if it is a 'Presidential War' then Congress can invoke the War Powers Act. In the UK the making of war, and of peace, are part of the Royal Prerogative. The issue arose during the build up to war with Iraq in 2003. The banning of trade union membership at GCHQ in 1984 was a prerogative act and as such was declared legal by the Law Lords.

If an election or the Parliamentary situation were to produce circumstances in which no party has a majority the monarch might play a more active role in encouraging negotiations between party leaders aimed at the formation of a government. Certainly, in the inter-war era of 'three partyism' with hung parliaments and coalition governments the norm, the Monarch was much more involved in politics than in the post-war era: witness George V's highly controversial role in the formation of the National Government in 1931. If the duopoly really is breaking down, then maybe the role of the monarch in choosing a Prime Minster will again be politicised. The precise course of events would depend on the situation in the House of Commons and the Queen would, as far as possible, be guided by precedents and by the advice of those best fitted to give that advice including former Prime Ministers, constitutional theorists such as Lord Blake, as well as the Queen's personal advisers. There would be a heavy responsibility placed on the party leaders to try to resolve any difficulties among themselves in order to avoid embroiling the Queen in party political controversy, thereby perpetuating the typically British myth of a totally apolitical monarchy.

The continuing importance of the Monarchial element in the Constitutions of the Dominions was revealed in 1975 when the Queen's representative in Australia, the Governor General, dismissed the Labour PM Gough Whitlam. To radicals such as John Pilger this merely revealed the reality of elite rule which is normally concealed by a facade of democracy; Whitlam had threatened vested interests therefore he had to go. To Monarchists such as Andrew Roberts the intervention was democratically justified when at the subsequent election Australians returned a Liberal Government under Malcolm Fraser.

Just as the Royal prerogative in reality means the government's prerogative, so the Monarch's power of patronage has passed to the PM, including the appointment of Peers. Constitutionally, the power to request the creation of peers has been important and has been used to resolve serious disputes between the two houses by creating or threatening to create peers. The residual power of the Monarch, an unelected position, was being used to make the political system more democratic.

According to Norton; 'the Queen fulfils the task of representing the unity of the nation as well as carrying out certain political functions largely but not exclusively governed by convention.... The monarchy occupies a central position in the British polity, a real and valuable one.... in embodying the unity of the nation, and a formal but nonetheless necessary one in fulfilling certain political duties. In the eyes of some, it is the most efficient element of the constitution.'

Not everyone would agree that a hereditary Head of State is a particularly efficient institution for the 21st century. Tom Nairn has argued powerfully for a reassessment of the 'glamour of backwardness' symbolised by Britain's obsession with the Monarchy. It is a myth that the Monarchy has always been popular. When George the Fourth died, the Times said that no-one would mourn; Professor Crick points to the unpopularity of Victoria, the 'Widow of Windsor', for most of her reign. When the House of Windsor gets concerned about is current difficulties it comforts itself with the fact that it was a lot more unpopular in the late 19th century and yet it went on to reinvent itself.

The Abdication crisis of 1936 could have seriously injured the standing of the Crown and fear of doing so is one reason why the current Monarch will not abdicate. Monarchy is not a career choice; it is supposed to be a vocation, a sacred trust.

Bernard Crick ties the position of the Monarchy in with our position as 'subjects' rather than 'citizens' and implies that it should be reformed or abolished as part of a new constitutional settlement. Since 1992 the Royal Family has had its share of traumas with marital failures galore, the Windsor fire, the introduction of income tax, the opening of Buckingham Palace to tourists, the divorce settlement and the public reaction to the death of Diana. The Queen is apparently concerned about the current unpopularity and also believes that Labour might try to reform the institution to create a 'peoples monarchy'. That is why she has co-operated over tax and in reducing the coverage of the Civil List from eight members of the family to four.

Labour hinted at reform, hence Jack Straw's talk of a more economical Monarchy and Mo Mowlam's talk of doing more to open up Royal Palaces. Yet Labour remains as pro-Monarchy as ever, witness the public humiliation imposed on the Shadow Welsh Secretary Ron Davies when he suggested that Charles was not fit to be King and Blair's involvement in the Queen's 50th wedding anniversary celebrations. Despite the arguments of the Republicans, abolition or even serious reform is not likely to be on the agenda for some considerable time.

The Monarchy: A summary

Arguments For	Arguments Against
Financial	**Financial**
Tourist revenue US tourists particularly want to see Royal aspects e.g. 1986 Andrew and Sarah wedding boosted tourism after Libyan pay bombing had scared Americans off. Royal visits abroad boost export earnings	Cost of Civil List Galling that some of the richest people in the world receive money from the taxpayer Queen only recently began to income tax
Symbolic	**Symbolic**
Unifies the nation; cuts across class, sex and racial divides, witness popularity of Diana and the Queen Mother	Apex of outdated class structure, how will this country ever modernise if the tone is set by a medieval legacy?
Royal Family acts as role model, a real extended family, a living soap	Dysfunctional family; poor example, divorces, can't accommodate outsiders
Constitutional	**Constitutional**
Hereditary Head of State prevents politicisation, contrast USA	Non-elected Head of State unacceptable in democracy; contrast Eire
Loyalty to Monarch is safeguard preventing coup; officers swear oath of allegiance to Queen	Monarchy clearly pro-conservative force e.g. role in constitutional crises of 1911, 1912-1914, 1931

The House of Lords

Bagehot, writing in the 1860s, described the Lords as one of the 'dignified' elements of the constitution. The Lords was traditionally dominated by Conservatives. In 1909 it broke convention by rejecting Lloyd George's 'People's Budget' leading to a constitutional crisis and finally the passage of the Parliament Act of 1911. The maximum length of a Parliament was reduced from 7 years to 5 years, the Lord's power of veto was removed and replaced by a power of delay over non-money Bills for 2 years. Money Bills must be passed by the Lords within a month of being received from the Commons, after which they go for the Royal Assent regardless. Money Bills certified as such by the Speaker of the Commons are those which exclusively authorise public expenditure or the raising of revenue.

The Parliament Act of 1911 reduced the power of the Lords but it did nothing about its composition. Attempts at modernisation of the world's oldest legislative assembly have met repeated frustrations. In 1917, the Bryce Conference recommended major reform, and in 1948 there was an all-party conference on possible reform but little was done. Facing a potentially hostile Conservative dominated Lords the Labour government of 1945-51 reduced the power of the Lords even further by the Parliament Act of 1949 as a result of which the Lords can now only delay for one year. This of course can still be significant as a government approaches an election.

Between 1949 and 1999 there were only two reforms. The 1958 introduction of Life Peerages and the Renunciation of Peerages Act (1963) by which Hereditary Peers can give up their title and become eligible for election to the Commons and hereditary peeresses could now be admitted in their own right. The Act was passed at the instigation of Lord Stansgate (Tony Benn) and his example was followed by Lord Home and Lord Hailsham (both Conservatives) among others. Since 1963 less than 20 Hereditary Peers have disclaimed their titles.

Although it is not an Act of Parliament, there is one further important development - the Salisbury Convention of the late 1940s. The Labour government of 1945-51 expected major problems with the Tory-dominated Lords, and this could have led to abolition. Understanding this, Salisbury, the leader of the Tories in the Lords, argued that the Lords should not reject a bill for which the government can claim a *mandate*. Arguably, it is this convention, combined with the new blood injected by the Life Peerage which has prevented the Lords from being abolished.

Composition

The British system is referred to as one of parliamentary democracy, yet extraordinary though it might seem in a supposedly democratic state the Upper House is totally unelected. Up until 1999 it consisted of approximately 1,250 members, about two thirds of whom were Hereditary Peers; the remaining ones were either Law Lords, Bishops of the Church of England, or Life Peers. It was one of the largest legislative assemblies in the world but only 300 to 400 members of the Lords regularly attended. The majority of these were Life Peers; most Hereditary Peers attended very rarely, and were often referred to as "backwoodsmen". The Lords was still overwhelmingly male, conservative and elderly, an easy prey to radical critics.

Hereditary Peers

A vast number of the roughly 800 Hereditary Peerages were created in the 20th century, especially under Lloyd George's Premiership (1916-1922); however, some of the more ancient ones were the Dukedom of Norfolk created in 1483 and the Baron of Mowbray (1283). Few Hereditary Peers gained government office; if they were ambitious they renounced their peerage. The absence of constituency responsibilities gives peers certain advantages. Not all Hereditary Peers were 'backwoodsmen', Home, Shackleton, Carrington and Gowrie were all active.

No PM between 1964 and 1983 created any hereditary peers. In 1984 Thatcher created 3 - Lord Stockton (Macmillan) Conservative, Viscount Tonypandy (ex-Speaker of the Commons); Lord Whitelaw (ex-Deputy PM) Conservative. Labour particularly opposed the hereditary peerage; as George Cunningham put it: "There is no justification for giving a person a voice and a vote merely because he is the son of his father.

Life Peers

Before the introduction of Life Peers in 1958 Conservative peers outnumbered Labour by 8:1; after it the ratio was about 3:1. Many Peers are ex-MPs or Councillors. As the Conservative peer Ian Gilmour puts it: "The Lords does something to reduce the hazards of a political career and embalms without burying a number of useful politicians."

Life peers have experience from varied walks of life such as Lady James the thriller writer, Lord Murray ex-General Secretary of the TUC, Lord Sieff from Marks and Spencer, and Lord Callaghan former Labour PM. In 1982 there were 43 female Life Peers. The aim of the 1958 Act was to introduce a wider cross section of society into the Lords thereby making it more legitimate and harder for a future Labour Government to reform or abolish.

Every PM finds the Life Peerage a useful way of rewarding friends, Wilson made 183 Life Peers, including some very controversial nominations such as Lady Falkender, Wilson's former Political Secretary, and Lord Kagan who later went to jail for fraud. Callaghan was much more circumspect and some of his nominees such as Jack Jones the TU leader refused a peerage which is very rare. Thatcher made great use of patronage. Altogether Thatcher created 214 peerages, Lord Weinstock of GEC, Lord Matthews a pro-Conservative 'Press Baron', Lord Forte of Trust House Forte, Lord Dacre the conservative historian, Lord Jacobovitz the ex-Chief Rabbi. Blair has appointed so many of his supporters that critics refer to 'Tony's cronies'. These include Lords Puttnam, Gavron, Bragg and Levy. Critics of Prime Ministerial power such as Benn point out that the patronage exercised by 10 Downing Street has created over 700 peerages since 1958, yet over 40 million voters between them elect just 659 members of the Lower House.

Functions of the Lords

The Bryce commission of 1917 identified 4 functions of the Lords. Firstly, legislative delay - only 3 Bills including the 1949 Parliament Act itself, were passed under the provisions of the Parliament Acts, i.e. were 'forced through'. The Act was 'threatened' in 1974/76 over Labour's Trade Union and Labour Relations Act and Aircraft and Shipbuilding Act, but a compromise was reached. It eventually happened over the War Crimes Bill in 1990. On the whole, the effect of the act is to inhibit the Lords in the exercise of even the limited degree of power they still possess. The Lords are reluctant to resist the Commons because such a conflict would lead to a questioning of the status of the Lords.

Secondly, legislative revision - this is its principal function. It is generally recognised than in cases of conflict the Lords should yield to the Commons. This does not mean that the Lords should not amend legislation passed by the Commons, even when it knows that the latter feels strongly about the matter, but that if the Commons persists in its view the Lords should normally give way.

The Lords meet for approximately 130 days per year (the Commons meets 160 days per year) but because of the financial primacy of the Commons the Lords can spend more time discussing other matters. The pressure on time in the Commons means that Bills are often inadequately discussed. The Government may have had second thoughts about some of the details of the Bill and these can be incorporated during its passage through the Lords.

The legislative process is the same as the Commons, except that most Bills are dealt with in Committee by the whole House. Most Bills start in the Commons then go to the 'Other Place'. If amendments are made to a Bill which has already passed the Commons then the Bill is returned to the Commons for consideration. They may reject or accept the Lord's revisions; if they reject them then the Lords may decide not to press their amendments, or there may be negotiations between the two Houses, or the Parliament Act may be used or the Bill may simply be 'lost'.

Thirdly, initiation of non-controversial legislation. Between 1974 and 1979 140 out of 315 Government Bills were initiated in the Lords. This saves the Commons time because Bills introduced in the Lords require little amendment in the Commons. Most Private Bills originate in the Lords, giving a local authority power to construct an airport or an oil company power to lay a pipeline across private land. The Commons would probably pass fewer Bills and certainly less adequately drafted bills were it not for the Lords, but ultimately which bills and how many bills become law depends on the Commons.

Fourthly, the sheer diversity of its membership and the weakness of party ties is said to allow for some very well-informed debates. The debate on the Criminal Justice Bill in 1996 saw much of the legal establishment savage Howard's proposals. However, five-sixths of Labour MPs and half of Conservative MPs say they pay little or no attention to the debates in the Lords.

In addition there are the judicial and oversight functions of the Lords. In total, there are 19 Law Lords, including the Lord Chancellor, 11 Lords of Appeal, ex-senior Judges etc. A minimum of 3, but usually 5, Law Lords hear appeals - sitting in Appellate Committee. Unlike the US Supreme Court, the Law Lords can only interpret the law - not decide what is constitutional and what is not (see section on Judges). The Lords scrutinises the executive through Committees such as the Joint Committee on Statutory Instruments and the Select Committee on the EU.

Reform
Supporters of the Lords such as Professor Shell believe that the Lords has proved its worth by amending Tory legislation since 1979 but Damien Welfare states that for most of the last century the Lords has acted in the interests of the Conservative Party. It caused havoc with the 1974-79 Labour government's legislative programme. Interestingly it was Conservative governments who were responsible for two major reforms of the Lords.

Notionally they perform the same functions as the Commons; in practice as Adonis points out they perform all except the judicial role half heartedly and even that role could be performed by an alternative appellate court in the absence of the Lords. Their legislative role is essentially a revising one as even Shell accepts. Their ability to oversee the executive is even more limited than that of the Commons. They clearly cannot be representative in the sense that the term is most often used. Their ability to air the concerns of the nation is inevitably impaired by their lack of democratic accountability and their somewhat elitist composition. All governments have to recruit a few members from the Lords but it is a small minority of the political executive. The implication is clear - the Lords is in need of replacement, however the option poses difficulties.

The Parliament Bill of 1968 would have introduced a two-tier system, 250 peers, appointed by the government of the day and with voting rights, plus non-voting existing hereditary peers, but not their heirs. It would have had a delaying power of 6 months over non-financial legislation. The proposal was introduced by Wilson's Labour government and was supported by Heath and the Conservative front bench. It was opposed by the Labour Left led by Michael Foot because it did not go far enough, and the Tory right led by Enoch Powell who opposed any change. Wilson was forced to abandon the attempt through lack of parliamentary time. This experience discouraged subsequent governments but the role and composition of the Lords remained a matter for debate and reform of the Lords was included in Labour's 1997 manifesto.

Donald Shell and Philip Norton have stressed that since the late 1960s the Lords, or more accurately, the working peers, have exhibited a "new professionalism". They are more and more willing to use their limited powers to criticise the government and Thatcher's government in the 1980s frequently encountered opposition from the Lords. This combative mood survived into the 1990s as the Major Government's defeat in February 1996 over Sky getting a monopoly of big sporting events demonstrates. Andrew Adonis and Peter Riddell have both rebutted this view of the Lords as the 'watchdog of the Constitution'. Whilst it is true that it has not exactly been Mrs Thatcher's poodle, neither did it stop the Conservatives getting their way on any of the major issues of the post-1979 era. It barked a lot, even nibbled occasionally but very rarely showed real teeth for the simple reason that it has long since lost them.

Options for the Lords

According to Professor Norton writing in 1982 there were the following options for the Lords.

Remove	Replace	Reform	Retain
Left-wing Lab	Labour leadership /Lib Dem	liberal Tory	Right-wing Tories
e.g. Benn /Skinner	e.g. Blair/Ashdown	e.g. Lord Home	e.g. Enoch Powell

Retain

Defenders of the Lords claim it does a useful job. As the then Tory MP (now Lord) Norman St John Stevas put it in 1968: "The case for the Lords is a highly practical one...It. is an assembly which works"

A dwindling number of traditional Tories such as Sir John Stokes believed that the Lords could be retained in its then condition. They argued that the hereditary peers were trained for the job from birth onwards, attended the right schools and universities and owed allegiance to no one, independent of constituents. When in February 1996 the Labour Party unveiled its plans to abolish the hereditary peerage there were critical editorials in the right wing press arguing that what mattered was not the lack of democratic legitimacy but the contribution made to Britain by hereditary peers. Yet even the Conservatives accepted the inevitability of change hence the compromise over allowing 92 hereditary peers to survive.

Reform

It is the fear of abolition which led most Tories to believe that reform is inevitable and therefore they have come up with some proposals. In 1978, the Home Committee advocated a House of 400 members, one-third nominated by the parties, two-thirds elected by PR but Thatcher was not interested.

Remove

Removing a second chamber altogether and putting nothing in its place means unicameralism. Labour leaders have always opposed this; in the 1979 election campaign Callaghan had vetoed a proposal to include abolition in Labour's Manifesto. However, after 1979 the old idea of abolition resurfaced and in 1980 became Labour policy. Benn proposed to create 1,000 new peers to vote for abolition. However, unicameralism would remove a safeguard, a check and a balance and make 'elective dictatorship' more likely. Israel is unicameral however it has PR which prevents elective dictatorship. In the absence of PR in the Commons this option appears too threatening because it removes one of the few checks and balances.

Replace

By 1997 both the retain and reform options were no longer viable, whilst removing altogether and putting nothing in its place was also not an option, Labour wanted to replace it.

Replacing the Lords would mean a new Upper Chamber probably called the Westminster Assembly or just the Upper House. It could be appointed, by reviving the old functional chamber idea to allow pressure groups a formal say in the political process. This was suggested by Leo Amery and Winston Churchill in the 1930s.

In 1989, as part of their Policy Review, Labour adopted a proposal to replace the Lords with an elected Upper Chamber, probably elected by Proportional Representation. The Liberal Democrats agreed. Yet in Government Labour have shied away from this idea. Stage 1 of Labour's reform involved abolition of the hereditary peers. This was achieved by 1999 although 92 were given a reprieve until such time as Stage 2 is completed - if that ever happens. The Conservatives saw it as Labour simply removing a check and balance which happened to be dominated by Conservatives. In their eyes it had nothing to do with democratisation, it was merely enhancing the government's power. The Liberals saw it as a necessary first step en route to a democratic upper chamber.

Labour have yet to go ahead on Stage 2 claiming a lack of consensus as to what this should involve. Blair appointed the Wakeham Commission to consider options for Stage 2. He reported in January 2000 recommending a chamber of 550 members with 12%, 16% or 35% elected. In October 2001 the Government responded with the White Paper 'Completing the Reform' written by Lord Irvine. It favoured 20% election. In the face of huge opposition from Labour backbenchers the plan was abandoned, a rare example of a Government climb down. Robin Cook, then leader of the House of Commons, was said to favour more radical reform. The Commons Public Administration Committee favoured 60% elected with the Law Lords removed and forming instead a Supreme Court. This would impact upon the power of the Lord Chancellor. The Human Rights Act states that there should be an 'independent and impartial tribunal' which also questions the party political Lord Chancellorship.

For once the Conservatives were prepared to be more radical than Labour and suggested the creation of a Senate of 300 with 80% elected. Blair said such a body would challenge the Commons leading to gridlock. A 24 member joint Lords/Commons committee now looked at the issue and reported in December 2002 setting out 7 options for the Lords ranging from fully appointed to fully elected. The various options were debated in the Commons in February 2003 but none were approved. Blair made it clear that he favours 100% appointment. Cook openly disagreed with this but within a few weeks he had resigned over Iraq. Meanwhile the Lords had voted for a fully appointed chamber. As of summer 2003 the Government appear to have lost interest in the issue. Thus the Conservative suspicion that Labour would never progress on to Stage 2 and that all they had really wanted was to abolish the hereditaries looks plausible.

Conclusion

? Why has it proved so difficult to reform the Lords fundamentally since 1911?

The Lords survives because there is no consensus on what to do about it. Shell implies that reform of the Lords is an irrelevance, what really matters is reform of the Commons. Vernon Bogdanor agrees; there is nothing democratic about an upper chamber based entirely on Life Peerages as it would enhance the patronage powers of the PM, and anyway reform of the Lords should have come after reform of other political institutions not before.

As Democratic Audit argues 'the Lords continues to offer a more independent check on government than the Commons, but it lacks democratic legitimacy and accountability to the public.' Andrew Granath points out that the partially reformed House has proved more difficult to manage and has blocked the government on a number of issues including the repeal of Section 28 relating to the 'promotion' of homosexuality in schools, lowering the age of homosexual consent to 16 and elements of the anti-terrorist bill.

? 'Reform of the Lords is not urgent, reform of the Commons is.' Discuss.

There is an additional problem for reformers of the Lords and that is the implications reform would have for the monarchy given that they are both based on the hereditary principle. If the only source of legitimacy in a democracy is election, what possible justifications are there for the continued existence of the hereditary element in British politics?

Congress

Madison believed that 'in republican government the legislative authority necessarily dominates.' Hence the assumption that the Congress would emerge as the central policy making body apparently confirmed by the fact that it is Article One which deals with Congress.

There are two Senators per state regardless of population, California with getting on for 30 million people and Alaska with a third of a million both have two Senators. The 50 states therefore are served by 100 Senators. Before 1913 they were appointed, but the 17th Amendment of 1913 introduced direct elections. They serve 6 year terms with a third being elected every two years. The Senate is probably the most powerful and prestigious Upper Chamber of any legislature in the world. The British House of Lords has authority, it has very little power. The American Senate has both power and authority. Members of the House of Representatives often go on after a few terms there to seek election to the Senate. Many Presidents, such as Harry Truman, John Kennedy, Lyndon Johnson and Richard Nixon have served as Senators. The only President of recent times to come from the House was Gerald Ford and special circumstances applied in his case.

There are 435 members of the House of Representatives all of whom face election every two years The number per state depends on the state's population with roughly one Representative for every half a million people so that in 2000 California was divided into 52 congressional districts. Former Speaker O'Neill stated that in the USA *'all politics is local'*. Representatives, even more than Senators, regard their primary function as the articulation of local concerns because, if they are neglected, a Congressman may find him or herself unseated at the next election, which is never more than two years away. Perhaps Representatives are therefore closer to Burke's description of a delegate than their British counterparts. Of course, they try to take account of the party line, party voting has actually increased in recent years, especially if their party holds the Presidency; however, in any conflict of interests the wishes of the "folks back home" will probably prevail.

Most Representatives are relatively anonymous, ignored by national and even their own state's media. The same is true of MPs, but they are more beholden to their party because generally it was the party label that got them elected whereas Representatives exploit the advantages of incumbency through "pork barrel politics". This will often involve collusion with local pressure groups.

The Enumerated Powers specified in Section Eight include the power to create a currency, **the Implied Powers** therefore include the power to create a Federal bank. Under Article I, Section 3 of the Constitution, the

House has the sole power to impeach a President (and other senior civil officers) whilst the Senate tries the impeachment. The House (under Section 7) is empowered to initiate all 'money Bills', though such Bills still require Senatorial consent. The Senate alone has the power (by simple majority) to confirm or reject the President's nomination of Supreme Court Justices, Ambassadors and senior government officials. If there is no clear 'Electoral College' majority for any Presidential candidate, it is the House that chooses by ballot from the top three candidates This almost happened in 2000. The constitutional position is reflected in the greater authority and prestige of the Senate although the two Houses are approximately co-equal in their powers.

The Speaker

The House is controlled by the Speaker, elected by the whole House but in practice chosen by the majority party. The Speaker, currently Dennis Hastert, is 3rd in line to the Presidency and is far more powerful than his British counterpart because in addition to acting as 'referee; he also acts as the 'captain' of the majority team. He presides over the House and interprets its rules and although he puts questions to the vote, and can vote himself he rarely takes part in debates. Aided by the 'Parliamentarian', he decides on the allocation of Bills to the Standing Committees, and as Chairman of the Party's Steering Committee he helps decide the allocation of members to those committees. The Speaker can appoint Select Committees to carry out special investigations as with the Watergate Committee 1974. Speakers were even more powerful before the revolt in 1910 which deposed Speaker Canon. Speaker Thomas (Tip) O'Neill was a leading political personality after he replaced Carl Albert in 1977, Jim Wright (Texas) replaced O'Neill in January 1987. When Wright was forced out through scandal, Tom Foley took over.

Such was the scale of Democrat losses in November 1994 that Foley himself was defeated and was replaced by the radical Republican Gingrich, previously the Republican Whip. Gingrich was discredited by the Republican losses in the 1998 elections and was eventually replaced by Dennis Hastert. Hastert is a moderate much less dominant than Gingrich and has at times been overshadowed by the Majority Leader Dick Armery and the Republican Whip Tom Delay. In spring 1999 Hastert wanted the House to support Clinton's actions over Kossovo but Delay persuaded the Republicans to oppose it.

Even if the Congress is controlled by the President's party, it will not necessarily support his proposals. Bush cannot rely on Congressional Republicans to support him. In contrast with the weakness of the Select Committee system in Britain, the "Irangate Affair" revealed the strength of Congressional Committees. However, it also revealed the way in which both Senators and Representatives use the televised hearings for their own political advantage. They offer Representatives a welcome chance to get national exposure. Although committees in the Senate are obviously very important, most issues are resolved on the floor of the Senate. This is because power is more evenly distributed within the Senate than in the House where the Committees are the vital power centres.

The very fact the Senators serve six year terms allows them to take a broader perspective than their House colleagues. Senators tend to take a less parochial view because they speak for the whole state rather than just a district. Senator Clinton must speak for the whole of New York state not just a district of New York city. House Districts have big electorates in British terms, but all but the least populated states such as Alaska have more. Because there are only 100 Senators, they tend to get more media coverage than the 435 Representatives. "Freshmen" Representatives have to "serve their time" before they get chosen for the key committees whereas Senator Clinton, elected in 2000, is already on a prestigious committee. The convention of **"Senatorial Courtesy"**, whereby Presidents consult Senators over appointments to their State, demonstrates the high esteem in which Senators are held.

The formal powers of the Senate include the right to ratify Treaties and to approve high ranking Presidential appointments, including Federal judges. The Senate rejected the Treaty of Versailles in 1919, with monumental consequences for American foreign policy. Carter withdrew the SALT-2 Treaty before the Senate could reject it. He was only able to get the Panama Canal Treaty through by making a lot of concessions. The INF Treaty of December 1987 was ratified by the Democrat-controlled Senate. Presidents have increasingly resorted to making Executive Agreements instead of

Treaties, as they do not require Senatorial approval. The Bricker Amendment of 1953 would have made Executive Agreements subject to Senatorial approval, but it failed to get enough support. The Case Acts of 1972 force the President to disclose Executive Agreements to Congress

Generally speaking, the House is less concerned with foreign and defence policy than the Senate, preferring to concentrate on financial issues. The House of Representatives wields both negative and positive power. Whereas the Commons can be accused of acting simply as a "rubber stamp" for Government proposals, the Representatives are accused of blocking Administration plans without proposing suitable alternatives. They are alleged to be too concerned with local sensitivities to be able to offer coherent policies for the nation as a whole.

It is still relatively rare for the Senate to reject a Presidential nominee, but since Nixon the Senate has scrutinised nominees very closely. Ten (a post-1961 record) of Carter's nominees to the Executive Branch were either rejected or withdrew rather than face the detailed hearings. Ed Meese faced a real grilling when Reagan appointed him Attorney General, as did Rehnquist when he was made Chief Justice. Reagan's appointee to replace Justice Powell, Robert Bork, was rejected by 58:42. Even the Director of the OMB, part of the EOP, needs Senatorial confirmation. In the post-Irangate era appointees to the National Security Council will be very closely scrutinised.

Retiring after 30 years as a Senator, Barry Goldwater is alleged to have remarked, "if this is the world's greatest deliberative body, I'd hate to see the worst". However, for all the frustrations its members sometimes feel, the Senate is still very powerful and prestigious.

The Oligarchy

The Committees are the power centres of Congress and their chairmen are amongst the most powerful people in Congress. According to John Owens from the 1910 rebellion against Speaker Cannon to the 1960s, congressional politics was transformed into committee government as the congressional careers of Representatives and Senators came to revolve around their committee activities. Central party leaders were reduced to brokering agreements among committees and particularly their Chairmen who formed an **oligarchy** made up predominantly of Southern Democrats. These were the days of the Solid South when Southern Blacks were denied civil rights including the right to vote and the South was effectively a one party - Democrat - region.

Traditionally, chairmen were chosen by Seniority. The longest continuous serving member of the majority party of the Committee automatically became chairman. From 1931 onwards, the Democrats were the dominant party in Congress. This meant that Southern Democrats often became chairmen because they had the safest seats. The chairmen had the power to decide the Committee's agenda and block bills they disapproved of. Presidents such as FDR (Democrat) 1933-45, Truman (Democrat) 1945-53 and Eisenhower (Republican) 1953-61 had to work with the southern oligarchy led in the Senate by Russell (Georgia), Kass (Oklahoma), Dicksen (Illinois), Bird (Virgina) and Fulbright (Arkansas) and in the House by Rayburn (Speaker), Smith (Rules), Vinson (Armed Services) and Mills (Ways and Means) or risk losing their bills. Power was thus highly centralised and centrifugal.

The 11 former Confederate states had 22 Senators and with about one quarter of the country's population they had over 100 seats in the House. In 1960 94% of southern House seats and 100% of southern Senate seats were Democrat. Over one third of all Democrats in Congress were from the South. As late as 1967 over half of all Committees in Congress were chaired by southerners and these were the 'blue ribbon' committees.

If a President did attempt to get Civil Rights through Congress, then the oligarchy blocked it, and if all else failed, there was always the filibuster (the obstruction of Senate action on a bill by taking advantage of the rule of unlimited debate and "talking the bill to death"). It was LBJ, an ex-Senate Majority Leader and an extraordinarily skilled legislative tactician who got civil rights through. In the 1968 Presidential election, southern whites deserted the Democratic party. The Solid South was over, by 1980 there were only 12 Southern Democrats and 30 House Southern Democrats. The changes were due to the transformation of the South, industrialisation and urbanisation and the success of civil rights. A new breed of moderate southern Democrat had emerged such as Carter (Georgia) and Reuben

Askew (Florida). By November 1994 the Republicans were the dominant party in the South, including the 5 Democrat Representatives who switched parties the Republicans had 69 of the 125 House seats of the deep South, whereas in 1992 the balance was 77-39 in favour of the Democrats.

'The New Congress'

With the break up of the Solid South the oligarchy was undermined. Within a few years the Presidency was to be undermined by two separate but related crises - Watergate and defeat in Vietnam - bringing disgrace at home combined with defeat abroad. In response the 93rd Congress did two things which went a long way to rectifying the 6 decades of continuous decline: it reasserted itself over the President by passing measures such as the War Powers Act of 1974, the Impoundment and Budget Control Act 1974, the Jackson Amendment 1974, the Case Act. New Intelligence Committees have been established in both houses.

Secondly Congress reformed itself. Seniority was diluted, the power of Committee chairmen was reduced, it became easier to block a filibuster and the "Sunshine" laws opened up the Committees to public scrutiny. The oligarchy was broken up and a dual power structure emerged in which committees shared power with party organisations and leaders.

The combined result of these changes was what Orenstein calls a "New Congress", more democratic, more fragmented, more individualistic than before, but much more difficult to work with because the old power centres have gone. This would not be a problem if Congress had the capacity to set the country's course as a substitute for Presidential leadership but there are severe limits on the capability of the legislature to develop integrated and coherent policy, except perhaps in the financial sphere but even there it is unable to prevail.

This has produced gridlock where very little gets done. A weakened Presidency faces a centripetal Congress which is susceptible to lobbying by pressure groups under the ever present eye of a distrustful media. Martin Walker argues that well intentioned reform of the seniority system had led to a kind of political anarchy. There is so little party discipline in Congress that in the 1990, stand off between Bush and the Congress over the budget,

Gingrich, then the deputy leader of the Republicans in the House, led the rebellion against the deal his President and his party leader had just agreed. Bush tried to blame Congress 'The American people know that the President does not pass the budget, it is the Congress that does it.'

November 1994 Onwards

Republican control brought about important changes in the Congress' internal organisation. In the House of Representatives power became much more centralised than at any time since the beginning of the C20th as levels of party unity approached exceptional levels. The dual power structure was temporarily replaced by party rule. Gingrich, together with Dick Armery the new House majority leader, strengthened and centralised majority party organisation in a new steering committee dominated by the Speaker who together with the Republican Conference now exercised far greater control over committees. In the post-Gingrich era the party leadership has become less centralised and the committees have grown stronger.

Changes in the Senate have been less dramatic though here too some important changes occurred as Republican Party unity Increased. Senate Committees and their chairs have been made more accountable to Republican Conference and there is a six year term limit on Chairs. Robert Dole became the Senate majority leader, using the position as a stepping stone for his Presidential ambitions. However by late spring of 1996 with his campaign in trouble Dole stepped down from the Senate altogether. He was replaced by Trent Lott. Lott was a close ally of Gingrich and the two worked closely together from the summer of 1996 to Gingrich's resignation in December 1998.

The mid-term elections of 1998 produced a House with 223 Republicans, down from 228, 211 Democrats up from 26 and 1 independent. In the Senate a 55:45 Republican majority was unchanged. The first ever female black Senator Carol Moseley-Braun lost in an ill tempered race in Illinois. In New York the Democrat Charles Schumer ousted the Republican incumbent Alfonse D'Amato. The Republicans lost 1 Governorship to an Independent - the former wrestler 'Jesse 'the body' Ventura the Reform

Party candidate - giving them 31 to the Democrats 17 with 2 Independents. The Democrat Gray David won the Governorship of California, the first in 16 years. The Democrats did well in the South.

The Democrats retook control of the Senate in May 2001 under Tom Daschle. The mid-term elections of 2002 restored a Republican majority under Lott. He had to resign in 2003 following indiscreet comments about racial segregation. The new Majority Leader is Bill Frist.

Even though the highly centralised party leadership of the days of 1995/6 have not lasted nonetheless the Republican takeover has had lasting effects. Institutionally it has created term limits for Chairs, in terms of policy it led to the welfare reform bill of 1996 and the balanced budget agreement with Clinton in 1997. The 2000 elections produced an incredibly even Congress. The Senate was 50:50 but even in the House there was one of the narrowest margins in US history 221-211 Republican majority. The mid-term elections have enhanced Republican control.

? There is no question about it, Congress is the most powerful legislature in the democratic world. The question is, is it too powerful? Does it use its powers in a negative way - to block rather than build? Is it a bastion of negation?

1) The Legislative Process

The UK

Government Bills

Most government bills are based on manifesto commitments such as the Devolution for Scotland and Wales Bills which despite huge controversy went on to become Acts in 1998. Sometimes the government will float its ideas in the form of a **Green Paper** for consultation with pressure groups. The more serious proposals are put in a **White Paper**. The first time the Commons sees the bill is in its **"First Reading"**, but there is no debate.

The first serious stage is its **"Second Reading"**. The bill is introduced by the relevant Cabinet minister. The Shadow minister then responds. There is then a more general debate, involving all MPs, on the principles of the bill. After a debate of 1 or 2 days there is a vote. If it gets a majority, as it almost always will if there is a Majority Government, then it goes to a **Standing Committee**. Only one government bill since 1979 has been defeated at this stage, the Shops Bill 1986.

Standing Committee consists of 20 to 30 MPs from the major parties, drawn in proportion to party strength in the Commons as a whole, who look at the bill in detail in committee rooms over a few months. The Committees are whipped, the government have a majority of supporters on the committee and therefore the government will get their way.

Once the committee have finished with a bill then they report back to the whole House. The **Report Stage** is followed by its **"Third Reading"**, with a debate and a vote. Assuming that there is a majority, the bill then goes to the Lords.

The War Crimes Bill of 1990 was rejected by the Lords but was pushed through under the Parliament Act, one of the few times the Act has actually been used, to become the War Crimes Act .

Finally the bill goes to the monarch. Approval is automatic, no monarch has rejected a bill since 1707 and no Monarch will do so in the future. What if it is a Bill to abolish the Monarchy? For such a Bill to have reached the Monarch it must have passed through both Houses, no Monarch will attempt to flout the will of Parliament in such a way.

Former Speaker of the Commons - Betty Boothroyd. The Speaker has a much less important political role than the Speaker of the House of representatives, but still has a very important adjudicating and ceremonial role. She presides over debates and technically has a higher status than the PM.

Private Member's Bills

These are put forward by back benchers. Only those MPs who win in the ballot get the opportunity to do so. However, even these are unlikely to become acts unless they get government backing. Most private members bills that do become law are on moral issues which governments are wary of such as the abolition of the death penalty in 1965, the reform of the abortion law in 1967; reform of the laws on homosexuality in 1967 and reform of the divorce law in 1969

All these were backed by the Labour Party which was in office at the time but they were not government bills. The vast majority of private members bills fail because they don't get government backing therefore they don't get enough time on the Parliamentary calendar. Enoch Powell wanted to reform the law on testing of foetuses - he failed. Pressure groups representing disabled people tried to get through a bill to make working conditions better - again it failed. Mike Foster's bill to ban fox hunting failed in the late 1990s because it lacked government backing. Thus to sum up; the government dominate the legislative process at every turn, from the timetabling of the Commons to the voting in Standing Committees. This is why it is often said that in practice the Government legislates and Parliament simply ratifies the legislation.

Advantages of such a system - The electorate have the near certainty that the winning party will be able to turn most of their manifesto into legislation. It is also possible to act decisively in a crisis such as after the Dunblane massacre in 1996 when the Opposition parties promised to support a 'fast track' for legislation curbing gun ownership or after the IRA resumed their terror campaign and Parliament immediately agreed new powers for the police.

Disadvantages of such a system - Parliament is unable or unwilling to check legislation properly which is why we end up with ill thought out statutes such as the Dangerous Dogs Act which is very difficult to implement; the Child Support Act which had bi-partisan support but which when implemented generated huge controversy; the Police and Magistrates Courts Bill which Howard's senior Mandarins had warned him about and which Chief Constables described as 'inept and

101

incompetent' or even worse the Poll Tax which had to be abandoned within a few years of implementation because it was so unpopular. The same Parliament that passed the Poll Tax also repealed it. One of the reasons there have been so many Criminal Justice bills over the last few years is because the legislation is rushed and partisan. For example the attempt to link motoring fines to the income of the offender.

The USA

The legislative process is enormously complicated and very few bills actually complete the legislative obstacle course The Congress of 1993/94 saw just 5.9% of the bills introduced go on to become Acts.

If it is a finance bill, it has to begin in the Representatives although it still has to go through the Senate (there is no equivalent of the Parliament Act of 1911). Any other type of bill can start in either House, or both concurrently. In the Representatives, a bill is allocated to the relevant Standing Committee by the Speaker, so an agriculture bill goes to the Standing Committee on agriculture.

Unlike Standing Committees in Britain those in Congress have autonomy. Indeed they are the power centres of Congress. The Committees look at the bill in detail, they hold hearings, consult pressure groups, interview members of the relevant executive department (this could be described as obstacle 1). Most bills never get any further, they are not rejected but "pigeon holed".

If the Committee want the bill, it then has to go to the powerful **Rules Committee** (obstacle 2) which is responsible for organising the timetable of the floor of the House. The Rules Committee is the most powerful committee in the House. It has a bi-partisan membership (2:1 in favour of the majority party). Containing senior party members, the Committee allocates Bills from the Standing Committees to 'Calendars' (on the House time-table) and can effectively determine their fate. A Bill sent to the 'Whole House' calendar may be a finance Bill for general discussion; the 'Open Rule' calendar allows amendments, the 'Closed Rule' limits debate. The old seniority system allowed the Committee to be dominated by

'Southerners', but reform in the 1970s made it more 'liberal' though it is still powerful. There is no real equivalent in the Senate.

The Committee can kill a bill by pigeonholing it and, although it is possible to force them to give the bill a ruling through a discharge petition, it is very difficult. The Civil Rights Bills of the early 1960s were pigeonholed by the Rules Committee which was at that pre-Congressional reform stage even more powerful than it is today and controlled by Southern Democrats. If the Rules Committee want the bill it then goes to debate on the floor of the House (obstacle 3) which is relatively straightforward because if it has got this far, it must have quite a lot of support. In the Senate, the bill is referred to the relevant Standing Committee by an officer, the Parliamentarian.

The Committee go through the same process as their equivalent in the Representatives. Again, most bills die in Committee. Floor debate in the Senate is far from a formality because each Senator feels that they have something to contribute to debate and there is the possibility of a **Filibuster** (obstacle no 4).

If the bill gets a majority in the Senate and in the Representatives, then the chances are that the two versions of the bill will be very different, so they have to be reconciled. This is the job of a **Conference Committee** made up of Senators and Representatives from the appropriate Committees (obstacle no 5). If they can agree a compromise, then it goes back to the floor of the House and the floor of the Senate for approval or rejection (obstacles 6 and 7). Even if both agree, there is another obstacle (8), the President.

Presidential Action

In the UK the Royal Assent is a formality but in the USA but the President has various options:

a)   sign the bill into law, e.g. Clinton's Crime Bill in 1994 even though the eventual version bore little resemblance to the original bill proposed by Clinton.

b)   do nothing, then after 10 working days, the bill becomes law anyway,

c)   veto the bill - the President cannot veto particular sections, he has to veto the whole bill. There is no general line item veto and an attempt to introduce one was ruled unconstitutional in 1998 in the case of Clinton v New York City. The President has to give a written explanation as to why he is vetoing the bill. Congress can overturn the veto, but it requires a two-thirds majority in each House. Reagan vetoed the Highways Bill 1987, describing it as "pure pork", but Congress overturned the veto. Clinton used the veto to great effect after 1994.

d)   the President could leave the bill and if there are fewer than 10 working days left of the Congressional Session, then the bill will fail. This is known as the Pocket Veto, and unlike the regular veto, it cannot be overturned by Congress. If they want the bill, then it has to start the whole obstacle course again in the next Congress.

Advantages of this legislative system - There is no elective dictatorship, no group can push bills through, they must build a consensus. Congress' procedural devices reflect the separation of powers.

Disadvantages - It is very difficult to act in a crisis. There have been only two occasions this century when the Congress has responded urgently to a President's domestic programme - both involved special circumstances. Between 1933 and 1939 President Roosevelt (Democrat) pushed the New Deal through a Congress controlled by his party. So successful was he in doing so that he was branded a 'democratic dictator'. LBJ in the 1960s got the Great Society reforms through a Democrat-controlled Congress. It is easy for a determined minority to apply pressure at one of the several access points and be able to block the bill - Standing Committees, filibusters, Rules Committee etc. This could be said to create a 'tyranny of the minority'.

? 'The structure and operation of Congress reflect the decentralised and heterogeneous nature of the American political system.' Discuss.

The US Budget

There are particular problems with budgetary politics. There is no parallel in the Commons where the Government's Budget is almost guaranteed passage. The Office of Management and Budget gathers information from the various Departments and Agencies before submitting the President's Budget to Congress. In 1974, Congress passed the **Impoundment and Budget Control Act** preventing the President from impounding funds. At the same time, it set up its own budget committees, giving Congress more influence over the annual budget.

The House and the Senate each have their own Budget Committees, advised and co-ordinated by the Congressional Budget Office. Each Standing Committee sends its budget proposals to the House or Senate budget committee, and the two bodies then formulate a budget resolution.

This resolution contains overall figures for income, expenditure and borrowing, as well as items for particular services (such as health, defence, etc.) Authorisation Bills (concerning the spending of money) and Appropriation Bills (income) are then reconciled and agreed. Constitutionally, Money Bills must originate in the House, but they do not necessarily agree with the President's

By 1980 the Carter Presidency presided over a budget deficit of about $40 billion a year, the Federal government was spending $40 billion more than it collected in taxes. Reagan argued that this was totally unacceptable claiming that he would balance the budget. In fact, by 1984 the deficit was about $200 billion per year. The memoirs of David Stockman, Reagan's ex-Director of the budget, reveal the lengths to which the Reagan Administration had to go in order to get its Budget proposals through. Stockman, in charge during Reagan's first term (1981-5), resigned in protest at failure to curb the deficit blaming, "pork barrel politics" in Congress. In 1985 Congress passed the **Balanced Budget Act**, sometimes named after its sponsors Gramm, Rudman and Hollings, an attempt to get rid of the deficit in stages. The Supreme Court ruled the act unconstitutional in the Synar case. So, in 1987, Congress had to pass a revised version of the act but this did not work; the deficit remained extremely high. Hence Bush in 1990 and Clinton in 1993 having to raise taxes. Clinton finally got the deficit down with the US economy growing very rapidly and with Clinton doing a deal with the Republican Congress in 1997. Bush managed to get a $1.3 trillion tax cut through in May 2001. However he is struggling to get more tax cuts through in 2003 and meanwhile the deficit has returned.

2) Scrutinising the Executive

The UK

The fusion of powers makes it much harder for Parliament to keep check on the Executive because the government controls the legislature. There are various mechanisms and processes through which Parliament in particular the Commons attempts to scrutinise the executive.

The Official Opposition

This is the second biggest party. Since 1997 it has been the Conservatives. It has a dual role: to constructively criticise government policy and to act as a government in waiting. The separation of powers means that there is no equivalent in the USA. The two-party system encourages an adversarial atmosphere in the Commons which the very shape of the chamber enhances; the Government benches versus the Official Opposition benches, whereas Congress and indeed most legislatures are circular reflecting a more consensual approach. However even in the UK there are also considerable areas of agreement and consensus over foreign policy, Europe, Northern Ireland, the Monarchy the war on terror. Adversarial politics 'makes better copy' - and now TV - than consensual politics but actually there is a large, mostly unseen, element of co-operation between the two front benches. The PM will, from courtesy, consult the Leader of the Official Opposition on issues such as terrorism, war, major crises, as Major did with Blair over the renewed IRA terror threat and Blair did with Smith over war with Iraq.

Despite disagreements about policy, there is an underlying consensus over procedure on the role of Parliament. The Opposition are consulted about the timetable; they get so many Opposition Days when they choose the subject for debate, they have the right to choose topics in their reply to the Address from the Throne (the Queen's Speech) they are represented on various committees in proportion to overall party strength and occasionally they provide the chairmen of Select Committees, the expert and widely respected Labour backbencher Frank Field chaired the Select Committee on Social Security.

Party competition is an essential part of British democracy. The Official Opposition has been part of British politics for centuries but was only formally recognised in 1937 with the Ministers of the Crown Act which provided a salary for the leader of the Official Opposition. Since 1975, the party as a whole has received public funding. Adversary politics makes Parliament an arena for struggle between two main groups competing for electoral support. The Opposition offer themselves as an alternative government, a government in waiting, and this means their opposition has to be *constructive* not merely *obstructive*.

The Conservative Shadow Cabinet consists of about 20 senior spokesmen. There are another 40 or 50 Conservative spokesmen and 10 Opposition Whips all bound by collective responsibility. In 1968, Enoch Powell was sacked from the Conservative Shadow Cabinet because of his public disagreement with party policy on race. Clare Short resigned from Kinnock's Shadow Cabinet because she opposed the continued bombing of Iraq in 1991 and Bryan Gould resigned from Smith's team in 1992 because he favoured devaluation of the £ within the ERM. There was a lot of pressure on Clare Short - again - in 1995 for suggesting a wider debate on the legalisation of cannabis and for stating that she favoured a tax increase for the middle class and on Harriet Harman in 1996 for sending her son to a grammar school, both apparently at odds with Labour policy. Hague lost two colleagues over his line on E.M.U. In May 2001 Crispin Blunt resigned from the Shadow Government in protest at Smith's ineffective leadership.

By common consent the Labour Party between 1979 and 1987 had not been an effective opposition. Partly, because for much of the time, Labour had to concentrate on reforming itself. Partly because for much of the time the Tories had huge majorities; it was very dispiriting for Labour MPs to win the debate and yet lose the vote and in such circumstances it became very hard to galvanise the Opposition. With Labour as a relatively ineffective opposition throughout most of the 1980's, commentators argue that real scrutiny of the Government often came from Conservative Backbenchers

After 1987, particularly after 1992, Labour was far more effective in both the tasks of an opposition. Since 1997 the Conservatives have largely failed to provide effective opposition despite Hague's assured performances in the Commons.

Blair

Critics such as Professor Finer, author of 'Adversary Politics and Electoral Reform' believe that British politics is too adversarial and that is a product of the first-past-the-post electoral system. Certainly the public seems to feel that sometimes Oppositions seem to oppose for the sake of it.

Rebellious Backbenchers

Although a government with a majority dominates Parliament, it can never take for granted the automatic loyalty of its Backbenchers, if they oppose the government then it will normally have to back down. Norton traces the history of backbench dissent back to the late 1960's. In the late 1970s minority government/very small majorities gave Backbenchers enhanced power.

With the huge government majorities of the post-1983 parliaments, Backbenchers had the luxury of rebelling knowing that they would not defeat 'their' government. Under Major backbench rebellions were common because the government was seen as weak. The Government lost votes over Maastricht and had to use a vote of confidence to get their way;

they were defeated over the extension of VAT on domestic fuel; they lost votes on the Nolan issue and on European fisheries policy. In February 1996 they faced possible defeat over the Scott Report and once more there was talk of 'the ultimate deterrent' a vote of confidence. In the event they won but by just one vote.

Peter Riddell points out that the real problem with the Major Government after 1992 was not its small majority; after all the Churchill Tory Government of 1951-1955 had a majority of just 17 but it was never defeated by backbench rebellions. The problem was that unlike the early 1950s when the Tory party was united, the party of the 1990s was bitterly, ideologically divided and this manifested itself in both Cabinet division and backbench dissent.

Backbench rebellions in Blair's first term were relatively muted indeed Labour backbenchers were accused of being too subservient. In November 1997 many Labour Mps voted for cuts in benefits to single parents despite the fact that it was against their principles. However it is a different story in the second term. One Labour MP, Paul Marsden, defected to the Liberals complaining of unacceptable pressure from the Chief Whip Hilary Armstrong. There have been threatened rebellions over the failure to democratise the Lords and over foundation hospitals. The huge anti-war rebellions of spring 2003 revealed the opposition to war within the Labour Party and even led to talk of Blair resigning. They were the biggest rebellions against a Government since 1886.

Select Committees

Arguably the most effective form of scrutiny is the Select Committees of the House of Commons, particularly those that were set up in 1979. Select Committees are not a new thing. One of the first, and still the most important, Select Committees was the Public Accounts Committee set up by Gladstone in 1862. It has the largest back-up staff (approximately 400 auditors under the Comptroller General) but still faces the impossible task of monitoring public spending - currently running at over £300 billion per year over £30 million per hour. It was very critical of waste in the Health Service Trusts, especially the expenditure by a Health Authority of £60 million on the 'wrong' computer system and of mismanagement at the Welsh Development Agency. The PAC is the only select committee which includes a front bencher because by convention it is chaired by a member of the Shadow Government.

As the 'power' of Backbenchers declined in the 20th century, there were demands for more Select Committees as a way of redressing the imbalance of power between front and back benches. Various attempts at reform in the 1960s and 1970s failed to make an impact.

In 1976 the Select Committee on Procedure was set up. This was a broad inquiry into the working of the Commons. Reporting in 1978 it made several positive suggestions including radio broadcasting of the Commons. It recommended ways in which the procedures and practices could be improved so as to enable "The House as whole to exercise effective control and stewardship over Ministers and the expanding bureaucracy of the modern state for which they are answerable and to make the decisions of Parliament and Government more responsible to the views of the electorate."

The Procedure Committee was unanimous that the PAC should remain but whole system of select committees, which had grown piecemeal since the war, should be recast with 12 new subject committees charged with examining all aspects of expenditure, administration and policy within the various departments. The various select committees would co-operate, as often a topic spans more than one government department.

The Labour Government was largely unenthusiastic, particularly Foot the Leader of the House who thought select committees would *"drain away attention from the Chamber, the strength of parliament being increasingly transferred to such committees"*. The Conservative opposition promised "A Conservative Government will present positive, constructive proposals based on this report", which it duly did in June 1979.

There are now 17 of these committees. Each has 11 Backbenchers on it except for the Northern Ireland Select Committee created in 1994 which has 13. The Backbenchers come from all parties in proportion to party strength. A few are even chaired by Conservative MPs. The Procedure

Committee had recommended that Standing Committee membership should be drawn largely from the relevant Select Committee. Bills after 2nd Reading still go to Standing Committees not to the Select Committees. Of course there may be overlap of membership, but a fundamental distinction is still being drawn. Standing Committees are whipped and adversarial, Select Committees are bi-partisan and more consensual. This distinction reflects a basic duality in British procedures not found in the USA where the two functions - legislative and investigatory - are performed by the same committees. Jones and Kavanagh refer to the introduction of the Select Committee system as *"the most important procedural change that the British Parliament has adopted in a century"*.

The 'New' Select Committees have not changed the balance of power within the Commons - back benchers had more power in the hung/near hung Parliaments of 1974/79. George Jones argues that they have had little impact other than to encourage the proliferation of lobbyists.

They have produced over 1,000 reports since 1979 but very few Select Committee reports have led to direct government action, the 1980 report of the Home Affairs Select Committee recommending abolition of the 'Sus' laws was one of the few exceptions. The 'sus' law was immediately repealed, but then the Home Office may well have intended to legislate anyway.

However they have had an impact, there have been several occasions where a Select Committee investigation has embarrassed the government and drawn attention to problems which the government may wish to hide. This was certainly true of the Select Committee on Foreign Affairs in their investigation of the sinking of the Belgrano which led to the Ponting leak and one of the biggest crises of the second Thatcher term. It was even more true of the Select Committee on Defence's report over Westland. Thatcher's refusal to let certain Ministers and Civil Servants give evidence to the committee is an illustration of the limits of their power but also of their ability to force an issue on to the top of the agenda. The same was true of the Select Committee on Trade which criticised the way the government, and Lord Young in particular, had handled the privatisation of Rover. The Trade and Industry Committee carried out an investigation into exports to Iraq after discovery of the super-gun barrel parts in April 1990. The

Treasury and Civil Service Select Committee has been the most influential and the government adopted some of its recommendations in its 1995 White Paper on the Civil Service.

Edwina Currie's initial refusal to give evidence to the Select Committee on Agriculture and their subsequent threat to force her to attend and the refusal of the Maxwell brothers to prejudice their case by giving evidence to the Select Committee on Social Security in its investigation into pensions, also illustrate the limits of Select Committee power. In the USA, these people would have been subpoenaed.

It is instructive to contrast the two main types of Commons Committee

Standing Committees Select Committees

Standing Committees	Select Committees
Legislative	Investigator
Whipped	Not whipped
Partisan	Bi-partisan
Ad-hoc	Permanent
Front and Backbenchers	Except for PAC purely Backbenchers
Backbenchers chosen for loyalty	Backbenchers acquire expertise
Have power (at least in theory)	Have authority and that is growing all the time

Opinion is divided as to whether the Select Committees are 'useful new weapons' or whether they simply divide along party lines, whether they are 'watchdogs' or 'poodles'. In opposition Labour claimed to support the Select Committees as a way of holding government accountable. In Government since 1997 it has predictably seen these committees as a threat and has tried to have rebels removed from them. Under Labour more reports have been issued and more ministers have given evidence than under the Conservatives. In 1998 Harriet Harman was attacked by the Social Services Committee and Robin Cook and his Permanent Secretary Sir John Kerr were questioned over the Sierra Leone Affair. Labour's response to the Liaison Committee's 2000 Report 'Shifting the Balance' indicates that they are unwilling to extend Select Committee power. No new resources or staff and continued monitoring of appointments by the whips.

Labour whips tried to get Gwyneth Dunwoody chair of the Select Committee on transport and Donald Anderson chair of the foreign affairs select committee sacked because they were too critical. Backbenchers refused to allow this.

However Blair does now appear before the Chairs of the Select Committees. According to Democratic Audit 'reforms to the select committee system and the management of business in the commons have not remedied its inadequacy in scrutinising legislation and holding government to account, due to the government's continued single party domination of the chamber and its committees.' The Commons has agreed a package to strengthen the role of Select Committees but it has rejected a proposal for a new committee of senior MPs to take responsibility for selecting their members away from the whips.

There are various other ways in which Backbenchers can hold the government accountable, amongst the most famous is Question Time. MPs can table written questions as frequently as they wish but to ask an oral question an MP has to be drawn from a ballot. Oral questions may get publicity but written questions are a useful way of digging out facts. In 1985 the Foreign Secretary, Howe, announce guidelines on the sale of arms to Iraq and Iran. It is alleged that in 1988 Ministers secretly changed the guidelines without announcing the change to Parliament. Right up to November 1992 Ministers were replying to questions saying that the 1985 guidelines remained in place. The change only came to light following the collapse of the Matrix-Churchill case which led to the setting up of the Scott Inquiry. One of Blair's first actions after becoming PM was to change PM's Question Time from twice a week to once a week.

The USA

Congress has been described as **'the most powerful legislature in the democratic world'**. It is when we come to look at the way in which Congress scrutinises the US executive, that we appreciate how powerful

Congress, and in particular, its Committees really are. There are two key reasons why Congress is more powerful than Parliament despite the fact that Parliament is legally sovereign: firstly the separation of powers, which means that the administration (with the exception of the Vice President) does not sit in Congress. Secondly party discipline is so much weaker than it is in the House of Commons. However in the 1980s and 1990s party voting and party leadership strength did increase whilst committees lost a degree of influence. These tendencies were enhanced by the Republican take over in 1994 and for a while it did look like there would be a period of party government. However party loyalty peaked in 1995/6 and by 2003 party loyalty has waned a little.

The relevant Committees of Congress oversee the appropriate department of the executive The Senate's Foreign Relations Committee and the Foreign Relations Committees of the Representatives oversee the State Department. Bush's nominations of Secretary of State and of US Ambassadors had to be approved by the Senate's Foreign Relations Committee. The House of Representatives Foreign Relations Committee grilled the Secretary of State, Colin Powell, about US policy towards Iraq.

If no appropriate Committee exists, then one is created as with the Committee which investigated Watergate in 1973/4. These Congressional Committees have the power to subpoena evidence and witnesses. When President, Ford, gave Nixon a pardon the House Judiciary Committee summoned Ford to explain why. Contrast these examples with the weakness of the British Select Committees. Even the Scott Inquiry of 1992 to 1996 found that it was criticised by people such as Lord Howe for being too hard on witnesses, an accusation that would be risible in the USA.

As Tim Hames point out, Congress has exerted a much greater degree of oversight even over foreign policy since the early 1970s and not just through the Case Act and the War Powers Act. The Foreign Assistance Act of 1974 monitors covert operations by the Executive. The Trade Act - 1974 - states that trade talks must be approved by Congress. The Arms Export Controls Act 1976 allows Congress to reject arms deals and the Intelligence Oversight Act of 1980 tightens Congressional control over the CIA.

However the War Powers Act did not prevent Ford committing troops in the Mayaguez incident, nor did it inhibit Reagan in the invasion of Grenada. It certainly did not inhibit Bush in either Panama or Kuwait. The Supreme Court ruled the Legislative Veto unconstitutional in the *Immigration Service v. Chadua* case (1983) thus casting doubt on the constitutionality of the War Powers Act, and probably invalidating impoundment restrictions too.

Section 4 of Article 2 of the USA Constitution states that a President shall be removed from office if impeached and convicted of treason, bribery or other 'high crimes and misdemeanours". The power of 'impeachment' belongs to the House of Representatives which would set up a committee to consider the evidence. If the House agrees to the impeachment with a two-thirds majority, the case is then referred to the Senate which tries the impeachment. When a President is being tried, the Chief Justice of the Supreme Court presides, and a conviction is secured by a two-thirds majority. Andrew Johnson had been impeached in 1867, but the Senate failed to convict by one vote. The House of Representatives were in the process of impeaching Richard Nixon but he resigned in August 1974 before it could be completed. The attempt to impeach Clinton over the Lewinsky scandal failed.

3) Representation

The UK

Representative Democracy where the people elect representatives, MPs or Senators, to make decisions for them is the dominant form of democracy in the modern world. Parliamentary government is a form of representative government in that through the House of Commons the representatives of the people share in the governmental process.

A.H. Birch argued that the UK has 'Representative and Responsible Government'. Representative, in that there is government by consent, and the people participate in the political system; responsible, in that government is responsive, rational, considered and accountable. Birch discusses the meanings of 'representative'. A 'representative' may be a person or group who is typical of a class; this is concerned with social, economic, racial, gender and age attributes of a group of people. An agent or delegate, on the other hand, is someone whose function is to protect and if possible advance the interests of the individual or group on whose behalf he is acting, for example, barristers, ambassadors, delegates to the TUC.

British MPs are representatives not delegates. The Lords is totally unelected however it has traditional authority and this might give it a limited degree of representative legitimacy. On the surface, the Commons is obviously a representative body; it has **legal rational authority** because its members are chosen by the people every few years.

There are, however, two problems with the representativeness of the Commons: The electoral system is not based on PR, so therefore the result is not necessarily representative, as is shown by the following table;

The General Election, 2001

Party	UK % Votes	No. Seats	% of seats
Labour	40.7	413	62.7%
Tory	31.7	166	25.2%
Lib Dem	18.3	52	7.9%

The House of Commons is not representative in the sense that it is not typical, it is not a microcosm of British society. MPs are part of an elite. Peter Riddell has talked of the increased professionalism of MPs, more and more in both major parties have a background in politics making them even less representative. They are overwhelmingly white, male, middle aged and middle class, as, to a lesser extent, are Congressmen.

White

Until the 1987 election, there had not been a single MP from the ethnic minorities for over 50 years; even after 1987 there were only four - all of them in the Labour Party - Bernie Grant, Paul Boateng, Keith Vaz, Diane Abbott. An Asian MP was elected in a by-election only to lose his seat in

1992. In the 1992 election attention focused on the black Tory candidate for Cheltenham John Taylor who had been the subject of racist comments from some within the local party. Taylor was defeated but Nirj Deva was elected in Brentford as the first non-white post-war Tory MP. All 12 ethnic minority MPs represent Labour. Paul Boateng has become the first ever black Cabinet Minister. Lady Amos has replaced Clare Short and become the first ever black female Cabinet Minister.

Male

There are too few women; few women seek to become candidates and therefore there is a lot of prejudice against female candidates despite, or perhaps because of, Thatcher. The 300 Group is a pressure group formed in 1980 by Leslie Abdela which aims to increase the number of women MPs. Their original target was gender equality by 2000 but this has been abandoned as unrealistic. Since 1918 only 166 women have been elected to the Commons. At the 1992 election the Tories only had 62 women candidates to Labour's 143 and the Liberal's 138. 23 Tory women were elected, 35 Labour women. 1997 saw a big increase in the number of women MPs. By 2003 there were 118 female MPs, 94 of them Labour.

Labour introduced positive discrimination in favour of women parliamentary candidates in 1988 and in 1989 Kinnock established a quota system for Shadow Cabinet elections. Emily's List (named after Emily Davidson the suffragette, but also an acronym for Early Money Rises Like Yeast) formed in 1993 by Barbara Follet argues that women must take more urgent steps to increase representation but in 1996 the Labour Party's attempt at introducing all-women shortlists in winnable seats was ruled contrary to the sex discrimination laws. A reform of the law gives political parties leave to adopt measures of positive discrimination to raise the proportion of female MPs. Britain has one of the lowest number of female MPs of any European democracy, still under 20% of the House. In 1992 Greece had 4.3% of its legislature made up of women, Norway had 34.4% The Scottish Parliament and Welsh Assembly have much higher proportions of elected female members.

Middle Aged

Most MPs are 'older' because they need to gain experience before they are adopted as candidates for 'safe' seats. Very few MPs are under 30, few Ministers are under 40, few cabinet Ministers are under 50. Few MPs are over 70.

Middle Class

In the 1983/87 Parliament, 96% of Conservative MPs and 57% of Labour MPs were 'middle class' - mostly lawyers, teachers, lecturers, journalists. In the February/October 1974 Parliament, 60% were graduates (compared with 4% of adults), over one-third of MPs graduated from Oxbridge.

One half were ex-public school (4% of adults), 60% of Conservatives and 16% of Labour MPs (still 4 times the national average) had been to public schools. Only one-sixth, mostly in the Labour Party, were 'workers'. Thus the Commons, even Labour MPs, is in socio-economic terms unrepresentative. It is substantially middle class and has become increasingly so as the number of working class Labour MPs has declined. Even the embodiment of labourism John Prescott has admitted to being middle class.

The Tories were more upper class, but these days they are also middle class, the party of the estates has become the party of the estate agents.

Whether any of this really matters is debatable. The Powell argument is that MPs do not have to be a microcosm in order to be representative but Polly Toynbee claims that it certainly does matter that there are so few women MP's, that is why much legislation on social issues is so badly drafted. It is all part of the problem that Anne Phillips is referring to when she calls for there to be a 'gendering of democracy.'

Congress as a Representative Body

Congress is still (although to a lesser extent than the Commons) overwhelmingly 'white, male, middle aged and middle class'. There are 39 black members of the Representatives who form the Congressional Black

Caucus. It has been described as 'the conscience of Congress' since its formation in 1969. However there are currently no black Senators. Similarly there are relatively few women members of the 107th Congress, 74 in the House and 13 in the Senate. Most Senators and Representatives are professional men, often lawyers, businessmen, accountants, journalists or doctors. The Representatives tend to be younger than the Senators partly because the Constitution says Senators have to be at least 30, Representatives have to be at least 25, but more importantly Senators have often served several terms in the House first, or they have been involved in State politics. Because American elections are such expensive affairs, the majority of successful politicians tend to be wealthy. Indeed the criticism is that American politics is fast becoming a rich man's pastime.

One big difference between Congress and Parliament is that both Houses of Congress are elected and can therefore claim to represent US citizens. Representatives serve two year terms and therefore have to pay more attention to the "folks back home". They are therefore more involved in "pork barrel politics" (Congressmen doing something for their districts/states purely for re-election purposes).

However, Senators also have to make sure that they serve their state because Senate seats are so fiercely contested. The average senatorial election costs £6 million to fight; which means that Senators have to raise £20,000 a week for each week of their six year term. Given that well over 90% of incumbents seeking re-election are successful. then the Congress really is representative. As Thomas Cavanagh put it in 1975 'a near idiot who has competent case work can stay in Congress as long as he wants. You can do whatever is good for the district. Nobody is going to criticise you for not devoting enough time to the broad issues.' The power of incumbency was one of the reasons behind the campaign for term limits.

Pork barrel politics may please constituents but if Senators and Representatives push up public spending whilst refusing to increase the taxes to pay for it, then the outcome is a bigger and bigger Budget Deficit.

4) Parliament and Congress as Sounding Boards

In Britain both chambers do attempt to air the main concerns of the nation. Arguably, the Lords has a higher standard of debate than the Commons but it is the debates in the Commons which usually generate media interest. Whether they are of a high standard is of course debatable, but commentators such as Simon Hoggart believe the standard of oratory has fallen since the war. Arguably, the televising of the Commons has added to this and some commentators are concerned that the growing importance of TV in politics is at the expense of Parliament. However to counter that it could be said that televising the House has raised the profile of parliamentary debates which assists the opposition, Select Committees and back benchers. Parliament can push stories and issues on to the media and the public agenda.

In the US, Congress debates all of the major issues concerning US citizens and it's proceedings are televised and have been for some time. Whether debate is of a very high standard is questionable, the debate over the Crime Bill in 1994 was rather ill-tempered. The debate over Haiti in 1994 shows that even on foreign policy, the President cannot take Congress for granted. However the debate on war with Iraq was very one sided.

5) Parliament is the Recruiting-ground for Ministers

This particularly applies to the House of Commons although every Cabinet/Government has, by law, to include a certain number of Lords. Riddell emphasises that the Commons is still the place where political reputations are made or broken. Mrs. Thatcher really impressed her fellow Conservative MPs in 1974 by her performance in committee stage on the Finance Bill. This is one reason why she was elected leader of the party in February 1975. As for the Labour Party, in the late 1980's Gordon Brown so impressed the Commons during John Smith's absence through illness that he did extremely well in the subsequent Shadow Cabinet elections and was promoted. In contrast the Tory MP John Moore, once tipped as a future leader, failed to consolidate his reputation during the crisis over the health service in 1988, was soon demoted and shortly afterwards disappeared from sight.

Our system of Parliamentary government has the advantage of offering a 'career structure' - apprenticeship as an MP, followed by office. Norton has talked of a 'new breed' of MP citing Redwood as an example of a career politician. The US system is very different because the administration is not part of Congress. This is one reason for the system of primaries and caucuses which choose the party's nominee to fight the Presidential elation. Congress, unlike Parliament, is not really a recruiting ground for the administration because the separation of powers prevents membership of more than one branch. Some former members of Congress do take posts. In Clinton's first administration the Secretary of the Treasury was the ex-Senator, Lloyd Bensen.

? To What Extent Does "The Decline of the Legislature" Thesis Still Have Validity?

Introduction

In the 20th century legislatures have lost power to the executive. Congress has lost power to the US administration, Parliament has lost power to the British executive. The Supreme Soviet never really had power, the Russian Duma is subordinate to the powerful Executive and the Chinese NPC is a rubber stamp. The reason for this decline is the expansion in the role of government. All over the democratic world government is now held responsible for welfare and for running the economy. By the 1960s it was clear that this had led to shift in power from the legislature. However on both sides of the Atlantic, the last 20 odd years has supposedly seen a resurgence of the legislature such that it may no longer be valid to talk of the decline of the legislature.

Paragraph 2 - Yes it has validity in relation to the UK legislature. The decline of Parliament through "Elective Dictatorship" and "Overload".

Paragraph 3 - Yes it has validity in relation to the US legislature. The Imperial President - the emergence of the US as a superpower and the growing importance of the President as Commander in Chief - Hiroshima,

Cuban missile crisis, the Vietnam war, Desert Storm. Federal government intervention in economic and social policy after 1933. Massive expansion in the size, power and complexity of the US executive. All caused a decline in the power of Congress.

Paragraph 4 - No it no longer has validity in relation to Parliament. Norton's argument, supported by Riddell, Judge and Rush about the resurgence of Parliament. New professionalism of the Lords, far more importantly the increase in backbench rebellions and the growing authority of Select Committees.

Paragraph 5 - No, it no longer has validity in relation to Congress. The 'New Congress' since the early 1970s, the decline of the "Solid South" and break up of the oligarchy all saw a resurgence of Congress which has continued into the 1990s under Gingrich.

Even the Duma and the NPC are asserting themselves although with obvious limits in the case of the latter.

Conclusion

Talk of the resurgence of Parliament is exaggerated. Only one Government Bill has been defeated in the Commons since 1979 - the Sunday Trading bill in 1986. Most backbench rebellions turn out to be damp squibs. Select Committees are weak. In contrast Congress really is powerful, particularly over domestic policy. Talk of an Imperial Presidency was always an exaggeration, it is better to use Richard Rose's notion of a post-modern President almost inevitably doomed to fail to meet the absurdly high expectations of the office. The Israeli Knesset has certainly not lost power; it is a genuine policy making legislature in contrast the NPC is even more powerless than the European Parliament. Thus the thesis does still have validity in relation to certain legislatures, but it never really did have validity in relation to others.

Chapter 4
Executives

If the separation of powers principle was adhered to as closely as liberal democratic theory suggests then the role of the executive would be to implement domestic and foreign policy and execute legislation passed by the legislature. In reality executives have far more extensive powers than this.

It was because liberalism emerged as a reaction against the despotic powers of the Crown that it was so keen to constrain the powers of the executive. The American Constitution provides a classic example of this. The Founding Fathers, having just escaped the 'tyranny' of the British Monarchy wanted to hold their own executive in check so that the President was intended to be a figurehead. The emergence of the activist Presidency of the C20th illustrates the difficulty of limiting executive powers in an age when citizens expect government to deliver welfare and a managed economy. If even the America executive with all the checks and balances it faces can become so powerful that it is sometimes described as 'imperial' then there must be certain forces at work centralising power.

It could be argued that the USA is an exception because in this century it has come to be the superpower which effectively acts as the world policeman and therefore inevitably the President is bound to become more powerful. However this cannot explain the rise of strong Presidencies in France and Russia and the apparent emergence of Prime Ministerial government in Britain and Chancellor government in Germany. When Foley talks of the rise of the British Presidency he is thinking about the same factors which have personalised power across the democratic world. The media focus on individuals rather than parties and at time when ideology is once more said to be at an end this may well have a certain logic to it. The rapid rise of the almost 'apolitical' Berlusconi and the American equivalent Ross Perot indicates that people are looking for a strong man removed from conventional party politics. Yeltsin took the process to its logical conclusion by refusing to be associated with any particular party

Power does not necessarily depend on formal position it can owe more to sheer personality. At the same time as the political executive seems to be becoming more personalised we have seen the development of powerful bureaucracies with the apparent ability to defend their own interests. In theory bureaucracy under liberal democracy operates according to Weber's ideal typology. The civil service is recruited and promoted on merit, it is neutral, officials loyally serve whichever party wins office. This view was always suspect to the left who argued that senior bureaucrats coming, as they tend to do, from elite backgrounds are inherently conservative and use the powers of their office to block socialism.

With the rise of the new right since the late 1960s a new critique of bureaucracy has become fashionable. This is variously known as public choice theory or the bureaucratic over-supply model and it sees bureaucrats as a budget maximising pressure group at the very centre of government linked to other insider groups in iron triangles or issue networks defending the interests of their clients rather than serving the public interest in a Weberian sense.

This critical view of the official executive has had a pervasive influence all over the liberal democratic world even on parties of the left. The notion of 'reinventing government' came from America and was adopted with enthusiasm by Clinton and Gore but a variant of it has been adopted by the Australia Labour Party, the Conservative Government in Britain, the

British Labour Party, the French government under Chirac and the Russian government.

Marxists claimed that under Communism the state would wither away, therefore official bureaucracy would disappear. In contrast Weber warned that irrespective of the form of economy societies were becoming more complex and would be increasingly subject to rule by bureaucrats, an **'iron cage'** of bureaucracy. Arguably Weber was proved correct. In fact it could be said that bureaucracy is even more powerful in Communist regimes. Thus both wings of the executive, political and official, are the source of lively debates within liberal democracies as well as Communist states as to their true political role.

Australia - Formal executive authority is vested in the Governor General appointed by the British Monarch in consultation with the Australian PM but in practice power lies with the Cabinet chaired by the PM, the leader of the biggest party.

China - The President is elected to a five year term by the NPC but this is a ceremonial position and real power lies with the State Council headed by the PM and the General Secretary of the CCP. However for a long time Deng dominated Chinese politics without having a formal position.

France - The President is directly elected for 7 year terms. He appoints the PM and the rest of the Cabinet and chairs Cabinet meetings. There are serious disputes as to the balance of power and responsibilities between the President and the PM so it is referred to as the **'dual executive'**.

Germany - The President is elected by the Bundestag and representatives of the state legislatures for a five year term. Power lies with the Chancellor, appointed by the President he must maintain a majority in the Bundestag. The Chancellor heads a Cabinet which in theory at least makes policy but there are suspicions of 'Chancellor Government'.

Israel - The President, elected by the Knesset is a figurehead, power lies with the PM who is now directly elected but who in practice has to command a majority in the Knesset. The PM heads a Cabinet which almost always includes spokespeople from several parties.

Russia - The President is directly elected for 5 year terms. He appoints the PM. Putin has powers formally greater than those of any other democratically elected President of a major state.

UK - The Monarch appoints as PM the leader of the largest party in the Commons who chairs the Cabinet which, in theory at least, is the main policy-making body.

USA - The President is directly elected for four year terms, maximum length of office 10 years. The Cabinet is purely advisory. Some fear that 'the President exercises a dangerously personalised power'.

The British Executive

Introduction

The Executive comprises the government - the political executive - and the Civil Service - the administrative or official wing. The government consists of approximately 100 ministers of whom the 20 or so most important sit in the Cabinet, the remainder being Junior Ministers. Every member of the government, from the Prime Minister down to the most junior of junior Ministers is either an MP or a member of the Lords. In a typical department such as the Home Office there is a Cabinet Minister, the Home Secretary, currently David Blunkett, supported by 6 or 7 Junior Ministers, perhaps one of whom is a member of the Lords. Each Junior Minister, will have specific responsibilities, such as prisons, immigration or the police. The Treasury is the exception. The PM is the First Lord of the Treasury, but in practice it is under the control of the Chancellor of the Exchequer, currently Gordon Brown. It is the only department to have another member sit in the Cabinet - the Secretary of the Treasury, currently Paul Boateng. There are in addition two junior ministers in the Treasury.

The Civil Service is appointed, not elected. They are *permanent*, that is they do not change when the government changes. The most senior bureaucrats who have day to day contact with ministers are known as "Mandarins". Civil Servants can vote but senior officials are not supposed to make their political views public, so they cannot join a party. They are supposed to be *neutral*. Civil Servants have a low public profile, they are generally *anonymous*.

Collective Responsibility

Co-ordination of policy is supposedly achieved through the convention of collective responsibility which means that all members of the Government are collectively responsible for the decisions of the Cabinet and must be seen publicly to support them, even if they have private doubts. The alternative is resignation as Frank Cousins (1966), George Brown (1968), Michael Heseltine (1986), Nigel Lawson (1989), Geoffrey Howe (1990), John Redwood (1995) Robin Cook and Clare Short (both 2003) among others demonstrated. The convention applies to junior Ministers, such as Keith Speed (1982) and Ian Gow (1985), who will not even have been present at Cabinet when policy was decided. The USA has a single man executive, the President; therefore there is no collective responsibility.

However, there have been examples in Britain of Ministers in clear disagreement with government policy and yet allowed to remain in Cabinet. This was as true of Benn in the Labour Cabinets of the 1970s and Peter Walker in the Thatcher Cabinets of the 1980s as it was of Portillo under Major. Clare Short finally resigned a few weeks after describing the war as irresponsible.

Individual Ministerial Responsibility

The politicians are accountable to Parliament, it is they who are responsible for the running of the department and if things go wrong, they get the blame. If there is a major policy failure then the Minister is expected to resign. In 1982 the Foreign Secretary, Lord Carrington, resigned when Argentina occupied the Falklands. 1986 saw the Trade Secretary, Leon Brittan, resign over Westland. In 1988, the Junior Minister for Health, Edwina Currie, resigned over her comments on salmonella in eggs. In 2002 the Education Secretary Estelle Morris resigned because of problems in the schools particularly over A' Levels.

The convention of individual ministerial responsibility shields the Civil Servants, hence the focus in the Scott Report on the Ministers - Lyell, Waldegrave and Clark - rather than the officials. According to this convention Mandarins advise, Ministers decide and Civil Servants implement policy decisions Thus there is said to be a **clear distinction between the policy advisory role of mandarins and the policy making role of ministers**.

Again though the convention appears to be weakening, or at least changing, because there have been many examples of Ministers not resigning despite apparent failure. In 1994 Sir Robin Butler the Cabinet Secretary argued that it is important to *distinguish between accountability and responsibility*. Ministers must be **accountable** for everything that goes on in their departments but they cannot be held **responsible** for operational matters which is why Howard did not resign over prison break-outs. This was an operational matter, not a policy matter. In 1995 the head of the Prisons Agency, Derek Lewis, was sacked by Howard. Lewis subsequently claimed that Howard's attempt to distinguish policy and operational matters was spurious given that he interfered all the time with operational details. In 1995 Major refined IMR further by stating that a Minister need only resign if he had **deliberately** mislead Parliament which is why Waldegrave did not resign over the Scott Report although even some Tory MPs like Richard Shepherd felt he should. The Democratic Audit describes the convention as 'a fiction' and argues that 'Labour is now seen as a sleazy and disreputable party alongside the Conservatives.'.

All of these features of the way the Executive is supposed to function have been subject to argument, debate and interpretation. Some critics believe that Cabinet government is a myth, the Cabinet has become simply a rubber stamp and we actually have **Prime Ministerial Government**. Others argue that neither the PM nor the Cabinet really make policy and that we have **Civil Service government**. Another view is that the whole policy making process is so fragmented and lacking in co ordination that we have **Departmental government**.

Prime Ministerial Government or Cabinet Government?

The modern Cabinet is able to trace its origins back to the middle ages.. Traditionally, it was a council closely connected to the Sovereign. By the 18th century the Cabinet was liberated from the domination of the monarchy and by the 19th century, the rise of organised political parties and the triumph of a dominant PM further influenced and changed the character of the Cabinet. Cabinet is a committee which has both political and executive functions which include co-ordination, decision making, planning, and arbitration. In the Cabinet major decisions are made or ratified and interdepartmental conflicts are resolved.

As a response to the overload of Cabinet and the need for expert advice, Cabinet Committees serve an important function. Standing Committees of the Cabinet are permanent for the duration of the PM's term of office. Ad hoc Cabinet Committees are set up to deal with specific issues. Major referred to Cabinet Committees as 'the sinews of the body politic'. They continue to be so under Blair. The Democratic Audit cites the examples of Prescott getting a more prominent position on such committees to balance Brown's power and the way in which devolution was orchestrated by the Lord Chancellor through a Cabinet Committee more than the Scottish Secretary Donald Dewar.

The powers of the PM can be divided into *fixed powers* such as the right to appoint or dismiss Cabinet ministers, the right to seek dissolution of Parliament, the right to summon and chair Cabinet meetings and *variable* powers such as the power to dominate Cabinet proceedings if his colleagues are willing to allow it. There have been strong PM's in British history, in the 1860s and 1870s, Disraeli and Gladstone, and during and after WW1 and WW2, Lloyd George and Churchill respectively. However, starting in the early 1960s and continuing to this day there is a school of thought which says that the PM has acquired so much power that we now have a 'presidential' style system.

The Labour MP and academic Richard Crossman argued this in 1963 in his introduction to a new edition of the Walter Bagehot classic, "The English Constitution" (original edition 1867). Bagehot had distinguished between **the dignified elements** of the constitution such as the Monarchy and the Lords which looked impressive and had authority but little power and **the efficient elements**, the Commons and the Cabinet. Crossman argued that since 1867 the Commons and the Cabinet had lost power, they had become merely dignified. The efficient elements now were the PM backed by the Civil Service.

Crossman identified certain trends pushing power towards the PM. Firstly the rise of disciplined, ideological parties, united behind their leaders. Secondly the rise of big government, the interventionist state which can be traced back to the Liberal governments of 1905-14 which laid the foundations for the welfare state. The shift in power to the executive inevitably strengthened the position of the head of the government, the PM. Thirdly the growing impact of the media which more and more focused on personalities so that election campaigns were becoming more and more "presidential".

The combined result of these changes, Crossman claimed, was that **"the post war epoch has seen the final transformation of Cabinet government into Prime Ministerial government."** Crossman cited various examples purporting to show Prime Ministerial government; Chamberlain's policy of appeasement in the late 1930s, Churchill during the war, Attlee's decision in 1948 that Britain should have the atom bomb which Crossman alleges Attlee pushed through without Cabinet involvement just as the Suez Crisis of 1956 was allegedly orchestrated by Eden without the involvement of his Cabinet. Macmillan was supposed to provide another example in 1962 when on "the night of the long knives" he sacked a third of his Cabinet in one go.

In October 1964 Wilson formed a Labour government with Crossman in the Cabinet. In his diaries which were published after his death in 1973, Crossman comments that Wilson showed the domination of a PM, backed by the Civil Service. For example he vetoed discussion of devaluation of the pound until November 1967 when Britain was forced to devalue.

Crossman's arguments have been adopted by other commentators such as Tony Benn and Michael Foley. Benn himself served in the Labour Cabinets of the 1960s and 1970s and from personal experience he supports the thesis that power has shifted to the PM in conjunction with the Civil Service. However, it was the experience of **Thatcherism in the 1980s** which convinced many that we do have Prime Ministerial government. Foley accepts that a comparison of the PM and a US President is flawed because in many ways the President is weaker than a PM given the checks and balances he faces. Foley argues that we have created a *British Presidency*, not encumbered by formal constraints and therefore dangerously powerful.

The theoretical powers of a PM certainly are very impressive. PM's appoint their Cabinet and their government with no screening mechanisms such as the Senatorial ratification that a President has to cope with so in theory Prime Ministers can appoint whoever they want. The PM decides when to call a General Election within the 5 years maximum length of a parliament. In theory the Monarch dissolves Parliament but in practice the Monarch does so at the request of the PM. The Liberals argue for fixed term Parliaments which would remove the power of dissolution from the PM.

The Premier chairs the Cabinet, decides its agenda and is responsible for the minutes. The PM is head of the Civil Service, responsible for the appointment of mandarins, a role which Thatcher took very seriously. A Prime Minster has enormous powers of patronage such as appointing Life Peers. The PM (together with the Lord Chancellor) appoints judges, the PM even appoints Bishops of the Church of England, the heads of the nationalised industries and certain Oxbridge Professorships.

Despite all of this not everyone believes that Cabinet government has been replaced by Prime Ministerial government. The strongest advocate of the continuing relevance of Cabinet government is Professor George Jones of the LSE. Jones argues that Crossman, Benn et al have only looked at the potential powers of the PM; they have not considered **the practical constraints on the exercise of those powers**.

Jones believes that even Thatcher had to work with her Cabinet; she was not as dominant as the media implied, even at the height of her power in 1988. For every theoretical Prime Ministerial power there are some very real constraints. In practice there are very real limitations on appointments to the Cabinet. Some of the party MPs are too old for office, some are too young, some are just not up to it, and some don't want it. The PM has to achieve some kind of balance, to reflect the spread of views within the party.

If the Cabinet and wider government consists entirely of people from the Prime Minister's wing of the party then other groups within the party will be disaffected. Thus Wilson and Callaghan had to include Labour right wingers such as Roy Jenkins, but also Labour left wingers such as Benn. Major found just the same thing, he had to include critics such as Portillo and Lilly within his Cabinet. Redwood broke ranks in 1995 to challenge Major and became an irritant stalking the backbenches but an independent Portillo would have been far worse from Major's point of view.

Even the supposedly all-powerful Thatcher had to include non-Thatcherites, often in key positions, hence Hurd the former Heathite was Home Secretary from 1985 to 1989 then Foreign Secretary. Chris Patten, the embodiment of Christian Democrat style Conservatism held various Cabinet posts under Thatcher for whom such corporatist ideas were anathema. She was equally dependent on that 'One Nation Tory' Kenneth Clarke. Indeed by 1990 the Thatcher Cabinet included very few Thatcherites. Blair as PM has had to be equally eclectic in his appointments, including non-Blairites such as Clare Short.

There have been several PMs who have "got the timing of an election wrong". Wilson did in June 1970 just as Heath did in February 1974. Heath then lost the leadership of his party in February 1975. Callaghan in autumn 1978 committed a sin of omission. He might have won an election held then, instead he opted to wait. The ensuing 'Winter of Discontent' of 1978/9 saw Labour plummet in the opinion polls and the vote of no confidence in his government in Spring 1979 removed the power of dissolution from him. In other words not calling an election can be just as fatal as calling one. Arguably Major got it wrong by waiting until April 1992. Had he called an election in November 1990 when he became PM or in March 1991 after the Gulf War he could have asked for a fresh mandate and conceivably won more decisively.

Crossman argued that chairing Cabinet, controlling its agenda, determining the minutes were all formidable powers. In practice though the agenda largely writes itself and the minutes obviously have to reflect the mood of the Cabinet. Apparently, Thatcher did have a different approach to chairing Cabinet; she stated her views at the outset and then invited disagreement, but she appears to be the exception rather than the rule. The PM is the head of the Civil Service, but very few PM's actually get involved in appointing or promoting mandarins, again Thatcher was the exception.

The Dynamic Relationship Between PM and Cabinet

Academics such as Peter Hennessey and Dennis Kavanagh argue that both the Prime Ministerial government view and the Cabinet government view are misleading because they are static whereas political relationships are dynamic. Prime Ministerial power depends upon at least three variables: the style of the PM, the circumstances of the time and the degree of party support.

James Callaghan
'Chairmen' such as Attlee from 1945 to 1951, Callaghan between 1976 and 1979 and Major after 1990 try to pull the teams together. Dominant PMs such as Chamberlain are not necessarily the most effective, just as less charismatic leaders such as Attlee are not necessarily ineffective

There is no one approach to the job of PM, there is no job description. Each PM approaches it in a different way. Norton goes into great detail about different types of PM talking of balancers, innovators and reconcilers. To simplify there are 2 main approaches. 'Managing Directors' such as Wilson

133

'Mark 1' between 1964 and 1970 and most obviously Thatcher 1979 - 1990. These Premiers try to lead from the front, they are interventionists who attempt to push the Cabinet in their direction. Blair appears to fit into this mould. Many of the Premiers who are supposed to have demonstrated that Britain has Prime Ministerial government have in some sense ultimately failed, including Thatcher. The other approach is the Chairman of the Board who adopts a collegiate approach. Examples include Callaghan and Major. Attlee was this type of leader and his government of 1945-51 is generally seen as a great success.

Circumstances constantly impact upon the PM and his or her Cabinet, party, Parliament and the public. In 1951 Churchill came back and had his 'Indian summer' as PM from 1951-55, but circumstances had changed and he was a lot less dominant than during the war. Wilson 'Mark 2' in 1974 was very different to the Wilson of 1964, partly because his colleagues had recent Cabinet experience. However, circumstances don't just change between governments they also change within the lifetime of a government. Look at the ups and downs of Thatcher between May 1979 and November 1990, or the changed position of Major after November 1990. Had the war against Iraq gone badly then Blair would have been seriously damaged politically.

Ultimately a PM is as powerful as his or her party colleagues, in Cabinet, in Parliament and in the country, will allow. British politics is party politics, British government is party government. If the party is fractious or lacks a majority the PM's position is clearly weaker. Callaghan led a minority government, inevitably therefore Callaghan was less dominant than Blair who has enjoyed huge majorities.

Thatcher

There are so many alleged examples of prime ministerial government under Thatcher that it is hard to know which to choose. Whether they really do show prime ministerial government or not is debatable.

In March 1981 came Howe's third Budget when almost everyone expected a U Turn - it was instead a very deflationary budget at a time of rapidly increasing unemployment. The summer of 1981 saw riots. Thatcher was very vulnerable at that point but the 'wets' never managed to co-ordinate opposition to her. Autumn 1981 saw the purge of the 'wets' - Gilmour, Soames, Carlisle - all were dismissed and replaced with Thatcherites - Tebbit, Brittan, Lawson; James Prior was 'demoted' from the Department of Employment to Northern Ireland. In spring 1982 came the beginnings of an economic boom which was to last until 1988/1989. The Conservative's poll ratings were improving even before the Falklands conflict of April/June 1982 engrossed public attention. It boosted both the Conservative party and more specifically Thatcher herself.

Margaret Thatcher
In May 1979 Mrs Thatcher won her first General Election with a Conservative majority of 43.
According to Professor Kavanagh what was striking about Mrs Thatcher's governments was not her
domination of the Cabinet, Parliament or Conservative Party, but her approach to leadership

In June 1983 came the landslide victory, an overall majority of 144. Pym was sacked, Howe became Foreign Secretary, Lawson became Chancellor. The first term had seen Thatcher preoccupied with domestic affairs. In the second and third terms Thatcher was able to play the role of world stateswoman. Anglo-American relations were extremely close in the mid-1980s, the 'special relationship' was very much in evidence during the Falklands war. Thatcher was a useful intermediary between Reagan and Gorbachev.

In the winter of 1984 came the privatisation of BT; it was not the first nationalised industry to be privatised, but it was the first real popular success - the enterprise culture had arrived, **popular capitalism** was a key strand of Thatcherism.

In November 1985, the Anglo-Irish agreement was signed; it gave Dublin a role in the running of Northern Ireland, a major concession from such a staunch 'Unionist' as Thatcher. An excellent illustration of the impact of 'events' upon the position of the PM is the saga over Westland a helicopter company based in Somerset which by 1985 was going bust. An American company wanted to take it over and Thatcher and the Trade Secretary, Leon Brittan, were content to see this happen. Heseltine, the much more pro-European Defence Secretary, wanted a European take over, so that British defence capability was not entirely in US hands. He more or less openly breached collective responsibility. In January 1986 there came a Cabinet meeting at which Thatcher told Heseltine that from then on all statements on the issue had to be cleared through her Press Secretary, Bernard Ingham. Heseltine resigned, declaring that Thatcher was not listening to her Cabinet.

A few days later, an internal inquiry revealed that Brittan had told a Civil Servant, Collete Bowe, to leak a letter from the Solicitor General to Heseltine. This led to Brittan's resignation. Thus Thatcher had lost 2 key ministers and was in a very weak position, indeed on the day of the crucial debate in the Commons she told her Downing Street staff that when she returned she may no longer be PM. Instead Thatcher survived although it marked the closest Thatcher came to resignation before 1990 and left her in a weaker position. For example she had to abandon plans to sell Land Rover to an American bidder In April 1986 the Sunday Trading Bill was defeated but it coincided with the US bombing of Libya and the media gave it little attention.

In autumn 1986 a successful Tory Conference was used as a springboard for the next election. There were tax cuts in the spring 1987 budget and the economy was booming. In April 1987 Thatcher had a successful trip to the USSR, a great PR success perfectly timed for the election. A third election victory saw the Conservatives win an overall majority of 101 despite a poor Tory campaign.

There was more privatisation but to some extent the popularity of this had diminished after the Stock Exchange crash of October 1987. In order to avoid a recession Lawson relaxed monetary policy, interest rates were reduced at the same time as fiscal policy was expansionist, the 1988 budget cut taxes from 60% to 40% (top rate), and 27% to 25% (standard rate). Politically it was very popular. Thatcher described Lawson as 'my brilliant Chancellor'. Economically, it was very dangerous - it fuelled an already inflationary situation.

By autumn 1988 the economy was overheating with the trade deficit approaching £15 billion p.a., interest rates were raised leading to higher mortgages and an end to the house price boom. By 1989 with the economy close to a recession and high mortgages hurting the Conservatives politically, Labour went into sustained leads in the opinion polls which they held until Thatcher's resignation in November 1990.

June 1989 saw the European Elections - a poor Tory campaign led to their first national defeat since 1974. At the June 1989 Madrid Summit Howe and Lawson got agreement from a reluctant Thatcher on the conditions for eventual entry into the Exchange Rate Mechanism. The memoirs of the participants all tell a different tale showing how hard it is to get accurate information about the inner workings of government even after the event

Thatcher mishandled the summer 1989 Cabinet re-shuffle; Howe was demoted, he became Leader of the Commons and, as compensation, Deputy Prime Minister. Major became Foreign Secretary. Autumn 1989 saw the resignation of Lawson in a row over Walters and ERM. Major moved to the Treasury, Hurd to the Foreign Office.

In November 1989 Thatcher was challenged for the leadership for the first time - Sir Anthony Meyer, a stalking horse. Throughout 1990 the Government was increasingly unpopular. Spring 1990 saw anti-poll tax demonstrations all over the country, in London it turned into a riot.

On August 2nd 1990 Iraq invaded Kuwait, Thatcher quickly backed Bush in his despatch of a force to protect Saudi Arabia and liberate Kuwait. The Friday before the Tory Conference the UK went into ERM and interest rates were cut creating short-term euphoria. However, in the Eastbourne by-election of autumn 1990 a safe Conservative seat was lost by the Conservatives to Liberal Democrats. In November 1990 came the resignation of Howe, his 'bitter' resignation speech made a Heseltine challenge inevitable. Thatcher was brought down by her own party, not the voters and it was her own Cabinet which on Wednesday November 21st 1990 conveyed to her the crucial message that she must go or risk defeat in a second ballot at the hands of her personal and political enemy Heseltine. The British political system is based on party not personality despite the widespread assumption that British elections are increasingly 'Presidential'. She was the author of her own misfortune. Conservative back benchers in marginal seats were not willing to let her be the author of their destruction at the next election.

It was her longevity in office which lends credence to the notion of Thatcher as an 'ism'. Before becoming Prime Minister she had stated that she 'would not waste time having internal arguments' and she always described herself as a 'conviction politician' rather than a 'consensus politician'; she described herself as 'the Cabinet rebel'. Whereas most Prime Ministers tend to get closely involved only in certain policy areas - the economy, defence, foreign policy and security/intelligence matters being the most obvious example, Mrs Thatcher appeared to attempt to intervene across the range of policies and Departments. She held well-publicised seminars on topics such as football hooliganism and she made a big point of personally taking on - literally - the problem of litter in London. In 1988 she lectured the General Assembly of the Church of Scotland on morality and in the summer of 1990 Thatcher convened a conference of academics to discuss Germany's past, present and future.

The memoirs of disaffected former colleagues such as Pym, Prior and Stevas and the public criticisms of her by people such as Heseltine and Lawson all superficially confirm the autocratic style of leadership which became Mrs Thatcher's trademark but these are hardly unbiased sources. Just because Thatcher had a forceful, perhaps even autocratic, style does not 'prove' that Cabinet government has given way to a more Presidential style. On various occasions her policy was blocked or diluted by her colleagues or by the Whitehall machine. The ability of the PM to dominate the government is dependent upon circumstances and upon the degree of party cohesion, it does not just depend upon the style of the incumbent.

If even Thatcher, clearly the strongest peacetime PM this century is removable in such way it must cause us to doubt the notion of Prime Ministerial government.

Major

The Conservatives were by 1990 very divided over Europe, especially Maastricht, and within the party there was a strong divide between right and left. Major has also had to contend with the fact that he had a small majority after April 1992 making it not only difficult to agree policies, but also acting as a catalyst for backbench rebellions. Thatcher clearly by-passed her Cabinet on occasions, relying heavily upon her Policy Unit, Cabinet Committees, bilateral meetings between herself (with her advisors) and the departmental minister or high powered inter-departmental task forces of able civil servants reporting to her. Under Major Cabinet meetings were apparently more relaxed, more like genuine discussions. The Cabinet met regularly to prepare the negotiating position of Major and Hurd at the Maastricht Summit in December 1991 and to approve the replacement of the Poll Tax. Major was concerned with representing and reflecting the Cabinet view.

Catterall argues that 'the extent to which the Major government distanced itself from its predecessor can easily be exaggerated'. Thatcher was defeated, Thatcherism remained. The classic example was privatisation of the railways under Major.

Blair

It is still too early, even after 6 years, to say how the Blair government will develop, but it does seem presidential. Michael Foley argues that the tendency towards presidentialism within the UK political system, tendencies which have been evident for decades, have reached their logical conclusion under Blair. The fact that he had won the leadership of his party by a landslide in 1994 obviously put him in a strong position within the party. He was able to stamp his ideological views on the party *before* he became PM, as in the removal of Clause Four, whereas Thatcher had to fight ideological battles with her own party *after* she became Prime Minister. Thatcher was battling the wets in her Cabinet two years into government. At no point as PM has Blair faced a concerted ideological challenge to New Labour's agenda. The fact that in 1997 Blair had gone on to win the general election by a bigger margin than any previous Labour PM made him even stronger. Labour's election campaigns in both 1997 and 2001 focussed very much upon Blair. As he told the newly elected Labour MPs in 1997 *'we were elected as New Labour, we will govern as New Labour'.*

Blair had never served in government before and neither had most of his colleagues. Nonetheless he was concerned that Prime Ministers often lack the power to impose their will upon the Whitehall machine. Blair was determined to assert the power of the PM over departments and ministers. Andrew Rawnsley quotes Blair's advisor Jonathon Powell warning civil servants to 'expect a change from a feudal system of barons to a more Napoleonic system.' Blair strengthened the PM's office and the Cabinet Office. According to Peter Riddel the shift from co-ordination to central control was 'the biggest centralisation of power seen in Whitehall in peacetime.' His former colleague Mo Mowlam has accused him of acting like a president, exactly the same charge made by Clare Short in her resignation speech.

In practice the Blair government has operated as a duopoly with power shared between Blair and Brown. The Treasury is stronger than ever and through a system of Public Service Agreements it effectively controls the spending departments. Both the decision to give the Bank of England control over interest rates and the criteria for determining whether the pound should join the Euro were effectively taken by Blair and Brown. The Cabinet was informed afterwards although following Short's resignation Blair and Brown have promised that the Cabinet will discuss the key issue of the Euro.

Apparently Blair has only voted in 5% of the divisions in the Commons since becoming PM. He holds fewer Cabinet meetings than his predecessors, when Cabinet does meet it lasts for a shorter time and above all its role has changed. Instead of deciding policy the Cabinet is *informed* of the policy that has been decided by Blair in a bilateral with the relevant Minister in conjunction with his own advisors. Clare Short talked of centralisation in the hands of 'an increasingly small number of advisers.' According to her 'there is no real collective responsibility because there is no collective.' Cook is said to have been replaced as Foreign Secretary in 2001 by the more compliant Straw because Cook was too independent. Blair uses advisers such as Lord Levy to act as his unofficial envoy to the Middle East. The resignation of Estelle Morris was allegedly because Blair listened more to his own education adviser Andrew Adonis.

At the time of the war with Serbia in 1999 Blair gave a speech in Chicago outlining his belief in humanitarian interventionism, the Foreign Office was supposedly taken by surprise. After September 11th Blair effectively became, in Mandela's words, Bush's Foreign Secretary, touring the world to drum up support. The war with Iraq was conducted by Blair in a presidential manner with the Defence Secretary Hoon, in effect, a mouthpiece. It may be that this overstates Blair's dominance. For example it is possible that in the first term he wished to move towards PR for the Commons but was unable to persuade the Cabinet. The media inevitably focus on personalities and leaders. Even so Blair does appear to dominate the Government more than any post-war Prime Minister other than Thatcher. We do not talk about Blairism but it is very much Blair's government and as of May 2003 Blair had been PM for just six years whereas Thatcher was PM for eleven and a half years. Unless Blair chooses to quit he looks set to become the first Labour PM to serve two full consecutive terms. Now that the war with Iraq is over Blair's position looks stronger than ever. The media speculate as to whether Blair will use his power to move Brown from the Treasury or to take on Murdoch by holding a referendum on the Euro.

Of course all of this personal domination carries risks. Peter Oborne argues that Blair's Napoleonic approach has generally worked well and produced more efficient government but during a crisis such as the war then the system breaks down. Blair has personally identified himself with the cause of reform of the public services, if reform is not seen to make a difference then Blair is vulnerable. If the war with Iraq had gone badly Blair may well have had to resign because he had gone out on such a limb over the issue. Blair has been lucky in that the economy has performed well under his government, the wars Britain has fought under his leadership have been short and successful and so far the Northern Ireland peace agreement has held up. He has also benefited from two enormous majorities. If the economy goes down or if the peace in Iraq proves more difficult than the war or if it provokes a terrorist attack on the UK or if terrorism returns to Northern Ireland or if he gets a Euro referendum wrong then Blair will be in a very different position.

Conclusion

Questions as to whether the UK has Cabinet government, or Prime Ministerial government are ultimately unanswerable in a factual sense because so much depends upon interpretation. Major had to endure almost five years of attacks from within his own party and had to take the unprecedented step of calling a leadership election, a vote of confidence in himself. It might be objected that Major is the exception but as a comparison with Callaghan, Wilson, Home, Macmillan and other Premiers reveals he was more like the norm, it was Thatcher who was one of the exceptions. However Democratic Audit conclude that 'Labour has further concentrated the power of decision in the hands of the PM and the Chancellor and accelerated the decline in cabinet government. Their aim is to produce effective government but there are doubts about their 'control and command' strategy and the continuation of inadequate checks and balances in the policy process and a weakened civil service still produces policy fiascos such as the Dome and the handling of the foot and mouth crisis.'

Prime Ministers and Presidents

It was Richard Crossman writing in the 1960s who popularised the notion that a British PM is becoming more like a US President. The UK supposedly has Cabinet Government but the Cabinet was becoming increasingly dignified and therefore more like the US Cabinet, which is a purely advisory body. General elections in the UK are increasingly portrayed by the media as presidential contests, Thatcher versus Foot in 1983, Kinnock versus Major in 1992, Blair versus Hague in 2001. If the broadcasters get their way and the campaign includes a leader's debate then the process will be even more Americanised. However, Michael Foley has pointed out the flaws in the comparison of a British PM and an American President. A British PM exercises power within a unitary state with an uncodified constitution. An American President is head of a federal system in which much power is reserved to the states. They are checked and balanced by Congress, which is referred to as 'the most powerful legislature in the democratic world'. They are constrained by a codified constitution upheld by a Supreme Court, which has been described as the 'most powerful tribunal on Earth'. In Clare Short's words 'we have the powers of a presidential system with the automatic majority of a Parliamentary system.'

So who then is more powerful, a UK prime Minister or an American President? As always much depends upon what we mean by power. US Presidents tend to be more powerful abroad than they are at home, UK Prime Ministers tend to be more powerful at home than they are abroad. There is now only one military superpower. The US spends as much on defence as the next nineteen nations combined. The UK may still lead the Commonwealth, be the world's fourth biggest economy, have a leading role in the EU and a permanent seat on the Security Council of the United Nations but still has a limited influence in global affairs. Any President operates within a system based on a separation of powers. They may well face a Congress controlled by their opponents. For six of Clinton's eight years in office the Republicans had majorities in both houses of Congress.

A British PM operates within a system based on a fusion of powers. They are almost always PM because their party has a majority in the Commons. When Clinton visited Blair shortly after Labour's first victory Clinton joked that he whose he had a majority of 179. In reality even when the Democrats had a majority in Congress in 1993/4 it did not help Clinton very much because party loyalty is much weaker than in the UK. However when it comes to foreign policy or defence partisanship matters less than patriotism. The fact that the Congress is split, with the Democrats enjoying a wafer thin majority in the Senate and the Republicans in control of the House of Representatives will not much hinder Bush when it comes to prosecuting the war on terror. However when it comes to domestic matters such as tax and spend or the appointment of Supreme Court judges Bush may well find himself restrained. Blair still commands a majority of 165 and can almost guarantee that his domestic agenda will get through Parliament. However his attempts to act as an international statesman are constrained by the relative weakness of the UK in a world dominated militarily at least by the USA.

Despite all the talk over the last 40 years of Prime Ministerial government and more recently of President Blair the fact is that any British PM holds office within a parliamentary system of government. Blair is a member of and accountable to the Commons as witnessed by PM Question Time. He calls elections (within the maximum five years laid down by the Parliament Act of 1911) and can theoretically be removed by a vote of no confidence. Not only is the President not a member of the legislature neither are any of his Cabinet or Administration with the solitary exception of the Vice President. Bush's only appearance before Congress is the annual state of the Union address. Elections are at regular intervals, November 2002 saw the last mid-term elections and November 2004 is when the Presidency will next be contested. The only way the Congress can remove a President is through impeachment and this has never actually succeeded. President Johnson survived by one vote in the 1860s, Nixon resigned before it reached the Senate and Clinton survived relatively easily. In the UK the vast majority of government bills become law whereas in the USA most bills fail to get through Congress and even bills supported by the President often get radically amended. No PM need worry that his government's bills will be rejected by the Head of State, no Monarch has refused to sign a bill since 1707. US Presidents can veto bills and do so if they can derive political advantage from it.

It is precisely because UK Prime Ministers face far fewer formal checks and balances that fears arise. A Labour MP, Graham Allan, recently introduced a bill, which would have recognized the reality of Prime Ministerial power by restructuring British government around a separation of powers. Of course the bill got nowhere and Blair downplays notions of a Blair presidency. If past precedent is any guide then Blair will find his powers reduced at some point as his party or his Cabinet or Parliament reassert themselves. Powerful PM's such as Thatcher are allowed to dominate for a while and are then constrained, in her case to be eventually replaced by the more collegiate Major. US Presidents in contrast are able to invoke their personal mandate as Reagan in the 1980s, Johnson in the 1960s and Roosevelt in the 1930s and 40s were able to do. However they are hemmed in by so many constraints that in the end 'the power of the President is the power to persuade'. There could be little talk in the USA of 'an elective dictatorship.'

The British Civil Service

Introduction

The modern British Civil Service began with the Northcote-Trevelyan report of 1853. It was generally admired for its ability to work for whatever party was in power. The Labour government of 1945-51 experienced no problems with the Civil Service. From the late 1950s onwards the Civil Service began to attract criticism. The right argued it was "a bloated bureaucracy", the left argued that the mandarins were elitist. Ministers in the 1964 to 1970 and 1974 to 1979 Labour Governments are supposed to have met with obstruction. At least that is the verdict of the diaries of Crossman, Benn and Castle. Healey sat in the same Cabinets as the three diarists and yet in his autobiography he has nothing but praise for the mandarins.

The Labour governments of 1964-70 tried to reform the Civil Service as part of their overall attempt at modernising the British State. In 1966, Wilson set up a Royal Commission under Lord Fulton to investigate the structure of the Civil Service. **The Fulton Report** came out in 1968. Its opening lines were a damning indictment of the mandarins;

"The Home Civil Service today is still fundamentally the product of the 19th century philosophy of the Northcote-Trevelyan report. The tasks it faces are those of the second half of the 20th century."

The criticisms were that the Civil Service was too much based on the philosophy of the amateur, the generalist. Fulton made 22 recommendations, Wilson accepted 21 of them. The most important were that control of the Civil Service should be transferred from the Treasury to a new Civil Service Department. A Civil Service college was set up to train officials in modern business techniques. The 1,400 classes were to be abolished and replaced by a unified grading structure. Recruits were to be encouraged from outside Oxbridge and there was to be less secrecy, more openness. Wilson claimed that the Fulton Report was the greatest shake up of the Civil Service in over a century, yet one of the most widespread assumptions in recent political history is that the Fulton report failed to radically alter the culture of Whitehall.

Professor John Griffith argues that Fulton failed because he looked at the wrong issue, recruitment and promotion. He should have been looking at the bias of mandarins, but Wilson specifically excluded this from the terms of reference because it touches on the sensitive issue of relations between Ministers and Mandarins.

According to the left wing journalist, Peter Kellner, and a member of the commission, Norman Hunt, Fulton failed because it was "sabotaged" by the Mandarins who paid lip service to the reforms but carried on recruiting and promoting public school, Oxbridge 'chaps'. Ponting in 'Whitehall; Tragedy and Farce' agrees with this.

The timing was wrong. Fulton reported in 1968 by which time Wilson had a lot more pressing priorities than the reform of the Civil Service. Heath came in 1970 with his own ideas about reforming Whitehall. He set up the CPRS - Central Policy Review Staff or "Think Tank". When Wilson came back in 1974 he set up the No. 10 Policy Unit. It was not until 1979 that a PM came in determined to reform the bureaucracy. According to Professor Fry, Fulton didn't fail in the long run. It takes a generation to change the structure of Whitehall and Fulton laid the foundations on which Thatcher was to build.

The Civil Service under Thatcher

Thatcherism was committed to *"rolling back the frontiers of the state in the social and economic spheres"*. This involved cutting government spending on welfare, cutting income tax, privatising the nationalised industries, selling council houses to their tenants and cutting the size of the bloated bureaucracy. The Thatcherites were convinced that the Civil Service needed to be made slimmer, more efficient. They had been heavily influenced by books such as Leslie Chapman's 'Your Disobedient Servant' and Bacon and Eltis 'Britain's Economic Problem - Too Few Producers'. The three Es - economy, efficiency and effectiveness were her watchwords. As Mark Wickham-Jones points out, the radical free-market right, following the thinking of theorists such as the American economists Buchanan and Tullock, are very suspicious of public sector bureaucracies.

Thatcher brought in businessmen as advisers who, she believed, understood how to achieve efficiency. Lord Rayner from Marks & Spencer set up an Efficiency Unit working in the Cabinet Office. Civil Servants working for Rayner monitored civil service functions to see if cuts could be made. If waste could be cut, then either taxes could be cut, or the money could be spent on politically rewarding areas like health and education.

Rayner left in 1982 but 'Raynerism' survived. The Efficiency Unit has apparently identified savings worth billions. The financial-management initiative (FMI) asked departments to set (and where possible quantify) their objectives and to measure the extent to which they had been achieved. The number of civil servants fell by about 18%. In 1979, there were 730,000 servants; ten years later there were about 590,000 but mostly the cuts were of 'industrial' civil servants; for example, those who worked in now-privatised munitions factories. Whether the Civil Service was more efficient is debatable. Critics argue that services have been cut, not waste.

Another business adviser, Sir John Hoskyns, was the first head of Thatcher's Number 10 Policy Unit (a tiny equivalent of the President's White House Office). He was very influential in the early stages of Thatcherism such as the Spring 1981 budget. However he left in 1982 frustrated at what he saw as Civil Service obstruction of radical Thatcherism and has subsequently campaigned for a switch to the American style system whereby when a government changes so do the senior advisers. *"How can we have radical government without radically minded officials?"* The argument for a politicised Civil Service is that at least the government can guarantee support from the bureaucracy. Even Thatcher found this too radical because of the loss of continuity it would lead to.

Relations between the Thatcher government and the Civil Service deteriorated. Thatcherite policies such as privatisation, must have encountered Civil Service "opposition" because they were reducing the size and role of the state.

Poor morale amongst officials was intensified by the government's refusal to increase Civil Service pay leading to a Civil Service strike in 1981 which even involved GCHQ (Government Communications Head Quarters) in Cheltenham. In November 1981, Thatcher abolished the Civil Service Department, the centre-piece of Fulton's report. Control was restored to the Treasury which Thatcher believed would keep a clearer eye on costs. In 1983 she abolished the 'Think Tank'. Thatcher felt that her government did not need its advice, she had a strategy.

In January 1984, apparently without consulting her Cabinet, Thatcher banned TUs at GCHQ. The Ponting case was followed by what Piper calls 'the inadequate Armstrong memorandum'.

By the late 1980s Thatcher's government had made huge changes to the Civil Service. However, the biggest change of all began in 1988 when the Efficiency Unit under Sir Robin Ibbs produced **"Improving Management in Government: the Next Steps."** Ibbs believed that, in Piper's, words 'substantial obstacles were thwarting the introduction of lasting improvements in Whitehall efficiency.' The Report advocated breaking up the Civil Service into autonomous agencies which would have control over their own budgets and could ultimately be privatised. According to Ibbs 'the Civil Service is too big and too diverse to manage as a single entity'.

Thatcher was given the report in spring 1987 but because it was contentious it was held back until after the election. The report was gradually implemented from 1988 onwards. The 'Next Steps' programme, when fully implemented, would hive off most governmental functions to quasi-independent agencies, many of whom would contract out their business to private-sector firms. 'Agencies would carry out the executive functions of government within a policy and resources framework set by a department.' The ultimate aim was to reduce the Civil Service to just a core of policy advisers. It was the biggest shake up of Whitehall in the C20th.

Politicisation?

Whether Thatcher politicised the Civil Service or not depends upon how we define politicisation. If we take the broad definition, that is changing the culture of Whitehall to make it more efficient, then yes, Thatcher did politicise it. However, if we take a narrow view of politicisation, Thatcher appointing and promoting officials who agreed with her, then according to Peter Hennessey no, she did not politicise it.

By 1990 most Permanent Secretaries - the heads of Whitehall departments - were appointed by her but basing his argument on a survey by the non-partisan Royal Institute of Public Affairs Hennesey concludes that appointment was based on merit not on whether the mandarin was 'one of us'. Even the officials who became very closely identified with her and her policies such as Ingham her Press Secretary, Sir Charles Powell one of her Private Secretaries, and Sir Peter Middleton, Permanent Secretary at the Treasury, were **all appointed on merit**. She preferred to appoint 'can-do' types, interested in the quick implementation of their political bosses' decisions. There was a reduction of the opportunities for civil servants to make government policy reflecting a greater use of think tanks outside the Whitehall machine.

As Professor Fry argues perhaps the changed culture of the 1980s and 1990s is really a reflection of the longer term changes promoted by Fulton. Obviously it takes a long time for change to an institution as slow moving as Whitehall to manifest itself; one generation, at least, of Mandarins had to be replaced by post-Fulton figures.

The Civil Service under Major

Majors 'big idea' in terms of the public sector was the **Citizens Charter** published in July 1991. The Independent commented 'it offers an agenda for action which neatly points up the difference between Thatcherism and the policies that the Prime Minister intends to make his own'. However, Peter Catterall argues that there is a great deal of continuity from Thatcherism to Major, the Charter 'marks a progression from the policies of Mrs Thatcher as much as a clear break.' The 1992 Tory manifesto 'The Best Future for Britain' described it as 'the most far reaching programme ever devised to improve quality in the public services... the Charter will be at the centre of government's decision making throughout the 1990s'.

By 1993 there were 30 charters ranging from a passengers charter for British Rail to a patients charter in the NHS. British Rail had to refund £1.5 million in 1993 because of the charter yet their definition of a train being late is that it has to be one hour overdue.

A White Paper published in 1994 claimed that three years experience showed the Charters to have been a success. However a Financial Times audit published at the same time said that little had been achieved.

Adonis pointed out that the notion of citizenship involved is a consumerist one, the model is the private sector. Tony Wright a Labour MP and author of 'Citizens and Subjects' agrees with Adonis, giving more power to consumers and pretending that this constitutes citizenship is to fundamentally cheapen the concept.

Continuity and Change

Responsibility for the civil service was given to William Waldegrave, the head of the Office of Public Services and Science. He argued in a speech in July 1992 'there will continue to be areas where we must ask the question; is this really any business of government', a British version of 'reinventing government'. Waldegrave denied that increased use of QUANGOs represented any kind of threat to democracy, accountability is maintained through the appropriate Minister and the power of citizens as consumers creates accountability.

In July 1992 the official in charge of the government's civil service reforms, Sir Peter Kemp, was removed because he was critical of the way reform was being implemented. Kemp, a former Treasury official, had been the Next Steps Project Manager but he had argued with Waldegrave. In November 1993 Kemp spoke out against the management of the Civil Service arguing that it was becoming 'littered with policies that do not work'. In March 1994 Sir Clive Whitmore the top Civil Servant at the Home Office quit his job, allegedly because of his opposition to Howard's style of policy making, a few months earlier Sir Geoffrey Holland had resigned as

Permanent Secretary at the Education Department again supposedly because of bad relations with his Minister, John Patten. These incidents revealed a tension between Ministers and Mandarins, a tension perhaps born out of the changed approach to policy advice on the part of the government.

The 1994 White Paper on the Civil Service, 'Continuities and Change', argued that much had been achieved since 1979 but much remained to be done. The goal was to continue market testing, introduced in 1992 following the 'Competing for Quality' White Paper of 1991, and complete the implementation of the Ibbs Report. By April 1995 108 agencies employing 370,00 people, two thirds of the civil service, had been set up. The Prior Options process means that when agencies review their activities every five years one of the things they should consider is privatisation. Sir Peter Levine the head of the Efficiency Unit favoured full blown privatisation of agencies.

The Treasury and Civil Service Select Committee welcomed the Citizens Charter and the creation of more Agencies but was concerned about the weakening of IMR particularly in relation to such high profile agencies as the Child Support Agency and the Prisons Agency. It had been concerned about this issue ever since its first report on the Agencies and in 1994 it argued that Agency Executives should be directly accountable to Select Committees and that a new Civil Service Code should be introduced. Ibbs had wanted Chief Executives to be directly accountable to Parliament but when Thatcher introduced the Report in February 1988 she had stressed that there were to be no changes to civil service accountability.

A PAC report in 1994 brought together the findings of 17 earlier reports into the Agencies, Health Service Trusts and so on. It set out details of 26 cases of mismanagement, incompetence and fraud costing taxpayers £80 million. Perhaps this was the consequence of replacing the old public services ethic with a more commercially driven one.

The Government responded to the Select Committees with another White Paper in January 1995 'Taking Forward Continuity and Change' which rejected the suggestion that Agency heads be directly accountable to Select Committees but accepted the idea of a new Civil Service Code and an independent appeals system through the Civil Service Commissioners for civil servants who felt the code had been breached.

One general concern had been the increasing number of civil servants leaving Whitehall for lucrative careers in the private sector. The list includes Sir William Armstrong the ex-Head of the Civil Service who went to work for Midland Bank, Sir Edward Playfair who left the Department of Defence for International Computers, Sir Lesle Rowan who after the Treasury went to Vickers.

The first Nolan Report in May 1995 recommended that the new Civil Service code should be introduced immediately and that to avoid suggestions that both Ministers and Mandarins were abusing public service by leaving it for well paid work in the private sector Nolan recommended an automatic three month waiting period.

Labour and the Civil Service

The promotion of a more managerial culture in Whitehall met with applause, even, if muted, from the Labour Party. As The Guardian argued in 1997 there is no question but that a Blair government anxious to keep spending down would be just as keen on 'efficiency' as Thatcher and Major. As the election approached senior Labour figures met Civil Servants. Labour had been out of office for a very long time and the hope was that by exchanging ideas with the Official Opposition the mandarins would be better prepared for a change of government if it occurred. Peter Hennessey has long argued that such contact needs to be increased and formalised with senior civil servants seconded to work with the Opposition for a while. According to Hennessey many within Whitehall eagerly awaited a change of government. The Labour 1997 manifesto had nothing specific to say about the civil service other than the plans for a Freedom of Information Act.

The first six years of the Blair government has seen few problems with the civil service except for the Treasury where Brown's advisors have been resented and seven resignations occurred. The most prominent was Sir Terry Burns, the Permanent Secretary, who resigned in summer 1998 as Brown appeared to pay more attention to his own adviser Ed Balls. The influx of political advisers, especially spin doctors, caused friction with the civil service. In 1998 Richard Wilson replaced Butler as Cabinet Secretary and Head of the Civil Service. Blair thanked Butler for helping achieve a smooth transition.

Labour have completed the implementation of the Next Steps programme. Ten years on from Ibbs and over three quarters of all civil servants (377,480) worked in executive agencies. Both the Child Support Agency and the Pensions Agency - the two most controversial agencies - have been made more directly accountable to Ministers and Parliament. The Citizens Charter was re-launched under a new name - Service First. Robert Pyper summarises Blair's challenge to the civil service and the government's agenda

Tony Blair's seven challenges for the civil service

1. Implement constitutional reform in a way that preserves a unified civil service, ensure close working between UK government and the devoted administrations

2. Staff in all departments to integrate the EU dimension into policy-making.

3. Public services to be improved, more innovative and responsive to users, and delivered in an efficient and joined-up way.

4. Create a more innovative and less risk-averse culture in the civil service.

5. Improve collaborative working across organisational boundaries.

6. Manage civil service so as to equip it to meet these challenges.

7. Think ahead strategically to future priorities.

Modernising Government
The White Paper Modernising Government, March 1999, promised to create a civil service for the C21st.

Central Objective
'Better government to make life better for people'

Aims

Ensure that policy making is more 'joined up' and strategic.

Focus on public-service users, not providers.

Deliver high-quality and efficient public services.

New Reforms

Government direct: public services available 24 hours a day, seven days a week, where there is a demand.

Joined-up government: co-ordination of public services and more strategic policy making.

Removal of unnecessary regulation: requirements that departments avoid imposing new regulatory burdens and submit those deemed necessary to Regulatory Impact Assessments.

Information age government: target for all dealings with government to be deliverable electronically by 2008.

Learning labs: to encourage new ways of front-line working and suspend rules that stifle innovation.

Incentives: for public service staff - including financial rewards for those who identify savings or service improvements.

New focus on delivery within Whitehall: permanent secretaries to pursue delivery of key government targets, recruit more 'outsiders', promote able young staff.

Key Commitments

Forward-looking policy making

Identify and spread best practice via new Centre for Management and Policy Studies (which will incorporate the Civil Service College).

Joint training of ministers and civil servants.

Peer review of departments.

Responsive public services
Remove obstacles to joined-up working through local partnerships, one-stop shops and other means.

Involve and meet the needs of different groups in society.

Quality public services
Review all government department services and activities over five years to identify best suppliers.

Set new targets for all public bodies with focus on real improvements in quality and effectiveness.

Monitor performance closely to strike balance between intervention when things go wrong and allowing successful organisations freedom of management.

Information-age government
An IT strategy for government to co-ordinate development of digital signatures, smart cards, Web sites and call centres.

Benchmark progress against targets for electronic services.

Public service
To be valued, not denigrated.

Modernise the civil service (including revision of performance management arrangements; tackle under-representation of women, ethnic minorities and people with disabilities; build capacity for innovation).

Establish a public-sector employment forum to bring together and develop key players across the public sector

Pyper stresses that the really important changes to the civil service will come about as a result of devolution. Labour have not done what constitutional reformers wanted which is to introduce a Civil Service Act with clear rules for executive conduct.

Conclusion

Tony Butcher argues that Major sought to combine a continuation of the Thatcherite emphasis upon efficiency with a maintenance of the traditional Whitehall features - permanence, impartiality and recruitment and promotion on merit. Blair has maintained this approach. In 2001 the Public Administration Select Committee produced a report 'Making Government Work' which recognised the civil service as 'a resource of immense value to government' but was critical of its generalism. As Democratic Audit put it 'overall there are doubts about the capacity of the civil service to improve and deliver the public services that are at the heart of the government's electoral mandate.' As the Guardian commented back in 1995 'the revolution rolls on - but not quite as radically as some in Whitehall would prefer'.

 Has the Civil Service been politicised since 1979?

Departmental Government

Both Cabinet Government and Prime Ministerial government appear too simplistic as ways of explaining the workings of a machine as complex as Whitehall. According to commentators such as Hugh Heclo what we actually have is departmental government where the Ministers and the Mandarins in a particular department co-operate in promoting the interests of that department. Ministers spend on average two years in a department so their loyalty is transient but the Mandarins are permanent and therefore are the guardians of the **departmental view**. The Treasury will always try to balance the budget by insisting on public spending cuts. The Foreign Office is accused of being too pro-Arabist and too pro-Europe. Thatcher always distrusted the Foreign Office as 'quisling' and her Foreign Secretaries, Carrington, Pym, Howe, Major and Hurd were always regarded warily in case they had succumbed to the departmental view. MAFF is regarded as the 'sponsoring Ministry for the NFU' and so on.

Government is often a battle for resources so the politicians and officials are in alliance attempting to get the maximum budget for 'their' department. The divisions within Whitehall are thus vertical - between departments - rather than horizontal - between Ministers and Mandarins. Departments have on-going links with insider pressure groups. There is a form of log-rolling as politicians and officials make interdepartmental deals to help get their programmes adopted. Blair has attempted to avoid this *departmentalitis* by creating inter-departmental bodies such as the social exclusion unit in an attempt to promote **joined up government**.

The Civil Service do not actually govern but they do get involved in policy making. They have to, because of the size and complexity of modern interventionist government. The problems are lack of co-ordination, with each department pushing its interests there is little incentive to look to the national interest, and the associated problem of short-termism. Everyone's eyes are fixed firmly on the next election but the problems facing the country are often deep seated and require long term solutions. This links with overload, as politicians are 'forced' by the democratic process to make promises that in government will prove impossible to implement.

The US Executive

Powers of the President

Article 2 of the US constitution states that, "the executive powers shall be vested in a President". The constitutional powers of the President are briefly set out, they mostly concern national security: the President is the Commander in Chief of the Army, and can make treaties subject to Senate approval. On law-making, the President can make recommendations to Congress.

The modern Presidency is much more powerful than the wording of the Constitution suggests. The Presidency today has a variety of functions within the political system, as Clinton Rossiter described. Presidents are elected by the nation every four years and no President may now serve more than two full terms. He is the 'Head of State', carrying out the formal and ceremonial duties done in Britain by the Monarch.

Country	Head of State	Head of Government
USA	President (elected by the people)	President
UK	Queen (hereditary position)	PM
Japan	Emperor (hereditary position)	PM
Israel	President (elected by Knesset)	PM
Germany	President (elected by politicians)	Chancellor
France	President (elected by the people)	PM
Russia	President (elected by the people)	PM
Ireland	President (elected by the people)	PM
China	President (elected by the NPC)	PM

The President is **the defender of the constitution**. That was why Watergate was so shocking, Nixon did not defend the Constitution he abused it.

The President is Chief Executive that is Head of Government. He organises the executive branch, with the 'advice and consent of the Senate' they appoint the heads of all government departments, other members of the administration and all federal judges including the Supreme Court. The Vice President is his deputy but has little real power although Cheney is a key figure within the Bush Administration. There are 16 secretaries who head departments employing 3 million Federal Civil Servants all working for the President. The **Executive Office of the President (EOP)** also works for him. Fewer than two thousand work in it but they are his *personal bureaucracy*.

The President is Commander in Chief, in charge of the armed forces and therefore he wages war such as in 2003 the decision to attack Iraq. **The President is Director of Foreign Relations**, he is Chief Diplomat. In 1787, the US was just 13 states, with a population of 3 to 4 million, isolated from Europe, therefore it did not really have much of an army or much of a foreign policy. Today, there are 50 states, 280 million people, it is the only military superpower and one of the economic superpowers. Tim Hames points out that for most of the 216 years of the Republic the Congress has favoured a more isolationist stance than the President, irrespective of party. The exception was the period from 1941 to 1973 but since then the normal relationship has reasserted itself.

Most of Article 2 is taken up in describing the Electoral College however the Presidency has acquired more power, more roles. **The Constitution states that the President shall be allowed to recommend legislation to Congress.** In the 19th century, with the passive Presidency, this was not particularly important. In the 20th century, with the active Presidency, the role of **Chief Legislator, or Legislative Leader** became critical. Most of the laws passed by Congress originate in the Executive, even though formally they can only be introduced into the legislature by a member of Congress.

The tribune of the people. The President is the only nationally elected politician, the only one who can claim to be the spokesman of the nation. With the modern media this role has become much more important. The media focus on the President means that any mistakes or failures receive widespread publicity. The President ends up having a love-hate relationship with the media, they use the media, particularly television, to try and get their message across, but at the same time they often feel hounded by unfavourable coverage. FDR used the radio for his "fireside chats". Kennedy distrusted the press but believed he could use TV to his advantage, for example during his debate with Nixon in the 1960 election. JFK was the first "telegenic President".

Johnson blamed the growing unpopularity of the Vietnam War on television coverage which he believed was anti-American; Nixon was paranoid about both the press and television; Carter clearly failed to come over well on TV. Reagan 'the Great Communicator', used the media more effectively than any President since Roosevelt, but his first reaction to the Irangate scandal in November 1986 was to blame it on the 'sharks' in the media. Bush Senior complained of hostile media coverage whereas Clinton appeared to have a good relationship with the media. The present Bush is not particularly effective at communicating through the media but the US public appear to find his style endearing.

Manager of the economy. This effectively determines whether the incumbent wins or loses the battle for re-election, as Clinton's campaign slogan in 1992 put it **'its the economy, stupid'**. The President is now expected to deliver low unemployment, economic growth, generous public services and low taxes all somehow magically combined with low inflation. Of course the same is true of a British government but at least they control the key levers - fiscal and monetary policy. A President has to try to persuade the Congress to endorse his fiscal stance, hence Bush has to try to get his budget through the Congress.

As for monetary policy he has even less control because there is an independent central bank. In terms of the economy at least a US President has responsibility without power. The Bush family blame the defeat of Bush senior on the Fed's refusal to cut interest rates.

Presidents are now party leaders. Every President since 1856 has been either a Republican or a Democrat. The President is both the effective national leader of his party and tries to work closely with his party in Congress in order to get his legislative proposals through. Washington warned Americans to *"beware the divisive influence of party"*. Parties are not mentioned in the constitution, but they had already developed by the 1790s. However, party loyalty is very weak. A President cannot threaten to call an early election as Major repeatedly did. FDR got party backing as did LBJ and, to a certain extent, Reagan. Truman, Kennedy, Carter and Clinton were opposed by many Democrats and thereby failed to get some of their policies through. Republicans tried to distance themselves from the Reagan Administration to avoid the 'fall out' from the 'Irangate' scandal as Democrats 'disowned' Clinton - and vice versa - after the elections of November 1994.

Professor Schlesinger provides a very useful and necessary historical perspective. It is often said that recent Presidents, such as Kennedy and Carter, faced great difficulties because the party system is in decline, but the parties have never been as strong in the USA as in Europe and Presidents such as Theodore Roosevelt and Wilson managed to overcome opposition from within their parties. Similarly, pressure groups are not a recent phenomena, James Madison warned about their dangers in the 1780s. The anti-slavery lobby in the 19th century and the Prohibition movement in the early 20th century were classic examples of single issue groups. As to the quality of the candidates who have emerged through the primary system in the last 30 years as the power of the party leaders to choose Presidential nominees has declined, it is difficult to argue that George W. Bush was less well qualified to be President than say Warren Harding in the 1920s or Ulysses Grant in the 1870s, both of whom were corrupt and both of whom were chosen by party bosses in 'smoke filled rooms'.

World Statesman - In the 20th century, as the US became a world power, then the President became more important globally. The process began in 1901 with Theodore Roosevelt and the first US colonies, it continued in April 1917 when the US joined WW1. The decisive turning point though was 1941 when America entered WW2. There is no doubt that George W Bush is politically the most powerful person in the world.

The job is multidimensional and clearly requires exceptional skills, if it is to be performed effectively.

The President's Administration

The President heads the executive branch, a giant organisation with numerous specialist divisions. Most of these have been created in the last seventy years. The first President created three departments - State, War and Treasury, with a total staff of less than a hundred. Today there are 16 departments, almost 60 independent commissions, agencies and boards and the bureaucracy is so vast it is referred to as the fourth branch of government. The federal government employs over three million officials but the states employ over 13 million.

The Cabinet

The President chooses a Cabinet (with the consent of the Senate) made up, mostly, of the heads of the most important government departments such as the Treasury. Members of Cabinet cannot be members of Congress, usually they have no large popular following, and have often never run for the electoral office. They can be powerful by virtue of the Department they head, but the Cabinet as a collective entity rarely plays an important role. Nixon only held 11 Cabinet meetings in the whole of 1972. It is up to Presidents who they wish to include in their Cabinet. Clinton for example gave the US Ambassador to the UN Cabinet status as a way of indicating the significance of the UN.

As the responsibilities and functions of federal government have gown, so has the size and complexity of the bureaucracy needed to implement decisions. There are not only 16 departments but also hundreds of commissions, agencies, boards, authorities and other institutions that have being built up over the past century to deal with particular problems as they arose. The structure of the bureaucracy is the result of piecemeal evolution rather than any rational plan, presenting the President, as Chief Executive, with immense problems of co-ordination and control as he attempts to direct the work of the executive branch.

Each department is headed by a Cabinet Secretary below whom there are Under Secretaries, Deputy Under Secretaries, Assistant Secretaries and Office Directors all appointed by the incoming President. Below them are the civil servants, permanent career officials. Initially civil servants were appointed according to the spoils system but this began to change with the Pendleton Act of 1883 which introduced appointment on merit, which now applies to 90% of the staff.

There are more than 5,000 senior civil service positions (in departments, agencies and commissions) to be filled by each new President on political grounds. This does have certain advantages. The President can bring in people from outside the civil service who have experience of the matters they are going to administer. It allows the President greater control of the civil service. The higher civil servants in the USA are politically accountable because they are identified with a particular set of policies. However, there are also obvious disadvantages. The changeover of civil servants with each new President destroys the continuity of government. A permanent, non-partisan civil service as in the UK is a useful source of independent and constructive advice and criticism. In the US friction can easily occur between the permanent career officials in the lower ranks of the civil service and the 'outsiders' who are brought in as their superiors.

The vast majority of the officials are based outside Washington and will never come into contact with the President. They are permanent, just like British Civil Servants. It is easy to tell in the British political system who are the politicians and who are the officials. The ministers are elected politicians; the mandarins are permanent officials. It is not as easy to tell the division in the USA.

Within the departments there are bureaux which deal with a particular area of administration, there are 25 such bureaux within the Department of the Interior. Bureaux operate with relative independence from the control of the Cabinet Secretary and other high Civil Servants. Congressmen, pressure groups and even the President himself develop direct links with the Bureau Chiefs, thus by-passing the more senior Civil Servants in the department. The most extreme case is the FBI operating within the Department of Justice but with its own career structure. The relative autonomy of the bureaux means that power in the cabinet departments is diffused among different centres of decision making.

The political appointees are often not career politicians and they work alongside permanent officials who are often able to persuade the political appointees to their way of thinking. The political appointees are said to "marry the natives" so that the Department of Defence (the Pentagon) tends to have a "hawkish" view. The Department of State has a "doveish" view. This is true of most political systems. In Britain though disagreements are hidden behind collective responsibility, in the US there is no collective responsibility. All disagreements are public.

In the Carter Administration, Brzezinski, the National Security Adviser, wanted to support the Shah of Iran to the bitter end; the State Department, led by Cyrus Vance, thought that Iran would be lost to American influence unless contact was established with the anti-Shah factions. Secretary of State Haig's row with Jeanne Kirkpatrick (then the American Ambassador to the United Nations) in 1982 over American policy in the Falklands War. Both Haig and Kirkpatrick were Cabinet members pursuing differing policies and not bothering to hide their disagreement. The result, as often happens, was that American policy was unclear. Haig's differences with Bush, Weinburger, Richard Clark (the then National Security Adviser) and Larry Speakes (then Reagan's Press Spokesman) over American policy in the Middle East led eventually to Haig's resignation. Reagan's new Secretary of State Schultz believed that the US must respond constructively to Gorbachev. His Secretary of Defence, Weinburger, took the opposite view, arguing that the Soviets could not be trusted. Powell has publicly disagreed with Rumsfeld over the future direction of the war on terror.

Economic policy sometimes suffers from divided responsibility, as the Chairman of the Federal Reserve, the Treasury Secretary, the Council of Economic Advisers and the Director of the Budget all battle, publicly, over which policies the President should adopt. Financial policy under Reagan was extremely chaotic with four of Reagan's people saying different things.

The "active Presidency" of the C20th has meant a much bigger bureaucracy. In 1933, there was 1 federal bureaucrat for every 280 Americans but by 1953, the ratio was 1 to 80. In 1937 the Brownlow Committee on the Re-organisation of the Executive Branch reported that the "President needs help". The response was the setting up in 1939 of the EOP - the Executive Office of the President, the President's personal bureaucracy.

White House Office

This includes the President's closest advisers, his speech writers, press secretary, working under a Chief of Staff who can sometimes be second only to the President in terms of power. The Chief of Staff of WHO in Reagan's first time was James Baker and he is credited with the success of that term. After Irangate, Reagan sacked his Chief of Staff Regan and bought in the experienced, ex-Senator Howard Baker who became known as Reagan's Prime Minister. Nixon's Chief of Staff, Bob Haldeman and his deputy, John Ehrlichman both served prison sentences over Watergate. Bush's Chief of Staff is Andrew Card.

National Security Council

The NSC consisting of the Secretary of State, Secretary of Defence, Vice President, military chiefs and the NSA (National Security Advisor) advises the President on all aspects of US foreign/defence policy. The NSA supposedly has a policy advisory role, not a policy making one. However, there have been occasions when the NSA has made policy such as from 1969 to 1973 when the NSA was Henry Kissinger. It was Kissinger rather than the Secretary of State, William Rogers, who was responsible for Nixon's foreign policy. Irangate is an example of the EOP working badly. Both Schultz and Weinburger opposed the sale of arms to Iran. The policy was very much that of key figures in the EOP, the Director of the CIA, William Casey, and the NSA, Bob MacFarlane, his replacement, Admiral Poindexter, and finally Lt. Col. Oliver North. The current NSA Condoleeza Rice is a hugely influential figure.

Office of Management and Budget

The OMB was set up in 1921 but known originally as the BOB (Bureau of the Budget) working out of the Treasury. Transferred to the EOP in 1939, in 1970 it was renamed the OMB. It collates the President's budget requests. The OMB has become extremely important over the last 20 odd years as budgetary issues have come to dominate domestic politics. The Director and his deputy have to be confirmed by the Senate, which is unusual for the EOP and indicates the importance of budgetary politics. The Director of OMB under Bush is Mitchell Daniels.

Council of Economic Advisers

Set up in 1946 it is a three man panel of economists advising the President on macro economic policy. The current Chair is Glenn Hubbard.

In addition to these agencies Presidents can create additional offices such as the Office of the US Trade Representative and the Office of National Drug Control Policy both created by Bush senior.

Independent Executive Agencies

About 40 agencies exist outside the structure of the main departments. These have been set up to deal with particular problems or areas of policy, e.g. Environmental Protection Agency, National Science Foundation,

National Aeronautics and Space Administration (NASA). They are run by a Director, rather than a Cabinet Secretary, appointed by the President.

IRCs - Independent Regulatory Commissions

The Independent Regulatory Commissions' function is totally different from the Executive Agencies: they take the supervision of certain other activities entirely out of the President's hands. Run by an independent board of commissioners (usually between 5 and 7) who serve fixed terms of office, they are not responsible to the President for the work of the commission, are part of the executive branch, but are not under the direct control of the President. He appoints their members, but only when there is a vacancy. His nominees have to be confirmed by the Senate and once appointed, they have *"security of tenure"*. They serve long terms, up to 14 years, therefore a President has to work with IRC's run by people he did not necessarily appoint.

The oldest IRC is the **ICC (Interstate Commerce Commission)** set up in the 1880s. The most important is the **FRB (Federal Reserve Board, 'the Fed.')**. The Chancellor of the Exchequer no longer tells the Bank of England when to raise or lower interest rates but he still sets the inflation target. The American situation is much more like Germany where the Bundesbank is independent of the politicians. The US President does not have the power to tell the Fed. what to do and yet monetary policy can have a huge impact on the fate of his presidency. In 1979/80 President Carter facing re-election wanted the Fed. to relax monetary policy, that is to cut interest rates. The Fed refused believing this to be inflationary and this may have helped defeat Carter in 1980. The same thing happened in 1991/2. The IRC's have been referred to as the 'headless fourth branch of government'.

The Power of the Bureaucracy

The bureaucracy has expanded at the behest of Presidents, according to classical democratic theory it can also be controlled by them if they desire. A very influential book which came out in 1992, 'Reinventing Government', by David Osborne argues that the government should be a purchaser rather than a provider, enabling rather than doing. It has had a big impact on Clinton and indeed on British politics too.

 Why is it so hard to co-ordinate the US Executive?

The Vice-Presidency

As Vice President Truman was not even told about the development of atomic weapons and yet as President he had to make the decision about their use against Japan. It is a perfect illustration of the strange way the office of the Vice Presidency operates. Its holder generally has little status within the Administration and yet is literally "a heartbeat away" from the most important post in the "free world".

Three Vice Presidents in the last half a century have had to take over the Presidency; Truman in April 1945 when FDR died, Johnson in November 1963 when Kennedy was assassinated and Ford in August 1974 when Nixon resigned. Two Vice Presidents have had to carry a heavy workload because the President was incapacitated, Nixon, in 1955 when Eisenhower suffered a heart attack and Bush in 1981 when Reagan was shot. Spiro Agnew, Nixon's Vice President, attracted attention for another reason, he resigned in 1973 rather than face criminal charges.

The Constitution says little about the vice-presidency. The Vice President is the formal head of the Senate but plays little part in its affairs, only being able to vote in the event of a tie. Until twenty years ago there was no constitutional procedure for replacing a Vice President. The 25th Amendment ratified in 1967 states that whenever there is a vacancy in the office of the Vice-President, the President shall nominate a Vice President, who shall take office upon confirmation by a majority vote of both Houses. In October 1973 Nixon had to replace Agnew and in August 1974 Ford had to choose a Vice-President.

Whatever the formal constitutional position, the amount of authority a Vice President has depends upon their personality and the leeway a President allows them. Eisenhower's choice, Richard Nixon, was

167

controversial. In 1952, during the campaign, Nixon was accused of corruption and had to clear his name in the famous "Checkers" speech. Eisenhower gave Nixon no help at all and, eight years later, when Nixon ran for the Presidency, Eisenhower refused to endorse him. Yet as Stephen Ambrose argues he was actually a very effective Vice President. Because Eisenhower chose to remain aloof from partisan politics, Nixon was in effect the leader of the Republicans during the 1950s.

The last person either John or Robert Kennedy actually wanted as the Vice President was Lyndon Johnson. Liberal Democrats opposed Johnson who they regarded as too conservative. Kennedy told them "we may have to look towards Texas", in other words Johnson would "balance the ticket". The narrowness of his margin of victory shows the choice of running mate was crucial. "Running mates" are often chosen, not for their intrinsic merits but because of what they can add to the "ticket". The conservative Reagan's choice of the more 'liberal' Bush and Mondale's choice of Ferraro are classic examples of this. Clinton was unusual in choosing a fellow Southerner as his running mate, thereby indicating the importance the Democrats attach to regaining the votes of the white South.

Kennedy in office, made little use of Johnson, except to send him on "fact finding" missions to South East Asia and then disregard the proposals Johnson made. Johnson's own choice as Vice President, Hubert Humphrey, toured Europe defending Johnson's policy in Vietnam. Nixon's choice of Ford to replace the discredited Agnew owed much to Ford's "clean" record as House Minority leader. Congress was obviously going to scrutinise Nixon's appointee very closely. Ford's own Vice-President, Nelson Rockefeller, chaired a presidential Commission of Inquiry into the CIA.

Carter made more use of his Vice-President, Walter Mondale, than most Presidents do and retained him on the ticket in 1980. Alexander Haig, Reagan's first Secretary of State, describes in his memoirs the power struggle within the White House when Reagan was shot. Bush, the formal second in command, was elbowed aside. This is the problem Vice-Presidents face; if they take a back seat role, as Bush did, they are accused of lacking charisma; if they try to take a higher profile, as Johnson did, they are accused of disloyalty and of distracting attention from the President.

Bush's own choice for the post, Dan Quayle, came as a complete surprise. Bush passed over his rival from the primaries, Bob Dole (perhaps because the campaign had been so bitter) and chose the relatively unknown, wealthy, youthful senator from Indiana. Presumably Bush was balancing the ticket as Quayle was a hawk on defence. The choice was greeted with derision because of Quayle's alleged avoidance of service in the Vietnam war. Quayle was effectively hidden from sight during the campaign. Bush's collapse in Japan in 1992 reminded Americans how close Quayle was to the Presidency.

Vice President Gore in contrast had a very good reputation. Gore had a higher profile than most VPs. In September 1993 Clinton gave Gore responsibility for the 'Reinventing Government' initiative. He was tainted by campaign funding scandals from 1996 and of course failed to get elected as President in 2000.

Those who do seek the office do so because they hope to use it as a springboard for their own Presidential ambitions rather than as an important post in its own right. In this century, six Presidents succeeded to the office directly from the Vice Presidency - Theodore Roosevelt, Calvin Coolidge, Harry Truman, Lyndon Johnson, Gerald Ford and George Bush. Of these, all except Ford went on to win office in their own right at the next election. In addition to these, Nixon's spell as Vice President helped him become a national name and therefore gain the nomination in 1960 and again in 1968. Only Mondale might be said to have suffered in his Presidential ambitions through his experience of Vice President. Bush became the first Vice President since Van Buren in 1837 to go directly on to win the White House. Vice President Cheney is extremely powerful. Perhaps the office is not so insignificant after all.

The Development of the Presidency

The vagueness of Article Two of the Constitution implies that the President was expected to be a figure head, a symbol of national unity. In fact, the first few Presidents were charismatic leaders of real authority: **George Washington** 1789-97; **Thomas Jefferson** 1801-9 (Democrat); **James Madison** 1809-1817 (Democrat); **James Monroe** 1817-25 (Democrat) and

Andrew Jackson 1829-37 (Democrat). Apart from **Lincoln** 1861-5 (Republican), the remaining 19th century Presidents were "passive". The dominant branch was Congress, indeed in the 1880s Woodrow Wilson in his book on US politics talked of "Congressional Government".

In the 20th century a much more active Presidency has emerged. It started with **Theodore Roosevelt** 1901-9 (Republican) and **Woodrow Wilson** 1913-21 (Democrat). However the modern presidency really began in 1933 with FDR (Democrat). This marked the beginning of the supposed, *"Imperial Presidency"*. It was to last for 40 years and during that time Congress allowed the President a relatively free hand over foreign and defence policy, but not over domestic concerns:

President	Party	Dates	Programmes
Roosevelt	Democrat	1933 - 1945	New Deal
Truman	Democrat	1945 - 1953	Fair Deal
Eisenhower	Republican	1953 - 1961	A passive President
Kennedy	Democrat	1961 - 1963	New Frontier
Johnson	Democrat	1963 - 1969	Great Society
Nixon	Republican	1969 - 1974	New Federalism
Ford	Republican	1974 - 1977	A caretaker President
Carter	Democrat	1977 - 1981	Carter was active but perhaps ineffectual
Reagan	Republican	1981 - 1989	Reaganomics
Bush	Republican	1989 - 1993	No domestic agenda
Clinton	Democrat	1993 - 2001	New Covenant
Bush	Republican	2001 -	Compassionate Conservation

FDR 1933-45, Democrat

FDR's domestic polices were known collectively as the New Deal. It shaped US politics for the next 30/40 years laying the foundations for the US political consensus in the same ways that Attlee's Labour governments of 1945/51 laid the foundations for the post-war British consensus. Both FDR and Attlee introduced a massive extension of the role of government. They both embraced welfare programmes and they both adopted Keynesian full employment economics. In terms of foreign policy between 1933-41 Congress was isolationist but in 1941 Japan attacked Pearl Harbour and the US entered the war. By 1945 it was a superpower and highly interventionist.

According to William Leuchtenberg every President since FDR has been in his 'shadow'.

Truman 1945-53, Democrat

Truman's domestic policies were known as the Fair Deal. Congress, controlled for most of his time in office by the Democrats, blocked Civil Rights for Southern Blacks.

By 1946 war-time co-operation between the USA, UK and USSR had given way to the Cold War. The underlying goal of every US administration since 1945 or perhaps even 1917 has been to combat and constrain Soviet power. The US had to take over Britain's former role of 'World Policeman': hence, in March 1947, the **Truman Doctrine** was announced - the US would intervene in Greece and Turkey to prevent the spread of Communism through the so-called Domino Theory. "It must be the policy of the USA to support free peoples who are resisting attempts at subjugation by armed minorities or by outside pressure." The susceptibility of the majority of Congress to the rhetoric of the Cold War was established. The adoption of the Truman Doctrine marked a decisive moment in American history because it launched over 40 years of containment and the military-industrial complex.

Both Democrats and Republicans shared fears of Communism spreading, although intervention was opposed by isolationists such as Taft. Truman was given a relatively free hand over foreign policy, Congress backed the creation of NATO in 1949, and the Korean War of 1950-3.

Eisenhower 1953-61, Republican

Ike was a passive President but by then the Civil Rights Movement had emerged and the Brown judgement forced him to act, hence the despatch of the National Guard to Little Rock in 1957 and the, admittedly weak, Civil Rights Act of that year. In terms of foreign policy Ike and his Secretary of State Dulles talked of 'rollback' but practised containment and were backed by Congress such as in the despatch of US marines to the Lebanon in 1958.

By 1960 the Sino-Soviet split was apparent and the Soviets had withdrawn their aid and advisers from China. However US relations with both the USSR and China remained poor for years to come.

Dwight D. Eisenhower

Kennedy 1961/63, Democrat

JFK's domestic policies, the New Frontier, were partly blocked by a Democrat controlled Congress which opposed Civil Rights for Southern blacks. Kennedy's Presidency promised much but delivered very little. The aura of "Camelot' which surrounded the Kennedy White House gave the Presidency enormous glamour, but there was little of substance to match the impressive style. Congress backed him over foreign policy where he opposed the Soviets, over Cuba and Berlin

LBJ 1963-9 Democrat

Lyndon Johnson was a skilled political operator who shrewdly played on the feeling of national grief to push Kennedy's Civil Rights Bill through Congress, as a tribute to Kennedy's memory. Over the following two years, Johnson was to achieve more social reform than anyone since Roosevelt. Johnson's "Great Society" legislation included the Voting Rights Act, Medicare, Medicaid, an Open Housing Act, Affirmative Action programmes, the expansion of the Food Stamp scheme and of Aid for Dependent Children, the Elementary and Secondary Education Act, the Office of Equal Opportunities and the Head Start programme.

He was helped by two factors, the enormous Democratic majority in Congress after the 1964 elections, 295-140 in the House and 67-33 in the Senate and the riots which occurred in most of the big Northern and Western cities after 1965 and which highlighted the need for urgent action. The 1965/67 Congress was dominated by liberal Democrats who worked with the President in a rare display of Legislative/Executive harmony. In a sense, the 89th Congress completed the work of the New Deal and the Warren Court.

Chapter Four

The War in Vietnam

American's part in the 30-year Vietnam War really began in August 1964 when a US ship, *"The Maddox"* was allegedly fired on by the North Vietnamese in the Gulf of Tonkin, off the coast of North Vietnam. LBJ asked Congress to pass the Gulf of Tonkin Resolution giving him the power to take whatever action was necessary over Vietnam. It passed the Representatives unanimously and only two Senators voted against it. It was a blank cheque to wage war in South East Asia.

In the 1964 campaign, Johnson branded his Republican opponent, Barry Goldwater, a war monger, yet, within a few months of his landslide victory, Johnson authorised the mass bombing of North Vietnam and by 1968 America had over half a million troops fighting in Vietnam, without Congress ever officially declaring war.

By 1966/7, as American television showed US forces fighting a guerrilla battle they could not win, a large section of the public turned against the war. The "domino theory" stated that, if Communism triumphed in Vietnam, then the rest of Indo-China, the Philippines, Burma, Thailand and eventually all of Asia would succumb. Johnson was determined that he would not be branded the President who "lost" Vietnam as Truman had "lost" China. The urban riots and the anti-war demonstrations merged into one huge protest movement. By 1968 and the Tet offensive, the anti-war movement gathered strength and support spread from "draft-dodging" students to "middle of the road" Americans.

1968 was in every sense the critical year of the decade. In March, following the strong showing of the anti-war Democrat candidate, Eugene McCarthy, in the New Hampshire primary, and the entry into the race of Robert Kennedy, Johnson withdrew from the campaign. In April, King was assassinated in Memphis by a southern white, James Earl Ray and there were riots in 125 cities, including Washington. In June Bobby Kennedy was also assassinated by a Palestinian activist. The Democratic Convention in Chicago in 1968 saw the party regulars, led by Hubert Humphrey and Mayor Daley, regain control of the party from the anti-war student protesters and their candidate, McCarthy. Daley had no scruples about using the Chicago police to "deal" with the "unpatriotic" demonstrators.

US Ally
Neutral
Areas largely under Viet Cong control in 1973
★ Major US Bases
◄ Ho Chi Minh Trail

Richard Nixon, 1969-1974, Republican

As public opinion reacted against the traumas of war, riots and assassinations, by swinging to the right, Americans turned to 'the new' Nixon who scraped a narrow victory in the November 1968 election which broke the "New Deal Coalition" and ushered in an era of Republican domination of Presidential politics which was to last for 24 years.

Nixon took over a badly shaken nation and appealed to the "silent majority" of "patriotic, law abiding" Americans to support his efforts to end the war "honourably" and help him return order to the nation. Surprisingly, black militancy subsided, although the anti-war movement continued to flourish. In 1970 at Kent State University in Ohio, four protesters were shot dead by the national guard. Nixon's domestic policies were often blocked by a Democrat controlled Congress however Nixon was more concerned by foreign policy.

Detente

By 1969, the two Superpowers had entered a period of detente. It was to last for a decade and produce two major Superpower agreements, SALT 1 and the Anti-Ballistic Missile Treaty as well as the Helsinki Accords of 1975, whereby the post-war European frontiers were finally, 30 years after the end of the war, formally recognised. Nixon and Kissinger also exploited the Sino-Soviet split by opening up relations with China. America hoped to benefit from the hostility between the two most important Communist nations by playing one off against the other. The breakthrough to China came in 1972, just in time for the election.

The End of the Vietnam War

Nixon 'secret plan' for ending the war meant cutting down on US troops, but extending the bombing into neutral Cambodia. Hugh Brogan calls this Nixon's "worst crime". In 1971, Daniel Ellsberg, revealed confidential documents to the New York Times. Nixon tried to stop publication of the Pentagon Papers; he failed because the Supreme Court upheld the freedom of the press under the 1st Amendment. The papers revealed, amongst other things, that the "Maddox" incident had been grossly exaggerated

In April 1975, South Vietnam, Cambodia and Laos all finally fell to the Communists. Ford wanted to intervene, but Congress refused. The Vietnam War traumatised US politics. It broke the bi-partisan consensus which had characterised US foreign policy since the late 1940s; it divided public 'opinion; it split the Democratic Party and it caused a major shift in attitudes towards the use of American military power. Understanding the 'Vietnam syndrome' is essential to understanding US foreign policy in the 1990s. The British journalist, Christopher Hitchens, refers to the 'stab in the back' theory promulgated by the right since Vietnam, the US did not lose the war on the battlefield, rather the solders were 'betrayed' by the politicians.

OPEC raised oil prices in 1973-4 by a 400%, this caused economic problems all over the West. The relative economic decline of the USA had massive implications for US power. The energy crisis served to emphasise what had long been evident: the USA had lost its dominant position in the world economy. Of course, it remains an economic superpower but the eclipse of US domination pre-dates the oil crisis. "The fundamental problem faced by US business was that rivals in Europe and Japan were accumulating capital at a far faster rate." Vietnam, Watergate, oil crisis - all reached their climax in the years 1972/74.

Chapter Four

Watergate

The "Watergate Affair" dominated American politics for over two years. It paralysed the Nixon Presidency and led eventually to the first ever Presidential resignation. It led to the imprisonment of some of his key White House aides, as well as a former Attorney General, John Mitchell. Together with the debacle in Vietnam, it brought an end to the "Imperial Presidency".

In the wake of Watergate, Congress reformed itself and sought to reassert its power through measures such as the War Powers Resolution of 1973, the Congressional Budget Act of 1974, and the tightening of the Freedom of Information Act in 1974. There was closer scrutiny of the CIA and greater Congressional involvement in foreign policy through measures such as the Jackson Amendment of 1974 (limiting trade with communist nations unless they liberalised their emigration policies) and the Clark Amendment of 1975 (prohibiting covert operations by the CIA in Angola).

British commentators believe that, if a similar scandal was to occur in this country, the truth would not emerge because Parliament, the courts and the press are much more inhibited than in the American system, as the Scott Inquiry has demonstrated.

If Watergate had appeared to fade into history the Irangate crisis, Nixon's death and 'Whitewatergate' certainly brought it back into focus. "Watergate" is used as a short-hand term for the corruption and aggrandisement of the Nixon White House, what Godfrey Hodgson calls the "plot that failed".

Nixon tried to overcome the constraints of the separation of powers by impoundment and by organised deception. The White House "Plumbers Unit" forged documents, burgled offices and wiretapped illegally in order to blacken the reputations of those the Nixon White House decided were "enemies". Ellsberg's psychiatrist's office was burgled in the hope of finding information which would incriminate him and discredit his evidence. Democrat opponents were smeared as alcoholics and rumours were spread about the failure of their marriages. Nixon was paranoid about opposition, believing that the press were "out to get him". He was also suspicious about the loyalty of his own Cabinet members and only really trusted his White House advisors. Consequently, apart from Mitchell, the people implicated in Watergate came from the Executive Office of the President, not from the Cabinet.

The main details of the two year affair can be briefly stated. On June 17th 1972, as the Democratic Party was preparing for its National Convention, five men were caught attempting to burgle the offices of the Democratic National Committee, housed in the Watergate hotel and office complex in Washington. On June 22nd President Nixon categorically denied that any member of the White House staff had been involved in the raid. His Special Assistant, John Dean, conducted an inquiry into the affair and established that no-one in the Nixon Administration was involved in any way "in the very bizarre incident". However, two journalists on the Washington Post, Carl Bernstein and Bob Woodward, established that the five men worked for CREEP, the Committee to Re-elect the President. Whilst their investigations were proceeding, Nixon defeated McGovern in one of the greatest landslides of the century.

In February 1973, Judge John Sirica threatened the burglars with harsh prison sentences unless they revealed who it was that had authorised the burglary. One of the burglars, James McCord, an ex-CIA employee, confessed. Sirica suggested a Senatorial Committee to get to the bottom of the affair. In April 1973, Nixon dismissed Dean and announced the resignation of Haldemann and Ehrlichman. Dean claimed that Nixon had authorised a "cover up" to conceal the link between the burglars and the White House. Nixon vehemently denied this. In May, a Select Committee of Congress (under the Chairmanship of Senator Sam Ervin) began its hearings. Nixon, claiming "executive privilege", refused to allow his aides to appear before the committee. Ervin dismissed Nixon's claim as "executive poppycock" and, over the next few months, the top Nixon aides testified before the committee.

In July 1973 one of those aides, Alex Butterfield, disclosed that Nixon kept tape recordings of all his conversations in the Oval Office. A long legal battle now ensued as the Committee tried to get hold of the tapes. In a separate but related development, Nixon's Vice-President, Spiro Agnew, resigned rather than face criminal charges. For as long as Agnew was Vice

President, people were reluctant to consider impeaching Nixon because Agnew was regarded as even more corrupt. In October 1973 Ford replaced Agnew. Now it was possible to talk of impeaching Nixon.

In October 1973, Nixon dismissed Archibald Cox, the Special Prosecutor he had appointed to look into the affair, because Cox refused to accept an edited version of the tapes. The battle went to the Supreme Court which ruled in August 1974, by 8 - 0, that Nixon should hand the tapes over to the new Special Prosecutor. Nixon had consistently claimed that he knew nothing about a "cover-up" until March 1973. However, the tapes revealed that on June 22nd 1972 he had ordered Haldeman to get the CIA to stop the FBI investigating the case. As Alastair Cooke puts it, Nixon had lied 'steadily and unblinkingly" for two years.

In July the House of Representatives Judiciary Committee voted to recommend impeachment on the ground of obstructing justice. On August 9th 1974, Nixon became the first President ever to resign the office. The new President, Gerald Ford, gave Nixon a free pardon. Ehrlichman, Haldeman and Mitchell all served prison sentences for their part in the affair.

In 1973 Professor Schlesinger, a Democrat who had been an adviser to JFK. wrote the *"Imperial Presidency"*. If the President is like an emperor, then clearly the constitution has failed. Schlesinger had supported a strong presidency when the Democrats were in the White House, but with Nixon there he feared that the Presidency had become too powerful, reminiscent of Hailsham's concern about 'Elective Dictatorship' when Labour was in power

Gerald Ford 1974-1977, Republican

Congress re-asserted itself, even over foreign policy, the Imperial Presidency supposedly gave way to what Ford called an Imperilled Presidency. The "dual crisis" of the Presidency undermined the authority of the White House and made Congress, pressure groups, the media and public opinion much more wary of the Presidency. Ford was a Republican President facing a Democrat Congress. Not surprisingly, there was little that Ford could accomplish, he was a caretaker serving out the remainder of Nixon's term. Altogether Ford used the regular veto 48 times and the pocket veto 18 times.

Jimmy Carter, 1977 - 1981, Democrat

Jimmy Carter became President in January 1977 following his narrow victory, 297-240 in the Electoral College and roughly 41 million to 39 million in the popular vote, over the incumbent, Gerald Ford who having beaten off the strong Reagan challenge for the Republican nomination fought a better campaign than had been expected. Carter probably owed his election to the anti-Republican mood engendered by Watergate. It was hardly a resounding success, Carter was voted into office by just one quarter of the electorate.

Carter, a former Governor of Georgia, had no experience of national politics, of Washington power broking; he was an outsider who as late as 1975 had little 'name recognition' outside his own State. Carter had taken the 'primary route' to the Democratic nomination, beating established party figures along the way. In the anti-corruption atmosphere of the mid-1970s, Carter was the perfect candidate, arguing that it needed an outsider to 'clean up this town'. Alastair Cook rates Carter as one of the most intelligent and hard working Presidents. Other commentators and 'insiders' stress Carter's ability to handle complex issues and his mastery of detail.

Yet the consensus is that the Carter Presidency was a failure. He was criticised by 'left wingers' such as Walter Dean Burnham, Arthur Schlesinger, Lane Kirkland and Ted Kennedy for being too conservative. He was attacked by 'right wingers' such as Jeanne Kirkpatrick, Norman Podhoretz and David Stockman for refusing to take a firm line with the Soviet Union and for failing to cut the welfare budget and reduce inflation.

It is extremely unusual for an incumbent seeking nomination from his party not to be successful, but by 1979 Carter was registering approval ratings as low as Nixon's at the time of Watergate and there was every possibility that he would lose the nomination to Kennedy. The Iran hostage crisis actually helped Carter at first as the nation rallied behind its leader and he was able to win the nomination struggle. However, the long hostage crisis and particularly the failed rescue attempt destroyed his chances of re-election and led to the landslide defeat at the hands of Reagan in 1980, 489 to 49 in the Electoral College and around 35 million to 44 million in the popular vote.

The Breakdown of Detente

The most controversial aspect of Carter's foreign policy was his attempt to make human rights the litmus test of American attitudes towards other nations. Long time friends and allies such as the Shah of Iran, South Korea, the Marcos regime in the Philipines, Duvalier in Haiti, Pinochet in Chile and various other autocrats were told to improve their human rights record or face losing substantial American aid. This policy gave hope to those within such countries who were struggling for democracy. The right-wing was outraged, claiming that totalitarian states such as the USSR had far worse human rights records than the autocracies Carter and his United Nations envoy, Andy Young, were attacking. By 1978, as relations with the Soviet Union deteriorated, Carter began to dilute the 'human rights' policy. Andy Young was dismissed and Carter began to take a more traditional approach to American interests; however, even as harsh a critic as Schlesinger is prepared to give Carter some credit for his attempt to re-direct American foreign policy.

The Camp David agreement between Egypt and Israel with America acting as 'honest broker' was an historic achievement and represented the biggest move forward in the Middle East since the State of Israel was set up in 1948. Even though America's vital interests were not at stake, Carter risked major domestic problems over his even-handed approach to this issue. His other important foreign policy success, the Panama Canal treaty, did involve America's security and Carter had to lobby hard to overcome right-wing opposition. Carter's failure to have SALT 2 ratified owed much to the hostile superpower climate created by the invasion of Afghanistan and the emergence of Solidarity in Poland.

Carter had begun his Presidency with a positive attitude towards the Soviet Union, but he ended it with a grain embargo and a boycott of the Moscow Olympics. Both these gestures were symbolic, they actually achieved little but they illustrate the breakdown of detente since its high-water mark in 1972. Whoever was in power in 1977/1981 would have had to cope with this problem.

Some of Carter's problems, such as poor presentation of policies, were self-inflicted and arose from over-dependence on the 'Georgia Mafia', inexperienced advisers such as Hamilton Jordan and Jody Powell who neglected key party leaders such as Tip O'Neill, the then Speaker of the House of Representatives. On the campaign trail, Carter had emphasised his lack of familiarity with Washington and the voters had approved; now as President it cost him dear.

The biggest problems Carter faced, such as the energy crisis, the Iranian revolution and the breakdown of detente, were (as Godfrey Hodgson stresses) not Carter's fault and would have tested, and probably defeated, any President. Carter did have some successes, especially in the foreign policy field. However Presidents are judged by the voters on 'bread and butter' issues, such as prices and jobs, and Carter scored badly in this area. Again the causes of America's economic difficulties in the late 1970s were largely outside Carter's control. The second oil crisis, brought about by the fall of the Shah, provoked higher inflation and threw the world economy into recession. Even before 1976, the US was already suffering from Japanese and German competition and 'de-industrialisation'. Unemployment rose to 11% in 1980 and the budget deficit soared as welfare payments increased and tax revenues fell.

Carter mishandled the all-important Energy Bill, he committed his administration to the bill claiming that the energy crisis was the 'moral equivalent of war' but did not lobby hard enough to counter the powerful oil and automobile lobbies. In desperation, he sacked most of his Cabinet and told the nation that it was suffering from a deep 'malaise'. The public responded by blaming the President. It was undoubtedly his worst domestic defeat. Carter did succeed in establishing two new Federal Departments, Energy and Education, and in tightening controls over the covert operations of the CIA. Carter had not worked well with the Democrat controlled Congress, he had neglected the vital task of liaising with Congressional Democrats. He had also offended the union leaders by distancing himself from labor. Carter had always been a conservative

Democrat, rather than a Kennedy style 'New Dealer', and after 1978 he had moved further from liberalism in an opportunistic attempt to steal the thunder of the emergent 'New Right'. According to Walter Dean Burnham, Carter was "the most conservative Democratic President for his time since Grover Cleveland left office in 1897".

The Iran hostage crisis was the final straw; Carter's response was contradictory rather than weak. He disclaimed any intention to use force and then mounted the rescue operation. Had it succeeded then perhaps Carter would, despite all his problems, have won in 1980, but it failed and so did Carter. Reagan defeated him by 10% and the Republicans took control of the Senate for the first time in over 25 years. Carter was the first elected incumbent to be defeated since Hoover in 1932. Like Hoover, his reputation is now being reassessed and his record shown to be not as bad as people once imagined.

Ronald Reagan

Ronald Reagan - The Resurgent Presidency, 1981 - 1989

In the same way that Thatcherism marked a radical shift to the right in the UK, the Reagan administration marked a radical shift to the right in the USA. Neither Thatcher nor Reagan were the reason for the shift: they were effect not cause.

No President since Eisenhower had managed to serve two full terms - part of the attraction of Reagan was that he offered a return to stability. To understand the appeal of Ronald Reagan and the way in which he was (arguably) able to restore some of the authority if not the power of the US Presidency, one has to consider the trauma and dislocation the US had been through in the two decades between JFK and Carter.

Reagan offered a simple message: there was no malaise in American society, the government was not the solution, it was the problem and it must get off the backs of the people. The remedy for America's ills was a return to a more limited government intervention in the economy and social policy combined with a return to more traditional values, taxes must be cut as must welfare spending. The deceptively simplistic message had a very strong appeal.

If the essence of the 'Reagan Revolution' was to curb 'big government' then it failed. Reagan certainly cut welfare programs. The poor got much poorer. Even so, Reagan was not able to reduce welfare entitlements to the extent that the 'New Right' believed necessary, because the Democrat-controlled Representatives blocked him.

The Second Cold War

As Fred Halliday argues by 1980 there was a second Cold War. "Within six years no fewer than 14 states were taken over by revolutionary movements, and in 3 others significant radicalisations occurred." US administrations blamed the Soviet Union for adventurism in the Third World as Ethiopia (1974), Angola (1975), Yemen (1979), Grenada (1979) and other nations 'fell' to Marxist regimes. Even where the Soviets were clearly not to 'blame' for upheaval - Iran (1979) or Nicaragua (1979) - they were assumed to have benefited from revolution. Reagan believed that Soviet expansionism underlay Third World upheavals: "Lets not delude ourselves. The Soviet Union underlies all the unrest that is going on. If they were not engaged in this game of dominoes, there would not be any 'hotspots' in the world."

The USA must stand up to the evil empire (USSR) and to terrorists; there must be no repeat of the humiliation of the Iranian hostage affair. With the election of Reagan, Superpower relations deteriorated even further. The Reagan Administration abandoned Carter's 'human rights' foreign policy believing that it had damaged American allies such as the Shah of Iran and Somoza of Nicaragua.

Jeanne Kirkpatrick, the US Ambassador to the UN and a very influential 'New Right' figure, drew a clear distinction between authoritarian regimes such as Chile, the Philippines, South Korea, Saudi Arabia and South Africa and totalitarian states such as the USSR, Vietnam, Nicaragua, Angola and Cuba. Human rights abuses in the former could be forgiven because the regimes were capable of reform, not so in the latter. In his first press conference, President Reagan alleged that the USSR 'reserved unto themselves the right to commit any crime, to lie, to cheat'. Reagan 'Mark 1', i.e. 1981-1985, believed that the Arms Control agreements of the 1970s had weakened America's defences and allowed the Soviet Union to overtake America as a military power. Hence the enormous American arms build up of the 1980s and the announcement of the Star Wars programme in 1983.

At first the Russians had thought that Reagan would be another Nixon who, once elected, would drop his emotional anti- Communism in favour of realism. In fact, relations got steadily worse with incidents such as the imposition of Martial Law in Poland in December 1981 and the shooting down of the Korean airliner in autumn 1983. The nadir came in December 1983 when, in response to the arrival of Cruise and Pershing missiles in Western Europe, the Soviets pulled out of the Geneva negotiations.

As late as 1983, Reagan was describing the Soviet Union as "the focus of evil in the modern world". The deteriorating relations between Moscow and Washington alarmed many people in the West and caused a renaissance of CND. American public opinion, while suspicious of Soviet ambitions, was also concerned by the prospect of war and this was a possible threat to Reagan's prospects of re-election. Accordingly, in 1984, the rhetoric softened and Reagan indicated his desire to reach an Arms Control Agreement.

One of Ronald Reagan's strongest, publicly-stated beliefs was that the USA must not bargain with terrorists. During his first term (1981 -85) US forces came into conflict with Libya (the dogfight off the Gulf of Sidre, 1981) and in November 1983 (days after the Beirut US Embassy bombing) the US invaded Grenada to expel a communist regime. In 1985, the US reacted strongly over the hijacking of the Achille Lauro and in spring 1986 US planes bombed Libya - in response to alleged Libyan involvement in the Berlin-disco terrorist attack. Even Reagan found that, despite episodes such as Grenada and Libya, it is very difficult to create the broad national consensus which is needed to justify the potential loss of American lives in foreign countries, thus Reagan's withdrawal from Lebanon in 1983 after the embassy bombing.

Reagan had his failures in his first term, particularly the failure to balance the budget. However, overall he was judged to be very successful and in November 1984, Reagan won one of the biggest landslides of the 20th century, 59% of the popular vote to Mondale's 41%, 525 in the Electoral College to Mondale's 13. Reagan seemed to have restored the authority, if not the power, of the Presidency after a decade of disillusion.

Irangate

Irangate is a short-hand term used to refer to the two-edged scandal which hit the USA in the last quarter of Reagan's Presidency; it involved arms sales to Iran and the illegal funding of the Nicaraguan Contras. It would have damaged any President, but it hurt Reagan disproportionately precisely because of Reagan's tough stance on terrorism.

Because Reagan had restored American pride in their political system, it came as a great shock when in November 1986 it turned out that Reagan had been doing deals with terrorists. The US had been selling arms to Iran, the very country which had humiliated the US in 1979/80, in return for Iranian help freeing the hostages in the Lebanon. Reagan's explanation was that he had come under pressure from the hostages' families and that he wanted to build bridges with the Iranians so that when the Ayatollah died, the US would have some influence. The Tower Report of 1987 showed that despite Reagan's denial, he had traded arms for hostages.

Even worse was the fact that profits from the arms sales were illegally diverted to fund the Contras, the anti-Communist forces fighting the left wing Sandinista government of Nicaragua. Reagan still denies knowledge of this. Either he is lying and should have been impeached, or he is telling the truth and therefore the USA was led by a President who did not even know what his own administration was doing, in a policy area with which he was passionately concerned. Either way it damaged the authority of the Presidency all over again.

In November 1986, within days of the mid-term elections, a story leaked to the Lebanese press that the US had traded 'arms for hostages'. Reagan's approval ratings, which had been over 60% as late as October 1986, immediately plummeted.

When the story broke Reagan argued that the real reason behind the sale of US arms was strategic, or geopolitical. The US was trying to develop links with 'Iranian moderates' so that when the Ayatollah died the US would have some influence on Iran - he firmly denied trading 'arms for hostages'. This could be seen as reversing Carter's mistake of 1979 when he 'backed the wrong horse' in the power struggle to succeed the Shah. David Mervin points out that there could be perfectly good diplomatic, strategic reasons for building bridges to a country as important as Iran.

Two of Reagan's aides, Admiral Poindexter (NSA) and Oliver North who worked in the National Security Council, took the blame; Poindexter resigned, North was dismissed, although Reagan continued to refer to North as a 'patriot'. Reagan asked his Attorney General, Ed Meese, to investigate. However, North was allowed to spend time shredding documents. This turned out to be crucial later on as it became clear that without a 'smoking gun' comparable to the Watergate tapes, Reagan could not be impeached. Meesse's investigation revealed a second strand to the scandal. The profits from the sales had been diverted to fund the Contras in Nicaragua. This was illegal under the Boland Amendment of 1985. Congress, dreading 'another Vietnam', had refused to allow military aid to the rebels.

Reagan was convinced that the Contras should be helped to overthrow the left-wing government of Nicaragua; he compared the Contras to the Founding Fathers. Reagan, like previous Presidents, argued that Congress was impinging on the President's right to control US foreign policy. Reagan denied, and continues to deny, any knowledge of 'Contragate' the Nicaraguan end of the whole affair. He appointed a bipartisan Commission of Inquiry to look into the whole scandal. It was a three-man board headed by Republican Senator John Tower, with Brent Scowcroft a former and future NSA, and Ed Muskie a former Democrat Senator.

The Tower Report was published in Spring 1987. It criticised Reagan for his 'hands off approach' to the Presidency; regarding the policy of selling arms to Iran, it specifically stated that there had been a trade-off arms for hostages. Reagan went on TV to 'apologise'; 'my heart stills tells me I was right, but my head tells me I was wrong'.

The Tower report also exonerated Vice President Bush and the Secretaries of State - Schultz - and Defence - Weinburger. Most of the blame was put on people within the EOP - Admiral Poindexter, North, Macfarlane the former NSA who in 1987 tried to commit suicide; the director of the CIA Bill Casey who died in 1987 shortly after testifying to the Congressional Committees but who according to Bob Woodward, the journalist who 'broke' the Watergate story, was the 'brains behind the covert operations of the Reagan White House'; most importantly, Tower blamed Donald Regan the Chief of Staff at WHO.

In the summer of 1987, Congress began investigating Irangate. The committee hearings were televised and the most senior officials of the Reagan administration, but not Bush or Reagan, were called to give evidence. Schultz, and Weinburger, stated their opposition to the policy of selling arms to Iran. Irangate demonstrates the problem with the EOP and in particular the NSC: a body which is supposed to be policy-advisory had become policy-making. This was the same problem as Watergate only much, much more serious - the NSC had been operating a foreign policy which was the diametric opposite of officially stated US policy. Not only was policy kept secret from the American people and Congress, it was also hidden from the people within the executive branch who were supposedly responsible for defence/foreign policy.

If one believes Reagan, which in the absence of tangible proof one must, part of the policy was even kept secret from the President himself. It was the privatisation of foreign policy, a negation of separation of powers and checks and balances. In that sense, Irangate was more important than Watergate. Reagan did not suffer politically anything like as much as Nixon. There are two reasons for this: firstly, in the absence of a 'smoking gun', it was legally impossible to prove conclusively that Reagan was lying, no matter how sceptical critics such as Senator Moynihan might be. Moynihan argued that to be asked to believe that Reagan did not know about the Contra link was like being asked 'do you believe in the tooth fairy?'

Secondly it could be argued that no-one, even the Democrats, wanted Reagan impeached because this would damage the Presidency and the American political system. The Democrats hoped to win the Presidential election of 1988 and the last thing they wanted was a discredited Presidency. Reagan was saved from the threat of impeachment by the spectre of Watergate. Hence, the Congressional Committee failed to follow up certain controversial points, such as the drugs connection.

To many people's surprise, the Democrats failed to make much of the Irangate issue in the 1988 elections. Legal proceedings against the Irangate 'culprits' led in 1990 to fines, not prison sentences. It could be argued that Irangate had a beneficial effect on American politics because in future the NSA will be confined to policy advice. Thus, it was noticeable that Scowcroft kept a low profile during the war against Iraq. Baker, a long time friend of Bush, was the second in command in Washington. Maybe the NSC, after the problems of the Kissinger/Brzezinski/Irangate era, is now firmly subservient to the State Department. The structural problem of American government, how to allow for the President to receive confidential advice without a conflict developing between the EOP and the bureaucracy, is far more important than what Poindexter did or did not say to Reagan, or whether North is a patriot or a fraud. Woodward's book, 'The Commanders', stresses that Bush was very much in charge in the White House: there was no hands off approach.

Just as there was more to Nixon than Watergate, so there was much more to Reagan than Irangate. Mervin argues that he was the most successful President for decades.

The End of the Cold War

Many people credit Reagan with ending the Cold War. There were no summits during Reagan's first term but in 1985 Reagan met Gorbachev in

Geneva and in 1986 they met again at Reykjavik and came very close to an historic arms reduction deal. A deal, which for the first time ever led to nuclear weapons actually being cut, was eventually signed in 1987.

In the post-Cold War world, maybe even the military-industrial complex would find it impossible to prevent real cuts in defence spending. Paul Kennedy's book, The Rise and Fall of Great Powers, the main thesis of which was that great powers often suffer 'Imperial overstretch', came out in 1988 and it chimed in with the public mood in the USA. Despite the fact that the USA was on the verge of winning the Cold War, there was a very real sense of a nation in decline.

George Bush 1989-1993, Republican

Some people argued that November 1988 marked Reagan's third election victory - he had become the first president for decades to choose his successor. The Democrats chose an uninspiring candidate, Michael Dukakis. In summer 1988 he was 17 points ahead of Bush in the polls, but it was turned around by a combination of the Democrats' incompetence and 'attack politics' organised by Lee Attwater who told Bush that if he was serious about winning he had to go negative, hence the Willie Horton ad leading to the allegation that Dukakis was soft on crime and blacks. Bush attacked Dukakis for lack of patriotism, for being against the death penalty, for having a poor record on environmental issues but above all for being a 'card carrying member of the American Civil Liberties Union.'

At the August 1988 Republican convention, Bush made the surprising choose of Dan Quayle from Indiana as his running mate. It backfired on Bush when Quayle's war record was publicised. The one memorable moment from the campaign was in the Vice Presidential debate when Lloyd Bentsen said to Quayle, when Quayle compared his youthful age to Kennedy, "I knew Jack Kennedy, Jack Kennedy was a friend of mine, you are no Kennedy." It is a measure of how unimpressive the Democrats campaign was that Bush was able to turn the word 'liberal' into a term of abuse - the L word. Dukakis shied away from the description 'liberal' until the very closing days of the campaign when he turned it to his advantage, saying that he was a liberal in the Roosevelt and Kennedy tradition rather than the McGovernite version. By then it was too late

The Democrats claimed that Bush had no mandate. Like most Presidents, Bush made more of an impact over foreign policy than over domestic. The situation was not unique but it was exaggerated under Bush because of the changed world order. At their summit in December 1988 Bush and Gorbachev pledged themselves to work towards strategic arms cuts of up to 50%. This led to a treaty in June 1990.

Bush took office in January 1989 and in June the Chinese students were slaughtered in Beijing. Bush appeared not to respond. In Autumn 1989, 'the velvet revolutions' of Eastern Europe led to the collapse of communism in Hungary, Poland, East Germany, Czechoslovakia, Bulgaria and eventually, at Christmas 1989, Romania. The Cold War was finally over and the USA had won it. The collapse of the Soviet Empire was the single biggest success for US foreign policy this century and Bush had not had to do anything. Robert Gates, Director of the CIA, has argued that Bush's inaction was itself an act of statesmanship.

In December 1989, Bush, anxious to dispel the 'wimp' factor', made his first decisive foreign policy move, the invasion of Panama. Despite military incompetence and questionable methods, it was enormously popular with the US public.

The Bush victory was less impressive than either of Reagan's but it was still decisive. Bush received 54% of the popular vote and won 40 states; Dukakis gained 46% of the popular vote winning 10 states plus Washington DC. The Bush campaign had avoided any specific party commitments, except one negative promise: 'Read my lips. No new taxes'.

The Gulf War

However, Bush's 'greatest' foreign policy 'triumph' was yet to come. On August 2nd 1990, Iraq invaded Kuwait. US forces were sent as the main components of a 28-nation coalition under UN auspices. As Michael Cox points out the end of the Cold War provided the USA with retrospective justification for their anti-Soviet stance. It also undermined the liberals who had argued that the USA was in decline, instead the US now had freedom to act without worrying about Soviet constraint. As Bush put it Saddam and his ilk 'could no longer count on the East-West confrontation to stymie concerted UN action against aggression.' Saddam Hussein had not understood that with the end of the Cold War the Soviets would now not back Iraq.

Originally the UN aim was to protect Saudi Arabia - Desert Shield - while letting sanctions do their work. Sometime in late Autumn 1990, Bush increased the level of US forces and changed strategy. In December 1990, an ultimatum was given, January 15th 1991 was the deadline. On January 16th 1991 Desert Storm began. The air war was an enormous technological success story, or at least that was how it was presented. The military industrial complex certainly benefited. The land war was even seen as an 'anti-climax'. The war was over within weeks, but Saddam was allowed to survive and eventually to taunt Bush and later Clinton over their failure to destroy him. Bush claimed that the war proved that the Vietnam syndrome was over. Perhaps the most important bit of evidence that it is not over is Bush's decision to end the war and his reluctance to topple Hussein or protect the Kurds.

The New World Order

As a world power, America has global interests. All American administrations believe that the US has a particular need to ensure that communism does not spread through Central and Southern America, the USA's back-yard. This was one of the few areas of disagreement between Bush and Gorbachev at the 1988 summit. All US administrations are very supportive of Israel, partly because of the Jewish lobby, partly because Israel is a pro-Western force in such a vital area. Hence, the general surprise in 1991 when the US, for once, appeared not to endorse Israeli hawks and instead supported the Israeli Labour Party.

In August 1991 the USSR itself imploded. The Cold War was over and the USA had won it. Far from helping Bush, the US victory in the Cold War simply turned the spot light on his domestic policy. But Bush had no domestic agenda. As Will Hutton put it in October 1991 'this may be the President who won the Cold War, vanquished a Third World dictator and dared to confront the pro-Israel lobby - but he is also the President running a US economy with the slowest growth rate since the war.' GDP had gone up by roughly 1% a year. Felix Rohatyn argued that what was really needed was 'a new domestic order'.

Bush's presidency illustrated the traditional view of US presidents - they are neither imperial nor imperilled but they have much more impact over foreign policy than they do at home. Abroad, Bush appeared to 'control' the 'new world order'; at home he could not even get a budget through.

As Martin Walker pointed out at the time the budget impasse sent signals of US ineptitude around the world and created the biggest domestic crisis since Irangate. In October 1990 with 200,000 US servicemen on the front line in the Gulf the political establishment back in Washington locked itself into stalemate and started to close down the government.

The biggest criticism of Bush is that he almost completely ignored America's domestic problems, he did little to curb the budget deficit, although he did go back on his promise over taxes. In 1990 he put them up. He neglected America's enormous urban problems, the growth of America's underclass, the drugs problem, falling standards in schools, the crumbling infrastructure and Japanese penetration of US markets. The Democrat campaign of 1992 focused on domestic concerns such as the Savings and Loans scandal, when the equivalent of the building societies had to be bailed out, because this is where Bush was vulnerable.

By 1992 there were signs of alarm within the White House. Bush cancelled a visit to Asia and he cancelled $1 billion of aid to the Soviets on the grounds that, with the US in recession, the money should be spent at home. The embarrassment of the visit to Japan and of Buchanan performing so well in the New Hampshire primary indicated that Bush was experiencing some of the problems faced by Carter and of course Bush faced the same fate - a one term Presidency.

The Democrat Nomination

By April 1991 with Iraq expelled from Kuwait at minimum casualties for the Allies, Bush was so popular that leading Democrats such as Mario Cuomo, Bill Bradley and Al Gore decided not to run leaving the field open to less experienced Democrats such as Clinton.

Clinton was elected Governor of Arkansas in 1978 at the remarkably young age of 32 and apart from 2 years out of office in the early 1980s he held the post until he became President. He chaired the DLC for a year emphasising that he was a 'new Democrat' to distance himself from traditional liberal Democrats. He retained a liberal stance on abortion, affirmative action and other issues. Walker argued that Clinton was hawkish on foreign policy, liberal on lifestyles, fiscally cautious and opposed to traditional liberality on welfare. Critics of Clinton such as the radical journalist Alexander Cockburn claim that Clinton was so scared of being seen as soft on crime that during the primary elections Governor Clinton refused to waive the death penalty even over James Rector a mental incompetent.

Clinton won the Democrat nomination against the opposition of the liberal Senator Harkin, the centrist Paul Tsongas and the idiosyncratic ex-Governor of California Jerry Brown. His campaign survived so many set backs such as an alleged affair with a night-club singer, Jennifer Flowers, that he christened himself the 'comeback kid'.

Bill Clinton

The Clinton Presidency, 1993 - 2001

The First Two Years

Candidate Clinton said that he would focus like a laser beam on the economy. In his Inaugural Address in January 1993 Clinton argued that 'we must invest more in our own people, in their jobs, and in their future, and at the same time cut our massive debt ... it will require sacrifice but it can be done and done fairly.' In his first State of the Union speech he was even more blunt 'spending must be cut and taxes must be raised.' His first budget, which raised taxes, got through the Representatives by 218 to 216 and the Senate was split 50 to 50 so Gore had to use his casting vote.

The transition team was headed by Vernon Jordan, later on to be involved in the Lewinsky affair. Clinton was slow getting his administration organised, partly because having said on the campaign trail that he wanted a Cabinet that 'looked more like America' he now had to persuade the Senate to ratify women and minority appointees. It did not always work, as with Zoe Baird and Kimba Wood who were both turned down for the post of Attorney General. It was not until February 11th 1993 that he nominated Janet Reno who was confirmed by the Senate, third time lucky. Lani Guinier the controversial nominee for the post of head of the civil rights division in the Justice Department was also rejected. Partly this was because the Republicans were looking for an opportunity to 'revenge' the Democrat controlled Senate's rejection of Tower in 1989.

Altogether there were four blacks in the Cabinet, two Latinos and six women. However not all the appointees were 'politically correct', some were traditional elite figures and they tended to get the 'top' jobs. Warren Christopher, an LA lawyer and former Carter adviser, became Secretary of State, ex-Senator Bentsen went to the Treasury and Les Aspin a former Chairman of the House Armed Services Committee became Secretary of Defence. Ron Brown, a former Chairman of the DNC became Commerce Secretary, Leon Panetta Director of OMB. Anthony Lake the National Security Adviser and Madelaine Albright the Ambassador to the UN were both Carter appointees. There were lots of 'Friends of Bill' from Arkansas who had helped on the campaign. George Stephanopoulous, for example, who became Clinton's spokesman. Five months into Clinton's term the Republican David Gergen was brought in to 'save' the administration's communications effort. Relations between Gergen and Stephanopoulous were appalling. By mid-1994 Panetta had replaced the ineffectual McLarty at WHO.

There were so many early glitches that Clinton had to 'restart' his Presidency with the unveiling of his economic programme before Congress in February 1993, just one month into his term. Clinton antagonised some powerful figures such as Sam Nunn by seeking to implement his pledge on gays in the military. After four months in office Clinton had an approval rating of just 36%, lower than all his predecessors at that stage. NAFTA was approved in November 1993 even though it antagonised the labor movement and took Republican help to pass. A crime bill was signed by Clinton in August 1994 even though it bore little resemblance to the bill he had originally proposed and the Brady bill was passed a limited gun control measure. Ironically the economy which had so damaged Bush began to boom from late 1992 and the concern became inflationary pressures in an overheating economy rather than sluggish performance.

Health Care

The biggest domestic policy issue was health care. Health costs eat up 13% of the GDP, 38 million Americans are uninsured. In January 1994 Clinton had told Congress that if they sent him a health care bill that did not guarantee every American health insurance that could never be taken away he would veto it. Hillary Clinton was given responsibility for the policy. She impressed observers by her grasp of detail. The DLC chairman Dave McCurdy was opposed to her plan on the grounds that it smacked too much of the old style 'tax and spend' Democrat approach. The DLC favoured a more market driven plan put forward by Congressman Jim Cooper of Tennessee. Gephardt introduced a bill into the Representatives, Mitchell into the Senate. July Clinton was backing down and by September both houses had abandoned the bills. According to commentators such as Andrew Sullivan the Clinton health care plan was simply too ambitious and too statist for a people who regard low taxation as a priority and regard government intervention as a threat to individual enterprise. Health care reform has not just gone away, the issue remains vital with 38 million Americans including 12 million children without any form of insurance, by 1996 Medicare was costing $180 billion per year, but Clinton lost interest.

Foreign Policy

In terms of foreign policy he took a tough right wing stance on Cuba welcoming refugees from Communism. There was a very different response over Haitian refugees and Clinton ended up virtually pleading with the military junta to leave the island. The disaster in Mogadishu when US servicemen were murdered and their bodies paraded through the streets appalled US opinion. Clinton promised to quit Somalia by March 1994. There was more equivocation over Bosnia although to be fair to Clinton no-one else seemed to have a consistent, practical approach either.

Scandals

A lot of things went wrong that should have been contained; for example the $200 airport haircut, the White House travel office fiasco, the enforced departure of Agriculture Secretary Mike Epson over corruption, the problems over Housing Secretary Henry Cisneros, the firing of Surgeon-General Jocelyn Elders over incautious remarks over sex education and the problems over her replacement, Henry Foster, who claimed to have done just a few abortions and turned out to have performed hundreds.

By December 1994 a federal judge ruled that Clinton would have to face questions over the allegations of sexual harassment made by Paula Jones. However the bigger embarrassment came over a land deal made 16 years earlier. Whitewater itself is 230 acres of land in Arkansas. Whitewater Development Corporation was half owned by the Clintons when he was Governor of Arkansas, the other owners being the McDougalls. James McDougall owned Madison Guaranty Savings and Loan which collapsed in 1989, the Whitewater venture collapsed soon after. Questions were raised about Clinton's involvement, for example had Governor Clinton given Madison preferential treatment, had Madison improperly helped fund Clinton's election campaigns?

The scandal cost Clinton several scalps such as Webster Hubbel from the Justice Department, Roger Altman and Jean Hanson from Treasury and Bernard Nussbaum from WHO. More seriously in July 1993 Vince Foster the Deputy White House Counsel and an adviser to the Clintons over Whitewater committed suicide. The administration waited four months to reveal that in Foster's office at the time of his death had been documents relating to Whitewater and they delayed again when it came to releasing them to a Department of Justice investigation into Madison.

In January 1994 Clinton reluctantly agreed to the appointment of an independent investigator - Robert Fiske - into both the Whitewater scandal and Foster's death. By March 1994 Fiske was subpoenaing administration officials and the Congressional Republicans were demanding a Congressional investigation and Congressional Democrats felt obliged to agree, the Senate and the House Banking Committees would each look at the issues. The subsequent Congressional committees beginning in July 1994 were highly partisan with Democrats using their majority in both Houses to limit the scope of the investigations and Republicans complaining of obstruction. By the autumn attention was turning to the mid-term elections.

Clinton as a 'lame duck'?

The Republicans won a 54 to 46 majority in the Senate and a 236 to 199 majority in the Representatives. Polls showed that disapproval of Clinton was a factor and some Democrats distanced themselves from him during their campaigns.

Anti-Clinton sentiment was especially evident in the South but in general the Republicans benefited from an anti-tax, anti-big government feeling. The mid term election results appeared to have made Clinton effectively impotent, they certainly scuppered any talk of health care. By Christmas of 1994 Clinton was accepting that mistakes had been made and beginning to sound like a Republican with talk of tax cuts for the middle class.

The Republicans wanted to balance the budget in seven years, Clinton argued for balance over a decade. However the Balanced Budget Amendment which passed the Reps by 300-142 in February 1995 failed in the Senate because it needed two thirds, it actually got passed by 66 to 34.

For many commentators Gingrich was the new focus of attention so that when 'King Newt' said 'I am determined to get to a smaller federal government. I am determined to return power to the states and local governments and to private citizens' the assumption was that Clinton had become the lamest of lame ducks.

Whitewater Resumed

In July 1995 a Senate Committee composed of members of the Senate Banking Committee with two members of the Senate Judiciary Committee began investigating Whitewater under the Chairmanship of Senator D'Aamato (Republican) of New York.

The investigation was broader than in 1994 in that it also considered whether Clinton helped to maintain the insolvent Madison Guaranty Bank in return for money to fund his 1984 and 1986 gubernatorial election campaigns.

In the House the Banking Committee now under Jim Leach (Republican, Iowa) reopened its inquiry in August. The Senate inquiry focused on questions surrounding the suicide of Vince Foster, in particular had the Administration removed certain documents from Foster's office before investigators arrived. Neither the Congressional Committees nor the special Prosecutor Kenneth Starr found any evidence on the key issues.

Clinton Resurgent

In fact Clinton's fortunes began to improve in 1995 for three reasons. Firstly the Republicans began falling out amongst themselves, over who should get the nomination and over policy. To simplify the House Republicans, particularly the freshmen zealots, wanted to move quickly to implement the Gingrich programme. The Senate Republicans under Dole were much more cautious. Secondly over domestic policy Clinton stole the Republican thunder, by his January 1996 State of the Union Address he was sounding almost like Reagan when he declared that "the era of big government was over." At the same time Clinton appeared to develop a surer grasp of foreign policy issues. By late 1995 he was able to boast of helping to broker peace deals in the Middle East, Northern Ireland and Bosnia.

By spring 1996 the first two of these achievements looked a lot less secure. Rabin had been murdered by a Jewish extremist, dozens of Jews were killed by Islamic terrorists, Israel was bombing Lebanon and Likud had won the Israeli election. The IRA had renewed their offensive, only the Daytona peace accord on the former Yugoslavia seemed to be holding. Even so Clinton was given credit for his efforts, a curious turn of events given his attack on Bush for ignoring domestic policy at the expense of playing the world statesman in 1992. In June 1995 Clinton finally vetoed a bill which would have cut federal spending; the Congress did not even attempt to override it. By the end of the year he had vetoed 10 bills, two of them concerning the budget. Only one of the ten was overridden by Congress, the Securities Bill

The Whitewater scandal rumbled on, Hillary Clinton faced criminal charges and in May 1996 several of Clinton's former Arkansas associates were found guilty over Whitewater, rejuvenating the Republican Congressional investigation just as it appeared to have run out of steam.

Whitewater appeared simply too complex and apparently remote to concern ordinary Americans. There were more allegations of sexual impropriety but by the summer of 1996 the whiff of scandal did not seem to be damaging Clinton.

Clinton was able, as Reagan was, to articulate the public mood, as his impressive performance after the Oklahoma bombing of April 1995 demonstrated. Clinton invoked lofty ideals, however vaguely. In contrast, Dole, talked of legislative details at a time when Americans were in rebellion against Washington insiders; that is why Dole resigned from the Senate, but Clinton went on to win re-election comfortably. However the Republicans kept control of Congress and Clinton remained dogged by scandal as the Monica Lewinsky affair demonstrated. Yet with the economy booming most Americans appeared to turn a blind eye to his behaviour. The attempt to impeach Clinton failed. Not a single Democrat Senator voted for his removal. However the whole affair wasted time and distracted Clinton. There were no initiatives in the second term to compare with the overhaul of the federal welfare system in 1996.

Despite facing a relatively united Republican party controlling Congress from 1995 to 2001 Clinton was able to undermine the Republicans. By combining the veto with a concerted public campaign and extensive use of executive orders Clinton not only blocked many Republican reforms but emerged with substantial victories.

Throughout the Lewinsky scandal Clinton continued to exercise real power over foreign policy. In the summer of 1998 just after his public 'apology' Clinton authorised the bombing of terrorist bases in Afghanistan and Sudan and in December 1998 as the House voted for impeachment the US and the UK attacked Iraq. By the spring of 1999 the US was leading the war with Serbia over Kossovo.

The economy continued to boom throughout the late 1990s. It proved to be the longest boom in the history of the USA with talk of a 'new economy'. Clinton was still popular by 2000 but there was a general sense of wasted opportunities. Right wingers such as Peggy Noolan and left wingers such as Christopher Hitchens loathed everything the Clinton's stood for and wrote damning accounts of the administration. To Hitchens Clinton's famed triangulation simply meant that the left got all the words but the right got all the deeds. However even former associates such as Robert Reich and George Stephanopolous talk of a flawed Presidency. Liberal commentators such as Elizabeth Drew ('On the Edge') saw Clinton as indecisive, a judgement echoed in Bob Woodward's 'The Agenda'.

Martin Walker argues that Clinton will go down in history as the free trade President because even though Bush laid the groundwork it was Clinton who completed the job over NAFTA and GATT in 1994 and who pushed for the Asia-Pacific Economic Conference. Clinton was the first President to understand the importance of globalisation. As he put it *'everything from the strength of our economy, to the safety of our cities; to the health of our people depends on events not only within our borders but half a world away.'* Clinton foreign policy was based on 'engagement' and 'enlargement'. For example China would be integrated into global institutions and seen as a 'strategic partner'. NATO was expanded to the very borders of Russia. The World Trade Organisation, the IMF and the World Bank all dominated by the USA have unprecedented influence.

Clinton deserves credit for promoting prosperity, eliminating the deficit, safeguarding free trade, sticking up for minorities and simultaneously helping the poorer sections of American society. Clinton was able to show that the Democrats are different to the Republicans. The economy grew by 3% a year from 1992 to 1996, 4% from 1996 to 1999 and 5% in 2000. Unemployment was 6.8% in 1992, 3.9% in October 2000, the lowest level for 30 years. Unemployment among blacks fell from 14.1% in 1992 to 7.8% in 1999 and among Hispanics from 11.3% to 6.5%. Meanwhile inflation was down to 2%. Productivity was up as was consumer spending and the stock market. The deficit of $164 billion in 1995 had given way to a surplus of $236 billion by 2000. However the trade deficit was massive and the stock market was already falling by spring 2000. Greenspan had warned of 'irrational exuberance' and by the time Bush was sworn in all talk of a 'new economy' appeared spurious. Within two years of Clintons departure the US faced a recession, a budget deficit, tax cuts aimed at the rich and an ongoing war against terror. In truth it is too early to be able to assess the success or failure of the Clinton Administration.

The Presidency of George W. Bush

The election of George W. Bush was marked by such controversy over ballot papers in Florida and the actions of an allegedly partisan Supreme Court that many felt he lacked a proper mandate and that his would be a tainted, somehow illegitimate, Presidency. However the terrorist attacks on the USA on September 11th 2001 and the way in which, so far, the Bush administration has responded to them has served to rally support for the President and to sweep aside any lingering doubts over the election result. Since September 2001 Bush has enjoyed record approval ratings and his popularity benefited Republican candidates at the mid-term elections in November 2002. Inevitably any assessment of the Bush administration after its first 30 months in office will be dominated by the war on terror but it is important consider other aspects of the Bush Presidency to get a more rounded picture.

Bush was given a lot of credit for choosing an experienced and well-respected team of senior advisers. Vice President Cheney was seen as a very important figure, far more so that most Vice Presidents. There was talk of Cheney as a kind of Prime Minister and significantly when a gunman tried to attack the White House, Cheney was working whilst Bush was 'working out'. Colin Powell as Secretary of Defence, Donald Rumsfeld as Secretary of Defence and Condoleeza Rice as National Security Adviser were all seen as able counterparts to the inexperienced Bush, a man who had rarely left the United States. His Chief of Staff, Andrew Card, had worked in Bush's fathers Cabinet. Like other Presidents Bush staffed his White House Office with people he had worked with in his home state. Communications consultant Karen Hughes and political strategist Karl Rove had worked with Bush for a decade.

The Bush Administration argued for a less interventionist United States and there was talk of disengagement from the Balkans - where US soldiers were escorting children into schools - and from the Middle Eastern peace process. It was always unlikely that the USA would retreat from such a crucial region as the Middle East and even if September 11th had never happened it is probable that Powell and the State Department would have pushed for active American involvement in the peace process. Talk of a new isolationism was always exaggerated. An early clash with China over a US plane was resolved relatively amicably and Bush managed to establish good relations with the Russian leader Putin. The world's only superpower was however willing to act unilaterally as seen in its rejection of the Kyoto accords on the environment and its willingness to abrogate the Anti Ballistic Missile Treaty despite Russian objections.

In terms of domestic policy the Bush agenda was more controversial. Bush is very influenced by the ideas of Marvin Olasky the leading proponent of compassionate conservatism. Whereas Reagan and Gingrich wanted to curb government, compassionate conservatives wish to use the power of government to enable citizens to help themselves. For example Reagan wished to abolish the Department of Education whilst Bush wishes to promote education to help achieve social mobility and a more efficient economy. This is not so different to New Labour.

On other issues Bush is a traditional right winger. The religious right were heartened to see the ideologue John Ashcroft appointed Attorney General. He is an outspoken opponent of abortion and of affirmative action and his tenure is likely to generate conflicts over these and other issues. Bush had been supported by big business, particularly defence contractors who wanted to see big spending on national missile defence, tobacco companies who wanted an end to legislation against them, the oil industry who wanted exploration and drilling rights in Alaska and the gun lobby who opposed any more restrictions on the right to buy a gun. All these groups saw a return on their investment as the administration brought in policies favourable to them.

In August 2000 Bush had told the Republican Convention 'America has a strong economy and a surplus'. However by January 2001 Greenspan told the Senate Budget Committee 'we have had a very dramatic slowing down of economic growth.' In February Bush stated 'a warning light is flashing on the dashboard of our economy'. By late March Bush's approval rating was down to 53%. However the White House was able to get the huge - $1.3 trillion - tax cut it had promised through Congress by spring of 2001. It was helped in this by fears that the recession was worsening despite repeated cuts in interest rates. However the tax cut was aimed primarily at the wealthy and it was the rightwing nature of the administration that led the moderate Republican Senator Jeffers to defect. This meant that by May

2001 the Democrats chaired all the Senate committees giving them the power to block controversial appointments to for example the Supreme Court.

The events of September 11th completely changed the political dynamic. After a hesitant response, he did not return immediately to Washington, Bush recovered and is felt by most Americans to have handled the crisis well, his approval rating rocketed to 86%. The Congress passed a resolution permitting him to 'use all necessary and appropriate force against terrorism'. Only one member of the House voted against it. The US did not retaliate immediately; it waited to build a coalition against terrorism and then on October 7th 2001 attacked Afghanistan. Critics warned of the dangers of fighting a country which had caused huge problems for the British in the nineteenth century and had defeated the Soviets in the 1980s. However Afghan resistance collapsed quickly, the Taliban were defeated and so far the pro-Western government of Pakistan has not fallen. The apparent failure to catch or kill Bin Laden or Mullah Omar or to find those responsible for the use of chemical weapons in the USA has not so far dented Bush's popularity.

The confrontational tone of the Administration in general and Rumsfeld in particular may well dismay Europeans but is popular at home. Talk of extending the war on terror to Syria, or Sudan or most importantly Iraq is seen by most Americans as entirely legitimate as is the treatment of prisoners at the US base in Cuba. Colin Powell changed his approach and came round to the view that 'regime change' in Iraq War was vital. The use of the phrase 'axis of evil' to describe Iraq, Iran and North Korea was dismissed by Jack Straw as campaign rhetoric but has been defended by Powell. China is seen as a strategic competitor and Russia, France and Germany appear determined to resist what the French call American hyperpower. Relations between the US and Europe have been damaged by the development of the European Rapid Reaction force as well as arguments about the reconstruction of post-war Iraq. Blair is largely isolated in his support for Bush.

Bush has proven again the old truth that a US President is more powerful abroad than then is at home. However Powell, Cheney and Rumsfeld know that a successful war does not guarantee re-election. George Bush was extremely popular in spring 1991 having defeated Iraq but then lost to Clinton because of the economy. George W. Bush has finished off Saddam's regime and is determined to make sure the economy does not drag him down in 2004. That is why Greenspan the head of the Federal Reserve is so important and has been under pressure to cut US interest rates. Treasury Secretary Paul O'Neill has been replaced.

Many people assumed that the Democrats and their supporters would get 'revenge' on the Republicans in the mid-term elections of 2002 when they would defeat Republicans in the Congress and at state level. In fact the Republicans made gains in the Congress and this has transformed the prospects for Bush in the remaining two years of his first term. Bush campaigned on behalf of Republicans in critical states and this gave him the rare experience of a Republican President making gains in a mid-term election. The Republicans took back control of the Senate with 51 seats to the Democrats 47 with 2 Independents. In the House the Republicans increased their majority to 228 over the Democrats 204 with 3 Independents. To understand why November 2002 happened it is necessary to look at the consequences of September 11th. These elections can be seen as given Bush legitimacy in a way that he did not have in 2000.

It is clearly far too early to know whether the Bush administration will be a success or a failure. However at the moment he is in a very strong position and having been elected when the country was at peace and prosperous he may well be re-elected with the country still at war and in a recession.

The Post-modern Presidency

In his 1960 study, 'Presidential Power, the Politics of Leadership', Richard Neustadt pointed out how hard it is for a President to govern effectively, given the separation of powers and weak parties. A President is forced to rely on an appeal to the public, often over the heads of Congress. A President's only true power is the power to persuade. In 1980 Neustadt updated his work. His conclusion was the same as it had been 20 years earlier, that except in times of political crisis, the President is in a weak constitutional position. Richard Rose argues much the same thing, a post-modern Presidency lacking the support mechanisms to do the job properly.

Theodore Lowi argues that there exists a 'law' of Presidential failure. Having raised the public's expectations on the campaign trail, Presidents try to fulfil their promises but they inevitably fail. They then try to create the illusion of success through foreign policy triumphs. Lowi argues that Presidential failure is due to *institutional factors*, not personality failings.

Professor Shannon argues that circumstances and personality explain the failure of recent Presidents. Schlesinger agrees, what has been lacking since Kennedy, according to Schlesinger, is impressive leadership. Godfrey Hodgson argues that the crisis of the Presidency cannot be put down to personalities, It must have more to do with the wider political context in which these Presidents operated.

There is no 'law' of Presidential failure. There is not even a clear way to measure whether a President has succeeded or failed. Electoral success is not a very accurate indicator of Presidential greatness. Two of the greatest victories of the 20th century were won by Calvin Coolidge in 1924 and Richard Nixon in 1972 neither of whom would feature on a list of great Presidents.

 'The President exercises a dangerously personalised power'. Discuss.

Chapter Five

Judiciaries

According to liberal democratic theory the primary role of the legal system should be the protection and enhancement of individual rights and liberties; not the control of citizens or the protection of the state itself. There should be tolerance or even encouragement by state and society of diversity, debate and dissent to enhance freedom of choice and the pursuit of truth.

Both the UK and the USA are supposed to be liberal democracies but whilst the American political system is based on a separation of powers, the British system is based on a fusion of the legislature and the executive. It is the case that in America the judges are entirely separate from the other two branches of government, whilst in Britain there is a degree of overlap through the Law Lords.

Both the UK and the USA together with other liberal democracies such as Germany, France, Italy, Japan, Israel, India, Canada, Australia and so on have an independent judiciary able to uphold the rule of law so that even when it is the government which has transgressed it does not go unchallenged.

In theory then judges are independent however they are not necessarily apolitical. The American system openly politicises judges as in a different way does the German or indeed any system in which there is a codified constitution requiring interpretation by judges. The Germans have a Basic Law which is superior to ordinary law and which is interpreted by a Federal Constitutional Court, the German version of the Supreme Court. Israel does not have a codified Constitution but it does have a declaration of rights and it has a court which is able to stand above the politicians and occasionally impose its will on them.

The UK does not have a codified constitution or a constitutional court but the absence of formal theories which constrain government power does not mean that no constraints exist. Dicey argued that 'the rule of law', *'the universal subjection of all classes to one law administered by the ordinary courts'*, was vital to the British constitution.

The rule of law insists that no alteration in private rights and privileges, no incursion into private liberty, can take place without clear legal justification. Dicey wanted no distinction in law between the citizen and public servants as with the 'administrative law' of Europe which seemed to place government officials in a privileged legal position. Drewery argues that Dicey misunderstood the significance of continental systems such as France - the 'droit administratif' - far from giving officials favourable treatment provides an additional legal curb on government over and above the ordinary law. Dicey's ideas have acquired a mystical quality which they hardly merit.

According to the Democratic Audit 'formally everyone in the UK enjoys equal treatment under the law and equal access to justice. However there is concern over how fair and effective the criminal justice system is as a result of a number of incompetent investigations and unlawful convictions. This concern is especially strong among racial and ethnic minorities who experience discrimination at the hands of both police and courts.' Public pressure to be tough on crime has led the Blair government to limit or threaten basic rights to due legal process such as the right to silence, the right to jury trial and freedom from double jeopardy. Access to the law has been denied altogether to certain categories of detainee under the anti-terror laws.

The sovereignty of parliament states that the highest source of power in the land is the body that is most representative of the people as a whole; and the highest form of law the emanations of that body. From this sovereignty derives the proposition that ministers are 'responsible' to parliament. It is not quite as convincing as it sounds as the Scott Report showed. It is not quite true that a government can do only what the law says it may do - at least if the law is given the narrow meaning of statutes passed by parliament. Government ministers may also exercise a range of 'prerogative' powers: strictly speaking, powers once exercised by the monarch which have been given statutory form.

It is important to avoid exaggerating the extent of separation of powers in Britain, with its uncodified constitution, where government is not based on immutable laws. When political decisions are translated into Acts, things do not come to a full stop. A policy can stand or fall by the approach adopted towards a new Act by the judges called upon to interpret and apply it. It is wholly misleading to see the political process as something entirely different from the legal process - there is constant interaction between the two. Government is a composite activity which embraces both.

The rule of law is one of the key principles of liberal democracy and its continuing absence is a sure sign of despotism in some form. However even in countries which do entrench rights and which do have a clearer separation of powers the rule of law is often best seen as an ideal type rather than as a working reality.

Judiciaries

Australia - The High Court of Australia consists of 7 members.

China - The 1982 constitution established the highest court is the Supreme Peoples Court which interprets the constitution and the wishes of the State Council.

France - The Constitutional Council reviews the constitutionality of law. It consists of 9 members, 3 appointed by the President, three by the Speaker of the National Assembly, three by the president of the Senate each serving non-renewable 9 year terms plus any former President of France has the right to sit on it. In 1974 its powers were enhanced and since then the number of referrals has increased.

Germany - The highest court under the Basic Law is the Bundesverfassunsgericht - the Federal Constitutional Court, the final interpreter of the Basic Law, very comparable to the US Supreme Court.

Russia - The Constitutional Court acts as the Russian version of the US Supreme Court but has yet to acquire the same authority.

UK - The highest court of appeal in the UK is the eleven member Law Lords.

USA - The judiciary is headed by the Supreme Court consisting of 9 judges

The best way to get a clearer picture of the role of the judges is to look at the operation of the courts in more detail.

The British System

An Independent Judiciary?

At the top of the British legal/political system the boundaries between law and politics are muzzy and conflicts between legal impartiality and political expediency are very evident. The Attorney General and the Solicitor General are both barrister/MPs and therefore intimately involved in politics as the Scott Report demonstrated. There are a lot of lawyers in Parliament but fewer than in Congress.

Prior to the 1920s, it was accepted practice for Lord Chancellors to treat judgeships as rewards for political services. Crude partisanship disappeared in the 1920s/30s, but there has been frequent speculation about the political bias of the judges. Denning argues 'The keystone of the rule of law in England has been the independence of the judiciary. It is the only respect in which we make any real separation of powers.' Griffith disagrees "The most remarkable thing about the appointment of judges is that it is wholly in the hands of politicians."

Although judges are appointed by the government of the day they should not, thereafter, be subject to political pressure from either Government or Parliament. To enhance the independence of the Judiciary judges are largely, though not entirely, separate and distinct from the other branches of government, in accordance with Montesqeui's theory. However the Lord Chancellor is a party politician. There were suggestions in the press that the former Master of the Rolls, Donaldson, was appointed by Thatcher on a partisan basis and that judges hearing politically sensitive trials including Tisdall and Ponting had been politically selected.

Under the 1701 Act of Settlement senior judges enjoy security of tenure as they are appointed until retirement and can be removed only by a joint address in both Houses of Parliament. This has not happened this century. Lower judges such as Circuit judges may be dismissed by the Lord Chancellor for incompetence, dishonesty or misbehaviour, but this is very rare. The only case this century was in 1983 when Judge Bruce Campbell was dismissed for whisky smuggling. Even the infamous Judge Pickles, who many people believed made too many outrageous statements, was not sacked.

Judges have a fixed salary paid from the Consolidated Fund and hence (like the Monarch's Civil List) not subject to party political debate in the Commons. The remarks and sentences of judges in court cases should not be subject to criticism in Parliament. However, this principle is sometimes breached. Thatcher and others have criticised certain judicial comments and decisions such as the low sentence imposed by Judge Stanley upon a man who twice raped a six year old girl. In a more obviously political case the Labour MP Martin Flannery was suspended from the Commons for referring to 'tame Tory judges' during the Miners' Strike. Hailsham said that such parliamentary criticism was 'subversive of the independence of the judiciary'. All those involved in court proceedings - judges, lawyers, juries, witnesses and accused - are granted immunity from the laws of defamation for remarks made in court.

At the very peak of the legal system is the Lord Chancellor, a member of all three branches of government, a living refutation of the doctrine of the separation of powers. A Cabinet Minister, presiding over the sitting of the Lords in its legislative and deliberative capacities, he can sit as a judge, he appoints other judges and he runs a governmental department. The post dates back to 605 AD. He is virtually a Minister of Justice.

Between 1970/1974 and again 1979/87 Lord Hailsham was Lord Chancellor. Hailsham believes that the independence of judges will loom larger as the powers of government increase. In opposition in 1976 he advocated a Bill of Right's to counter the 'Elective Dictatorship'. Mackay took a much more liberal stance in terms of allowing judges to make public comments and the former Lord Chancellor, Irvine, was a key supporter of constitutional reform. However many reformers would like to see the office itself reformed to create a more genuinely independent judiciary and Blair recently implemented this. Even some Conservatives such as Lord Alexander have suggested that a Supreme Court needs to be created and the ambiguous position of the Lord Chancellor reformed.

The senior judge below the Lord Chancellor; the Lord Chief Justice can decide which judges hear which cases; head of the Court of Appeal Criminal Division he makes public statements on important legal issues. The LCJ in the mid 90s was Lord Taylor, a liberal who publicly criticised the government and in particular the Home Secretary. In practice the court of Appeal Criminal Division is the final court of appeal in criminal cases. The Law Lords hears only a handful of criminal cases each year, those involving important points of law. Once a prisoner has been through the Court of Appeal and lost, his case can only be reconsidered if it is referred back by the Home Secretary.

An impressive list of critics - including the former Law Lords Devlin and Scarman - have accused the Appeal Court of falling down on its job over the Guildford Four and the Birmingham Six. In the wake of cases such as the Birmingham Six and Broadwater Farm pressure is growing for a body independent of the Home Office to investigate cases raising serious fears that justice has miscarried. In 1991, in the immediate aftermath of the squashing of the convictions of the Birmingham Six, Major set up the Royal Commission on Criminal Justice under Runciman. However the government ignored one of the Commissions key recommendations and removed the right to silence.

The Master of the Rolls is the head of the Court of Appeal Civil Division. From 1962 to 1982 this post was held by the most politically influential post-war judge, Lord Denning who did more than any other judge to highlight the inescapably political nature of the judicial process. Denning saw himself as a champion of the individual fighting for freedom against bureaucracies, Trade Unions etc. He was the son of a draper, he went to grammar school and dismissed the view of *'that man Griffith'* that judges are elitist. He stressed freedom of the individual leading to battles with 'collectivists' in the unions and the Labour Party.

In his Dimbleby lecture of 1980 - 'Misuses of Power' - he argued that judges should have the power of judicial review over legislation, the right to veto rather than merely interpret and enforce, parliamentary statutes. 'Every judge on his appointment discards all politics and all prejudices. You need have no fear. The Judges in England have always in the past - and always will - be vigilant in guarding our freedoms. *Someone must be trusted. Let it be the judges."*

Between 1982 and 1992 the Master of the Rolls was Lord Donaldson, former head of the National Industrial Relations Court (1971/74). His appointment was opposed by Labour. Donaldson secretly advised the government on anti-trade union legislation. Donaldson became an outspoken opponent of Howard's sentencing policy arguing that it contradicts judicial independence.

Judicial Bias?

By convention judges are above politics - they are apolitical; they interpret law but they do not make law. The existence of parliamentary sovereignty certainly means that the role of the British Judiciary is very different to that of the US Supreme Court and this is usually taken to mean that the scope for judicial discretion in the UK is very limited. However, this rather simplistic view, what Lee calls a 'fairy tale', has been challenged from various quarters. Lords Denning, Reid, Radcliffe and Devlin have acknowledged the part played by judicial discretion and creativity. As Radcliffe puts it of course a judge makes law, how can he help it?

A new style of Judicial activism can be traced back to the 1960s and decisions such as Ridge v Baldwin (1964) in which a police constable appealed against his dismissal by the local police committee. He succeeded on the grounds that he had not had a proper chance to present his case and the common law principle of natural justice demanded that he should. Since 1966 the Law Lords have no longer regarded themselves as bound by precedent, stare decisis, and this has led to a new creativity on the part of the judiciary. Judges seem more willing to challenge the executive on the grounds of ultra vires and natural justice than they were in the days when the judiciary was 'more executive minded than the executive'

The Left Wing Critique

The fact is that judge's cannot be neutral: every human is biased. What is worrying is the inbuilt conservatism of the legal profession, a product of *both social background and professional training*. In January 1987 of 465 judges, 464 were white, 448 male, 166 over 65 and the greatest majority had privileged backgrounds. In 1970, 81% had been to public school, 76% to Oxbridge. In the past all judges except circuit judges had to be appointed from the ranks of the barristers/QCs. The Thatcher governments legal reforms allows solicitors to go on to become judges.

Hailsham argues that the judges have a diversity of view's/backgrounds. *"It is impossible to imagine people with a wider view"*. However as Anthony Sampson put it; "their social background has changed less than that of senior civil servants or even diplomats".

Clearly this social background cannot automatically be linked to any particular view or bias. Occupational socialisation may be more important than background in the formation and reinforcement of attitudes. Professor John Griffith argues that senior judges; *"by their education and training and the pursuit of their profession as barristers, acquire a strikingly homogeneous collection of attitudes, beliefs and principles which to them represent the public interest."*

The phrase the public interest is important because it reminds us that judges not only sentence criminals, they are involved in legal judgements about industrial relations, political protest, race relations, governmental secrecy, police powers and sexual behaviour. They do not simply administer the law in a passive way, there is much potential for judges to make law when interpreting it.

Griffith argues that they are more enthusiastic in defending property rights than wider human rights or personal liberties as in cases involving squatters. Peter Hain cited the case of an anti-apartheid protester who despite having his conviction for assaulting a police officer quashed on appeal, was denied costs by the judge on the grounds that "it was not a social thing to demonstrate' and that being on a demonstration was by itself likely to cause a breach of the peace.

According to 'Manifesto' a left wing Labour Party document of 1981; "Their attitude to the political and social problems of our time is shaped and determined by their class, their upbringing and their professional life ... their attitude is strongly conservative, respectful of property rights and highly authoritarian.' According to the critics this conservatism undermines the appearance of neutrality in the judicial process. Judges themselves do not see things this way.

The left believe that it is particularly in cases involving trade unions, Labour Governments, Labour Councils and official secrecy that the bias of the judges is most apparent.

Cases Involving Trade Unions

The Labour Movement's suspicion of the judiciary goes right back to the early 20th century. In these cases there is sometimes a clash between two rival philosophies; the individualistic/liberalism in which our lawyers are trained and the collectivist assumptions of the Labour Movement with its emphasis on 'unity is strength'. Heath's 1971 Industrial Relations Act which set up the National Industrial Relations Court revived the suspicions of the Labour movement about the inbuilt bias of the judiciary.

On 22nd July 1972 five dockers were imprisoned for contempt of court for refusing to cease 'blacking' (refusing to handle) certain goods. The 'Pentonville Five' case prompted widespread strikes and a threat of a general strike. On the 26th July 1972 the Law Lords reversed the earlier judgement and the dockers were immediately released.

Griffith comments; "it appeared very much as if the judicial system had bent itself to the needs of the politicians and that in particular the principles of the rule of law had been sacrificed to the expediency of the political and economic situation.' The experience with the NIRC is a good illustration of the problems that judges face in interpreting and enforcing what are arguably partisan, party-political laws. It bestowed upon judges an overt and unavoidable political role which dented their image of impartiality. The law was repealed in 1974. In May 1977 there was fresh controversy when Michael Foot complained that the unions always had a raw deal from the courts.

Again with the Thatcher government's industrial relations laws there was conflict between the unions and courts; over Eddy Shah's newspaper (the Stockport Messenger), over the Murdoch papers and the Wapping strike, but especially over the miners strike of 1984/85. Home Secretary Leon Brittan publicly encouraged the courts to threaten life sentences for striking miners charged with causing grievous bodily harm.

Denning's obiter dictum in the ABC case was elevated to the status of legal doctrine in 1984 when the Appeal Court quoted part of it in their ruling for the government in the 1984 GCHQ case. The High Court judge ruled against the government in the GCHQ case. This was an example of procedural ultra vires; what the government did was lawful, but how they did it - without first consulting the unions - contravened the principles of natural justice. However, this ruling was overturned by the Appeal Court. The Law Lords and the European Court of Human Rights upheld the government.

Cases Involving the Labour Governments of 1974-79

Since the late 1960s judges, led by Lord Denning, have taken on a much more interesting and challenging role vis a vis the executive. Perhaps this has been because government has appeared to be encroaching more and more on individual liberties. In Congreve v Home Office 1975 the Court of Appeal ruled that the Home Secretary Roy Jenkins could not stop people from buying TV licences early in order to avoid a price increase.

The most important case though was Secretary of State for Education v Tameside Metropolitan Borough Council. In 1976 the newly elected Conservative Council in Tameside (Greater Manchester) announced that it did not intend to follow the plans of its Labour predecessor to introduce comprehensive education. Under section 68 of the 1944 Education Act the Secretary of State (Fred Mulley) had power to give directions to a local education authority if satisfied that the authority *"have acted or are proposing to act unreasonably"*. Mulley directed Tameside council to implement the scheme for comprehensive education. The dispute then went to the courts, eventually it reached the Law Lords where the case turned on the meaning of the word *'unreasonably'*. The government lost the case.

In Laker Airways Ltd v Department of Trade 1977 the courts ruled that Industry Minister Peter Shore could not prohibit Laker Skytrain from flying and undercutting British Airways. Gouriet v Union of Post Office Workers, 1977 (the South African Mail Boycott case) raised an important constitutional issue with direct relevance to the rule of law and the relationship between the courts and the executive.

In January 1977 the International Confederation of Free Trade Unions called for a week of international protest against apartheid in South Africa. British trade unions were involved, including the postmen's union. A member of the National Association for Freedom (NAFF) sought the Attorney General's permission to bring a *relator action*. This is not a prosecution but a means by which a member of the public can hear the court's view and perhaps get a court ruling. By convention the Attorney General has to give his consent; in this case he refused permission since he felt that any action in this matter might precipitate wider industrial action.

The Appeal Court issued a temporary injunction whilst the matter was clarified. The union called off the proposed boycott. The Attorney General, Sam Silkin, felt that the courts allowing even a temporary injunction would create a precedent. He told the Court of Appeal that he had the absolute right to exercise discretion, that his actions could not be questioned in the courts, and that he was answerable only to Parliament.

The Appeal Court ruled that a citizen could obtain a temporary injunction to prevent an alleged breach of the law occurring. In July 1977 the Law Lords overruled the decision of the Appeal Court, arguing that the courts had no power to review the Attorney General's decisions, private rights may be asserted by individuals but public rights may be asserted only by the Attorney General. The Economist on 30 July 1977 commented *'this judgement leaves open the political question of whether one politician has too much power to make wrong decisions about the judicial process.'*

Cases Involving Labour Local Councils

In 1972 the Labour councillors of Clay Cross in Derbyshire were surcharged nearly £7,000 for subsidising rents in defiance of the controversial Housing Finance Act of 1972. An even more politically controversial decision was the 'Fares Fair' case of 1981. In the GLC election of 1981 the Labour Party included in its manifesto a plan to reduce fares on London Transport and to pay for this by a subsidy from the rates. Labour won and in October 1981 introduced the scheme. It ordered the London boroughs to issue a supplementary rate demand to provide the subsidy. The Conservative controlled Borough of Bromley challenged the GLC's legal right to issue the supplementary precept. The Court of Appeal found that the GLC was ultra vires.

Their ruling was based upon the 1969 London Transport Act which required *'integrated, efficient and economic'* transport facilities. The judges took this to mean that London Transport must try to cover its costs. Lord Denning caused a storm of controversy when he declared; a *'manifesto issued by a political party in order to get votes was not to be regarded as gospel. It was not a covenant.'*

The decision was upheld by the Law Lords but it aroused protest mainly on the left. Denning was accused of having made a political decision. Even the Economist commented that. *"Lord Denning's view of the general behaviour of the GLC is hard to interpret as anything but a covert political counter-attack against a legally elected, if unpopular, local authority."*

In 1985 the surcharging of Liverpool and Lambeth Councillors for breaking the government's 'rate capping' legislation led critics to claim judicial bias. In 1990 the courts ruled against 19 Labour local authorities and in favour of the government. The judges ruled that *'poll tax capping'* was not ultra vires. Again the left saw this as judicial bias but it could be argued that in fact the judges were merely interpreting the law as laid down by Parliament.

Secrecy

Whereas the UK has traditionally had an Official Secrets Act, other liberal democracies, such as the USA, Sweden, Australia and Canada, have a Freedom of Information Act. The very terminology is revealing; in Britain the accent is on secrecy and the state decides what is to be published. In most democracies the onus is on open government and the state has to demonstrate that publication of information would be damaging in order for that information to be kept secret.

There were some well publicised prosecutions in the 1960s and 1970s amongst them the Sunday Telegraph revelations about British involvement in the Nigerian War of 1970 and the attempted suppression of the Crossman Diaries. The ABC trial of 1977 is an example of judicial deference to the executive. The Labour Government deported a radical American journalist, Mark Hosenball. The Home Secretary gave no reasons for his decision that Hosenball was a security threat.

According to Denning: "There is a conflict between the interests of national security on the one hand and the freedom of the individual on the other. The balance between these two is not for a court of law. It is for the Home Secretary. He is the person entrusted by Parliament with the task. In some parts of the world national security has on occasion been used as an excuse for all sorts of infringements of individual liberty. But not in England...

They have never interfered with the liberty or the freedom of movement of any individual except where it is absolutely necessary for the safety of the state'.

In 1984 Sarah Tisdall a junior civil servant leaked certain documents concerning the way in which the government would handle the arrival of cruise missiles into Britain, what Parliament would be told etc. She leaked the papers to the Guardian newspaper and was convicted and sentenced to six months.

More infamously, in 1985, Clive Ponting was prosecuted under the OSA Section Two. The consent of the Attorney General to a prosecution under the OSA is required, which may bring accusations of political bias in deciding which cases to pursue. This was the result when Havers, who denied pressure from Thatcher, decided to prosecute Ponting. Ponting leaked information to a Labour MP (Tam Dalyell) in the belief that it documented an attempt by the government to deceive Parliament as to the circumstances in which the 'Belgrano' was sunk during the Falklands War. Ponting's defence was that the leak was (in the words of Section Two) 'In the interests of the state' and so not an offence. Prior to the trial, the PM's Press Secretary, Bernard Ingham, said it was hoped that an 'appropriately severe' judge would hear the case.

Judge McCowan in his summing up did endeavour blatantly to influence the jury in favour of a conviction. He ruled that the phrase 'In the interests of the state' should be taken as meaning no more than 'the policies of the government of the day' and effectively directed the jury to convict Ponting. The Economist's commented that *'The judges bizarre description of the state in this case suggests that Britain's constitution really does need a charter to describe it'*.

Defence Secretary Heseltine also intervened directly to introduce classified documents as evidence, thus enabling some of the trial to be held in secret and the jury to be 'vetted' (their personal and political backgrounds were secretly investigated by the Special Branch). In fact, the jury acquitted Ponting and the government were wary of using Section Two again.

A former Civil Servant, Peter Wright, wanted to publish a book "Spycatcher" about the activities of MI5. Wright had been in MI5 and claimed that it had been engaged in "dirty tricks" such as trying to de-stabilise Wilson's Labour governments. The government tried to ban publication in both Australia, where Wright now lived and the UK. The top Civil Servant, the Cabinet Secretary, Sir Robert Armstrong, was sent to Sydney to argue in court that the book should not be published. It was during the case that Armstrong coined the famous euphemism, *"being economical with the truth"*. The government lost the case in Australia and finally the Law Lords ruled that the book could be published in Britain.

Following official embarrassment over the acquittal of Ponting and the government's defeat in the Spycatcher affair, the original Official Secrets Act was replaced in 1989 by an even more restrictive statute which removed the 'public interest' defence and introduced a duty of life-long confidentiality for servants of the State. Even now that a Freedom of Information Act has been passed its impact will be limited because the Act does not go as far as reformers wanted. It will not be fully implemented until 2005.

A New Breed of Judges?

In the light of the Thalidomide case when the British judges refused to permit the Sunday Times to publish facts of desperate public interest, Denning's comments over the Birmingham Six - that justice could not have miscarried because that would imply that the police had engaged in perjury - and the comments of the judge in the Ponting case; Labour believe we need a new breed of judges in the UK.

We speak of the judges as though they were a homogeneous group, in fact there are a whole variety of judges operating in different courts at different levels. Judges are not a small group of policy makers. Griffith emphasises their similarity, other authorities such as Gavin Drewrey and Simon Lee emphasise their diversity. The Law Lords are often divided as they were in the Gillick case. Lee and Drewery are questioning the convention of an apolitical judiciary not from a left-wing stance, but from an examination of the actual record of the judges at work.

In the 1989 dock strike over the abolition of the National Dock Labour scheme *the judges argued in favour of the unions and against the dock employers* who tried to get an injunction to stop the strike on the grounds that it was a political strike and as such banned by the 1980 Employment Act.

As Lee points out the argument of the left wing critics of the judiciary is based on a logical fallacy. 'There are many reasons why the judges might decide against trade unions other than their alleged political conservatism. It may be for instance that the trade unions are in the wrong. It may be, indeed it undoubtedly is on occasions, because the judges are rightly applying legislation specifically designed by the democratically elected Conservative government to defeat the unions".

Lee also cites the 1980 case involving the steelworkers strike where the Law Lords overruled the Appeal Court under Denning and the case resulted in a resounding victory for the union. Scarman specifically rebuked Denning; *"The constitution's separation of powers, or more accurately functions, must be observed if judicial independence is not to be put at risk".*

Things are definitely changing, there is a new breed of judges. Applications for judicial review have trebled in the last decade. Judicial review of central government decisions has become so common that all civil servants are now briefed on the dangers of falling foul of the 'judge on your shoulder', as one internal Whitehall document puts it.

As Hailsham put it: "Parliament is supreme and no judge can declare an Act of Parliament invalid ... the importance of an independent judiciary is greater when judges have to serve under an all powerful parliament dominated by a party cabinet". What better description could there be of the Thatcher era? Unusually for a Conservative government, the Thatcher Governments of 1979-1990 lost several cases in the courts, most importantly 'Spycatcher'.

In 1985, the Appeal Court ruled that the Department of the Environment had acted illegally in reducing rate support grant for Bradford City Council and Nottingham County Council. This was later overturned by the Law Lords. In 1985, when Nicholas Ridley was Secretary of State for the Environment, he lost three separate cases, mostly relatively minor, e.g.

GLC v Ridley over London Regional Transport costs. Similarly, in 1985 when Norman Fowler was Secretary of State at Health and Social Security, he lost a series of actions in both the High Court and the Court of Appeal as the judges outlawed his new controversial restrictions on supplementary benefit for claimants in board and lodgings. He had failed to consult as he was required by law to do, the Social Security Advisory Board.

No government has ever been subject to so much scrutiny by the courts, or had so many rulings against it. Kenneth Baker as Home Secretary, deported an immigrant in 1991 and was subsequently found in contempt of court because he had not followed the correct procedure. Douglas Hurd, then the Foreign Secretary was ruled ultra vires over the Pergau dam affair; Howard was overruled in his attempt to have the Saudi Arabian dissident expelled from the UK and he had already been ruled ultra vires for his attempt to reduce payments to victims of crime in disregard of the statute passed by Parliament. The Master of the Rolls described this as an 'abuse of powers'.

The judge in the Matrix-Churchill case threw the case out of court thereby causing Major to set up an inquiry under another judge, Scott, which was later on to cause him so many problems. Judge Tumin as Chief Inspector of Prisons was another judicial critic of the government.

Perhaps these cases are the best demonstration that the judiciary is not 'anti-left'. We have witnessed the then Lord Chief Justice - Lord Taylor - in open disagreement with a Tory Home Secretary. Taylor had to retire early but his replacement Lord Bingham, the former Master of the Rolls, and Bingham's replacement as Master of the Rolls Lord Woolf, author of the report into the Strangeways prison riot, were both reformers. Bingham favoured the incorporation of the European Declaration of Human Rights into British law becoming a British Bill of Rights and in the very week in which he was appointed he warned the government that if they did not introduce a privacy law then the judges would do so.

In May 1996 Taylor lead an attack on Howard in the House of Lords in which almost the entire legal establishment criticised the government's sentencing policy. Indeed some right-wing newspapers such as the Sunday

Times and journalists such as Bruce Anderson have leapt to the defence of the government and in particular Howard against what they see as an undemocratic attack by the liberal judges on elected politicians, how times appear to have changed.

It is important to get things in perspective. Despite the supposed new breed of judges most judges are men, there is only one woman judge of high court level or above and no non-white judges at that level. Less than 1% of solicitors are non-white and over three quarters are men. Over four fifths of barristers are male and that is where most judges will be recruited from for the foreseeable future.

Some left-wingers such as Benn continue to argue that the judges are biased and that any attempt to portray them as otherwise is propaganda by those such as Charter 88 who want a codified constitution The 'villain' that emerges from the Ewing and Geary book on civil liberties is not Thatcher but the supposedly independent judges. No one has coerced the judiciary it has simply seen as its task to act as 'a long stop' for the executive, even if it meant tying itself up in legal contradictions or inventing new doctrines on the hoof.

However as Taylor himself argued in 'The Judiciary in the Nineties' 'the suggestion that judges are biased towards the Establishment does not stand up to examination.' Blair's governments have so far had no serious problems with the judges and it may be that the old left wing idea of a judicial bias against Labour is no longer relevant. Ironically the biggest problems have come from Blunkett the Home Secretary demanding tougher sentences for murderers and the judges denouncing this as political interference with sentencing. However the Pinoichet case of the late 1990s shows how difficult it is for judges to avoid political controversy.

? Can the judges stay out of politics?

The US Judges

Article 3 of the US constitution which deals with the courts states that there should be a **Supreme Court** which will be the highest court of appeal in the US. Congress determines the number of judges on the Supreme Court and since 1869, this has been set at 9. The President nominates judges to the Supreme Court, but they have to be confirmed by the Senate. One in five of all such nominations have been rejected since 1787.

Article 3 also states that Congress shall set up whatever "inferior" (lower than the Supreme Court) courts it deems necessary. There are therefore three tiers to the federal court structure: at the bottom are the 90 US District Courts; above them are the 11 US Courts of Appeal and at the apex the Federal Supreme Court. All federal judges, of which there are several hundred, are nominated by the President and have to be confirmed by the Senate. Reagan-Bush appointees account for two thirds of the federal judiciary. When Clinton came in 100 federal judgeships, 15% of the entire federal bench awaited nomination. However the appointment of federal judges below the Supreme Court is subject to Senatorial Courtesy. This enhances the status and patronage powers of Senators and ensures the President that his appointees will be confirmed, it does not apply to the Supreme Court. State judges interpret state law and the state constitution and therefore their appointment is nothing to do with the Federal Government, in some states they even elect judges.

Once appointed, like judges in the UK, Federal judges have security of tenure, that is they cannot be sacked. They can be impeached, but this is extremely rare so they remain on the court until they die or retire. Some Presidents, such as Carter, never get to appoint Supreme Court judges. Carter did appoint lots of federal judges, as did Reagan and given that most cases do not get as far as the Court of Appeal, let alone the Supreme Court, these appointments are also critical.

Judicial Review

Judicial Review is the convention which allows the Supreme Court to interpret the constitution and to act as constitutional referee or arbiter. It is not explicitly mentioned in the constitution, although it is implicit. There has to be a body which interprets the constitution and it could not be Congress or the President because they are partisan. It therefore has to be the court. This latent function was made manifest in the key case of **Marbury Vs Madison 1803**.

The Appointment of Supreme Court Judges

The whole appointments process is politicised from beginning to end. Presidents often nominate for political reasons and the Senate equally often responds on a political basis. From 1896 to 1932, the Republicans dominated US politics. This meant that when FDR became President in March 1933, he faced a hostile court. The court rejected key elements of the New Deal as unconstitutional. FDR tried to get Congress to agree to an increase in the number of SC. judges. The President would be able to appoint an additional judge for every judge over 70 up to a maximum of 15. It was an obvious attempt at packing the court and Congress rejected it. Thus, the most powerful President of the 20th century was prevented from tampering with the court.

In November 1936, FDR was re-elected by a landslide. The Court had to accept that they were out of touch with the public mood. Hence, from 1937 onwards, the court stopped blocking the New Deal, "a switch in time saved nine". It is an excellent example of the court, "following the election returns". By 1945, FDR had appointed most of the Court. In 1953, Eisenhower (Ike) appointed a new Chief Justice; the former Republican governor of California, the moderate conservative, **Earl Warren**. Warren was a disappointment to Ike because the Warren Court of 1953-69 was the most liberal court this century. Ike is supposed to have said that "Warren was the worst damn appointment I ever made". It is a clear example of the appointments process backfiring on the President. Similarly Nixon found that his own appointees voted against him over the Watergate tapes case.

In the 1968 Presidential election, Nixon had campaigned against the liberalism, what he labelled the 'loose constructionism', of the Warren Court. In 1969, Warren retired and Nixon appointed **Warren Burger** as Chief Justice. The Burger Court of 1969 - 86 disappointed conservatives because it failed to reverse Warren's judgements. Nixon, as part of his 'Southern strategy' to win over disaffected Southern white voters nominated two Southern judges, **Haynsworth and Carswell**. The Democrat controlled Senate rejected both on the grounds that they were racist and incompetent.

Reagan had an enormous impact on the Supreme Court. In 1981 Reagan appointed the first ever woman member - **Sandra Day O'Connor**. In 1986, Burger retired and Reagan promoted **William Rehnquist** to Chief Justice. He had first been appointed to the court by Nixon in 1970. The vacancy was filled by **Antonin Scalia**.

In 1987 **Powell** retired and Reagan tried to replace him with **Bork**. When Judge Bork faced the Senate Judiciary Committee in Autumn 1987 they scrutinised his political stance and the impact he would have on such a finely balanced court. At the time of Scalia's appointment, in 1986, Biden stated that he would accept Bork as an associate justice; however, he later argued that the position had changed because Bork would give the conservatives a majority on the Court. Hence Bork's decisive rejection, 58:42, the biggest negative majority in the history of the Senate. Reagan had to settle for **Anthony Kennedy**.

Almost ten years after Reagan left office his appointees are still on the Court helping to make crucial decisions many of which in the UK would be left to politicians. It could well be that Reagan's most lasting impact will be the way he was able to push the Federal Courts to the right.

Bush appointed two Supreme Court judges, David Souter in 1989 and Clarence Thomas in 1991. The latter was an extremely controversial appointment. In 1967, LBJ appointed the first ever black Supreme Court judge, **Thurgood Marshall,** an eminent liberal jurist who had represented the NAACP in the seminal case of Brown v Board. In 1991, Marshall retired. It was felt that Bush had to replace him with a black. Bush nominated one of the few black Republicans, **Clarence Thomas**, even though the American Bar Association (ABA) which grades potential nominees argued that Thomas was not Supreme Court calibre.

Despite the ABA's verdict the Democrat controlled all white Senate Judiciary Committee worried that rejecting Thomas would look like racism. It was on the verge of reluctantly confirming Thomas when at the last minute, a black law professor, **Anita Hill**, testified to the committee that Thomas had sexually harassed her when she had worked for him years earlier. The nomination now raised the spectre of two potent forces, racism and sexism. The Judiciary Committee recommended confirmation and the Senate ratified because enough Southern politicians feared a backlash in the next election had they not backed Thomas. However even now millions of Americans, particularly women, believe that Thomas should not be on the Supreme Court especially as it has to consider such contentious issues as abortion. At the Democrat Convention in the summer of 1992 the most popular campaign badge amongst women delegates was 'I believe Anita'. The Bork and Thomas nominations demonstrated how politicised the whole process is provoking the obvious contrast with Britain.

From 1969 to 1993, every judge appointed to the Supreme Court was appointed by a Republican President. Consequently the Rehnquist Court is very conservative. By 1998 Clinton had made two appointments, **Ruth Ginsberg** and **Stephen Breyer**. The dominant figure on the Court is O'Connor, indeed it has been described as the 'O'Connor Court'. On election night 2000 she described the prospect of a Gore Presidency as a disaster. With Bush in power there is no likelihood of reversing the conservative drift of the Supreme Court. He had not made any Supreme Court appointments by summer 2003 but he had made it clear that he would ignore any advice from the ABA which he sees as too liberal. The Attorney General, John Ashcroft is a staunch conservative as is the Solicitor General Theodore Olson who had been Bush's lawyer in the election dispute.

1953 - 69	**Warren Court**	liberal
1969 - 86	**Burger Court**	transitional
1986 onwards	**Rehnquist Court**	conservative

Summary of of Important Cases

1803 - Marbury Vs Madison This was the first time the court had rejected a law as unconstitutional, *the Federal Judiciary Act of 1789.* The case established the precedent of Judicial Review. As Marshall put it; 'it is emphatically the province and duty of the judicial department to say what the law is. Those who apply the rule to particular cases, must of necessity expound and interpret that rule. If two laws conflict with each other, the courts must decide on the operation of each.' Congress accepted the legitimacy of the court's ruling and so, extremely reluctantly, did President Jefferson.

1810 - Fletcher v Peck, The first state law to be declared unconstitutional.

1816 - Martin v Hunters Lessee, First time the Federal Supreme Court over ruled a State (Virginia) Supreme Court .

These cases established the boundaries of Judicial Review which remains to this day the reason why the Supreme Court has such a key political role.

1819 - McCullogh v Maryland, This case established Congress's right to set up a national bank *(Article 1, Section 8, the "Implied Powers")*. Marshall argued; 'This great principle is, that the Constitution and the laws made in pursuance thereof are supreme, that they control the Constitution and laws of the respective states, and cannot be controlled by them.'

1824 - Gibbons v Ogden Established Congress's right to tax ferries operating between New York and New Jersey *(Article 1, Section 8 the "Inter-State Commerce Clause")*.

All these cases occurred whilst **John Marshall** was Chief Justice. Marshall, the fourth Chief Justice, was a Federalist (someone who believed in strengthening the powers of the federal government over the states) and as such came into conflict with Jefferson.

When Marshall died in 1835 the Democrat President, Andrew Jackson, a strong supporter of state's rights, appointed **Roger Taney** Chief Justice. The Taney Court 1835-1864, emphasised state's rights including the controversial **Dred Scott Case 1857 - Scott v Sandford**. Scott was a run away slave who attempted to establish his rights as a free man. The court ruled that as a black man, he was not a citizen, he had no rights - he was property. It also ruled that Congress's attempt to stop the spread of slavery, the **Missouri Compromise of 1821**, was unconstitutional. Bork has argued that this was the worst decision reached by the court in the 19th century. This case helped to provoke the Civil War of 1861-5.

1861 Ex Parte Merryman - the Court told Lincoln that he could not suspend habeus corpus; Lincoln ignored the ruling on the grounds that the public safety required it.

1895 - Pollock v Farmers Loan and Trust Company the Court ruled that a federal income tax was unconstitutional. It was not until the 16th Amendment in 1913 that this was reversed. This illustrates how difficult it is to change the constitution in order to reverse a Supreme Court ruling.

In **1896 in Plessy v Ferguson** the court ruled that, despite the 14th Amendment, de jure segregation was permissible, provided facilities were equal. One of the dissenting judges argued that the Court should be colour blind. The infamous separate but equal ruling remained until 1954.

The Republicans dominated the White House from 1896 to 1932 and therefore inevitably, the Supreme Court reflected their conservative outlook. Therefore, if politicians attempted to intervene in economic and social politics, the court often rejected such approaches as unconstitutional.

1905 - Lochner v New York. The Court rejected a law to regulate the working hours of bakers, the state had limited them to 60 hours/week.

1918 - Hammer v Dagenhart. The Court rejected a law limiting the hours which children could work.

Schencks v USA and Abrams v USA, both 1919, the Court upheld the constitutionality of the Espionage Act of 1917 and the Seditions Act of 1918 respectively. Justice Holmes dissent in the Abrams case is one of the classic defences of free speech. 'The best test of truth is the power of the thought to get itself accepted in the competition of the market.' Government should punish political speech only when it posed a 'clear and present danger to society'.

The election of FDR led to a clash between the White House and the Court. The Court rejected certain parts of the New Deal for example:

1937 - Schechter v US Poultry Corporation otherwise known as **the diseased chickens case**. The court argued that the federal government had no right to regulate industry and agriculture in the way in which the **NRA** (National Recovery Act) and the **AAA** (Agricultural Adjustment Act) were attempting. FDR's response in spring 1937 was the **Court Packing Plan** which was rejected by Congress.

However from 1937, the court began to change its attitude towards the New Deal. For example, they ruled the **National Labour Relations Act (National Labour Relations Board v Jones and Laughlin Steel Corporation)** and the **Social Security Act** constitutional on the grounds that it was 'taxing for the general welfare' **(Steward Machine Company v Davis)**. By the late 1930s, FDR's appointees were beginning to have an impact.

In 1936 the Court established that only the Executive is responsible for foreign policy. 'The President alone has the power to speak or listen as a representative of the nation'. Tim Hames argues that this is a hard argument to sustain since it is rejected by Congress and impossible to implement given that Congress demands a continued role in foreign policy.

1944 Smith v Allwright - declared the all-white primary unconstitutional, thus reversing a 1935 decision.

During the Civil War of 1861-5, President Lincoln had flouted the constitution, and got away with it. During WW1, President Wilson had done the same thing. During WW2, FDR infringed civil liberties and the Court turned a blind eye as in **1944 - Korematsu v USA**. FDR had interned a 100,000 perfectly innocent Japanese Americans living in California arguing that they were a security threat. The Court ruled that this was not unconstitutional. Decades later the government accepted that this had been wrong and compensated their families financially.

In 1952, during the Korean War, there was the threat of a steel strike. President Truman tried to avert this by seizing control of the steel industry. Three steel companies filed a complaint. In June 1952 in the case of **Youngstown Sheet & Tube Metal Company v Sawyer** the Court ruled by 6:3 that the President had exceeded his Constitutional authority. The President immediately returned the mills to the owners. The "Steel Seizure Case" demonstrates the limits on Presidential power, even during war time.

The Warren Court 1953 - 1969

1954 - Brown v Board of Education of Topeka County, Kansas. Linda Brown, a black girl, was not allowed to go to her local school because of segregation. The black pressure group, the NAACP (National Association for the Advancement of Coloured People) used this as a test case. In the 1950s, Southern states spent $45 per white pupil, $13 per black. The Court had to decide whether the 14th Amendment of 1868 allowed segregation. The majority of the 9 judges said no; two southern judges thought it should.

Warren persuaded them to change their vote because he thought that on such an important issue the decision should be unanimous. Therefore, by 9-0, the court ruled that segregation is inherently unconstitutional.

'We conclude that in the field of public education, the doctrine of separate but equal has no place. Separate educational facilities are inherently unequal.' It ordered the lower courts to bring about desegregation in schools 'with all deliberate speed'.

It is an excellent illustration of the Court responding to changing circumstances. In the late 19th century racist assumptions were widespread, by the 1950s they were being challenged. The USA had just emerged victorious from a war against the racist ideology of Nazism and was at that time engaged in a 'Cold War' against Communism. It was a battle of ideologies, liberalism versus totalitarianism and the acceptance of segregation in the South damaged America's claim to be a democratic, open society. The Brown judgement reflected all these factors. It overturned the Plessy judgement showing that the court is not rigidly bound by precedent. If they were then judicial review would cease to have much significance.

The Court has authority, but little power, it cannot enforce its rulings. In 1957 the governor of Arkansas refused to integrate the schools. IKE sent the National Guard to Little Rock to escort black children into white schools. Hodder-Williams points out that ten years after the decision barely 1% of black children in the 11 states of the former Confederacy attended integrated schools. It took acts of Congress and policy directives by the Executive to change this and even then change came slowly, in various places, protests, riots and demonstrations took place before the law was put into effect, an excellent example of how the court requires other bodies to help it enforce its judgements.

1961 Mapp v Ohio - the police prevented were from using materials obtained during unreasonable searches and seizures.

1962 - Baker v Carr The number of representatives per state depends upon the state's population. A census is taken every 10 years and adjustments are made accordingly. Between 1980 and 1990, New York lost population and therefore its number of Representatives was reduced from 34 to 31. The opposite was true of California. The drawing of electoral boundaries within the state is a responsibility of the State legislature. If it does not adjust boundaries to reflect the internal shifts of population some Congressional districts will have a lot bigger population than others. This is known as **Malapportionment**. If it deliberately manipulates boundaries to benefit a group or to discriminate against a group, it is known as **Gerrymandering**. Both have the same effect - they produce unequal electoral districts.

In **1946** in the case of **Colegrove vs Green**, the Court was asked to grant an order to reapportion state electoral districts in Illinois which were notoriously inequitable. The court had refused to rule on this issue describing it as a "political ticket".

Baker v Carr involved the state of Tennessee which had not redrawn electoral boundaries since 1910. One district had had a population of 2,340 another of 312,345. Again, the case revolved around the 14th Amendment.

If one electoral district had a much bigger population than another, then the value of the vote was not equal. By then the composition of the Court had substantially changed. The Court ruled by 6:3 that this was unconstitutional there must be *equal electoral* districts so as to achieve *"One man, One Vote, One Value"*.

Again, it was the 14th Amendment that was being interpreted. According to Weaver, the decision 'may prove to be the most far reaching action taken by the Supreme Court in the last 100 years'. Warren described this as the most important case his court had dealt with and the ramifications of it are still being felt today.

The principle established in the Baker case was built upon with **Reynolds v Sims (1964)** and **Wesberry v Saunders (1964)**.

1962 Engel v Vitale The court ruled that school prayer in publicly funded schools was unconstitutional (1st Amendment - "freedom of religion", separating Church and State). This was broadened in **1963 in School Districts (Abington) v Schempp** which ruled that bible reading in state schools was unconstitutional.

1963 - Gideon v Wainwright The court ruled that a defendant must have access to a lawyer for all felony cases in state courts. (Sixth Amendment - "Right to a Fair Trial"). This was broadened in **1964 in Escobedo v Illinois** which established a criminal defendants right to a lawyer.

1964 New York Times v Sullivan - the Court said that the First Amendment means that a public official cannot win a libel action against the press unless he proves not only that a statement made about him was false and damaging but that the statement was made with actual malice, that is journalists published it knowing it to be untrue. Dworkin claims that the Courts decision freed the press to investigate and report the news without fear. It is likely that the Watergate scandal would not have been uncovered had it not been for this ruling. Not everyone takes such an optimistic view of the impact - see section on the US media.

1964 Heart of Atlanta Motel v USA ruled that Congress could \eliminate discrimination in private businesses and so upheld the 1964 Civil Rights Act

1964 Katzenbach v McLung, 'Ollies Burger bar' case - Ollie could not refuse to serve blacks as he 'imported' burgers from outside the state and was therefore bound by the Interstate Commerce Clause so Congress could regulate his activities through the Civil Rights Act.

1965 Griswold v Connecticut. A state had no right to ban contraceptives. This was later to be cited in the Roe v Wade case.

1966 - Miranda v Arizona. A murder conviction was overturned by the court because the police had not followed "due process", i.e. had not read the suspect his rights (*5th Amendment - "Rights of a Suspect"*). Ever since, the police have read the suspect their rights from a 'Miranda Card'.

1967 - Katz v USA The court ruled that the FBI should not be allowed to bug a suspect without a warrant from the Attorney General (*4th Amendment - "Privacy Clause"*). This is an excellent example of the court adapting the constitution to changing circumstances because the 4th Amendment actually states that persons shall be secure against 'unreasonable searches and seizures'. They could not have known about electronic surveillance in 1791.

The Warren Court extended civil liberties thereby infuriating conservatives who talked of impeaching him. Nixon campaigned against Warren's liberalism in the 1968 Presidential election. Warren's liberalism is an example of Judicial Activism or Loose Constructionism. Nixon campaigned for Judicial Restraint or Strict Constructionism, known as a Jurisprudence of "Original Intent". Warren retired in 1969 because by then, the liberalism of the 1950s and 1960s had been replaced by a shift to the right. Warren was in a sense now failing to 'follow the election returns'. Nixon replaced him with Burger.

The Burger Court 1969 - 1986

1969 - Alexander v Holmes County Board of Education (Brown v Board 2). 15 years on from Brown, some states had still not desegregated their schools. This decision made desegregation of schools mandatory, the court told them to "Desegregate with all deliberate speed". Thus it took 15 years from the 'Brown Judgement' for it to be implemented.

1970, Oregon v Mitchell said 18 year olds could not vote. Subsequently overturned by the 26th Amendment.

1970 Reed v Reed ruled sexual discrimination unacceptable.

1971 Lemon v Kurtzmann established a three prong test for laws to comply with the first amendment separation of church and state.

1971 - Swann v Charlotte Mecklenberg (a school board) De jure segregation (based on law) was ruled unconstitutional in 1954. But, if blacks live in one part of town, then the local schools will be black, and if whites all live in the other part of town, then the local school will be white. This is known as de facto segregation. One way round this is bussing - taking black pupils over to white schools and vice versa. Nixon, like many Americans including Linda Brown by now herself a mother, was against bussing, but the court ruled it as constitutional in this case.

1971 Griggs v Duke Power Company ruled recruitment tests that appeared to benefit whites were unlawful.

1971 - The Pentagon Papers case - New York Times v USA. A high ranking former officer, Daniel Ellsberg leaked information concerning the Vietnam war to the NYT. These documents showed that LBJ had distorted the Gulf of Tonkin incident and Nixon had authorised the secret bombing of neutral Cambodia. Nixon's Attorney General John Mitchell tried to prevent publication, but the court upheld the right to publish (*1st Amendment - "Freedom of Speech"*). The obvious contrast is with British cases involving official secrecy such as Tisdal, Ponting and Spycatcher where the judges tended to rule in favour of the government.

In **1971 in Harris v New York** it was stated that confessions extracted in violation of Miranda could be used in court to help the jury decide whether a defendant was lying.

1972 Furman v Georgia. The Court abolished the death penalty on the grounds that its application varied so much from state to state that it constituted a 'cruel and unusual punishment' which is banned by the 8th Amendment.

1973 - Roe v Wade. Texan law banned abortion but the Supreme Court ruled by 7 to 2 that a woman has a constitutional right to an abortion within the first 26 weeks of pregnancy. The court argued that the 4th Amendment, known as the privacy clause even though those words are not used, and the 14th Amendment (equal protection of the law) gave women this right. Conservatives such as Bork argue that this is the worst decision the Court has reached in the 20th century because it is not just adapting the Constitution to changing circumstances it is bending it out of shape.

1973 San Antonio Independent School District v Rodriguez - it held that states did not have to finance school districts equally.

1974 - US v Richard Nixon - Watergate Tapes Case. The Court ruled by 8-0 that executive privilege did not apply in this case therefore Nixon had to hand over the tapes. This lead to his resignation as he would have faced certain impeachment.

1976, Buckley v Valeo court overturned restrictions on campaign funding introduced by the Federal Election Campaign Act of 1974. It did so on 1st Amendment grounds.

1976 Gregg v Georgia. The Court reversed the Furman decision, arguing that execution for capital crimes was acceptable under the Constitution.

1978 - Bakke v University of California. When the Civil Rights Acts were passed in the 1960s, they removed legal discrimination. However, they could not remedy past discrimination. The way to help blacks achieve equality was through Affirmative Action which the 1964 Act introduced. This led institutions such as universities to set aside a number of places for candidates from certain ethnic minorities - a quota. Bakke, a white man, could not get into medical school, even though his grades were higher than the 16 blacks who got in via the quota.

Bakke said that this was reverse discrimination and took the case to court. The case split public opinion. Liberals, for example Carter, supported quotas. Conservatives opposed them. Jews, who had traditionally sided with blacks, opposed quotas. The court's decision reflected these difficulties. The court ruled by 5-4 that Bakke had been discriminated against. They also ruled, by 5-4, that positive discrimination is not inherently unconstitutional provided race is not the sole criteria. It was an ambiguous judgement that satisfied no one and the issues remained unresolved.

United Steelworkers of **America v Weber** 1979 and **Fullilove v Klutznick** ruled voluntary quotas and set aside programmes constitutional and a host of other cases qualified the constitutionality of such programmes.

US v Havens (1980) the court said that illegally obtained evidence could be used if it contradicted a defendant's testimony. **New York v Quarles (1984)** ruled that if public safety was threatened a suspect could be questioned without having been read his rights.

1983 Immigration and Naturalisation Service v Chadha. The Court ruled the one House Congressional veto unconstitutional. This has implications for the constitutionality of the War Powers Act.

In **Memphis Fire Department v Stotts (1984)** the court stated that racial quotas do not take precedence over length of service in redundancy cases.

1985 Garcia v San Antonio Metropolitan Transit Authority the court declared that the states could not expect the judges to protect their powers through the 10th Amendment. This overturned the **1976** judgement **National League of Cities v Usery** which had upheld states powers in relation to the inter-state commerce clause for the first time since 1936. Rehnquist dissented in the Garcia case.

1986 Bowsher v Synar - ruled the Balanced Budget Act of 1985 unconstitutional because it infringed the separation of powers.

1986 Bowers v Hardwick the Court by 5:4 refused to extend the constitutional right to privacy to consensual homosexual sodomy.

The Rehnquist Court, 1986 Onwards

The Rehnquist Court is a conservative body. So far, the most controversial decisions reached by the court have been over abortion, electoral districting and affirmative action.

In **1980 in Harris v McCrae** the Burger Court had upheld the constitutionality of the Hyde Amendment which Congress had passed banning the use of Federal government funds and Medicaid for abortions. The bigger test came in **1989 Webster v Reproductive Health Services** when it looked as though the Court would overturn Roe v Wade and ban abortion. In fact it did not go that far, O'Connor baulked at that, but it did return the decision over abortion to the states (*10th Amendment - "the reserved powers of the states"*). Conservatives such as Bork want to go further and ban abortion altogether but subsequent cases such as **Casey v Planned Parenthood in 1992** have only further qualified the right to abortion, they have not banned it. Dworkin calls this decision 'one of the most important Court decisions of this generation.'

This time O'Connor, Kennedy and Souter all baulked, and were supported by Blackmun and Stevens. Casey stipulates that state restrictions are constitutional only if they do not place an 'undue burden' on a woman's right to an abortion.

1989 Texas v Johnson. By 5 to 4 the Court upheld the right to burn the US flag on grounds of freedom of speech. Dworkin argues that a conservative court still values freedom of speech and thinks it important to democracy even in cases they despise. Bush's Attorney General Richard Thornburgh persuaded him to float the idea of a constitutional amendment to reverse this but it never got off the ground.

In **1988/89 in Stanford v Kentucky** it ruled that the execution of juveniles i.e. 16 and 17 year olds was constitutional and in **1989/90 in Wilkins v Minnesota** it said the same of the execution of a mentally handicapped person. Another example of the Court following the election returns.

1989 Wards Cove Packing Company v Antonio the Court ruled that the burden of proof regarding discrimination must lie with the plaintiff not the employer but affirmative action received its biggest blow in **City of Richmond v Croson 1989**. The Court by 6 to 3 invalidated quotas for contracts going to businesses owned by ethnic minorities.

1990 Arizona v Fulminante - overturned precedent by ruling that allowing an accused's involuntary confession as evidence did not automatically make the trial an unfair one.

1991 Rust v Hill prohibits people working in family planning services to discuss abortion procedures, Dworkin calls this an 'appalling decision' that limits First Amendment rights.

1991 - Chisom v Roemer, in a rare victory for the liberals the Court ruled that it is constitutionally acceptable for Louisiana under the Voting Rights Act of 1965, as amended in 1982, to elect is own Supreme Court (41 states elect at least some of their judges) in a way that ensures representation of minorities.

1992 Lee v Weisman by 5 to 4 ruled that prayers at a graduation ceremony were unconstitutional.

1993 Shaw v Reno - the most controversial voting rights case of recent years; declared a black districting plan unconstitutional in North Carolina as it involved 'racial gerrymandering' which 'even for remedial purposes' could 'balkanise' the USA thereby moving the country 'further from the goal of a political system in which race no longer matters'. The aim had been to strengthen the black vote by creating a 'bizarre' snake-shaped district but the Court said it violated the 14th Amendment.

1993 Zobrest v Catalania Foothills School District - ruled that despite the 1st Amendment public schools may provide a sign-language interpreter for a deaf child who attends a religious school. Had Ginsburg been on the Court at that point the case may well have gone the other way.

1995 US v Lopez the Court ruled by 5:4 the Gun Fee Schools Act of 1990 unconstitutional because of the 2nd Amendment. The Clinton administration had supported the Act even though passed under Bush. The court has been increasingly willing to overturn congressional statutes based on the interstate commerce clause if they appear insufficiently related to interstate commerce.

1995 US Term Limits Incorporated v Thornton - ruled term limits for Congressmen unconstitutional.

In June **1995 in Adarand Constructors Incorporated v Pena** the Court ruled by 5:4 (Breyer, Stevens, Ginsburg and Souter) that affirmative action programmes were permissible only as a last resort. In July 1995 under pressure from Republican Governor Pete Wilson the University of California ended all campus affirmative action programmes.

1995 Missouri v Jenkins the Court overturned a federal judges desegregation order and in **Miller v Johnson** it prohibited the use of race as a predominant factor in determining voting districts.

1997 City of Boerne, Texas v Flores the court declared the Religious Freedom Restoration Act unconstitutional under the 1st Amendment

1998 Clinton v City of New York ruled the line item veto unconstitutional

2000 California Democratic Party v Jones the court struck down California's use of the blanket primary in which all voters can participate regardless of party affiliation. The Act had been passed as a result of a voter initiative.

2000 Gore v Bush the court ruled by 5:4 that manual recounts in selected counties in Florida was not permissible. This is one of the most controversial judgements of recent decades. Conservatives jurists such as Posner regard it as the correct decision whereas liberals such as Alan Dershowitz regard it as an outrage.

In 2003 the court heard a crucial affirmative action case involving the University of Missouri. The Bush Administration filed evidence opposing quotas but the Court upheld their constitutionality.

Conclusion

In 1968, the American political scientist John Weaver described the Supreme Court as "the most powerful tribunal on earth". Certainly the role of the court is central to American politics and has been so since the inauguration of the new republic in 1787. Although the constitution does not explicitly grant the Court the power of judicial review, the very existence of a codified constitution does imply that the Court would act as arbiter in the political process because it is the only institution without an obvious political axe to grind. In other words the very fact that it is unelected gives it a degree of authority which partisan politicians cannot match. Hence, from the outset, the Court has had a major political role. Indeed as Chief Justice Evans said in 1909 **'we are under a Constitution but the Constitution is what the judges say it is.'**

It is not only the Supreme Court which is involved in politics, this is also true of the several hundred Federal judges and the thousands of State judges. However the focus of attention is on the ultimate judicial authority, the Supreme Court, often known as "The Brethren". Some of the most controversial issues in US politics have actually been resolved, not by the elected politicians, but by the nine, unelected, justices who make up the Court. This seems strange in a country so proud of its democratic traditions.

Yet it does reflect the American concern, for restraint of State power and an abiding concern for the rights of the individual. Judges can take a detached view of political issues, free of electoral considerations. Certainly over the past half century or so the Court has often reaffirmed the notion of checks and balances and reminded the Congress and Presidents that there are clear constitutional limits to their power. It is misleading to talk of 'the Court" as though it were a fixed body with unchanging views. Different judges see their role in different ways. Under Warren the Court adopted a liberal stance and promoted social change and civil liberties. The Burger Court of 1969-86 was supposed to reverse the liberalism of Warren, but in fact it made several judgements which consolidated Warren's achievements. The Burger Court lacked both the distinctive liberal philosophy of the Warren Court and, to the disappointment of conservatives, including Nixon, a clear conservative philosophy. The Burger Court is best described as a moderate, transitional Court trying to achieve balance.

The political role of the American courts was particularly controversial in the 1980s as Reagan left his conservative mark on the courts and as the Supreme Court, which had often been narrowly divided on crucial questions, made the fundamental change in direction that conservatives such as ex-Attorney General Meese had long demanded. Meese has waged a campaign against judicial activism arguing that the Founding Fathers did not envisage an interventionist Court and that "there is a danger in seeing the Constitution as an empty vessel into which each generation may pour Its passion and prejudice". Meese favours a 'jurisprudence of original intention'.

By the 1980s the philosophy that the judges should confine themselves to a jurisprudence of 'original intent' was dominant under current Chief Justice William Rehnquist. However the Rehnquist Court has disappointed conservatives and gladdened liberals by failing to reverse many of the advances in civil liberties which had been gained in an earlier period, proof once more that the Court cannot be controlled by politicians. The Rehnquist Court's dominant figure is O'Connor and she is relatively moderate. The Court has tended to support the powers of states leading some commentators to talk of a return to 'dual federalism'. However this was not the case in Gore v Bush. Certainly the Rehnquist Court, despite talking of a separation of powers, federalism and judicial restraint has challenged both state and federal power. If Rehnquist retires and Bush replaces him with O'Connor this will continue.

It is this very absence of political control which Nathan Glazier worried about when he talked of an 'imperial judiciary'. Bob McKeever argues that the Supreme Court weakens American democracy because politically unaccountable judges make policy decisions and promotes citizen apathy. However Richard Hodder-Williams claims that the court's power is often exaggerated, it has to co-operate with elected politicians in what Louis Fisher calls 'constitutional dialogues' and that it frequently assists the democratic process. In the USA, a highly legalistic society, the existence of a codified constitution with its Bill of Rights ensures that the judges will act as the ultimate arbiters of the political process.

 'The Supreme Court is the final arbiter of the political struggle. ' Discuss.

Chapter Five

Chapter 6
Pressure Groups

Pluralism

Pluralism is the dominant perspective for portraying the organisation of power in the West which in political terms embraces Japan, Australasia, South Africa and Israel amongst others. It involves a system of competing elites, where no single group is able to secure a monopoly of power and manipulate the system consistently to its own exclusive advantage. Pluralists claim that Governments respond to a number of interest groups not just economic interest groups.

Pressure Groups and Parties

Both pressure groups and parties are concerned with **'the mobilisation of bias'**. Both are seen as essential to the effective running of a modern liberal democracy but they are clearly distinct in a number of ways. Pressure groups wish to **influence** policy but they do not wish to become the government of the country. Political **parties in a democracy aim to aggregate a range of policies** on a variety of issues so as to command the support of enough voters to win a majority at elections. This is the key difference between parties and pressure groups. Pressure groups are intent on influencing policy whilst disclaiming responsibility for the conduct of government. Political parties are fundamentally concerned with gaining political power.

Pressure groups grow out of interested sections of the population and do not have a mandate from the majority of the population. Political parties are democratically elected with, in Britain and the USA, the winning candidate being the one with the most votes in the constituency. They represent specific geographical locations which also heightens their accountability and representation.

Pressure groups often concentrate on a single policy issue or on the interests of a single group of people. Trade Unions are largely concerned with their member's rights and pay, Shelter is primarily concerned with housing and the homeless. For parties to gain the necessary majority for an election victory they must cover a broad range of issues. As a result they tend to ignore minority issues but there should be more to democracy than mere majority rule, minorities have rights too. Pressure groups are often in competition with another group who possess an opposing set of values, such as the two sides of the abortion debate.

Despite the differences between parties and pressure groups there is a considerable amount of overlap and it is not always easy to separate them. The British National Party really only has one issue. The TUC in contrast is interested in a whole range of issues. Members of Greenpeace are likely to vote for the Greens. Most importantly the TU's are structurally linked to the Labour Party. They helped to form it, they still provide most of its funding and they still have a role in determining Labour policy and in some case choosing candidates.

The Growth of Pressure Groups

The growth of mass democracy and increased government intervention, particularly since 1945, inevitably lead to an increased role for pressure groups As government intervention has increased so pressure group activity has followed so that today citizens in liberal democracies expect government to have a policy on everything from AIDS to football hooliganism and consequently there will be groups lobbying to affect that policy.

Governments accept that such groups can be of benefit to itself and as a result many now have strong links with government. Pressure groups extend democratic participation in the decision making process. If some issues are ignored then groups may stand their own parliamentary candidates but due to the power of the party system few get elected. It was hard to see the Referendum Party of James Goldsmith as anything other than a pressure group and immediately after the 1997 election it turned itself into one. If a group should persist and become a political party as with the Green Party, one finds they are still largely associated with one issue and therefore do not receive the broad support they need in order to win the mandate of the electorate.

Just as pressure groups differ in size, membership and aim, they also differ in strategy. The major areas for focus in the UK are firstly government and civil service, secondly and growing in importance all the time the institutions of the European Union, thirdly Parliament and individual MPs, and finally the public via the mass media. The first two **access points** apply mainly to powerful sectional groups, the others apply mainly to promotional or cause groups. Pressure group lobbying that occurs outside Parliament but within the law is known as **extra-parliamentary** activity; if a group adopts illegal tactics in an attempt to persuade then it is referred to as **anti-parliamentary** in that they are not accepting the rule of law. Pressure groups in the USA follow different strategies because the structure of government is different.

The European Union

One important change in the nature of pressure group activity is that pressure groups now have to present their case in European terms. As Maizey and Richardson point out the Single European Act of 1986 and the Maastricht Treaty of 1991 helped shift power away from the nation state towards the EU, including the European Parliament. The SEA removed the threat of a single nation veto from a lot of decision making. As they put it **'any British pressure group which continues to rely exclusively on**

lobbying Whitehall and Westminster is adopting a high-risk strategy because on a large range of issues policies are now being determined in Brussels'.

Subsidiarity means that issues should be resolved at the lowest level compatible with efficiency. There is no point environmental groups lobbying the nation state if other countries are simply going to emit acid rain. Trade unions are finding that to cope with multinational capital they have to operate at an international level. Britain's fishermen are having to lobby the EU to get a change to what they regard as unfair fishing practices. Again the BSE problem brought out the centrality of the European Union. We witnessed the sight of the British government attempting to use the European Court of Justice, a body it previously wished to denude of its power, to get the ban on British beef lifted.

Types of Pressure Group

The standard categorisation, offered decades ago by Finer, was into **interest** or **sectional** groups and **cause or promotional** groups. A 'sectional' or **protective** pressure group such as the Confederation of British Industry protects the interests and publicises and promotes the views of its members on any issue that concerns them. The National Association of Manufacturers, the US Chamber of Commerce, the Business Roundtable, the American Federation of Labour-Congress of Industrial Organisations and the American Farm Bureau Federation are all sectional groups. Members of sectional groups usually belong to the group whose interests, typically economic, are being protected and usually come from similar socio-economic backgrounds.

Promotional or attitude groups promote a cause, as in the case of the British Field Sports Society which defends field sports and opposes hostile legislation or the Child Poverty Action Group and Help the Aged which help those too young or old to help themselves, Stonewall and Outrage which campaign on behalf of homosexuals and Amnesty International which campaigns for political prisoners.

In the 1960s and 1970s, a new kind of pressure group emerged especially in the USA, single issue cause groups. They particularly attracted young, educated, articulate people who were disenchanted with the staid traditional political parties. Common Cause formed in 1970 to campaign for a more democratic political process and the Nader consumer organisations provide the clearest examples. These groups were perceived to be on the left of the political spectrum and, in the past, the people they attracted may have joined the Democratic Party. The much discussed decline of American parties seemed to accompany the rise of promotional pressure groups. Alan Grant argues that nowadays such groups are the most effective opposition to big business.

Promotional groups have members from a wider variety of backgrounds drawn together by their strong feelings on a particular issue. The people who opposed the export of live calves from the UK included representatives of both sexes, all age groups, all classes, all religious groups and none and presumably all political persuasions. Many of them appeared never to have been involved in any form of overt political activity before, they were simply driven to protest about something they saw as morally wrong.

Public opinion and the media are most relevant to promotional pressure groups with limited funds; they see their role as educating the public. For example, the Child Poverty Action Group, formed in 1965 by left-wing academics Peter Townsend and Brian Abel-Smith. It is a pressure group for the poor rather than one of the poor, the poor are often too inarticulate and disorganised to lobby. Shelter was formed in 1966 to raise funds for the homeless and publicise problems. Their first director was Des Wilson who, with a flair for publicity, raised huge sums and influenced legislation. Shelter consistently opposed the sale of council houses.

Promotional groups concentrate on finding sympathetic individual MPs to promote private members bills as in the 1960s on divorce, abortion and capital punishment. They do not concentrate on lobbying the executive.

In the USA private citizens' lobbies such as Mothers Against Drunken Drivers (MADD) clearly cannot be categorised as liberal or conservative. Such groups tend to lack political power because they have no leverage, they cannot threaten to strike or refuse to invest capital, if their demands are not granted. Cause groups tend to rely on publicity and propaganda campaigns, leafleting, petitions, demonstrations, letter writing, 'lobbying' Congressmen etc. Moral Majority pioneered direct mailing techniques, whereby likely sympathisers are targeted and then solicited for support. British pressure groups and political parties are now adopting such methods.

Insider and Outsider Groups

The British commentator Wyn Grant argues that the sectional/promotional typology is inadequate because all pressure groups can be seen as self interested and sectional whilst all will present their demands as being in the national interest.

Grant argues that it needs to be replaced by an insider/outsider categorisation which emphasises the access/lack of access to the executive. The 20th century political system saw a gradual shift in power from the legislature to the executive. Parliament is no longer as important in the decision-making process as it was in the 19th/early 20th century. Decisions are taken by Ministers on the advice of civil servants and then presented to Parliament for approval leading to the suggestion that **Parliament has less influence over policy than pressure groups do.**

The corporatist tendency saw Parliament decline in influence as the insider producer groups grew in influence. Ministers are protected from too much pressure by civil servants who control the flow of information - this makes the civil service itself a target for pressure. Civil service neutrality means they should not act in an openly political way but, as they provide information for Ministers, they inevitably have an effect on policy so pressure groups often develop links with the permanent civil service. New Right theorists see this as an aspect of the bureaucratic over supply model, civil servants seek to expand budgets and use pressure groups to argue the case for more funding. This is supposedly particularly true of welfare where client groups such as the BMA, the nursing unions and the Royal Colleges are said to demand more resources for welfare bureaucracies.

Insider groups are those with regular access to the executive; outsider groups either lack, as in the case of Trade Unions after 1979, or do not desire for ideological reasons, as in the case of Greenpeace, to have such access.

The insider outsider typology is less applicable to the USA because of the separation of powers.

Corporatist Tendencies

Keith Middlemas has traced the history of "incorporation", the process whereby pressure groups as well as political parties are involved in policy making. They do not simply supply information but actively engage in policy formation. Middlemas discusses the UK but in fact corporatist tendencies are far more prevalent in Scandinavia and continental Europe, particularly the Catholic societies where it is part of Christian Democracy's concern with the social market.

For roughly 30 years after the war consultation with leading pressure groups, particularly the powerful producer groups - the unions and the employers organisations - was assumed to lead to stability, efficiency and better government. Such attempts at bargaining were not always successful, occasionally the relationship broke down as in 1968-69 over Labour's attempt to reform the unions and again in February 1974 with the miners strike. Heath argued that 'the challenge is to the will of parliament and a democratically elected government'. However the incorporation of such groups into the policy-making process was a key feature of the post-war consensus. Whereas under pluralism the state is detached under any form of corporatist arrangement the state takes a more active, regulatory role.

Britain never became fully corporatist which implies the abolition of Parliament, authoritarian corporatism or corporatism from above. What Britain did experience was a drift towards corporatism, liberal corporatism or corporatism from below.

Chapter Six

The Rejection of Corporatism

Thatcherism was a rejection not only of consensus, but also of corporatism which gave the big producer groups too much power. Commentators such as Mancur Olson criticised corporatist tendencies as "pluralist stagnation". However other writers such as Schmitter cite the examples of the most successful European nations such as Germany, Sweden and Austria all of which have some form of corporatist arrangement or social market economy. Britain is therefore unusual in that, after 1979, the Government has firmly rejected any such deals.

Ardent monetarists argue that wage settlements do not cause inflation; only an increase in the money supply can do that, if firms pay wages higher than they can afford then they go bankrupt. Conservative Governments after 1979 avoided any form of incomes policy. However, in practice, all governments operate an incomes policy in the public sector where they are the paymaster and even regarding the private sector there is concern that high wage settlements n companies such as Ford will be inflationary.

When asked in November 1990 what he thought was Thatcher's greatest achievement Dr David Owen replied 'taming the unions'. Three governments Wilson, Heath, Callaghan - had allegedly fallen victims to union power. Yet Thatcher was able to confront the unions and render them less powerful than at any stage since the 1930s. Membership has fallen by about 20% since 1979, millions of union members voted Conservative in the 1980s and 1992, no major strike of the last 17 years was successful and several key unions were defeated - most notably the Miners in 1984/85 and the printers in 1986/87.

There is supposedly a new mood of co-operation on the shop floor; management now manages and the unions are supposed to be more realistic about wages and new technology. Union membership was actually banned at GCHQ in 1984. The unions are even voluntarily reducing their influence in the Labour Party.

New Labour have not repealed the Thatcher government's union laws and in 1989 Labour even decided to oppose the closed shop. The whole drift towards corporatism has been reversed; indeed, one criticism of Thatcherism is that the government did not listen enough to either side of industry - unions or employers. The government appeared to be far more interested in the views of the City and groups such as the Institute of Directors and Think Tanks such as the Adam Smith Institute and the Institute for Economic Affairs than in those of the CBI let alone the TUC.

What accounts for this turn-around? There are two possible answers to the question; mass unemployment or law. With Monetarism came rapidly-rising unemployment; by 1981 it had trebled to approximately three million, a level not seen since the 1930s. Mass unemployment weakened the unions, militancy subsided as workers were afraid to strike as too high a wage claim would cost them their jobs Thatcher intuitively understood that essentially unemployment affects the unemployed, inflation affects everyone and loses more votes than unemployment.

The Thatcher government's union legislation was certainly an improvement on Heath's 1971 Industrial Relations Act. His approach was to introduce one all-embracing statute; her's was to go slowly, slowly, gradually curbing union power. The combined result is that picketing has been restricted, closed shops are harder to establish; unions were made liable for officials calling unlawful industrial action and employers permitted to dismiss strikers even if a dispute is legal; it is compulsory for all members of a union executive to be elected by secret ballot at least every five years and all political funds are to be approved in a ballot. Most importantly strikes must be preceded by a ballot or the union risks sequestration of its funds. If one agrees with the left this has all 'castrated' the unions; if one agrees with the right it has **'given the unions back to their members'**.

During the Miners' Strike of 1984/85, the union asked fellow workers to support them. In the end, the union could not even get all the miners to come out on strike let alone other workers.

Why does it matter whether it was mass unemployment or the union legislation which weakened the unions? Because if the unions have only been cowed as a result of unemployment then the supposed change in attitudes among union leaders and members is an illusion and if unemployment falls then union power will reassert itself. If however unions have changed their approach because of the law, and if the Labour government keeps those laws then the change in industrial relations is real and permanent.

The Delors inspired Social Chapter of the Maastricht Treaty proved anathema to the Conservatives who say that state regulation of worker's rights imposes costs on industry. The reason that the UK has so much inward investment from Japan and South Korea is that we now have flexible labour markets. Thatcher said in a keynote speech in Bruges in 1988 that she had not spent 9 years rolling back the frontiers of the state in Britain only to see them re-imposed by a Brussels corporatist bureaucracy and on that issue Major was in full agreement. However within days of their victory the Labour government signed the Social Chapter.

Despite this Democratic Audit points out that 'the UK lags behind the rest of the EU in trade union rights, limitation on hours worked, maternity provision, equal pay for women and other employment practices. Trade unionists do not have a basic right to strike safe from reprisals.' The strike by fire fighters in 2002/03 led the Labour government to call for the removal of the right to strike by such groups.

Agricultural Groups

An example of a powerful insider group with regular access to the British government is the National Farmers Union. It has achieved an almost unique position of power. The NFU always claimed to be a neutral body not linked to any political party but inevitably it has closer ties to the Conservatives. However, it was the Labour government which enshrined the NFU's position by legislation in the 1947 Agriculture Act. According to this, the NFU should be consulted and play an active role in formulating policy.

There are no serious party divisions on agricultural policy as the BSE case has shown, all the parties want to defend the farming community and are disagreeing simply about how best to do so and who should bear the cost, the EU or the British taxpayer.

It is wrong to see the lobby as homogeneous when in fact there are internal divisions such as that between dairy and pastoral farmers or between organic farming and agro-business. The BSE scare reveals the growing power of consumers which is likely to intensify as public awareness of the 'politics of food' grows. The Health Minister Stephen Dorrel was able to seize the initiative from the Agriculture Minister Douglas Hogg. However despite these trends it is difficult to see how any pressure group could obtain a greater level of influence than the NFU. Its Central Information Division for public relations and regular publications lead to a good press. It is a member of the CBI and has a professionalism envied by most pressure groups and as recently as the salmonella in eggs scare of 1988 it was able to demand Currie's resignation for threatening the interests of farmers even though what she said appears to have been correct.

The agricultural lobby has also had a traditionally advantaged role in US politics. At least since the New Deal, US administrations have taken very seriously the views of the Farm Bureau and the American Grange. Reagan dropped Carter's grain embargo on the USSR because of the pressure from the Mid-West pro-Republican Farm Lobby. Grant argues that the agricultural lobby has lost influence in recent years, in the UK as it has in the USA.

Business Groups

The media focus on the power of trade unions, the power of financial interests, the City, banks, insurance companies and pension funds is less direct and less publicised but that power is undoubtedly far more significant. It always was, even before 1979 when the unions had some clout but now the disparity is even greater. The importance of invisible exports and the dire implications of runs on the £ as happened between 1974 and 1977 mean that no government can ignore the interests of the financial sector. This is what the elite pluralist Charles Lindblom means when he talks of the **privileged position of the business sector.**

The Labour left believe that it was the financial interests which forced the Callaghan government to accept the terms of the IMF in 1976. Since then such interests have grown even stronger with the abolition of exchange controls so that 'Keynesianism in one country' is now effectively impossible as the French Socialists discovered in 1983. That is why New Labour is so anxious to reassure the City otherwise it will switch capital abroad thereby provoking a sterling crisis. If Labour signs Britain up for a single currency then the freedom of action of a Labour Chancellor will be very limited which may well please the City but infuriate the Labour left because it could be deflationary and lead to higher unemployment.

The most powerful groups in the US tend to be the giant corporations such as IBM, ITT, General Motors, Ford and Exxon which wield political power. It was alleged in the early 1970s that ITT had been involved in the overthrow of the Marxist Allende Government in Chile. The CIA supposedly did ITT's bidding. Other equally controversial incidents include the United Fruit Corporation's political role in Central America. Certainly some of these corporations are so vast their budgets rival those of some nation states.

New Social Movements

Traditional, mass parties as we have known them for over a hundred years appear to be declining and arguably a new style of politics is emerging as new social movements develop around such concerns as animal rights, sexual identities, consumer protection and the environment and the more traditional class based pressure groups decline. If class is losing its centrality to politics so that more and more the issues that concern people are lifestyle issues such as vegetarianism, or identity politics such as campaigns for the legalisation of homosexual marriage then the pressure groups that are developed are more likely to be New Social Movements which are less structured, more amorphous than traditional pressure groups. NSMs tend to be formed around issue of consumption and lifestyle such as the movements concerned with animal rights and conservation. In recent years it has been the anti-globalisation movement which has attracted huge interest.

Environmental Groups

Wyn Grant argues that Thatcherism rejected corporatism but, contrary to the accusations of the left, she did not reject pluralism. Some pressure groups, particularly producer interests, have lost influence, other groups, particularly consumer interests have gained influence. The green lobby, or at least the 'moderate' groups within it such as the Council for the Protection of Rural England has gained influence. This does not mean that green interests always prevail, the groups organising against the Newbury by-pass or the M11 are clearly seen as beyond the pale, ideological outsider groups. The Major government was disappointed when Shell backed down over the Brent Spa issue. The new concern for environmental issues was reflected in the Greens' electoral breakthrough. They achieved 15% in the Euro-elections of 1989 although they have fallen back since and some refer to the 'stalled greening of British politics'.

Greenpeace presents a petition in the European Parliament

Environmental groups such as Greenpeace have flourished in some countries. Green politics does not seem anything like as far advanced in the UK or the USA, as it is in Germany. There has been a backlash against green concerns as they have been seen as increasing costs and standing in the way of economic growth. Reagan cut the funds for the EPA. Bush claimed to be concerned about green issues but he was opposed to the Clean Air Act. In Britain, the recession and the 'greening' of the main parties, as well as internal divisions, have weakened green groups in recent years.

However there has been an increased awareness of environmental concerns and this is presumably a lasting change. Colin Ward (an anarchist) claims that there are about 5 million members of green groups in the UK and the polling organisation MORI classified 40% of British adults as green consumers.

The American Sierra Club is one of the oldest 'green' pressure groups in the world and even in the last century the Congress was taking action to preserve the environment. The issue seemed to spring to life in the 1960s at the same time as the anti-war movement and the women's movement. The Environmental Protection Agency was created in 1972 and the energy crisis of the 1970s focused attention on non-renewable resources. Yet Waldstein talks of the failure of green movements in the USA with a survey of 1990 showing that voters ranked it as well down their list of concerns. Bush did not even attend the Rio summit in 1992 and George W. Bush rejected Kyoto.

The Energy Crisis

Carter's Energy Bill was a response to the OPEC energy crisis induced by OPEC's quadrupling of oil prices In 1974. Carter told the American public that the energy crisis was 'the moral equivalent of war'. His Bill would have introduced new taxes on oil and the revenue from them would have financed exploration into alternative energy sources, energy conservation schemes and so on.

The Bill was torn to shreds in what Godfrey Hodgson described as 'the heaviest lobbying ever seen on Capitol Hill'. The oil and car lobbies - both incredibly powerful - put pressure on Congressmen to reject the bill. The counter lobby, of conservationists and others favouring reduced oil consumption, stood little chance of success. His defeat on this issue marked one of Carter's greatest domestic failures.

Animal Rights

In exactly the same way as environmental concerns have become mainstream so has concern over animal rights, indeed 'The Economist' argued that this has emerged as the most important New Social Movement in Britain. Whether it be research on animals, the export of live calves or the complex issues raised by the BSE problem these dilemmas are now very high up the political agenda. When the demonstrations against the export of live calves occurred in Brightlinsea it is estimated that one third of the town's population protested and a similar process took place at the other ports. It may well be that the police's use of the new powers given to them by the Criminal Justice Act of 1994 were counterproductive in that they provoked normally 'law abiding' citizens into action.

Again some of the groups involved, such as the Animal Liberation Front are ideological outsider groups whilst the RSPCA is an insider group and Compassion in World Farming which had been campaigning on similar issues for years without getting much attention and then suddenly found its message taken seriously by the media is a relatively 'moderate' group. Groups such as the Political Animal Lobby and the International Fund for Animal Welfare are funding sympathetic politicians in an attempt to lobby Parliament.

Iron Triangles and Issue Networks

As far back as the 1960s commentators such as J.L.Freeman were arguing that bureaucrats, Congressmen and interest groups operated through sub-governments. Cater talked of agency capture and Lowi stressed the triangular nature of the relationships, 'iron triangles'. Pluralists such as Heclo argues that although such triangles exist in general the more open issue networks predominate. Similarly McFarland argues that economic groups no longer prevail, their interests are countered by powerful forces and by an autonomous state. McKay uses the term issue network to denote something looser and wider than an iron triangle, a cluster of groups involved in the issue from the Congress, the Executive, the pressure groups but also the media and the research institutes.

The Military Industrial Complex

One of the most famous, or infamous, of iron triangles is the military industrial complex which Eisenhower warned Americans about in 1961. "We must guard against the acquisition of unwarranted influence by the military-industrial complex... in order to balance and to integrate these and other forces, new and old, within the principles of our democratic system."

Eisenhower's thesis was not particularly original - it had been stated much more persuasively several years earlier by C Wright Mills. However, coming from such an impeccably conservative source, Republican President, military background, the warning carried extra legitimacy.

Forty two years on from that speech the demands of the Pentagon have escalated to the point where the Reagan/Weinberger five years arms build-up involved expenditure of approximately $1 .6 trillion. The enormous expenditure on arms $360 billion in 2003, approximately 30% of the total federal budget means that defence spending emerges as a major macro-economic variable - 'military Keynesianism'.

Meanwhile, the American economy is plagued by the twin deficits, a budget deficit of about $200 billion a year and a trade deficit of about the same amount. The added irony is that much of the trade deficit (arguably a more serious structural economic problem than the more publicised budget deficit) is blamed on imports from America's allies, Japan, South Korea, Taiwan and Germany. Indeed, the protectionist mood which this endangered was a major issue in the 1996 Presidential election with Buchanan arguing that the USA should impose tariffs. Bush has imposed restrictions on steel imports. Allied with this is the growing isolationist sentiment and a resentment at the cost of defending Western Europe and Japan when there appears to be no significant threat now and when Europeans and Japanese themselves refuse to make the necessary sacrifices to pay for their own security.

If the military warlords are so entrenched in the American political system that they heavily influence or dictate foreign, domestic and defence policy, then clearly the notion of pluralism is a liberal democratic myth. It is one thing to state that the US is a global power, another to claim that the effective decision-makers in the US are military and corporate leaders. Similarly, the enormous defence expenditure has to be put into context, at around $360 billion, or approximately ten times the total British defence spending: it represents perhaps 10% of US GNP, approximately $3 trillion. Clinton was able to cut defence spending and reap the peace dividend, does that not show that the power of the military industrial complex is a myth? Bush increased defence spending after 9/11, was that due to the military industrial complex?

Pressure Groups

Other states also have some form of military industrial complex. Even Britain, a much weaker power, has such a complex and all attempts at reducing defence spending incur its opposition. Clearly the precise form of the military industrial complex varies from state to state.

Of course in democracies military industrial complexes face countervailing pressures, in particular from peace movements of which the most famous is the British CND formed in 1958. It was and is a typical promotional pressure group, dependent on publicity and unsure whether to hitch its fortunes to one particular party, Labour, or to try to stay out of party politics and attempt to exercise a general influence. Its fortunes have waxed and waned with the Cold War. Membership rose as superpower tensions increased and fell as they eased. It was really an NSM, fluid and decentralised. By 1985 with the arrival of Gorbachev the so called second Cold War ended and CND once more disappeared, but it could of course come back as the massive anti-war protests in 2003 showed.

The American Trade Unions

The US labour movement with 18 million members is the biggest pressure group of all but it has never wielded commensurate political power. The biggest difference between the British labour movement and its American counterpart is that whilst the British unions have a structural, formal link with the Labour Party, the American unions are only loosely bound to the Democratic Party.

In the USA, the Democratic Party predated an organised union movement. The Democrats date back to the 1830s. The unions only really developed into mass organisations in the 1880s as the USA moved from a rural society to an industrial urbanised power. FDR and the New Deal gave a huge boost to the unions and they became one of the most important and reliable elements of the Democratic New Deal coalition. Their Democrat allies did not always give the unions what they wanted however, for instance Truman failed to stop the anti-union Taft-Hartley Act (1947). However in general, individual unions (such as the United Auto Workers) and the movement as a whole endorsed Democrat candidates for the Presidency and for Congress.

The AFL-CIO split over the Vietnam War. The AFL-CIO leader, Meany, supported the war. The UAW under Reuther broke away to take a more liberal anti-war, pro-Civil Rights stance. By the 1970s, the union-Democrat relationship was in disarray with the AFL-CIO refusing to endorse the liberal Democrat candidate George McGovern. The biggest union, the Teamsters, actually supported, Nixon.

By the late 1970s, the labor movement was in crisis as the Carter Presidency failed to deliver the reforms the unions wanted and, by 1980, they faced the anti-union Reagan Administration. Meanwhile recession and mass unemployment led to unions losing members. By 2003, union membership in the USA is down to 15% of the workforce and falling. In the Southern States it is even lower.

US unions remain huge pressure groups capable of mobilising millions of people but, millions more workers, particularly in the growth areas of the economy such as the service sector, remain unorganised. The decline of American parties, the growth of single issue pressure groups, such as Common Cause, the increased importance of primaries, have all served to diminish the union's political power. In the past, the AFL-CIO Leaders were "kingmakers" within the party. Now the nominee tends to be from outside their circle. The unions maintained a low profile in the 1992 nomination battles within the Democrat party and Clinton kept his distance in 1996. Gore was seen as possibly too close to the unions in 2000 and this may be true of Gephardt in 2004.

The Medical Industrial Complex

In the past medicine, broadly defined, was represented by the AMA but now as Frank Davis points out there are literally hundreds of groups involved in health care issues - ranging from health care providers such as the American Dental Association to patients groups such as Citizens Action, unions representing health care workers like the American Federation of State County and Municipal Employees, health insurance companies such as the National Association of Health Underwriters to other interested groups such as the Distilled Spirits Council. The professional medical group the AMA (American Medical Association) helped block Medicare and Medicaid for twenty years. They would have joined with many of the other groups in the medical industrial complex to mobilise the fight Clinton's health care proposals had he gone ahead with them. Some groups such as the unions would clearly have backed the plan but they could not have raised the same kind of money or political support. In July 1994 Hillary Clinton claimed 'we cannot surrender to the same interests that have de-railed health care reform in the past.' Five months later those same interests prevailed.

Pressure Group Funding of Parties in the UK

Party finance in Britain is a very complex topic and it is difficult to get accurate statistics. Declining membership as documented by Seyd and Whitely means the Conservatives become more dependent on business and individual donations and the Labour Party becomes more dependent on trade unions.

About 33% of Conservative revenue comes from the Constituency parties, the rest comes from business and individual donations. Business contributions have been declining; in 1974, 42 companies donated, by 1992 only 240 did so. In 1985 46% of all donations were made by companies but by 1992 this was down to 19%. Business donations have to be declared in company accounts but individual donations can remain anonymous hence the fuss about donations from wealthy foreign businessmen including Asil Nadir, Hong Kong shipping magnates and Serbian millionaires.

The Labour MP George Howarth has argued that the link between appointments to QUANGOs (Quasi Autonomous Non-Governmental Organisations) and contributions to the Tories revealed 'a sleazy picture of a government which appoints 'one of us', which in Major's era seems to be tested against financial donations to the Tory Party'. Nolan was not allowed to look at party funding despite Labour's urgings that he should.

The financial dependence of old Labour on trade unions was even greater, about 60% of Labour's money came from the trade unions. Trade union contributions come in two forms - the political levy and trade union sponsorship of candidates (they pay up to 80% of a candidate's election expenses). In 1979, they sponsored 165 candidates.

Blair has said that Labour will renounce such union sponsorship but Labour need to be careful about cutting links altogether and not just for the practical reasons of funding. Henry Drucker argues that whilst the doctrine of the party has mostly come from middle class socialists the **ethos** has come from the unions.

The problem of finance is even more acute for the Liberal Democrats. In 1976 the Houghton Committee examined the basis of party funding. He favoured a state grant to parties, as happens in other countries such as Germany, based on the level of their support at the previous election. He recommended about £21 million a year as a small price to pay for democracy. Opponents of the suggestion, such as the Conservatives, argued that it would reduce the activity of members and the level of membership. The Report was not implemented.

Lobbying

Lobbying of the Commons is not so well developed as in Congress although the number of public relations firms specialising in parliamentary activity is increasing which was, and is, one of Nolan's concerns. As Berry points out the lobbying of Parliament is nothing new but since 1979 'the lobby' has grown bigger and become more sophisticated leading to fears of a sleaze factor. By 1993 over 50 lobbying companies existed, with the largest such as Ian Greer Associates enjoying a huge turnover. By 1991, 384 MPs held over 500 directorships and 450 consultancies between them. One concern is that MPs become 'a commodity' for hire with Parliament as a 'marketplace'. This concern lay behind the cash for questions scandal in 1993 leading to the appointment of Nolan. Anthony King, a member of the Nolan Committee has commented on the committee's findings that the public hold politicians of all parties in very low regard, thus MPs must take care to improve their image. The Hamilton and Aitken cases were particularly damaging.

However as Alan Doig points out there is a difference between **advocacy** and **interest representation** and there were already safeguards even before Nolan, such as the Register of Members Interests introduced in 1974 after the Poulson scandal. The Nolan Report led to much tougher regulations. There is a proliferation of lobbyists at European level.

Political Action Committees

Corruption, although it undoubtedly exists, is not the main problem in the USA. The big worry, according to commentators such as Drew, is the rise of the PACs, especially business PACs, which tend to be pro-Republican. PACs are not a recent phenomena, the Congress of Industrial Organisations formed a PAC, the Committee on Political Education (COPE) as far back as 1941. However, the 1970s legislation led to their proliferation. In 1976 there were just 500 PACs; by 1983 there were 3,500. In the 1984 elections, the National Conservative Political Action Committee (NCPAC) spent $15 million promoting Republicans. COPE spent over $3 million supporting Mondale's campaign.

Drew is a Democrat who believes that the significance of 'big money' is corrupting democracy. Individual donations from 'fat cats' have been replaced by corporate donations but they have the same effect; they reinforce conservatism. The right-wing journalist Robert Samuelson disagrees; he points out that PACs' share of campaign expenditure is not as high as people imagine.

In 1982 they accounted for about 30% of the total raised by winning candidates. Individual fund-raising still accounts for the majority of the money raised. Herbert Alexander is also a Democrat but he disagrees with Drew; Alexander finds nothing sinister in the influence of the PACs.

In the 1980 elections, although the Republicans easily (as always) outspent the Democrats, the Democrats benefited more from PACs: $43 million as opposed to $36 million for the Republicans. One criticism of the PACs is that they tend to favour incumbents, particularly in House elections, regardless of party, because the incumbent is more likely to win. PACs have also had the effect of strengthening the Parties' National Committees, especially the Republican's. Thus, the PACs have probably had a tendency to reinforce the status quo and make it more difficult for third parties to break through.

Chapter Six

Is Britain Still Pluralist?

The Thatcher government was unusually resistant to pressure group demands. Even the non-Thatcherite Ministers such as Hurd and Clarke regarded much pressure group activity as at best an irritant at worst a pathology, producer interests were taking precedence over consumer interests. The government showed that it was prepared to confront even those groups previously regarded as pro-Conservative when it took on the BMA and other health service professionals over its health service reforms in 1988. As one BMA poster put it 'What do you call a man who does not listen to the advice of his doctors?' Answer Kenneth Clarke, the then Health Secretary. At about the same time the government was antagonising the barristers and the judges over its legal reforms and its traditional allies in the brewing industry over its attempts to weaken the oligopoly in the industry, although on this one the Tories backed down.

The failure to consult adequately was in evidence again with the Child Support Act where 90 pressure groups, such as the National Council for Single Parent Families, were given just six weeks in which to respond to government proposals. Even the police pressure groups, traditionally friendly to the Tories were antagonised by the Sheehy Inquiry into Police Responsibilities and Rewards launched in 1992. Sheehy, a businessman, reported in June 1993 advocating performance related pay. By October Howard had dropped significant sections of the Sheehy Report.

In some ways the 1990s saw a return to consensus but there was no return to corporatism. Pressure groups now operate in a very different environment from the 1970s. Baggot points out how even the unions have adapted to the change by for example using political lobbyists to argue their case against privatisation of the Post Office.

According to Rhodes and Marsh (from an extensive survey of the literature on the issue) there is no evidence of the existence in the UK of the broad issue networks that Heclo argues exist in the USA. In the UK policy networks are more exclusive, a limited number of groups, particularly producer groups other than trade unions and professional groups, enjoy privileged access. In their view if pluralism still lives on it is in a very different form from pre-1979.

The Changed Nature of US Pressure Groups

As McKay points out the nature of interest group activity in the USA has all but been transformed in the past 25 years with labor and agriculture groups declining in significance, business remaining extremely important and other groups emerging as important players in Washington politics. More than 70% of welfare and citizens groups in Washington in 1981 had come into existence since 1960. Hedrick Smith identified the proliferation of lobbyists as a key change in 'the power game'. In 1961 there were 365 lobbyists registered with Congress by 1987 there were 23,011. Heclo talks of 'the new political mobilisation' whilst Anthony King writes of a 'New American political system'. As Salisbury puts it (in the book edited by King) there is the paradox of more groups but less clout but then that is part of pluralism.

Pluralism Versus Elite Theory

The pluralist asserts that society is open and that individuals are free to form and join a variety of groups. The state is neutral and detached, it acts as an "honest broker", serving the government of the day whichever party wins office. No one group is dominant in the policy process, there is balance and equilibrium, although not equality. Although elections ensure that political parties represent the changing wishes of the people, pluralism calls for a more active engagement in the political process by the population. The **classical pluralists of the 1950s** believed that although an elite exists it is relatively open or open to competition. Real power lies with the political elite and is not "hidden behind the scenes" with some economic based power elite.

Dahl's 'Who Governs?' was a study of local politics in New Haven. He looked at 3 areas of decision-making - political nominations, educational policy and urban development. Over political nominations, there was an unequal power distribution. A small number of top party leaders made important nominations. However, no group was excluded and politicians still have to 'court' the electorate. Three groups influenced educational policies - education officers, teachers and parents. When it came to urban development the Mayor and development officer were the key figures.

They obtained the funds and organised advisory committees. Therefore, the power to decide was diffused. Decisions were a product of compromise.

Other studies by pluralists such as Rose showed that political and economic elites were independent of each other and that the American government often acted against the interests of economic groups. Hewitt did a study of 20 diverse policy decisions in British politics between 1944 and 1964 arguing that there was no evidence of a power elite or ruling class prevailing across the board. Similarly Marsh and Grant's study of the CBI showed that if anything it had more influence when Labour was in power than it did under the Tories.

By the 1970s with the resurgence of ideology and the breakdown of the post war consensus, acknowledgements of some faults in classical pluralism lead to the development of **elite pluralism**. Elite pluralists such as Galbraith, Dahl and Jordan and Richardson accept that business groups have much more influence than any other organised lobby and that not all members of society get involved in group activity but they remain pluralists because they claim that no one group dominates.

Pluralists such as Dahl looked at observable political processes - decision-making on issues. But what about the decisions that were not made, that were not on the agenda? The pluralist assumption is that people are aware of what is in their own best interests. However, the radical critic Steven Lukes argues that the most powerful groups are able to protect their interests by controlling how members of society conceptualise their interests. Through the **shaping of desires** critical attitudes to the most powerful groups never developed.

According to the elite pluralist Charles Lindblom's 'Politics and Markets', business is in a 'privileged position' in a capitalist economy. Governments take notice of business whether or not business organises as a pressure group. Because pluralists concentrate on overt interest group activity, the privileged position of business is not apparent. Marxists believe that the state needs to appear autonomous in order to disguise the fact that they are representing the ruling class. Pluralism thus ignores the power of 'non-decision-making', it examines the process of decision-making rather than the results of it. From a Marxist perspective, public opinion consensus represents false class consciousness.

Pressure groups exist in all societies, capitalist or communist, traditional or modern. They are a necessary part of what Marxists refer to as 'civil society'. However, pressure groups obviously have more impact in pluralist, industrial or post-industrial societies than in closed or traditional societies. Generally speaking the more affluent a nation, the more educated, articulate and politically literate its citizens, the greater the scope for pressure group activity, particularly if the political system allows for a number of 'access points' where groups can apply pressure.

Although both Britain and America are pluralist societies, pressure groups seem to have more influence in the USA than they do in the UK. Partly this is due to **structural** factors caused by the different governmental systems; partly it is due to **social** factors caused by the different approaches citizens have to politics and to those who wield power.

The existence of federalism provides a greater number of 'access points'; the weakness of the party system means that politicians are looking for support from organised groups rather than, as in Britain, from the party leadership; the importance of finance in election campaigns provides an opening for pressure group influence at the grassroots of American politics. The influence of lobbyists on Capitol Hill, and the state legislatures, is held by some critics to be all pervasive.

The USA is probably the foremost example of a pluralist society. Citizens are allowed to form pressure groups, vote for a variety of competing parties, read a free press, practice the religion of their choice, and protest against government policy. It is a liberal democratic society in which, as Professor Finer points out, the sheer diversity of ethnic, racial and religious groups makes pressure groups an inevitable aspect of the political process. Far from posing a threat to the democratic ethos, pressure groups complement political parties and allow citizens to take a more active part in public affairs.

Such a complacent view of pressure group activity is challenged by radicals such as C Wright Mill's and Bachrach and Baratz who argue that pluralism is a myth. According to them, power is concentrated in the capitalist elite anatomised by Domhoff. Thus there is a long running debate between pluralist theorists such as Dahl and Galbraith and elite theorists such as Mills, and his followers.

It is unwise to generalise about pressure groups. On occasion, groups have promoted social reform and contributed greatly to the democratic process. The National Association for the Advancement of Coloured People (NAACP) was instrumental in the Brown Board of Education (1954) case. Whilst all groups are free to campaign both in Washington and in the State capitals, clearly the richer groups have more access to decision makers. A corporation such as Ford can employ full-time lobbyists, whereas poorer sections of society lack the resources to mount effective campaigns. Given the nature of the American political system with its various access points, it is relatively easy for groups to block change; it is much harder to promote change. If a pressure group such as the National Rifle Association wanted to block a law or constitutional amendment, it can put pressure on a variety of points - the Senate, the Representatives, the State Assemblies, even the Supreme Court.

The long running dispute between radicals and liberals, as to the nature of Western pluralism will not be resolved because essentially it is a political, not an academic argument. To Marxists it is self evident that in a capitalist society elite groups such as businessman, big land owners, press magnates, military leaders and so on will use their wealth and influence to manipulate the political system in the interest of capital. Elite pluralists though, argue that whilst it is true that such groups wield real power, they do not monopolise it and a system based on political equality can help reduce, though not eradicate, the degree of economic inequality.

A Comparison of Pressure Groups in the UK and USA

UK

1.Fusion of powers leads to a concentration of power in the Executive so that pressure groups focus on Whitehall, hence the notion of insider groups such as the City

2. An uncodified constitution means that pressure group rights are not guaranteed, they can be taken away as in the ban on unions at GCHQ in 1984 or the Criminal Justice Act of 1994 which severely limits freedom of assembly.

USA

Separation of powers means that pressure groups have to lobby all three branches of government if they wish to get something done. They must persuade both houses of Congress; there is no equivalent of the Parliament Act. They must persuade the President because his approval is not automatic, they may even need to lobby the courts - amicus curaie - as in Brown v Board or Roe v Wade

If a group is trying to block something then it is much easier; they need only persuade a key committee, or enough Senators for a filibuster.

2. A codified constitution means that group rights are, at least in theory, guaranteed. A ban on unions or a restriction of freedom of assembly would be ruled unconstitutional under the 1st Amendment.

To change the constitution is enormously difficult. A pressure group wishing to block such a change need only persuade 34

Senators; thus any attempt at repealing the 2nd Amendment would see the NRA lobby the Congress. It is the same in reverse, a pressure group wishing to change the Constitution has a much harder job so that when NOW tried to get ERA through it failed to get enough support

3. A unitary state means that all legal power flows from Parliament therefore there is relatively little pressure group activity at local level; even with education which is the most expensive local government function, policy is decided nationally.

3. Federalism means that states have rights which are guaranteed by the constitution and therefore much - most - pressure group activity is at state/local level e.g. education is a state concern.

4. British politics is party politics, British government is party government. Britain has a strong party system, the parties are centralised and ideological. Funding of election campaigns is mostly done through the parties and pressure group influence, although real, is restricted. The Conservatives are not formally linked to business groups, TUs are structurally linked to Labour although even here Blair is weakening the links

4. The US has a relatively weak party system in that her parties are decentralised and supposedly non-ideological increasing the scope for pressure group influence. This was always the case but became more so following the passage of FECA in 1974, so that in the 'New Congress' there were a multiplicity of lobbyists. PACs help fund election expenses and can exert influence over policy to the point where some commentators have suggested they are replacing parties

5. A relatively closed system of government, where by much of the work of the executive is secret through the 30 Year Rule and the OSA. Finer said this means that much group activity takes place behind closed doors - particularly insider groups - and is therefore less accountable.

5. A more open system of government with the 1st Amendment (freedom of the press) giving the media more protection - Pentagon Papers case 1971, Sullivan v N.Y.T. 1964, a Freedom of Information Act 1974, and Congressional committees protected by the 'sunshine laws' of the early 1970s. All mean that pressure group activity is more exposed to publicity. Finer stresses that this does not make them more powerful; it makes the system more pluralist.

6. Even now the UK, a relatively small country has a fairly homogeneous society, 93% white, the vast majority Christian, which means that the most important social cleavage is class rather than race, region or religion.

6. A vast country, the size of a continent. This means that regional differences are huge. A 'nation of immigrants'; leads to important divides along ethnic and religious lines so that 'race, region and religion' are said to be more important social divisions than class. Regionalism has declined with the breakdown of the 'solid South' and class is clearly more divisive than the myth of the 'American Dream' implies - but even so it is true that society is pluralist, and that the divisions are reflected in terms of pressure group activity e.g. the NAACP, AIPAC, the Irish lobby the Italian community etc.

Pluralism is a relative concept. The UK and the USA are both much more pluralist than China but still it is possible to see the USA as a better example of a pluralist political system and a pluralist society for the reasons cited above, hence Lijphardt's description of the UK as a 'majoritarian' system.

Chapter 7
Political Parties

Political Parties

According to Scruton 'Parties are voluntary associations of individuals united for common political purposes, some of whom pledge support, some of whom run for election and some of whom will take office in government if the party is successful'.

Parties in the modern sense emerged with the enfranchisement of the masses at the end of the C19th century. Parties in liberal democracies have played a variety of roles. They aggregate interests, they provide a channel of communication between the citizens and the government, they offer citizens an ideological choice, they help staff the administration. Parties in totalitarian regimes play a very different role.

Two-Party Systems?

In contrast to the multi-party systems of Western Europe, Britain and the USA have tended to have two dominant parties. Maurice Duverger, in his book 'Political Parties' (1954), argued that 'first past the post' electoral systems tend to favour a two-party system, whereas Proportional Representation promotes multi-partyism.

Britain

The usual way of characterising British politics is that it has a two party system in which power tends to alternate between the two major parties, Labour and Conservative. This is partly a product of the electoral system and partly because of the importance of class as a basis of party support. In the 1920s the Labour Party replaced the Liberals as the main opposition to the Tories and Labour has alternated with the Conservatives ever since.

Thirty or forty years ago Britain had an almost exclusively two-party Commons which faithfully represented an almost two-party nation. However, the two party system or duopoly is not as strong as it used to be. At almost every election from 1951 to 1983 the proportion of total vote taken by the two major parties declined and has only recovered slightly since 1983. However, because of the way the electoral system works, this decline in their share of the votes has not really been matched by a fall in their share of the seats. The main victims were and are the Liberal Democrats. (See chapter on electoral systems for details)

The USA

US parties are always described as much weaker than British parties but if they are so weak why has the system been dominated by the same two parties for about 150 years? The operation of the Electoral College mechanism, with the need for an absolute majority of 270 votes, has certainly benefited the two major parties. However, the failure of third-parties in America owes more to the adaptability of the two major parties and their ability to assimilate smaller parties, than it does to institutional factors such as the electoral system.

Actually two-party hegemony is much more apparent in America than in Britain. The Republican/Democrat stranglehold on American politics has endured since the 1850s and has been much firmer than either the 19th century Liberal versus Tory or 20th century Labour versus Tory duopoly. The third parties which have emerged in the USA, (such as the Populists in the 1890s and the Progressives in the first decades of the 20th century) have tended to be absorbed by either the Democrats or the Republicans. Conversely, breakaways from the two main parties (such as the 'Dixiecrats' in 1948 or the American Independent Party in 1968) have within a few years returned to the mainstream of the party.

There have been third parties which did remain aloof from the two main movements, such as the Prohibitionist Party or the Communists, but they have been even less successful than the breakaways. At no time in the last century and a quarter has a third party seriously challenged for power. The Civil Rights' movement of the 1960s, the most effective challenge to traditional politics since 1945, was incorporated into the Democratic Party. Perhaps the effectiveness of two- party domination in America helps explain the strength of cause groups.

Realising the difficulties involved in challenging the two parties, campaigners turn to pressure groups instead. Certainly the Democratic Party takes more notice of groups such as the National Organisation for Woman (NOW) or the National Association for the Advancement of Coloured People (NAACP) than it would of a splinter 'Rainbow' group, such as has been advocated by Angela Davis and some other black leaders. Jesse Jackson faces the same problem as faced George Wallace in 1968, John Anderson in 1980 and Ross Perot in 1992, the difficulty of breaking through the two-party domination of American politics. It is only partly caused by institutional factors, such as the voting system. It owes more to the all-embracing, non-ideological nature of the two main parties.

The Post-War Consensus in the UK

Both major parties in the UK are very broad coalitions containing people of widely divergent views. The Labour Party has always included democratic socialists on the left, believing in nationalisation and a radical redistribution of wealth as well as social democrats on the centre and right of the party who wish to make a success of the mixed economy, are doubtful of the value of public ownership and would accept merely a limited redistribution of wealth. **The majority of party members have been democratic socialists, but the party leadership has been dominated by right wing social democrats.** Like all ideologies it is not easy to define socialism with any precision. As Herbert Morrison once memorably remarked 'socialism is what Labour governments do'. Anthony Crosland said that we should not waste our time scouring the dictionaries looking for a definition of socialism because there is no one definition that will be universally accepted. Tony Wright entitles his book on the subject 'Socialisms' precisely because he wants to emphasise the plurality of approaches and traditions.

The Conservatives have simultaneously been the paternalist, One Nation, party which embraced state intervention and yet at the same time the party of free marketeers. The party of Peel promoted free trade through the reductions in tariffs in the 1820s and the repeal of the Corn Laws in 1846. It promoted social reform in the 1860s and 1870s under Disraeli but then seemed to become more reactionary after the 1880s under Salisbury who believed that often the best thing government could do was leave problems alone for fear of making them worse. The Conservatives under Balfour and Law opposed the social reforms of pre-1914 with Cecil arguing that pensions and the dole would weaken self reliance but in the 1920s and 1930s under Baldwin and Neville Chamberlain it followed what Martin Pugh has called a more populist conservatism.

For the 20 to 30 years after WW2, there appeared to be a consensus over both policy and procedure. Kavanagh argues that the consensus over domestic policy had the following features: a commitment to full employment to be achieved through Keynesian policy; support for the mixed economy, part private, part public corporations such as the National Coal Board; a welfare state based on the 1942 Beveridge Report; finally, a willingness on the part of government to consult leading pressure groups over policy-making and policy-implementation. Unemployment averaged just 1.8% through the 1950s/60s.

The post-war Labour Government introduced a whole series of measures - nationalisation, welfare, independence for the colonies, creation of NATO, creation of an independent nuclear deterrent - which built on the work of the war-time Coalition and laid the foundations for post-war politics. To Eric Hobsbawm 'being the only Labour Government so far which was not patently disappointing, it has acquired a mythical halo in retrospect." However for David Coates "The Labour Government had merely created a system of "welfare capitalism" in which the concentration of capital and economic privilege remained". Certainly Attlee's reforms owed little to socialist doctrine. 1945 to 1951 completed the process begun in 1906 by the Liberals and owed as much to Keynes and Beveridge as to socialism.

Ideologues such as Hayek, later on a key figure for the 'New Right', might argue that Attlee's Labourism had proven the point of his 1944 warning that state intervention was 'The Road to Serfdom' but it was not the free market Toryism of the 1930s that was to appeal to voters it was a more interventionist Conservatism, prepared to accept most of the post-war settlement based on welfare and managerial capitalism. It was helped in this by the affluence of the period which allowed western governments to use the fiscal dividend of growth to finance welfare programmes without raising taxes.

Even though the Conservatives disputed the details, they tended to accept the basic principles and modify their free-market ideals in favour of the mixed economy. After 1945 the party came under the influence of younger Tories such as Butler who used the opportunity of opposition to rethink the party's philosophy via the Industrial Charter of 1947. By the 1950s it was able to compete - successfully - with Labour as the party which would best manage welfare capitalism.

Labour also modified its stance. Anthony Crosland in 'The Future of Socialism' (1956) argued that post-scarcity capitalism had resolved the problems of 'primary poverty' and unemployment. Class warfare and socialist revolution were no longer needed. Crosland judged nationalisation to be a relatively unimportant means of achieving economic planning and social justice. It was an attempt to revise Labour ideology in the light of post-war conditions and it attracted scorn from the left because it seemed to abandon some socialist doctrines.

Ideological conflicts had been displaced by a squabble about effective administration of an undisputed socio-economic system, politics was about pragmatism rather than ideology. Of course there were exceptions such as the Suez Crisis of 1956 which spilt the country but in the early 1950s, the economic policies of both parties were so similar that commentators coined the term 'Butskellism' - a synthesis of R.A.Butler (the Conservative Chancellor) and Gaitskell (his Labour predecessor and Shadow Chancellor).

In this period, leaders and PM's tended to come from the 'centre' of their party, such as Eden who was much more concerned with foreign policy than with domestic considerations, and as with Churchill had absolutely no desire to provoke social conflict by attempting to unravel the social contract created in the 1940s.

There was little prospect of domestic disharmony under Macmillan, 'the high priest of consensus'. By 1958 some of Macmillan's colleagues were anxious to restrain public spending but he believed his job was to manage decline and avoid damaging social division, if that meant maintaining relatively high levels of state spending then it was a price worth paying.

The paradox of the 1950s is that it combined an unprecedented degree of affluence with a growing awareness of relative economic decline. The Thatcherites were to look back to the 1950s, particularly Macmillan's government, when harsh, difficult decisions were avoided, as the time when the seeds of decline were really sown. Those Tories who stood out against 'noblesse oblige' style policies at the time, such as the entire Treasury team which resigned in 1958, have subsequently been lauded as proto-Thatcherites.

The British consensus has to be seen in world-wide perspective, particularly against the background of the long post-war boom of 1948/73 which even the relatively weak British economy benefited from; the rejection and discrediting of 'ideology' which, in the wake of Hitler and Stalin, was equated with extremism so that by 1960 there was talk of 'an end of ideology'.

Gaitskell had formally lost the battle to "revise" Labour, as Crosland had suggested, along the lines of the West German S.P.D. after their Bad Godesberg programme of 1959. However the reality under Wilson was that the party downplayed democratic socialism in favour of social democracy. McKie and Cook argue that the 1964 election 'was less between competing philosophies; much more about which set of managers was likely to get best results.' Labour appeared to be much more in tune with the modernising, progressive 'spirit of the times', capturing the mood by offering a modernising programme promising 'the white hot heat of a technological revolution'. The vagueness and lack of detail was compensated for by Labour's success in winning over the lower middle class and Wilson's personal triumph in copying Kennedy.

Labour went on to win the general election of 1964 and to be in power for 11 out of the following 15 years. Wilson's compromises over domestic policy combined with the attempt to reform the unions led to growing left-wing disillusionment and opposition. The failure of the Department of Economic Affairs to seriously challenge the Treasury (an issue now brought back to life by Gordon Brown's insistence on a bigger role for the Treasury); the failure of the National Plan to achieve its targets; the refusal to devalue until it was unavoidable; the failure of the reforms of the Lords, the Commons, local government, the civil service and the trade unions all caused disillusion. In addition Wilson's support for US involvement in Vietnam enraged the so called "New Left".

Although there were worthwhile achievements particularly in the areas of social policy and private morality the governments of 1964 to 1970 "appear empty and rudderless." For Miliband the Labour Government's unimpressive record between 1964 and 1970 can be traced back to the fact that the revisionists had really won the battle. Although not all of the opposition to Wilson's vacuity came from the left (Crosland for example was very frustrated by the lack of direction) the party seemed to divide as though the right had betrayed it. After 1970 the party moved to the left as its leading right wingers moved to the right.

The Resurgence of Ideology

Already by the late 1960s with a 'resurgence of ideology' across the West, the British consensus was beginning to fragment. The 'New Left' incorporated the Civil Rights, Black Power, Women's Liberation, student power and anti-Vietnam movements of the 1960s and 1970s, showing that ideology and conflict could not be excluded from politics for ever.

The student activism of 1968 was accompanied by the emergence of movements to liberate groups oppressed on the basis of sexuality. Radical protests in the 1960s provoked an authoritarian recoil from the alleged moral indiscipline and hedonistic frivolity of the new 'permissiveness'. Conservatives, such as Mary Whitehouse, emphasised the importance of self-restraint, decency, propriety, respectability, deference and discipline, 'law and order' and patriotism.

In June 1970 the Conservatives under Heath won a surprise victory. On January 1st 1973 the Government took the UK into what was then called the EEC. However in terms of economic policy by 1971 there was unemployment of around a million so the government reflated and tried to get a deal with the unions through the 'Chequers talks'. When this attempt broke down a statutory prices and incomes policy was introduced. Thus by 1972 Heath had largely abandoned the free market Selsdon Programme on which he had campaigned in 1970. Local government reform, decimalisation, the Industrial Relations Act all aroused opposition. By 1973/74 the miners were challenging the incomes policy and Heath felt he had no option but to call an election.

By February 1974 facing a miners strike which had led to a 'three day week' Heath called the **'Who Governs'** election and lost to Labour. In the early 1970s the Labour Party had moved to the left under the influence in particular of Tony Benn and Labour in opposition had worked out a 'social contract' with the unions. A left-wing economic strategy worked out by Stuart Holland and Tony Benn involved more nationalisation, planning agreements and workers control. It was embodied in Labour Programme 1973 "which makes possible a democratic transition to socialism in this country'. Its 1974 manifesto promised **'a fundamental and irreversible shift in the balance of wealth and power in favour of working people and their families.'**

In office the minority Labour government jettisoned its left wing policies. In autumn 1976, as a result of a sterling crisis, the government had to ask the IMF for a massive loan. Callaghan and Healey, against the wishes of the left, accepted their terms - the introduction of strict monetary targets, cuts in public spending and deflation. By 1977, Labour had become a Minority Government again. It was able to hold on to office, partly through the **Lib-Lab Pact.**

By 1978, with inflation down, the Callaghan Government appeared poised to call an election - which they may well have won. However, instead of calling an election in autumn 1978, Callaghan and Healey asked union leaders for one more year of wage restraint. The result was strikes throughout the private and public sectors.

By spring 1979 following the **'Winter of Discontent'** which had sapped the Government's authority and the rejection of the Devolution proposals in the Referendums in Scotland and Wales on March 1st 1979, the Conservative Opposition called a vote of no confidence in the Government. The Government lost by just one vote. By convention if a Government loses a confidence vote there has to be an election.

At the 1979 election, Labour had a 12 point lead on prices and unemployment but the Conservatives had a 15 point lead on the issue of strikes reflecting public support for Thatcher's promise to 'take on' the unions. The unions appeared as sectional, selfish, almost syndicalist, bodies threatening vital public services and maybe even Parliamentary democracy itself. The Tories also had a lead of 61 points on taxes - in 1979 the highest rate on earned income was 83%, the standard rate had risen at one stage to 35%. Thatcherism stressed the need for tax cuts and incentives. Polls showed resentment even among average income earners at what were seen as high taxes financing welfare.

With a resurgence of the 'troubles' in Ulster in 1969, increased racial tension, and a painful and growing awareness of Britain's relative economic decline, there was by the 1970s little of the complacent self-congratulatory talk of the 1950s. Instead, there was talk of 'Elective Dictatorship', 'overload' and the 'ungovernability of Britain'. Samuel Beer was no longer talking of consensus but of 'Britain Against Itself'.

Wilson, Heath and Callaghan's governments had witnessed failure over the economy, 'U turns' over income policy and Europe, the final flowering and then decline of the corporatist consensus and a general awareness that 'Butskellism' had 'failed'. This paved the way for intensified ideological conflict in the early 1980s. Marquand argues that the free market conservatism of the 1980s provoked Labour in to adopting Bennism.

Thatcherism revived the ideal of free market capitalism. This rejection of the 'all embracing dominance of socialism', what Thatcher had seen as the 'socialist ratchet effect', meant Conservative withdrawal from the commitment of successive post-war governments to plan and spend for full employment, social justice and, in limited measure, equality. Unfettered capitalism coupled with social authoritarianism was the new credo.

The Shift to the Right

The New Right is the collective name for the political theorists and practitioners who emerged on both sides of the Atlantic in the early 1970s and went on to become the dominant political force over the next two decades. The New Right was a diverse set of people and ideas, some of whom sat very uneasily together. In the USA the key politician was Reagan and the vehicle was the Republican Party, in the UK it was Thatcher and the Conservatives.

Some commentators such as the Marxist Stuart Hall and politicians such as the liberal Tory Ian Gilmour saw Thatcherite ideas as such a decisive break with traditional conservatism that it cannot really be called Conservative. In Gilmour's eyes 'a bunch of 19th century liberals' hijacked the Tory Party' and made it 'dance with dogma'. Hall believes that the Thatcherites were not just another version of Conservatism they were attempting to impose a hegemonic project, to change the values of British society.

Others such as Paul Hirst argue that this is to exaggerate the ideological novelty of the New Right and to grant its adherents a consistency which they did not display in office. One confusing point is that some thinkers revered by the New Right such as Hayek consistently refused to consider themselves Conservatives. Hayek believed himself to be a liberal and his aim was to create a 'Constitution based on Liberty'. For him Conservatism was a statist philosophy. Simon Jenkins endorses Hayek's doubts, far from reducing the role of the state as intended Thatcherism accreted power at the centre.

Thatcher, Joseph and her acolytes such as Redwood always maintained that they are within the mainstream Conservative tradition. Joseph argued that he only really became a Conservative in 1974 when he rejected the dirigiste polices of Heath and the post-war Tory leadership. Joseph experienced a conversion as he came to see that Conservatism was about the defence of British sovereignty and an almost quasi-religious adherence to the market place

If Thatcher and Joseph are correct in saying that they were returning the party to a free market tradition it was one which had been neglected since 1945. In this new, harsher economic climate, the ideas of Friedman, Hayek and their followers gained a new audience. Theorists such as Samuel Brittan and Patrick Minford saw the trade union as a dual threat; economically because they distorted labour markets; politically because they challenged the authority of the strong state and produced a crisis of governability.

They believed that inflation can be controlled, not by prices and incomes policies (such as had been adopted in Britain and even, in 1971, in the USA by Nixon) but by strict control of the money supply. In Friedman's words **'inflation is always and everywhere a purely monetary phenomena'**.

Thatcherism

For details on Thatcher in power see section in the UK executive.

Comments on Thatcher tend to divide into two camps: on the one hand, hagiography as in the autobiographies of Lord Young and Nicholas Ridley; on the other hand, demonology as in the accounts by critics such as Dennis Healey and Roy Hattersley. Mrs Thatcher was neither saint nor sinner; she was a formidable politician with an enviable record at winning elections and echoing popular prejudice but much of what happened in British politics in the 1980s would have happened without her, even if Whitelaw had won the 1975 Tory leadership election. The rhetoric would have been more conciliatory but the policies would surely have been at least comparable? Pimlott argues that even if Labour had won the 1979 election much of what was later described as Thatcherism, such as selling council houses, would have been introduced anyway by a Labour government.

Thatcherism is an essentially contested concept, there is no consensus about its meanings. It was coined in the late 1970s, before she became PM, by the Marxist Stuart Hall who defined it as **'authoritarian populism'**. Another Marxist, Andrew Gamble, defined Thatcher's project as **'free**

market, strong state', a combination of a neo-liberal approach to economic and social policy combined with a more traditional Conservative view of the need for strong government, law and order and strong defence of national interests. Thus, Thatcherism did not precisely 'roll back the state', despite privatisation, tax cuts, pruning of central and local bureaucracies, because as Simon Jenkins has stressed in other areas, such as the control of local government, the central state 'rolled forward, not back'.

According to Hall and Gamble, Thatcherism meant more, much more, than just a dominant Premier called Thatcher. The shift to the right pre-dated Thatcher becoming PM and it occurred throughout the liberal democracies. The international dimension is important, Thatcherism was simply the British version of the triumph of the New Right in the late 1970s; Reagan's election in November 1980 saw the American version capture the White House. The shift involved a rejection of Keynesian economic policy and of welfarism which was alleged to have created a dependency culture. Given that no one individual can be said to be responsible for such a fundamental change in attitudes, perhaps it is misleading to talk of Thatcherism at all. Pimlott disputes whether the fabled consensus which Thatcher is supposed to have dismantled ever really existed. In a contrary way, Hall warns that Thatcherism is still around even if the lady herself has departed the scene.

Professor Hirst denies that Thatcherism was ever a distinctive, coherent doctrine. He sees it as traditional Conservatism refashioned to suit the 1980s. Certainly, the idea that Thatcher was not pragmatic and never did 'U turns' does not bear close inspection. Whether it be the abandonment of crude monetarism in 1985 or the inability to cut certain areas of welfare spending or the (admittedly temporary) surrender to the miners in 1981, her governments' track record is just as lettered with concessions and retreats as any other government. All governments have limited room for manoeuvre; all are faced with obvious constraints, especially given the underlying weakness of the post-war British economy. It is not surprising that the governments in the 1980s had to be flexible - what is surprising is that people expected anything else.

'True believers' such as Cecil Parkinson want to argue that it was not just another Conservative government, it was a radical, consistent administration, determined to reverse Britain's post-war decline. Critics on the left want to show that the government broke the unwritten rules of the game and, from ideological motives, cut welfare, increased unemployment, politicised the Civil Service and so on. The prosaic truth is that the Thatcher governments held office not because of any seismic shift to the right but because of a combination of luck, the defects of the British electoral system, and the shrewd, very pragmatic, leadership of Thatcher.

'Majorism'

The Tories had ditched Thatcher but they had not abandoned Thatcherism. Major did not break with the New Right. He may have been less of a conviction politician but in many ways it was his governments which furthered the New Right agenda even in areas where Thatcher was reluctant to tread. Not only was there the privatisation of the railways and of coal, but there was also a much more serious assault on the welfare state.

As with the American Republicans who want to trim back welfare it was Major's Ministers, in particular Lilley and Portillo, who talked of moving away from universalism and towards a welfare society where the state provision will be a safety net and there will be large scale middle class opting out in favour of private provision. At the same time some of the original New Right true believers such as John Gray switched tack and looked to Blair's Labour Party to seek to repair the damage done to community by the free market fundamentalism of the last two decades.

Ultimately it is impossible to answer questions such as whether the New Right is Conservative or whether it is ideological because there is no agreement on what the terms mean. Just because Conservatives regard their approach as non-ideological does not mean that the rest of us have to accept this. If Conservatism is an ideology then the New Right can be seen as simply a recent manifestation of it. If we accept the Oakshottian view, then the New Right were ideologues with no place in the Conservative canon.

The British Conservative Party, the most successful election winning machine in the democratic world, has always contained widely differing viewpoints. The Conservative Party has traditionally regarded itself as non-ideological, indeed it has scorned ideology as synonymous with extremism. Pragmatic Tories such as Hailsham and Chris Patten have seen Conservatism as organic, flexible and adaptive. The doyen of academic Conservatism, Michael Oakeshott, emphasised the rejection of any ideological aim. For him the purpose of government should be the maintenance of order. The persistence of 'High Toryism' personified by people such as Gilmour, Pym, and Prior, the 'wets', or **'One Nation Conservatism'** in the shape of Clarke, Heseltine and Hurd is evidence that the Tory Party has not been entirely captured by the **neo-liberal New Right'**.

A Dominant One Party System

After the 1992 election there was much talk of the 'Japanisation' of British politics as the Tories appeared to be so dominant as to bear comparison with the Japanese Liberals who had been in office continuously since 1955. Among others Stuart Ball, Anthony Seldon and David Marquand argued that the historical record shows the Tories to be hegemonic. In the 111 years after 1886 when the Liberals split over Home Rule the Conservatives were in power either on their own or as the dominant partner in a coalition for over two thirds of the time. Even in the 52 years after 1945, the 'Peoples War' which was supposed to lead to a 'Peoples Peace' the Conservatives held office for two thirds of it, 35 years.

The Labour Party has existed for 103 years; prior to 1997 it had been in office for just 20 years but it had held power with majorities in double figures for just 9 of those years. There had only been three decisive non-Tory elections this century - 1906 when the Liberals won a landslide, 1945 and 1966 both occasions when Labour won huge majorities.

On each occasion the Conservatives managed to recover reasonably quickly. By 1910 they were two seats off the Liberals although they had to wait until 1915 to return to office; having been 180 seats behind Labour at the 1945 election, by 1951 they were back in power with a majority of 17 and although Labour won a majority of 100 in 1966 by 1970 the Tories had once more regained power. Despite their defeat in 1997 the historical precedents suggested a rapid return to power for the Tories.

If Britain was becoming a Japanese-style one dominant-party system it would fit in with Parkin's notion that Britain has a deferential conservative political culture. Clearly there are dangers in a dominant one party system and there were unhealthy signs of patronage in the creation of the **Quangocracy**. One Conservative Minister commented that she had never knowingly appointed a Socialist to such bodies. The neutrality of the Civil Service becomes questionable; the notion of parliamentary opposition changes, with the Official Opposition impotent many people turn to direct action which is what the 'New Statesman' argues has been happening in recent years over environmental and animal rights issues.

In effect the real parliamentary opposition comes from within the governing party which is what some commentators believe was happening in the 1980s and 1990s as Conservative Tory Backbenchers and the Conservative dominated Lords caused the government more difficulties than Labour. The leader of the dominant party is removed not by the voters at a general election but by an internal party coup as happened to Thatcher in 1990 and many people thought would happen under Major.

Richard Rose argued years ago in 'Do Parties Make a Difference?' that it is the continuity of post-war British politics which is more striking than the contrasts. He was writing at a time when the Thatcherite revolution had not really yet established itself and many would argue that his conclusions were invalidated by the experiences of the 1980s. Yet by the mid 1990s the scenario Rose described looked very familiar, governmental failure and parties converging on the centre. Ideology normally has to bend to pragmatism in office, in the case of New Labour the bending began well in advance of power. Crewe talks of a new consensus whereby even Labour have accepted the market ideology. This would imply that Thatcherism did achieve the hegemonic project which Hall talked of. However Kavanagh doubts whether public opinion really has rejected welfare; Keynes has gone but Beveridge remains.

Labour Since 1979

Within the Labour Party the 1979 electoral defeat was followed by several years of bitter faction fighting. In autumn 1980 Callaghan resigned and Foot was elected leader by the P.L.P. The Labour Party was about to enter an era of fratricide which diverted much attention from the problems of the early years of Thatcherism. Between 1979 and 1981 the left, democratic socialists, had an ascendancy within the Party unique in its history.

Democratic Socialism

Tony Benn's **'Arguments for Socialism'** and **'Arguments for Democracy'** written in the early 1980's stressed that participation in decision making should be extended to the economic sphere via public ownership of the majority of manufacturing and service industries, worker's control of industry and substantial government control and regulation of the private sector. It advocated increased democratic participation and accountability via more open economic, political and bureaucratic structures. It advocated an extensive welfare state, and enhanced economic and social equality. It advocated abolition of the House of Lords, unilateral disarmament and withdrawal from the European Union because it is a free enterprise economic community.

The Realignment of the Left - 1982 Onwards

By 1982 the centre/right in alliance once more with most Trade Union leaders, such as John Edmonds and Bill Jordan and this time in alliance with the 'soft', or Tribunite left began to reassert control. It was too late to affect the 1983 manifesto which committed Labour to unilateralism, withdrawal from the EEC and an £11 billion expansion package. To the Labour right it represented **"the longest suicide note in history"**. To Benn it was a source of pride that Labour fighting on a socialist programme could win eight and a half million votes.

Kinnock saw it differently 'Just remember how you felt then, and think to yourselves, June the ninth 1983, never again will we experience that'.

Under Kinnock, Labour began to reverse the shift to the left. Kinnock stressed the need for party unity, "unity is the price of victory".

Realignment involved changing policies which were perceived as unpopular or impractical. New policies regarding the E.E.C., the Trade Unions and 'Social Ownership' were clearly an attempt to appeal to the floating voters. Despite Labour's new found pragmatism and despite an impressive Labour campaign the party lost the 1987 election, it was Labour's second worst performance since before the war. Clearly four years could not reverse what Hobsbawm argued was a thirty six year old crisis. A third consecutive defeat led to more internal debate. The Policy Review of 1987/89 led to the abandonment of unilateralism and a more enthusiastic approach towards the EU.

By 1989 with supposedly Communist regimes collapsing all over Eastern Europe and with the Chinese Communists brutally suppressing dissidents there was much talk of the death of socialism. It is not only in Britain and the USA that the post-war consensus had been challenged. The New Right philosophy had a big impact throughout the liberal democracies as the post-war boom collapsed. Socialist parties were in power in Spain, Australia and France but in practice they had all abandoned the traditional socialist notions of a command economy and egalitarian social policies. Labour was simply fitting in with this broader redefinition that parties of the left throughout the democratic world were undergoing.

By 1992 Labour was offering a much more 'moderate' programme. Again though it was not enough, in April 1992 the Tories pulled off a fourth consecutive victory albeit with a heavily reduced majority.

Labour Since 1992

It took the further defeat of 1992 before the party moved to 'one member one vote' pushed through under John Smith (with Prescott's role being crucial) at the 1993 Conference. At the same time the weighting in the Electoral College was changed so that each component now had exactly a third. Smith emphasised caution. It was paying off in that the 1994 local election results were spectacularly good for Labour, as were the 1994 European elections held just after Smith's death.

Blair was elected under the revised Electoral College, with over one million people participating, the biggest exercise in internal democracy ever undertaken by a British party. Blair won decisively in all three sections giving him a personal mandate unrivalled by any former Labour leader.

Is 'New Labour' Socialist?

Labour leaders since 1983 had pulled the party ever further from socialist ideology, until by the mid-1990s in economic terms it was merely trying to create capitalism with a human face.

The roots of New Labour lie in the changes that Kinnock made after 1983. The Labour Left was now isolated even on the previously staunchly left wing National Executive Committee, and in a weaker position than at any time since the 1930s. Blair, Brown, Mandelson and the pollster Philip Gould were enthusiastic supporters of Kinnock's reforms. However they felt frustrated by Smith's cautious approach after becoming leader in 1992. Smith believed that the Labour Party had changed enough and that 'one more heave' would dislodge the Conservatives. The modernisers believed that the public needed to see how much Labour had really changed.

When Smith died Blair became leader and initiated radical change. By 1995 Labour had abandoned the old Clause 4. As Blair said **'Labour should say what it means and mean what it says.'** The leadership began to talk of *New Labour* and persuaded the media to do the same. At the same time Blair and Brown promised that a future Labour government would not raise the rate of income tax or increase Conservative spending plans for the first two years.

This early version of New Labour espoused all the distinctive features of social democracy - a mixed economy, predominantly private ownership, and enhanced state provision of welfare Social democrats perceive 'socialism' as the legitimate heir to liberalism in modern, mixed economy capitalism which is perhaps why Blair found it relatively easy to work with the Liberals and vice versa. A consultative committee on constitutional reform was set up including Cook. Blair was reasonably close to Ashdown and closer still to Lord Jenkins with whom he discussed 'the project ' - the long awaited realignment of the left.

'New Labour' stressed majority representation and participation via the peaceful, constitutional, democratic process. The danger was that this could degenerate into electoralism, opportunist vote-catching. Was the Labour Party still socialist? Social democracy stresses the idea of a 'social', rather than 'socialist', society; Blair talked of 'social-ism'. Blair stressed liberty before equality, equality of opportunity, because that necessitates a much less intrusive state and is again very close to modern liberalism. Its stress on social justice and fairness leads to the demands for traditional socialist goals such as abolition of educational privileges through the introduction of comprehensive schools which is why even in Blair's Labour Party the decision of Harriet Harman in 1996 to send her son to a grammar school roused such protest. It favoured an extension of industrial democracy which was now described in a key speech in Singapore by Blair as a **'stakeholder society'**. For a while this was a fashionable idea and its proponent Will Hutton seemed to be a major influence on Blair. Hutton had written a seminal book 'The State Were In' attacking the outdated nature of Britain's political, economic and social systems and advocating radical reform. However within a year or so the term was effectively dropped from Blair's vocabulary as was the word socialism whether hyphenated or not. Blair seemed to be experimenting with ideas, feeling his way towards a consistent philosophy.

The term Third Way was used by Blair and those around him such as Anthony Giddens to distinguish New Labour from pure free market ideology to its right and old style socialism to its left. It was an alternative to social democracy and neo-liberalism. Giddens saw the Third Way as a response to globalisation and the end of the possibility of Keynesianism in one country. The shift from a producer economy to a service economy, the decline of traditional class identities, the growing importance of supranational institutions such as the European Union, the transformation of traditional family forms as a result of feminism, changed sexual mores and increased participation of women in the workforce, the growth of secularisation and the increasingly multicultural nature of British society all rendered the traditional left right divide redundant.

By the time he became PM in 1997 it was clear that New Labour was to the right of social democracy. That is why authentic social democrats such as Hattersley are so critical of Blair. Blair has argued that what matters is not ideology but competence. 'What matters is what works.' Blair promised the Trade Unions that New Labour would deliver them fairness not favours. The Government introduced the minimum wage, signed the Social Chapter and introduced the New 'Deal but it is still clearly a more pro-business government than the unions are comfortable with. The big domestic battles of the second term are to do with reforming the public services and on this issue Blair has seriously antagonised the unions.

As the Democratic Audit points out the government has sought to address deprivation through 'a series of measures including; full employment policies, including a New Deal scheme to move unemployed young people into employment; legislation on a minimum wage, increases in child benefit, substantial increases in health and education spending; reversing the decline in social housing, the establishment of a Social Exclusion Unit in the Cabinet Office.' This all sounds like very traditional Labour objectives. However the Blairites have moved a long way from traditional beliefs. They have embraced the idea that what matters is not equality but an improvement in the absolute living standards of the poorest. Blair was asked repeatedly by Jeremy Paxman about the growth in inequality. His replay was that he accepted a growing gap between rich and poor, ie an increase in relative inequality, provided that the poor were better off in absolute terms. Equality of opportunity has replaced equality of outcome as the goal. Stephen Byers, at that stage Secretary of State for Industry, told businessmen that the 'reality is that wealth creation is now more important than wealth distribution.' He told them that the role of government was to make sure that markets work efficiently and help to create a 'strong, just society'. In his view 'the corporate state does not work'.

This is a long way removed from the classic social democratic position identified by Anthony Crosland and his supporters such as Hattersley. It may well also be a long way removed from the position of Gordon Brown and it is possible that the current argument over foundation hospitals is the first real ideological crack within the leadership of New Labour. It is worth looking at it as a case study. New Labour modernisers felt that some hospitals with high reputations should be free from Whitehall controls. The new foundation hospitals, with freedom to manage themselves, could ignore Whitehall targets. This independence would enable them to respond more positively to local needs, to set their own salary levels, to borrow money to build new wards or operating theatres etc. it was argued that on occasions in the past, top-down control had stifled local innovation. Foundation hospitals would compete with trust hospitals for primary Care Trust business, by offering reduced waiting times etc., which in turn would drive up improvements in the performance of rival trust hospitals.

Old Labour traditionalists saw foundation hospitals as a Thatcherite-style reform since they reintroduce discredited market forces into healthcare. However, old Labour lost the argument and Foundation hospitals will exist alongside non-Foundation hospitals. Whilst old Labour is not convinced that competition will result in overall improved standards. Finally, critics argue that government targets result in hospitals manipulating healthcare in a perverse way in order to meet a target. Labour has now taken the controversial step of attempting to 'drive up standards' by introducing competition into secondary health care.

New Labour have departed from traditional Labour views in all sorts of ways. It has considered the extension of privatisation or part-privatisation to air traffic control and the London underground. It has adopted Clintonite ideas on workfare rather than welfare, a 'hand up not a hand out' and it has appointed business advisers to key Government task forces. An early Blairite slogan 'tough on crime, tough on the causes of crime' showed the party moving away from its traditional approach that crime was the fault of poverty and inequality. New Labour's interest in constitutional reform is itself a departure because traditionally Labour have accepted the Westminster strong government model and seen reforms such as PR and devolution as a distraction. Labour wanted to capture control of central government and use the power to impose democratic socialism or at least social democracy across the UK. New Labour is more interested, at least rhetorically, in promoting a pluralistic, decentralised political system which takes it closer to the Liberals.

Haywood emphasises that whereas social democracy was ideological New Labour have been pragmatic; it emphasises globalisation instead of the nation state and the market economy not the mixed economy. On some issues New Labour are strikingly illiberal. Straw was a more authoritarian Home Secretary than Labour was used to but Blunkett has been even more hard line. Whether it be treatment of asylum seekers or the importance of 'life meaning life' for murderers New Labours policies are far removed from the liberalism of Roy Jenkins when he was Labour Home Secretary in the 1960s. On foreign policy Blair has seemed willing to ally himself with neo-conservatives in Washington as well as Berlusconi and the Spanish conservative PM Aznar.

Despite all of this there are obvious continuities between old and new Labour. These become more obvious when contrasting Labour with the Conservatives. The New Right emphasise markets and individualism, arguably at the expense of community. New Labour is **communitarian**, they believe that the individual operates best within a community. Whereas the Conservatives tend to see the private sector as the solution and the state sector as inherently inefficient Labour still look to the state to remedy the deficiencies of a market driven society. Brown has directed resources towards core Labour supporters such as poorer pensioners. After the self imposed restraint of the first two years there have been huge increases in spending on education and health. By 2003 Labour had effectively raised direct tax by increasing national insurance contributions. New Labour may no longer be socialist but there are still major differences between New Labour and the Conservatives.

The Conservatives Since 1997

Conservative moderates were concerned that Major was swayed by the Eurosceptic right wing who wanted to fight the 1997 election by putting 'clear blue water' between the Tories and Blair. They wanted Major to contest the middle ground

Major resigned immediately after the 1997 defeat and the party elected Hague. As Politics Pal puts it, at first Hague's leadership appeared to be offering a more 'inclusive' party. Michael Portillo told the Conservative Conference that they should welcome single parents and gays into the party. This represented a social libertarian phase of Conservatism which some referred to as 'compassionate Conservatism'.

The deputy leader, Peter Lilley, spoke out against Thatcherite values. Many Conservatives were furious about this and Lilley was sacked. Blair's attack on 'the forces of conservatism' in 1998 pushed Hague into defending Conservatism through his 'Commonsense Revolution'. To rally support within the party, in 1999 Hague moved to the right and made five guarantees about a future Conservative government which took the party back towards Thatcherism. Some guarantees were unrealistic and later dropped.

The party did relatively well in the local elections and the European elections of 1999. The leadership appeared to believe that a more right wing approach worked. Once he was back in the Commons and the Shadow Cabinet Michael Portillo repeated his Social Libertarian message but Ann Widdecombe took a contradictory social authoritarian position on soft drugs so the party remained divided.

The 2001 campaign saw the party offering unrealistic policies on reducing tax, emphasising asylum reforms and opposition to the Euro when voters were more concerned with the public services. Hague's leadership appeared 'knee-jerk', simply reacting to the latest story in the Daily Mail and Steve Norris accused his party of being 'nasty, exclusive, angry and backward looking.'

The 2001 election was an even worse result than 1997 for the Conservatives because it shows they have not bounced back as they did in 1906, 1945 and 1966. Hague resigned immediately and the party was plunged into a leadership election using the new rules. Portillo was the early favourite. He favoured a new inclusiveness and was supported by 13 members of the Shadow Cabinet. However he was eliminated and by the last stage it was Clarke v Smith. The party members chose Smith presumably because Clarke is too pro-Europe for the current Conservative Party. Leading Conservatives such as Oliver Letwin and David Willetts have called upon the party to accept that it represents more than simply free market economics. They argue that 'there is such a thing as society' and the party must be more sympathetic to the poor and the marginalised.

Smith is seen as a right winger but he has tried to promote inclusiveness and social liberalism. He insisted that Conservative MPs not be members of the Monday Club. He has campaigned strongly on the public services. There was talk of removing Smith if the party did not perform well enough in the local elections of 2003. In the event the Conservatives did well enough to give Smiths a reprieve. However they are still in a dire situation because they did not do well enough to be in a serious position to challenge Labour in 2005 or 2006.

The Liberals

In October 1974, the Liberals won 19.3% of the vote and 13 seats, a decisive breakthrough. However in 1979, they dropped to 13.8% and 11 seats. Yet the appearance of two party politics was deceptive. The centre flourished when the two major parties were polarised, and the ideologues in both parties moved from the periphery to the centres of power.

Within two years of the 1979 election, a new party - the SDP - had been formed, and was winning by-elections. In 1982 the SDP and the Liberals combined to form an Alliance, which lasted six years. During that time the two parties fought on the same policies, and with rare exceptions did not run candidates against each other. The SDP, in tandem with the Liberals, sought to replenish the centre ground with a pragmatic style of politics which was supposed to 'break the mould' of ideological sectarianism. They were able to win 25.4% of the votes in the 1983 election and it looked as though the Alliance might displace Labour.

In the immediate aftermath of the 1987 election the Liberals and SDP began merger negotiations. These were completed by 1989 and most of the SDP voted to join the Liberals in a new party, now known as the Liberal Democrats. A rump of the SDP, under Owen's leadership, remained independent.

The voters were not at all impressed with this performance and as the Labour Party moderated its policies and up-dated its image the anti-Tory vote in by-elections and European elections went to Labour or on occasions, as in the 1989 European elections, to the Greens rather than to the Centre.

However Paddy Ashdown's Liberal Democrats won 17% of the votes in 1997 and 46 seats. The 2001 election saw the Liberals win 52 seats, their highest number since 1931. There now seems to be an almost irreducible minimum of 15-20% of the electorate who choose not to support the two main parties. That is a far larger residual vote than exists in a genuine two-party system like America's. Also the Liberals have a very substantial base in local government. At the local elections of spring 2003 the Liberals polled over 30% of the votes, their highest share for decades. There will be no simple return to two-partyism.

US Parties

In a sense, it is precisely because America is such a pluralistic society that the two-main parties have been so ideologically flexible. Party loyalty has never had the hold on American politics that it has in Britain. Of recent Presidents, Nixon, Carter, Reagan and Clinton all to some extent operated 'outside' party. Clinton, founder member of the centrist Democratic Leadership Conference, won the nomination and then the election in 1992 as a 'New Democrat' deliberately distancing himself from the party's past He ran in 1996 almost as a figure above party, hence the notion of 'triangulation' Bush was more of a party 'insider' having been the Republican Chairman during Nixon's Presidency and Reagan's Vice President for eight years.

This weakness of party in America is not a recent phenomenon. Even Franklin Roosevelt, the creator of the modern Democratic Party, experienced great problems securing his party's backing; he had to drop several proposals because the Southern Democrats would have voted against them. There are almost as many differences within the parties as there are between them. In the past this was especially true of the Democrats. The Republicans, like the Conservatives, tended to be more united at least in public but in the 1990s we supposedly witnessed what was called **'the great Republican crack-up'** as the ideological divisions within the party appeared to be tearing it apart. The victory of Bush in 2000 seemed to unify the party but, by summer 2003 with the war against Iraq over, divisions within the party were resurfacing.

Republicans such as Christine Todd-Whitman, the Governor of New Jersey, are socially liberal and therefore pro-choice, and economically liberal and therefore in favour of tax cuts and reduced government spending. Right wing Republicans such as Bush himself are conservative on moral issues and pro-free market. The more moderate Republicans are often from the North and East and tend to vote with liberal Democrats from the same areas. Thus region can count for almost as much as party label.

Broadly speaking, Northern Democrats tend to be more liberal than their Southern colleagues. This regional/ideological difference is particularly true of issues concerning civil rights such as affirmative actions and 'bussing' but it also extends to economic and social issues, such as the role of trade unions, state intervention in the economy, defence, and equal rights for women. In Congress, Southern conservative Democrats known colloquially as Dixiecrats (or less flatteringly as 'boll weevils') often line up alongside Republicans to form a conservative coalition.

There are several reasons for the difference in the degree of party cohesion in the USA and the UK. Partly it is due to institutional, or structural factors, such as the existence of a separation of powers in America and its almost complete absence in Britain, or the effects of federalism in the US as opposed to the unitary nature of the British state. Partly it is due to political and social differences, especially the continued existence of consensus politics in America which contrasts with the breakdown of the post-war consensus in Britain by the late 1960s early 1970s.

The separation of powers in America ensures that even when the President's party controls Congress, as under Bush now, the system of checks and balances operate so as to prevent a concentration of power. Vile distinguishes between Presidential parties and Congressional parties. It is sometimes said that the US has a 100 party system because each state has its own duopoly. In the British system the Prime Minister is the head of government by virtue of being head of the party. In the USA it is the other way around, the President is head of the party, as it were incidentally, by virtue of being elected Head of State. That is why the party which does not control the Presidency is effectively leaderless, as the Democrats are at the moment.

The separation of government and legislature in the USA also reduces the potential for patronage and a 'pay-roll' vote. Very few Senators would risk exchanging their seat for a post in an administration which will last at most eight years. American administrations are generally staffed by 'non-politicians' such as Henry Kissinger, James Baker, and Colin Powell rather than established Senators and Congressmen, although there are exceptions such as Donald Rumsfeld.

With elections at regular intervals, a President cannot use the threat of dissolution to bring the party into line. In America, the voters seem to make the parties pay if they appear overly ideological. The 1980 election, when an ideologue, Reagan, was rewarded by the voters, was an exception and explicable only by reference to the disillusioned mood of Americans after the traumas of the 1960s and 1970s. By the 1984 campaign, Reagan was downplaying his radicalism and emphasising his desire for an Arms Control agreement. This is now also true of Britain where, having lost four consecutive elections, the Labour Party stressed its moderation and diluted its socialist message. Blair accepted that Thatcherism moved British politics to the right.

American parties are decentralised, regionally based, non ideological, and not very cohesive. The intra-party contests for the nomination are, as in the 2000 dispute between Bush and McCain, a lot more intensely fought than the inter-party battles in the general election.

The Evolution of the Party System

The first two party system emerged in the 1790s with a split between the Federalists such as Hamilton and the Democratic-Republicans lead by Jefferson. Followers of Jefferson emphasised states rights. However, the modern Democratic Party dates back to the 1830s and the Presidency of Andrew Jackson. It was seen as the party of the 'common man' whereas the Republican Party, the 'Grand Old Party' formed in the 1850s, was perceived as the voice of capitalist interests. The white South did not forgive the party of Lincoln for freeing the slaves and for the next 100 years the 'Solid South' was a one party region. Despite the 15th Amendment

303

(1870) the blacks of the South were effectively disenfranchised after the end of Reconstruction in 1877.

The Republican Party dominated American politics following the Civil War, especially after 1896. The Populist movement of the early 1890s made up of poor farmers was swallowed up by the Democrats within a couple of years. In the first decades of the 20th century, the Republicans under Theodore Roosevelt were seen as the reformers. It was only under Roosevelt's successor Taft, 1909-1913, that the party adopted a more conservative philosophy and, in response, Theodore Roosevelt led a break-away movement officially termed the Progressive Republican League but more memorably known as the 'Bull Moose' party.

This breakaway cost the Republicans the 1912 election and allowed the Democrats under Wilson to capture the Presidency for the first time since 1888. Wilson himself adopted many of the ideas of the Progressives.

Republicans dominated in the 'boom' years of the 1920s, but in 1929 the US economy collapsed and, by 1932, unemployment stood at around 25% so that the Republican laissez faire ethic was discredited. It caused a realignment in American politics as the nation moved to the left but it was the other Roosevelt - Franklin Delano - and the Democratic Party which reaped the benefit. Walter Dean Burnham described 1932 as a 'critical' election because it ended the Republican domination of US politics which had lasted a generation and ushered in a Democrat domination that was to last until 1968.

The New Deal Coalition

The 'New Deal' was the name given by President Roosevelt to the policies he put forward to deal with America's economic crisis in the 1930s. For the first time in US history the Government accepted the need for state intervention to regulate the economy and to promote the kind of state welfare schemes adopted in Europe 30 years earlier. Roosevelt shifted the consensus, but he wanted to save capitalism not to dismantle it.

Roosevelt was able to contain any radicalism that may have threatened the existing system. There were radical populist movements both to the left and right of the Democrats such as Senator Huey Long of Louisiana and Father Charles Coughlin's anti-Semitic movement.

The pragmatism and charisma of Roosevelt minimised the attraction of these radical forces and also helped establish a New Deal Coalition which was to survive for 30 or 40 years. The 'New Deal Coalition' consisted of those groups in American society who supported FDR and who formed the bedrock of support for the Democratic Party from the 1930s to the late 1960s.

The Democrats gained control of the Presidency and retained it for the next twenty years. Between 1932 and 1968 there was just one Republican President - Eisenhower - and he was a war hero almost 'above' party politics. The Democrat domination was not confined to the Presidency. Between 1930 and 1968 the Republicans controlled Congress for just 4 years that is 1946-1948 and 1952-1954. The Democrats also dominated state politics, for example the Governorships.

The New Deal had three lasting legacies for US politics. There was a transfer of power from the states to the Federal Government. There was a massive increase in the role and power of the executive. Thirdly, the creation of the 'New Deal Coalition'.

The Democrats had always been the party of ethnic and religious minorities. FDR simply strengthened the Democratic hold on these groups and added two other forces, the Trade Unions and the intellectuals. Curiously, the coalition also included whites in the South who were antagonistic to the very groups listed above. Thus, the coalition which Roosevelt forged was incredibly successful;

The Break-up of the New Deal Coalition

Like all coalitions it was inherently unstable because it was based on compromise. FDR was unable to do much on behalf of Southern blacks because if he tried then Southern white Democrats would have blocked his other programmes. FDR even refused to make lynching a Federal offence. Truman was unable to achieve civil rights for southern blacks. Eisenhower did not attempt to dismantle the New Deal in much the same way that in

Britain between 1951 and 1964 the Conservatives accepted many of Attlee's reforms. However, the New Deal Coalition began to fall apart in the 1960s.

The critical year for the Democrats was 1968 when the party split three ways just as they had in 1948. The anti-war, pro-Civil Rights, student movement led by Eugene McCarthy humiliated Johnson in the New Hampshire primary in February 1968. LBJ announced he would not run in 1968. Bobby Kennedy now entered the race. The loyalist, pro-Vietnam War, 'establishment' Democrats were now led by Hubert Humphrey, but were epitomised by Mayor Daley of Chicago.

Following his win in the California primary in June 1968, Kennedy was assassinated. LBJ's promotion of Civil Rights for blacks alienated the White South. This time the Dixiecrats called themselves the AIP (American Independent Party). Their candidate was the segregationist Governor of Alabama, George Wallace.

Humphrey managed to win the McCarthy followers back into the fold, although many of the 'New Left' wanted to avoid assimilation into the Democrats where they believed their radicalism would be diluted. Wallace was in the same position as all such candidates; he knew he could not win the 270 Electoral College votes necessary to win the Presidency, but if he could prevent either of the two main candidates getting 270 then the House of Representatives would have to decide and Wallace would trade his support for an influence on policy, particularly of course on civil rights questions. Wallace's strategy did not succeed, Nixon won 301 Electoral College votes to Humphrey's 191 and Wallace's 46, over 10 million in the popular vote, 13.5% of the total. It was the best third-party performance in the Electoral College this century and because not all of his votes were from the South, his intervention may have been enough to give victory to Nixon.

In 1972 Nixon's 'Southern strategy' paid off when he won one of the great landslides of the 20th century against the liberal Democrat George McGovern. The latter got just 37.3% of the vote. Alex Wadden argues that this was the beginning of the backlash against liberalism that Republicans such as Bush have exploited ever since.

The 'Contract with America'

The Republicans took both the Senate and the House of Representatives in the mid-term elections of 1994. In 1994 the House Republicans campaigned on a 10 point Contract with America which advocated the following:

1) A Fiscal Responsibility Act leading to a balanced budget amendment and a line item veto power for the President

2) A Taking Back Our Streets Act which would build more prisons, increase sentences, reduce the possibility of appeal against death sentences

3) A Personal Responsibility Act introducing welfare reform

4) A Family Reinforcement Act including tax incentives for adoption

5) An American Dream Restoration Act giving tax sheltered retirement accounts

6) A National Security Restoration Act limiting US participation in United Nations ventures

7) A Senior Citizens Equity Act expanding tax breaks for pensioners

8) A Job Creation and Wage Enhancement act leading to a 50% reduction in capital gains tax

9) A Common Sense Legal Reforms Act to reduce excess litigation

10) A Citizens Legislature Act introducing term limits

Significantly the Contract avoided such contentious issues as abortion and school prayer. Gingrich claimed that this represented a historic shift and promises 'to replace the welfare state with the conservative opportunity society'. Survey evidence though shows that most voters had never even heard of the 'Contract with America'.

Gary Wills wrote of **'the collapse of the Republican revolution'** less than two years after they took control of Congress. The main problem was that

Gingrich was outmanoeuvred by Clinton in the budget impasse of 1995/1996. Clinton was able to win again in November 1996 even though the Republicans retained control of Congress.

A more accurate description of US politics in the 1990s would be 'dealignment' - no one party dominated but conservative ideas prevailed.

The US Consensus

The American author, Gore Vidal, argues that there is only one party in America - the 'property party'. Certainly there are few major ideological differences between the Republican Party and the Democrats. They both share a belief in the 'American way of life', which they agree needs to be defended against the Communist threat; they both support capitalism, although the Democrats are more willing to allow state intervention in the economy. The structure of government in the USA promotes consensus. The separation of powers means that there are separate institutions sharing power and if they cannot work together then there will be deadlock. The same process applies at State level, where the legislature might have split control or the dominant party may not hold the Governorship, again the impulse is towards consensus.

Whereas in Britain the post-war consensus began to break down by the late 1960s, giving way to the adversary politics of the 1970s and 1980s, in the USA a high degree of consensus still exists. Indeed, in US politics, the differences within the parties often appear to be greater than the differences between them.

A liberal Republican such as Powell is closer to a moderate Democrat such as Clinton than he is to a right wing Republican such as Ashcroft. Similarly former Vice President Gore has more in common politically with the former Republican Governor Pete Wilson than he has with Jesse Jackson.

During the 1992 Presidential election, Clinton put forward policies which were not radically different from Bush's. Certainly Clinton put a different emphasis on issues such as taxation, welfare and attitudes towards foreign policy, but there were none of the ideological divisions which characterised the 1992 British election. Clinton was keen to downplay liberalism and portray himself as a 'New Democrat'. This was even truer in 1996

There is a 'left wing' within the Democratic Party including people such as Senator Edward Kennedy (Mass.), Congresswoman Pat Schroeder (Colorado) and Congressman Ralph Dellums (California). Kennedy opposed Carter in the 1980 Primaries because Carter had been too conservative. Schroeder was a strong advocate of the ERA who believes that Republican policies are particularly harmful to women and that the Democrats should do more to exploit this issue.

Dellums leads the Black Caucus in Congress and headed the successful 'sanctions against South Africa' campaign in 1986. Jesse Jackson wanted a 'realignment' of American policy, making it less obsessively anti-Soviet and more orientated to the Third World. Jackson strongly opposed the Nicaraguan Contras and, even more controversially, he favours the Palestinian cause and opposes American support for Israel. The DLC has always been very critical of Jackson and their hostility is reciprocated with Jackson referring to the DLC as 'Democrats for the Leisure Class'.

However, the mainstream Democratic Party rejects Jackson's policies and is less committed to welfare and the unions than the old style 'New Deal Democrats' such as Kennedy. The Democrat Leadership Council had been forged in the wake of Mondale's defeat in 1984. It was dominated by mid-western and southern Democrats such as Clinton and Gore. Clinton supports state intervention to help business but even the 1992 version was certainly no radical, even in American terms and by 1994 he had shifted to the right. Just like the British Labour Party Clinton was so anxious to win that he became a centrist candidate, unlikely to offend floating voters. He promised to end 'welfare as we know it' and arguably he did precisely that.

Nigel Ashford identifies six different rightist factions within the Republican camp. Edward Ashbee focuses on the distinction between 'paleo-conservatives' around Buchanan and supply-siders around Jack Kemp the former Congressman who became Housing Secretary under Reagan. Just as the Democratic party has a 'fundamentalist' wing, so the Republican Party have their own 'zealots' such as Jesse Helms and

Buchanan. Helms is a Senator for North Carolina closely associated with the 'Moral Majority'. His opponents allege that Helms supported the right-wing extremist 'death squads' in El Salvador. Helms sided with the Argentinean Junta during the Falklands War. He is a very powerful figure within the party and within Congress. He was Chairman of the extremely important Senate Foreign Relations Committee.

Buchanan is an ex-Nixon aide who worked in Reagan's White House office as Director of Communications, but left in 1986 to pursue his own Presidential ambitions. He believed that Reagan had nothing to apologise for in the Irangate affair and should certainly have pardoned North and Poindexter. Buchanan argues that Congress, which he describes as 'Israeli occupied territory' has tried to usurp control over foreign policy. He would introduce tariffs and stop US aid. The Republican primaries of 1996 turned into a battle between Senator Dole and Buchanan who knew he could not win but he could damage Dole. By 2000 Buchanan had left the Republican party and fought the election as the Reform Party candidate.

Thus each party has its ideologues, but they tend to be isolated. The growth of primaries after 1960 did make it more likely for 'outsiders' to get the nomination, McGovern was the classic example, but recently the party leaderships have reasserted more control over the nominating process. The ever increasing importance of TV means that the parties choose telegenic moderates who reassure rather than frighten voters.

Why No Socialism in the USA?

Werner Sombart pointed out decades ago that the USA is unique among major industrialised states in not having a mass socialist movement. This is a product of the ethnic divisions of US society; the liberal individualist ethos of American politics which is built into the very constitution itself; the fact that unlike Europe land was always plentiful it was labor that was scarce so that wages were relatively high and the frontier acted as a safety valve and promoted a mentality of rugged individualism which clashes with the collectivist assumptions of socialism; already by the end of the 19th century there were 'red scares' as union militancy and socialism were presented as 'Un-American' and lastly the fact that the Democratic party pre-dated the formation of the trade unions.

The American Marxist, Mike Davis, describes the AFL-CIO/Democrat relationship as a 'barren marriage' and proposes that the unions breakaway and form an independent Socialist Party. Mainstream labor leaders regard this as an unrealistic approach, as Socialist parties have never done well in the USA. The Socialist Party of the USA formed in 1901 and led by Eugene Debs polled nearly one million, 7% of the total vote, in the 1912 election, the high-water mark for his party. The British Labour Party was polling at the same level, yet within 12 years it formed a government.

The American Socialist Party never really flourished even in the Depression years of the 1930s. The 1948 election was probably the time when the 'left' within the Democratic Party came closest to breaking away. The Democrats split into three factions, the mainstream party led by Truman, the Dixiecrats led by Strom Thurmond who felt that the Democrats had moved too far to the 'left' because Truman tried to introduce Civil Rights for blacks as part of the Fair Deal. The Progressive Party led by Henry Wallace, FDR's vice-president from 1941 to 1945, felt that the Democrats had moved too far to the 'right' and that Truman's policies had caused the Cold War.

Wallace had the backing of the Communists, dismaying the liberal democrats such as Galbraith, Schlesinger and Reuther who had formed 'Americans for Democratic Action' as a 'left-wing' but anti-Communist force. Wallace polled dismally and despite Thurmond's insurgency Truman still managed to beat the Republican, Dewey. The chances of a left-wing breakaway were heavily diminished.

Party Organisation in Britain

The **Labour** Party has always claimed to **practise intra-party democracy** - the **Conservative** Party traditionally made no such claim. The Conservative Party have always been a leadership party. This fits in with their overall philosophy and history, their belief in hierarchy and strong leadership. Labour's claim to be a democratic party reflects its beliefs and history. Its ideology of socialism and equality, the belief that the leadership must be held accountable to the membership not just the MPs. Hence **Labour has traditionally been a membership party**.

However in practice the Labour Party is less democratic than it appears, a view put forward as far back as 1955 by Professor Robert **McKenzie** in his very influential book 'British Political Parties'. McKenzie argued that in practice the **Labour Party is a covert oligarchy** - it is controlled by the Parliamentary leadership and the Trade Union 'bosses'. Conference is manipulated by these groups through the use of the block vote. The experience of the Labour governments of the 1960s and 1970s seemed to vindicate McKenzie's argument. Time and again the Labour leadership simply ignored the wishes of Conference; as Wilson himself put it to Conference; "you say what you want, the Government's job is to govern".

Before 1981, leaders of the Labour Party had been elected by Labour MPs (PLP), hence they tended to come from the centre/right of the party; Attlee 1935-55, Gaitskell 1955-63, Wilson 1963-76 and Callaghan 1976-1980. Foot 1980-83 was the only post-war leader elected by the PLP to come from the left of the party.

The Left, led by Benn was determined to change Labour's constitution. It was able to push through two out of three of their demands for constitutional change - Mandatory Reselection and an Electoral College - although they lost the fight for N.E.C. control of the Manifesto. The left believed that the Electoral College in which the affiliated organisations had 40% of the votes with the remaining 60% shared between the CLPs and Labour MPs would produce leaders from the left. This was the final straw for some of the more moderate/right wing Labour figures such as Jenkins, Owen, Rodgers and Williams (the Gang of Four) who in 1981 broke away from Labour to form the SDP. About 25 Labour MPs and one Conservative MP followed them.

Never again would a Labour Government ignore the wishes of Conference or the NEC and it would be harder for Labour MPs to ignore the wishes of the CLPs because mandatory re-selection would make them more accountable to their local activists who tend to be on the left. CLPs would de-select MPs who were insufficiently left-wing. To Benn writing in 1981:

"The debate now going on in the Party is as important as any we have ever had. On the one hand it is about policy and on the other hand about party democracy, but above all it is about the inter-relationship between the two."

By 1981, therefore, it looked as if McKenzie's theory was no longer valid. The PLP had lost control of the party because their old allies in the union leadership had switched to the left. Under the guise of promoting party democracy the Bennite left (or 'hard left') had increased its influence. Critics argued that the Labour Party was **abandoning representative democracy and moving towards delegate democracy**. The leader and MPs were becoming delegates but not in the Burkean sense of being bound by constituents, they were bound by the wishes of the Conference, the NEC and the CLPs.

In summer 1981, Benn, against the wishes of the **'soft' or Tribunite left** - Foot, Kinnock et al, challenged Healey for the Deputy Leadership. This meant that the Labour Party spent the summer and early Autumn of 1981, when Thatcher was at her most vulnerable, not attacking the Conservatives but attacking each other. The hard left never forgave Kinnock for refusing to back Benn and the **Campaign Group** came into existence as a result of this split. The result was announced at the LPAC in October 1981; Benn got 49.6%, Healey got 50.4%. Significantly, in the CLP section Benn got 81% of the votes.

Having engaged in such a divisive contest, the Labour Party now began to reunite. However by then the damage had been done. Since 1983 Labour has become more and more of an overt leadership party. Labour's first party political broadcast of the 1987 campaign - 'Kinnock - the movie' - was so obsessed with the leader that it did not mention the Labour party at all. At the beginning of the 1980s the home-policy committee of Labour's NEC was a source of constant opposition to the leadership; Labour's annual conference was a week of ritual humiliation for the PLP. Now Conference is stage managed, the NEC is docile. Blair has abandoned the election of the Labour Chief Whip, the current occupant Hilary Armstrong was appointed by the leader. The leader's office is a powerful body including such close confidantes of Blair as Peter Mandelson and Alastair Campbell his Press Spokesman.

Blair has established a Labour Policy Forum which the leadership can control. The Liberal Democrat Party also has a constitution that gives more power to the leader than the old Liberal party did so there is less scope for the Conference embarrassing the leadership.

At the same time as Labour and the Liberals have been abandoning intra-party democracy the Tories have become less of a leadership party. Bonar Law said in 1922 that 'the party chooses the leader, and the leader chooses the policy and if the party does not like it, they have to get a new leader.' Macmillan retired in October 1963 plunging the Tories into a leadership battle during their party conference. In those days the Tory Party did not elect their leader, he was chosen by the 'Magic Circle' and they chose the least meritocratic of all the contenders, the 14th Earl of Home. Iain Macleod and Enoch Powell refused to serve under him.

After 1965 Tory MPs elected the leader. The formal process was that when the party was in power a challenger needed the support of 10% of Tory MPs, it only used to be 3 MPs but the rules were changed after 1990 to prevent 'frivolous' challenges whilst the party was in office. Had it not been for this rule change then Major might well have been challenged in Autumn 1994 around the time the 8 Tory MPs were having the whip withdrawn. The rule did not apply to the election of June 1995 because Major initiated it.

To win on the first ballot a candidate required a majority of Tory MPs plus a lead of 15% over the second place. In 1990 Thatcher achieved the first criteria with 204 votes out of a total of 373 but as Heseltine had 152 then she was four short of the 56 she needed to be clear of him. In the second ballot new candidates could enter. Thatcher's original intention was to fight on but she was dissuaded by her Cabinet. To win on the second ballot required an overall majority, Major on 185 was actually 2 short of the necessary figure but the other two candidates conceded defeat thereby preventing a third ballot.

The election of the leader led to a new kind of relationship between the leader and the MPs. The days of the 'magic circle' were well and truly over. Heath, Thatcher and Major were all meritocrats none of whom went to public school. Hurd's leadership bid in 1990 was handicapped by the fact that he had been to Eton, Major was seen as a man of the people, a theme exploited in the 1992 party broadcast showing Major going back to his roots in Brixton. Having become leader Major called for a 'classless society'. This all reflects a broader sociological shift whereby traditional institutions such as the Monarchy have lost authority and the Tory Party, previously the party of the elites, of the landed 'estates' has become the party of the 'estate agents'. Thatcher's election and leadership were both cause and effect of this change.

The new type of leader has had to face a far less obedient party. Thirty years ago Kilmuir said that 'loyalty is the Tory Party's secret weapon'. Those deferential days are long since over. Where once criticism of the leader would be muted and behind closed doors critical Tory MPs now rush to the cameras on College Green Westminster to air their views. Heath was removed by what the Tory MP Julian Critchley called a 'peasants revolt'. Thatcher, the most electorally successful leader the party has known since Salisbury was removed by an internal election. Major had to whip his troops into line by threatening to call an election and in June 1995 the leader had to take the unprecedented step of calling a leadership election, a sort of vote of confidence in himself. Hague was subject to constant sniping and so is Smith. Hague was the last leader to be elected purely by MPs, now activists play a role.

It is not just Conservative MPs who are displaying a new found independence of spirit, activists are demanding to be consulted. The fact that activists are more willing to threaten de-selection shows the way things are changing. Meyer was de-selected, Mellor, Gardiner and others have been threatened. It was his local party which got Yeo sacked from the government in 1994.

The former Conservative leader Bonar Law is said to have remarked that he would rather take advice from his valet than from the Tory party conference and until the 1960s the leader only arrived on the last day to give the assembled faithful the benefit of his wisdom. Tory party conference is still rigidly controlled to prevent internal dissent being publicised but Kelly argues that the Conference now exercises an informal policy making role, witness its involvement in the poll tax policy and even more so the two issues of Europe and law and order.

It could be argued that the old style Conservative leadership elections were more effective in that they were easy to organise, were soon over, were cheap and only involved the people the leader would be in charge of on a day to day basis i.e. the party's MPs. In contrast Labour contests were very complex, time consuming, expensive and give a role to extra-parliamentary forces. But it could not seriously be denied that the Labour system was more democratic. Efficiency versus democracy - the usual dichotomy. Hague democratised the Conservative party's procedures by giving members a say. In 2001 Smith became the first leader elected under this system.

The Conservative Leadership Contest 2001

	1st round	No. of MPs 1st round re-run	2nd round	Final round
Kenneth Clarke	36	39	59	39%
Iain Duncan Smith	39	42	54	61%
Michael Portillo	49	50	53	-
David Davis	21	18	-	-
Michael Ancram	21	17	-	-

Declining Membership

Until recently all the main British parties seemed to have fewer members. Though reliable membership figures are not available for the Conservatives, it is probable that they had around 2.8 million members in 1953, about 1.5 million by the 1980s. Seyd and Whitely show how Tory membership dropped even further in the 1990s so that by 1998 it was now down to about 700,000 and they were losing about 60,000 members a year. For Hague's internal ballot on party reform around 400,000 ballot papers were distributed although only 114,000 voted. Their average constituency membership is 2,400 but more worryingly for them the average age of members is high - 67 - and the party is literally dying, whereas in the

Labour Party only a quarter are aged over 66. 60% are male with most coming from social classes A/B and C1. John Bercow resigned from the Shadow Cabinet saying that the Conservatives were seen as 'racist, sexist, homophobic and anti-youth.'

Kenneth Morgan points out that declining membership in the 1960s, 1970s and early 1980s, made it easier for extreme left-wing activists to take control of CLPs. Their views did not represent the opinions of the average Labour voter. Labour's individual membership dropped from about 350,000 to around 300,000 during the 1980s, an average of 500 per CLP. Seyd and Whitely showed in 1993 how the grassroots Labour party was declining with obvious long term dangers.

Membership partially recovered under Blair so that it got back to over 400,000. However many of these new members paid a much reduced fee and their long-term commitment to Labour was questionable. To put this membership recovery in perspective in 1953 Labour had one million members. Since 1997 membership has again fallen, it is now down to about 280,000 ie lower than it was before Blair. Again 60% are male. According to Seyd and Whiteley only 14% of activists spend more than 5 hours a month on party work. By the local elections of 2003 Labour activists seemed very disillusioned indeed. The Liberals have about 70,000 members.

Declining membership is only part of the story. Parties have declined partly because of changing social conditions. People no longer want to spend their evenings in committee rooms, or think that their life revolves around a political party. To that extent the Green Party, a loose and occasional association of like-minded people, may be a model for the future. Partly, too, the decline of parties must have something to do with the power of TV. Leaders have been adroit at using TV to go over the heads of their parties direct to the public. With TV in the Commons these new political skills are vital while parties become far less significant. The process has gone much further in the USA.

Party Organisation in the USA

US parties are highly decentralised. They do have National Committees and these are gaining power, particularly in the Republican Party, but the national parties are in reality loose coalitions of State parties. This reflects three things. The sheer size of the USA which has led to **sectionalism**; it is obvious that the Democrats of California will have little concern over the condition of the Democratic Party in Florida or Illinois. In the US system, the local parties have enormous autonomy and would resent any national interference. Secondly the lack of ideology which allows for local adaptations. Thirdly the fact that it is a federal system where states have a high degree of autonomy. Federalism is alive and well in American politics and nowhere more so than in the continued fragmentation of American parties. Leon Epstein's 'Parties in the American Mould', 1986, emphasises their decentralised nature. It makes little sense to try and compare the Democratic Party of Duluth and the Democratic Party of, for example, Georgia. Duluth is in the heavily industrialised 'rust belt', the local Democratic Party is strongly left wing, indeed it is Communist influenced. In Georgia, the party has to respond to the innate conservatism of the South.

The only time that the US parties operate as national organisations is once every four years, during the Presidential election because the President is the only nationally elected politician. Each party's national committee organises the Presidential campaign - the Republican National Committee (RNC) and the Democratic National Committee (DNC). In non-Presidential election years the national committee has very little influence. Thus the DNC and RNC have very little control over candidates fighting mid-term elections. The exception was November 1994 when the Republican campaign was more centralised, especially that of the House Republicans fighting for the 'Contract with America'.

In America, the parties do not have a mass membership; they have activists who work for the party and they have 'identifiers' who broadly support the party but they do not have a dues-paying membership. Pressure groups seek to influence the parties at local level, where most decisions are made. For example, the United Auto Workers (UAW) virtually runs the Democratic Party in Detroit, Michigan

There is a great deal of cross-party voting in Congress. Southern Democrats, such as Senator Sam Nunn of Georgia and former Senator Lloyd Bentsen of Texas, tend to be more conservative than Northern Democrats such as Senator Kennedy from Massachussets. Southern Democrats, known as 'boll weevils', formed part of the conservative coalition which supported Reagan during his first term. In contrast, liberal Northern Republicans, known as gypsy moths', often opposed his more radical policies.

One way of looking at the US party system is to say that there are not really two parties at all; as Burns argues, there are really four parties: Congressional Democrats, Congressional Republicans, Presidential Democrats and Presidential Republicans. Or it could be argued that there are 102 parties - a two-party system in each of the 50 States and 2 Presidential Parties. Within each State the parties organise on a ward/precinct/county basis. The only politicians elected across the whole State are the Governor and the two Senators. Within each State the lower levels of the party organisations also have a high degree of autonomy.

Thus, the parties have a pyramid structure with the RNC/DNC at the top, below them are the 50 State Parties, then the county organisations of which there are thousands altogether. At the bottom are the Precincts/Ward committees of which there are tens of thousands. The state and county committees are the real power bases and they are more concerned with the nomination and election of Congressional candidates and State politicians than they are with the national party. Even the State party organisation has weakened as a result of the increased number of Primaries.

The Republicans are a leadership party, so power flows from the top to the bottom. In the Democrats power flows from the bottom to the top.

This allows the Republicans generally to appear more united but it is the Democrats who practise intra-party democracy. Both parties are said to be non-ideological and Clinton's 'New Democrat' ideas were centrist in much the same fashion as Blair's 'New Labour'. However the Republicans are displaying all the same signs of ideological division as the British Conservatives, split between Neo-conservatives such as Ashcroft and moderate Republicans such as Powell.

The separation of powers principle enshrined in the constitution has meant that the Administration cannot rely on party backing in the Legislature. They are elected separately, by different constituencies, with the President being the only nationally elected figure. The President is the nominal party leader but he has no sanctions against 'disloyal' party members. The opposition party do not even have a nominal leader. So the governmental system and the lack of ideological cohesion have prevented any national parties on the West European model. Critics, such as Walter Dean Burnham, blame this weakness of party for the problems in American politics since the early 1960s. They look to the strong party system of Western Europe as a model.

However, the two major parties in the USA have both endured for well over a century; their domination of American politics clearly does not depend upon national organisation. Thirty years ago, the conventional wisdom maintained that American political parties were in long term, irreversible decline. Authors such as Walter Dean Burnham ('Critical Elections and the Mainsprings of American Politics, 1970) David Broder ('The Party's Over', 1972) and Martin Wattenerg ('The Decline of American Political Parties, 1984) emphasised that parties were being replaced by pressure groups as the main channel of communication between citizens and the government. These studies tended to focus on the Democratic Party.

This 'decline of party thesis' is not confined to America; in Britain, for example, as Mulgan and Sayeed and Whitely point out membership has been steadily falling over the last 25 to 30 years. However the process has apparently gone further in the USA because parties there were never as formally entrenched, even in their heyday from the 1930s to 1950s, as they were in Britain.

However this party decline theory has been challenged by authors such as James Reichley ('The Rise of National Parties, 1985), Xandra Kayden and Eddie Mahe ('The Party Goes On; The Persistence of the Two Party System in the United States', 1985) and Gerald Pomper ('Party Renewal in America', 1982). These studies have focused on the Republican Party which has been very successful in Presidential elections over the past 35 years, winning six out of nine, and has also been able to overcome the long-standing Democratic domination of Congress and the State Legislatures and Governorships.

Under the Chairmanship of Senator Bill Brock, the Republican National Committee centralised power within the party through, for example, the use of direct mailing. Brock is given much of the credit for the very impressive Republican performance in winning the Senate in 1980. Many commentators heralded this as the beginning of the much discussed Republican realignment. However, according to Nicol Rae, the strengthening of the Republican National Committee has more of a response to dealingment than a harbinger of a new, centralised, disciplined, strong-party model.

The conclusion to be drawn from the recent literature on parties, together with recent election results and polling surveys, is that the parties have survived their long predicted demise but that they remain regional organisations responding to regional concerns except during Presidential elections. In the summer of 2004, the National Committees under their Republican and Democrat chairmen will swing once more into action.

Party Decline

Geoff Mulgan argues that in our post-industrial society political parties are declining in importance, they are like dinosaurs, unable to adapt to their changing environment. He claims that this is healthy, people are getting involved in a new kind of politics. Pressure groups, or more accurately New Social Movements such as the anti-road lobby, set what Mulgan calls 'weak control,' broad parameters allowing individual or local initiative. The anti-war movement of 2002/3 showed that people, especially young people, are capable of being politicised by issues they really care about. However for Peter Riddell the decline of party membership is the single biggest problem in British politics. Pressure groups find it hard to make the transition from a single issue group to more general demands.

As Democratic Audit point out 'UK parties are small by European standards and their memberships have halved over the last 20 years. ..Many local branches are now virtually defunct. Given the decline in their membership and in support from trade unions and corporate sponsors the two main parties increasingly rely on donations from wealthy individuals …..This fuels the suspicion that large donors exercise an improper influence over policy, or gain other advantages for themselves.' Blair got into trouble early on over a £1 million donation from Bernie Ecclestone which coincided with the government exempting Formula One racing from the ban on tobacco advertising. Mandelson's second resignation came over his connection with the wealthy Hinduja brothers and an apparent attempt to help them get passports. Lord Sainsbury recently gave a huge donation to Labour as did Lakshmi Mittal the steel magnate. Labour received £100,000 from Richard Desmond the 'soft porn king' before allowing him to go ahead and buy the Daily Express. Parties now have to conform to strict rules on finance and expenditure including a requirement to publish all donations over £5,000 and a complete ban on overseas donations.

The decline of party may well be accompanied by the rise of more personality centred politics as in the USA with people like Perot, Berlusconi, Goldsmith, perhaps Imran Kahn providing the role models. Seyd implies that the decline of party may well be unhealthy for democracy because the rise of candidate centred politics as in the USA will enhance the importance of the media and of money.

 'Parties are in decline all over the democratic world'. Is this true and does it matter?

Chapter 8
Open Government and the Media

One of the major differences between totalitarian states and liberal democracies is that, in closed societies, such as China, citizens are not allowed free access to information which may prove embarrassing to the state. In pluralistic societies, such as Britain and the USA, governments boast that their citizens enjoy democratic rights, such as a free media and access to information, provided its release will not threaten national security. In a democracy, where ultimately power rests with the people, the electorate must be sufficiently well informed about controversial issues to make an informed judgement. As Francis Bacon said 400 years ago **'knowledge is power'**.

Many critics argue that the British state is perhaps the most secretive of all the liberal democracies. The usual contrast is with America, where there is a Freedom of Information Act and a very vigilant media, as the Watergate, Irangate and Pentagon Papers examples demonstrate. However, most other democracies also have a similar commitment to openness. Canada, Australia and New Zealand are easily comparable with Britain because they have a parliamentary system of government. They have all introduced Freedom of Information legislation in the last 20 or so years. In Europe, nations such as Sweden have taken freedom of information even farther than the Americans and have opened current Cabinet records to public inspection.

In Britain, the 30-year rule was introduced in 1967. Cabinet papers and minutes are kept secret for a minimum of 30 years. Sometimes they are not released for 50 to 100 years and sometimes they are never opened to public inspection. Senior civil servants are responsible for 'weeding' the records to ensure that even after 30 years nothing which may prejudice national security is publicly available. Thus the government papers for the year 1972 were released in January 2003. Many documents relating to the still controversial Suez operation have still not been made available 47 years later.

Even when records are made available, they often tell us very little about how decisions were really made. Cabinet minutes provide a very bare record of the heated discussions generated by controversial issues. They ignore the political arguments, simply recording what decisions were reached. The diaries of Richard Crossman, Hugh Dalton and Barbara Castle divulge more than any government papers and the diaries of Tony Benn are the most revealing of all. However, such sources obviously have to be treated with caution.

The Official Secrets Act of 1911 became infamous in the 1970s and 1980s as the prosecutions under it received enormous publicity. On each occasion, except for Tisdal, the defendant was acquitted. Section Two was a 'catch all' clause, extremely vague and wide-ranging in its implications. Several 'establishment' figures such as Lord Franks and Leon Brittan suggested 'pensioning off' Section Two. Following the acquittal of Ponting and the embarrassing revelations of Peter Wright, the Act was effectively discredited. In 1989, the government introduced a new Official Secrecy measure which Hurd claimed would open up government but which critics, even on the Tory benches such as Richard Shepherd, argued would tighten secrecy.

A widely based pressure group, the Campaign for a Freedom of Information Act headed by Des Wilson and supported by some retired mandarins such as Sir Douglas Wass and Sir Frank Cooper, seeks the repeal of the Act and the introduction of something similar to the American, Canadian and Australian systems. They recommend the introduction of a 'secrecy ombudsman' to monitor the release of government papers; highly sensitive information, for example financial matters, would still remain secret. The Liberal and Labour Parties favoured such an Act although Labour's record on open government did not inspire campaigners with much confidence. The Conservatives remained unconvinced over the need for reform although Major did open up the system a little.

In Government Labour did introduce a Freedom of Information Act but it does not go anything like as far as reformers wanted. The original proposals of David Clark went too far for Blair so Clark was sacked in summer 1998. Responsibility was given to Straw who was not an enthusiast and his Bill was a heavily diluted version. Pyper suggests that civil service pressure may have been partly responsible. There are a large number of exemptions and the Government can override the independent Information Commissioner. The Act will not be fully implemented until 2005. Meanwhile the obsession with spin indicates a government unwilling to be open.

The Democratic Audit stresses that 'freedom of expression is circumscribed by the Official Secrets Act and ancient common laws of defamation, blasphemy and sedition. Defamation in particular enables the wealthy and powerful to protect themselves from adverse criticism and there is inadequate protection for whistleblowers'. The Shayler case shows that Labour is just as keen to prevent openness in the security services as the Conservatives were.

However Section Two was just the most notorious part of the whole edifice of secrecy in British government. The 'D Notice' system, whereby the press exercise a 'voluntary' restraint when reporting sensitive defence matters, is just as important. Similarly the 'lobby system' whereby a group of political correspondents were given unattributable, 'off the record', briefings by the Prime Minister's press spokesman sometimes even before MPs. This allowed the government to disseminate information whilst disclaiming responsibility. The newspapers did not have to go along with this system; indeed the Independent and the Guardian for a time boycotted such briefings. However Labour have reformed it. Lobby briefings are now on the record with journalists able to name their sources. Briefings are also open to all journalists not just a trusted few. Repealing Section Two by itself will do little to alter the 'culture of secrecy' which pervades British politics.

In the USA, government records are released within a few months unless there are good grounds, such as national security, for holding them back. The Freedom of Information Act dates back to 1966 but it was amended in 1974 in the light of Watergate. The report of the Tower Commission into Irangate, which was very scathing about how decisions were reached in the 'Arms for Hostages' affair, is publicly available. Indeed so much more open is the American system, that British historians and journalists often find out about British politics from American government records. In the 'Spy Catcher' case British visitors to America bought up the book which was freely available there long before it could be published in Britain.

It is important not to overstate the degree of 'openness' in America. For example, when Frank Snepp, the former CIA station chief in Saigon, wrote his account of the mismanaged American evacuation of South Vietnam, 'Decent Interval', the Carter Administration successfully prosecuted him. Under Reagan, the American system became less open. The proportion of documents declassified, made publicly available, has been cut. Lie detectors have been introduced and, in November 1985, were applied to all "individuals with access to United States Government sensitive information". Executive privilege provides a useful way for the President to deny information to Congress and the media. The scandal about the Clinton administration's use of FBI files shows that the US system is not immune to manipulation of information. However, despite these qualifications, it is undoubtedly true that the American system is much more open than the British not just because of the 1966 and 1974 Acts but because there is a healthy scepticism about the need for secrecy and a respect for the importance of the freedom of the press which seems absent in Britain. It is **the more open political culture** rather than any specific statute which makes government more accountable.

Clearly secrecy or openness in government is a relative concept. In comparison with China, the British system is very open. In comparison with the system used in America and most other democracies the British system is very secretive. Cabinet committees, where most important decisions are actually taken, did not even officially exist until Thatcher admitted to the existence of a handful of them. Neither did the government admit the existence of M15 or M16, until recently. This was despite the fact that their existence was taken for granted and they must have long had budgets running into millions of pounds. Major promised more openness and there was some movement for example the publication of more details on Cabinet Committees but in other areas there has been regression, in particular the increased use of QUANGOs.

As Democratic Audit puts it 'the Human Rights Act has transformed the law on privacy'. In 2003 Michael Douglas and Catherine Zeta Jones won their case against Hello magazine on these grounds. However 'privacy is also threatened by the actions of covert state surveillance agencies and the accumulation by public bodies of personal information obtained from private institutions and service providers.'

No one denies the need for secrecy in certain areas, but with British governments, of both parties, there almost seems to be a desire for secrecy for its own sake.

The way in which information is disseminated by the media is as important as the legal restrictions on the release of that information so in order to understand the way citizens are informed - or not - it is important to look at the operation of the mass media.

The Media

Introduction

The mass media includes TV, radio, film, video, satellite broadcasting, computers, the internet as well as newsprint. We live in a media saturated society where thinkers such as Jean Braudrillard have argued that the only reality is that which happens in the media. Thirty years ago Marshall McLuhan argued that TV had created a global village. The global broadcasting of events such as the Live Aid concert in 1985 and the release of Mandela in 1990, events which were watched by a majority of the world's population seem to have proved him correct. Over 95% of the world's TV sets were apparently tuned into the Live Aid concert. If Vietnam was the first televised war then the Gulf War of 1991 was the first satellite war and gave enormous publicity to CNN. However we need to put this into perspective; as Chomsky points out far from most people having access to the internet the majority of the world's population have probably never made a phone call. China with a population of about 1,200 million has about 15 million phones, France with a population about 4% of China's has 33 million phones.

About 40% of American households in 2001 had access to the internet. Many use it for political information, particularly younger, more educated Americans. They tend to be more liberal. The internet played a role in the 2000 election with Bush posting details of his financial backers, McCain raising funds through the net and Gore and Nader supporters using information on trading votes. Given the obvious centrality of the media, particularly TV to social life then it is important to examine its political impact. We need to consider who owns it, who controls its output and is the output biased?

Ownership and Control

In closed societies the state owns or at least rigidly controls the media. In Albania under Communist rule the authorities were so paranoid about controlling information that TV and radio were illegal and every typewriter had to be registered with the state. As for liberal democracies it is possible to give fairly accurate information about the *ownership* of media organisations; there have also been a number of studies about the end product, studies looking at the content of the media. It is clear that it is not easy to identify where *control* lies, and there is considerable disagreement about the relative amount of control exerted by owners, those working in the media, the government, the advertisers and the audience.

The UK is typical of liberal democracies in the sense that most UK media organisations are in the private sector; they are public limited companies; newspapers, magazine and book publishers, record companies, film, commercial TV and radio, satellite TV. A prime function of these companies is to be profitable. Through a process of mergers and take-overs, the number of companies involved has fallen, and the ones that remain are often very large, with a large share of the market - concentration of ownership. Concern has been expressed about the falling number of companies; is it a threat to the 'free press' because the consumer has less choice?

The larger companies also tend to be conglomerates, with interests in more than one area of the media, or with interests in completely different areas of business. They are frequently multinational with interests in different countries. As far back as 1970, Golding pointed out that 5 companies controlled nearly 75% of record sales, cinema audiences, paperback books, national daily newspaper sales. Murdoch's 'News International' owns the Sun, News of the World, Times, Sunday Times, Times Supplements, until he closed it down recently Today, some evening and weekly papers, American papers such as the New York Post, Australian TV, and BSkyB and he also has aviation interests. BSB attempted to compete with Sky for 8 months before amalgamating on Murdoch's terms. The law restricted newspapers to owning 20% of one TV station but this does not apply to satellite hence Murdoch can own BSkyB.

Maxwell's 'IPC' also had major newspaper, magazine and publishing interests. In Italy Berlusconi owns three TV stations commanding 45% of the audience. In France there are two TV channels controlled by the state and a strong tradition of 'arm twisting'. Murdoch owns 70% of the Australian popular press. Labour's proposed Communications Bill will remove all restrictions on foreign ownership and permit single ownership of ITV and Channel 5. To quote Democratic Audit 'the Government has brushed aside criticism from a parliamentary select committee to the effect that such a dramatic change will be achieved at the expense of creativity and pluralism, A new regulatory body, Ofcom, will have significant powers but may find it impossible to reconcile the twin aims of more competition and greater pluralism of content…A combination of deregulation and intensified competition has squeezed out a great deal of quality drama, news and investigative journalism from TV in favour of lightweight entertainment, a process that is mirrored in the broadsheet press. Both media collude in the trivialisation of politics, concentrating on personalities and splits rather than policy issues." TV coverage of the 2001 election was down on that of 1997. A special Question Time with Blair got 2.6 million viewers whilst 11 million switched channels to watch the British Soap Awards.

Silvio Berlusconi used his control of the media to promote his political agenda thereby becoming PM of Italy. Is this a sign of a new kind of politics, free from the traditional mass party, appealing via the media directly to the public? If so could it be that Britain's Berlusconi could be someone like Richard Branson?

Ownership can be identified; **the problem is still to explain who has control** over the content. One possibility is that control is in the hands of the owners or the major shareholders, who exert a powerful influence over their organisation. There are examples of 'newspaper barons' in the past such as Lord Beaverbrook of Express papers and in the present such as Murdoch who have used their position to be involved in appointing editors, sacking editors and print workers, making their views known to those responsible for the daily running of the paper.

Beaverbrook claimed 'I run the newspaper purely for the purpose of making propaganda'. Lord Mathews of Express Newspapers stated "By and large, the editors will have complete freedom … as long as they agree with the policy I have laid down." As Murdoch put it "I did not come all this way not to interfere" According to Harold Evans, former editor of The Times, Murdoch interfered by: "Sending me articles marked 'worth reading', which supported right-wing views, by pointing a finger at headlines which he thought could have been more supportive of Mrs Thatcher".

It is clearly difficult to unravel the relative power and control of all the groups involved. The owners of media organisations, the ruling class if there is such a class to which the owners belong and interact with; the journalists who work in the media, and are influenced by their social background, their idea of a good story, and the practical constraints under which they operate such as deadlines, what information is available. Journalists have a key role as gatekeepers. The market pressures exercised by advertisers and consumers upon whom the media depends for its income and those seeking access to the media such as pressure groups or seeking to keep information out of the media as with companies causing pollution or producing dangerous products.

The legal powers of the government are embodied in the BBC's Charter drawn up in 1927, and in the Broadcasting Act of 1990, which regulates the ITC and includes the statement that the Home Secretary may "at any time require the authority to refrain from broadcasting any matter or classes of matter specified." For some observers, such power comes uncomfortably close to political censorship, which is thought to have no place in a democratic society.

The relationship between the media and the state is one of interdependence. According to John Whale "The media and the state are in two minds about each other; a certain tension separates them, on the other hand undeniable ties bind them". Maintaining this delicate balance, by formal and informal means, is a continuous process which periodically erupts into open conflict. The French media is far more subject to government control than the British and the Russian media is virtually an arm of the Putin government, but even in the UK Governments are involved in several ways. The government appoints the Board of Governors of the BBC as well as the members of the Independent Broadcasting Authority which sets the standards for commercial TV and radio. Thatcher appointed 'Marmaduke' Hussey, a Tory, as Chairman of the Governors of the BBC although by convention if there is to be a Tory Chairman he should be balanced by a Labour deputy as Hussey was with

Joel Barnet a former Labour Minister. Blair was criticised for appointing Gavin Davies, a friend of Gordon Brown, as Chairman.

The government is also responsible for legislation which affects the media, such as the requirement that broadcasting is neutral. Government gets involved in the control of ownership as when Murdoch bought the Times, the bid had to be cleared by the Monopolies Commission. Prior censorship is rare in Britain during peacetime, but it occurred in 1986 over 'Zircon' when the Special Branch actually raided BBC Scotland, and arguably it occurred in 1985 over 'Real Lives At the Edge of the Union' a documentary about terrorism which the government 'requested' the BBC not to broadcast.

The Official Secrets Act prevents publication of information via civil servants. D-notices (the D stands for Defence) 'advise' the press not to report certain issues and makes it difficult for them to have access to the news in future if they disobey. This system is rarely used and has no legal backing, but it generally 'works'.

Controls are particularly significant in times of war as in the Falklands - decisions about who could go with the Task Force, censorship and delays in releasing reports and pictures which were not considered to set the right tone, or in 1991 in the Gulf War. By the Iraq war of 2003 the collusion between the media and the state was such that certain journalists were 'embedded' with the armed forces. The courts are used to enforce the laws, although they do not always support the government, ultimately they did not support it over Spycatcher.

Most of the 'insider' information that journalists really value comes from two sources, 'leaks' and 'the lobby'. Political leaks are not accidental - they are controlled releases of information through which members of the government ensure that information reaches the public via the media, but is not attributable to any one source. The Government, although having far less control than in, say, Russia, still has an important influence.

In the wake of various sensationalist stories about members of the Royal Family and politicians there have been growing demands for a privacy law on the grounds that self regulation through the Press Complaints

Commission is not working. In 1989 Thatcher set up the Calcut Committee which subsequently recommended stringent regulations including a statutory tribunal. The Select Committee on National Heritage rejected this idea but the issue remains on the agenda as the comments by the Lord Chief Justice, Bingham, in May 1996 indicate.

By 1993 the tabloid press which had backed him so fervently in 1992 were extremely critical of Major, particularly over Europe. Blair went out of his way, literally he flew 12,000 miles to meet Murdoch in Australia, to establish good relations with Murdoch, and Labour dropped their intention to reform the law on cross-ownership thereby reassuring Murdoch. Perhaps this is why 'The Sun' backed Labour in 1997 and again in 2001.

The Manufacture of News

In their book, 'The Manufacture of News (1981), Cohen and Young outline two models of the media: the laissez faire, commercial or market model and the manipulative model. The models make contrasting comments about both the content and the effects of the mass media.

In general, commentators reject an extreme version of the laissez faire model, they do not accept that the news is an objective account of what is happening. It is in fact the case that the news is a manufactured product; those who produce the news are involved in a process of selecting events for news coverage and also in making decisions about how to present the issues that have been selected.

A considerable number of studies have been conducted to illustrate the fact that the news is manufactured. James Curran points out the limited amount of news in the popular press which focuses on the human interest story. The Glasgow University Media Group's 'Bad News' (1976) ask how balanced the broadcast news is? There **is a hierarchy of access to the media and a hierarchy of credibility**. From the media's point of view, strikes equal bad news; the media deal with effects not causes, the workers are seen as solely responsible for strikes.

Clearly, there are different possible interpretations of the nature of the news. One explanation would accept the manipulative model and see news as an expression of the views of the powerful groups in society, the state in a society where government controls the media, the ruling class in a capitalist society. Miliband sees the link between the control of the economy and the control of ideas; for him, the owners of the media are clearly part of a capitalist class and, therefore, their support for this class and the one-sidedness of the press are to be expected.

But in Britain the government has limited control over the media and not all experts would accept that the media is simply the mouthpiece of the ruling class. Certainly both Young and Tunstall would reject this view as one-sided. Bilton says it is 'too simplistic to suggest a conscious process of collusion between the media and those in powerful positions in society.' Most papers give a centre or right of centre view of society and, by concentrating on human interest stories, give little analysis of social issues.

Those who prefer the laissez faire model point out that there is a free press which is not completely under government control and there is some diversity of views expressed. Colin Seymour-Ure argues that in the Thatcher years relations between government and media were marked by three features. Firstly, informal political pressure with occasional resort to the law; secondly, an aggressively free market approach both to the press and to the broadcast media including the promotion of trade union legislation favourable to the employers; thirdly, an indifference to the creation of cross-media conglomerates. There are plenty of instances of the media uncovering events that are highly embarrassing to the powerful in society such as 'Death on the Rock' the documentary about the SAS killing suspected terrorists in Gibraltar. The survival of the media depends on providing the consumer with what he or she wants. In broadcasting, 'due impartiality' results in balanced coverage. Those who produce the media, the gatekeepers, set the agenda. The sort of news they produce will be influenced by their social backgrounds, and their career plans.

John Pilger argues that the British media generally endorse the status quo and even The Daily Mirror which was once a radical, challenging paper has gone downmarket witness its deplorable chauvinism over the England-Germany game in 1996. However under Piers Morgan the Mirror has in some ways become radical again as in opposing the war in 2003. Pilger himself regularly presents iconoclastic documentaries on the TV, so clearly he is not censored.

The former Labour Home Secretary Jack Straw has drawn attention to the decline in the coverage of Parliament even in the so-called quality press. This has fed into a more general concern that TV is supplanting Parliament as the main political forum.

Northern Ireland

McCann argues that 'people have a distorted view of events in Northern Ireland'; he claims the reporting of the British troops has been over-favourable and the reporting of the IRA over-critical. He says that the British press is in a constant state of adaptation to the needs of the British ruling class. There is no free press. Those who have ultimate control over what is printed are drawn from a tiny segment of society, the owners of big business. One of the qualifications for editorship is general acceptance of the owner's values. Journalists know well what is expected of them and what their paper's line is. There is a fair mount of self-censorship. If a reporter does send through a report which is critical of the establishment it is at the mercy of news editors and sub-editors with years of experience of what is acceptable.

Philip Elliot ('Misrepresenting Ulster') is also critical of the coverage of Ulster, but doss not take a Marxist line. Elliot argues that official sources of information (the army, public relations departments) have sometimes misled journalists by, for example. blaming the IRA for violence caused Loyalists - in other words, they use the media for propaganda.

Media coverage has concentrated on acts of violence (especially violence in England, e.g. the murder of Ian Gow; violence in Ulster now appears 'less newsworthy') rather than on the political issues involved. By simply reporting what has happened 'who did what, to whom, where', journalists can say they are simply recording newsworthy events. It does not increase understanding of the situation, but it saves journalists getting involved in difficult judgements about the causes of the conflict.

Though the Northern Ireland conflict has for the last 35 years been one of the most tightly controlled areas of news reporting, there is still very little formal censorship, in the sense of directives or bans by government, which is why the ban on Sinn Fein received so much attention. The ban lasted from 1988 to 1994 when the cease fire began. But there hardly needs to be censorship, for both government and media know the informal values which make the system self-regulating.

As Barrat puts it, "There is no need to police a mass medium that is itself so well-regulated that it never steps out of line. The arsenal of powers that the state is able to deploy against the media is for the most part kept in reserve....a deterrent to deviance and a spur to self-control."

The Media and American Politics

The First Amendment to the Constitution states that 'Congress shall make no law abridging the freedom of the press'. Now in the electronic age, when 98% of American homes have televisions and the average American watches 30 hours of TV a week, the media have an even more important role to play in politics. The majority of people get most of their information about politics from television. In 2000 television earned $663 million from political advertising, more than double the 1992 figure. Certainly politicians themselves believe in the power of TV. They routinely arrange their schedule so as to ensure coverage on one of the three evening network news programmes. David Stockman, Reagan's ex-Director of the Budget, wrote scathingly of the Reaganauts, such as Michael Deaver and others, for whom 'reality happened once a day, on the evening news, they lived off the tube'.

As Lyndon Johnson put it, 'All you guys in the media, all of politics has changed because of you'. Johnson meant that politics had changed for the worse, and that television was most to blame, that it had trivialised political coverage. John Kennedy though believed that television coverage was politically neutral and helped compensate for the conservative bias of the newspapers. He was particularly angry over the papers' coverage of American policy in Vietnam. This is richly ironic in view of Johnson's later belief that TV had turned Americans against the war. In 1968, Johnson watched the well respected TV anchorman Walter Cronkite reporting critically from Vietnam. LBJ told his Press Secretary 'if I've lost Cronkite, I've lost Mr Average American'.

Indeed by the 1970s, television had become invested with 'semi-magical powers'. It was credited with helping to get rid of McCarthy after the Senate hearings into Communist infiltration of the Army were televised and McCarthy's demagogic character was revealed for all to see; with ending segregation as the callous, bullying tactics of racists such as 'Bull' Connor the Police Chief of Birmingham, Alabama were displayed to an appalled public; with discrediting American involvement in Vietnam, the first televised war, and with destroying Richard Nixon, as the televised Watergate hearings exposed the corruption at the heart of the Nixon White House.

This certainly exaggerates the power of TV. It is calculated that the entire output of the news programmes contains less information than the front page of the New York Times. There are 1,750 daily papers in the USA employing 56,400 journalists. However 98% of American towns and cities have only one daily paper. Most concentrate on local news. Only a handful really cover national or international politics.

Some politicians have learned to use TV to their advantage, for example Kennedy in the 1960 Presidential election debate with Nixon, and Nixon himself in his 'silent majority' speech condemning the student protesters in 1969. Just as Roosevelt used the radio to get his message across in his 'fire-side' chats, so Reagan used TV to appeal directly to the people, over the heads of Congress. Mondale was one politician who admitted he had never come to terms with the demands of TV and this did cost him votes in 1984. Dukakais was equally uninspiring as a television candidate, in particular during the second televised debate. One of the problems with Bush senior was that he could never articulate 'this vision thing'. Clinton was much more articulate than either Bush.

The 1980s witnessed the revival of radio as a political medium. Political radio is more3 conservative with 'shock jocks' such as Rush Lambaugh. The other important development is the rise of cable television. In the 1996 election only 21% of Americans obtained their political information from cable, by 2000 this was up to 35%. Within cable the previous near monopoly of CNN has been challenged by Fox among others. Fox coverage of the war on Iraq in 2003 was notably more hawkish than that of CNN.

Television responds to images much more than to content. During the 2002 elections the rival candidates promoted themselves, or more often attacked their opponents, through ten second advertisements. In the event, many voters seemed to react against such negative advertising and some of the biggest spending candidates were defeated. Despite some concern that the 2001 British election was too 'Americanised', American commentators were impressed by the way in which issues and policies were debated at length on the television and radio.

American TV is dominated by commercial concerns. In 1979, there were 746 commercial stations and 267 educational stations, the latter covered by the umbrella of the Public Broadcasting Services, there being no American equivalent of the BBC, although the three national news networks NBC, ABC, CBS, have impressive reputations for objective reporting. In this country, some of the most innovative news and current affairs coverage has come from the independent networks especially World in Action, News at Ten and Channel Four 7 PM news.

During the Falklands War, the Ministry of Defence was careful to control the access journalists had to the actual fighting; reporting of the war was in effect censored. The British government was responding to the 'lessons' of the Vietnam War, that too much coverage can turn public opinion against a war. The American government used the same technique in the Grenada 'invasion'. The ramifications of the media coverage of Vietnam are still being felt. In 1984, General Westmoreland, Commander of the American forces in Vietnam, sued one of the TV networks for implying in a documentary that he had 'squandered' lives.

However, John Pilger, an Australian journalist who covered the war in South East Asia, doubts whether the media was against the war. In his view the American journalists covering Vietnam supported the alms of the war but questioned the efficiency of the war effort. If so, they were following in a long tradition. William Russell of the Times created a stir and (helped bring down the Aberdeen government) by his reporting of the Crimean War in the 1850s.

The leak of the secret 'Jay Treaty' of 1795 infuriated President Washington as much as the leak of the 'Arms for Hostages' story infuriated Reagan. The war against Iraq in 1991 was a television spectacle, almost an extended advert for the Patriot missile and the Stealth bomber. Much the same was true in 2003. The US Freedom of Information Act of 1966, 'beefed-up' in 1974 after Watergate, allows American journalists much greater license than their British counterparts, as was demonstrated again in the 'Spycatcher' affair. However, even in the more open system prevailing in the USA, the government still has a vested interest in restricting information and, according to Godfrey Hodgson, Nixon wanted to introduce a British style Official Secrets Act.

Most recent controversial cases involving the media in American politics concern the press rather than television or radio. Nixon and his Vice-President, Spiro Agnew, were even more hostile to the press than they were to television. When he 'retired' in 1962, after losing the gubernatorial election in California, Nixon told the press, 'congratulations gentlemen, you won't have Richard Nixon to kick around anymore'. Agnew labelled the press 'an effete corps of snobs' and the "eastern liberal establishment". Reagan, a President who generally enjoyed a 'good press', claimed that their exposure of the hostage deal could have cost American lives.

The Pentagon papers case of 1971, the Woodward and Bernstein coverage of Watergate, the Time magazine accusation in 1984 that General Sharon approved the massacres in the refugee camps in Lebanon in 1982, the Miami Herald story about Gary Hart and Donna Rice and the Irangate story which actually 'broke' in a Lebanese paper in November 1986, are all examples of press stories seriously embarrassing and in some cases discrediting politicians. The Hart case is the most trivial but it does raise profound questions about journalistic ethics and privacy.

Not all politicians are damaged by adverse coverage. Geraldine Ferraro managed to overcome the setback to her campaign by the press revelations about her husband's finances. In the USA, the libel laws and the First Amendment often come into conflict. The 1964 case, New York Times v

Sullivan, was supposed to protect journalists making 'vigorous' comments' on the way public officials performed their duties, Instead it made editors more wary of controversial stories. Even though Sharon lost the case against 'Time', he won in the words of the magazine itself 'a moral victory of sorts'.

In the USA, as in Britain, newspapers are run as commercial concerns. American too has its 'Press Lords' such as Randolph Hearst on whom 'Citizen Kane' was based and the Chandler family. They too have their scandal sheets', such as the New York Post, owned by Rupert Murdoch, now an American citizen, and their 'quality' papers such as the Washington Post owned by Katherine Graham. Most owners, like businessmen in general, tend to be Republican sympathisers. Henry Luce, the founder of 'Time', waged a virulent campaign against the Democrats for having 'lost' China to the Communists. Agnew described the owners of the press as 'a small group of men with a concentration of power over American public opinion unknown to history'. In 1930, the British Tory leader Stanley Baldwin accused the Press Lords of seeking 'power without responsibility, the prerogative of the harlot throughout the ages'.

The press, radio and television combine into a curious form of pressure group whose purpose ought to be that of keeping government on its toes, but which sometimes seems to degenerate into sensationalism. All the scandal stories about Clinton did not appear to damage his support from the public, indeed perversely they improved his ratings. The media is particularly important in the USA where there is no official parliamentary opposition and they are able to scrutinise Executive policies more freely than in this country. Bush's occasional meetings with the press corps are the closest he gets to a 'Prime Minister's Question Time'- type grilling. In conclusion, a free media is essential to a pluralist society, but it must exercise responsibility.

? If knowledge is power, can government ever tolerate a free media?

Chapter 9
Electoral Systems

Introduction

As the interim report of the Plant committee set up by the Labour Party to examine electoral reform put it in July 1991 'There can be nothing more fundamental in a democracy than proposals to change an electoral system and it is imperative that we evaluate the reasons for such reforms, the criteria which we believe legitimate electoral systems should satisfy and that we examine in detail the major systems in the light of these criteria ... **Elections are central to democracy and their nature should not be determined by a few simplistic slogans.'**

Fundamental to all discussions of electoral reform is, or rather should be, the key question: **what are general elections for?**

In 'totalitarian' systems they serve a legitimising role. In liberal democracies elections are supposed to provide choice. Some people would answer that the primary function of a general election is to produce strong (by which they usually mean single-party), stable governments. Others, however, would argue that the aim is to produce a representative legislature. Most liberal democracies use some form of proportional representation but both Britain and the USA employ first-past-the-post, simple plurality, winner-takes-all electoral mechanisms, which do not necessarily guarantee a 'fair' result. To simplify greatly, PR is more representative than simple plurality systems but arguably it is not as effective at producing 'strong' government'.

Vernon Bogdanor argues that no government elected by less than 50% of the voters can claim to be 'strong', whereas Philip Norton argues that 'strong' government means one which is able to dominate the House of Commons'. If the main purpose of elections is to produce a representative legislature and government, then PR is the best mechanism. If the main aim is to produce a government assured of getting its proposals through the legislature, then simple plurality is preferable. The American system is more complex because, with a separation of powers and in the absence of strong parties, no government is assured of getting its measures through Congress.

Of course, it may be possible to produce an electoral system which can deliver both a proportionate result and an overall majority for one party. The Hansard Society's Commission on Electoral Reform in 1976 argued that it is possible to combine the two, as the German experience demonstrates.

However, the conventional wisdom maintains that this is unlikely. The debate about the validity of differing electoral systems therefore tends to revolve around this issue of priorities.

Features of FPTP

The present system is extremely straightforward. The UK is divided into 659 single member constituencies. A general election has to occur at least once every five years. Almost any British person over 18 can vote provided they have registered. The only exceptions are Peers, people in prison and the mentally ill. Similar requirements apply to candidates except that they have to be 21 and to lodge a deposit with the returning officer. This is returned if they achieve a certain threshold of votes. The candidate with the most votes wins, it does not need to be a majority. If an MP dies or retires during a Parliament there is a by-election and identical rules apply. We also used the system to elect our local councillors.

% UK votes					Number of Seats			
Election	Cons	Lab	Lib	Others	Con	Lab	Lib	Rest
1951	48.0	48.8	2.5	0.7	321	295	6	3
1955	49.7	46.4	2.7	1.2	345	277	6	2
1959	49.4	43.8	5.9	0.9	365	258	6	1
1964	43.4	44.1	11.2	1.3	304	317	9	-
1966	41.9	47.9	8.5	1.7	253	363	12	2
1970	46.4	43.0	7.5	3.1	330	287	6	
Feb1974	37.8	37.1	19.3	5.8	297	301	14	23
Oct1974	35.8	39.2	18.3	6.7	277	319	13	26
1979	43.9	36.9	13.8	5.4	339	269	11	16
1983	42.4	27.6	25.4	4.6	397	209	23	21
1987	42.3	30.8	22.6	4.3	376	229	22	23
1992	41.9	34.4	17.8	5.9	336	271	20	24
1997	30.7	43.3	16.8	9.2	165	419	46	29
2001	31.7	40.7	18.3	9.3	166	413	52	28

Arguments in Favour of FPTP

Accountability of MPs

Single member constituencies mean that voters know who their representative is and he or she is accountable to them. Most MPs hold surgeries to address constituents concerns and more and more MPs regard

343

such work as one of their main responsibilities. This is why if Labour does adopt a form of PR it is likely to be a variant of AMS.

Strong Government

Those who favour retaining the present British system of First-Past-the-Post (or simple plurality) tend to stress the desirability of strong government. Their approach is summed up by Professor Norton who argues that: "fairness alone should not be the sole criterion employed to determine the mode of election. Strong single-party government is central to the Westminster model of government. Given a choice between an allegedly fairer system of election and one that tends to encourage majority governments, supporters of the Westminster model plump for the latter".

Defenders of the present electoral mechanism in Britain argue that in contrast with say Italy, Israel and Ireland the British system produces strong, stable government. Italy where they had a very pure form of PR had 50 governments between 1945 and June 1992 yet the same old faces cropped up all the time. The elite just shuffled itself. In 1993 the Italian electoral system was reformed so that it now incorporates an element of FPTP. The Israeli election of 2003, following which it took weeks to cobble together a government, seemed to emphasise that PR can cause party fragmentation and tiny parties are able to decide the fate of governments. Such negotiations in smoke filled rooms are typical of systems employing PR.

No Representation of Extremists

Neither the British Union of Fascists in the 1930s, the National Front in the 1970's or the British National Party since the 1980s have ever had a single MP elected. In fact they never even kept their deposits in a parliamentary election. They have won a few local council seats. The Communist party only ever had 2 MPs at any one time, but since 1951 there have been none.

Thus in Britain, extremists have not gained representation and have therefore lacked a national platform; contrast this with France where Le Pen was able to use his party's electoral success in gaining seats in the

Assembly to promote racist views. Extreme right wing parties have also done well in Austria, Belgium, Sweden, Denmark and Norway and in Italy the Northern League and the reborn Fascists have attracted a lot of support. In May 1994 Berlusconi formed a government which included the former fascists the Italian Social Movement (MSI).

Arguments Against FPTP

To some critics of the whole operation of the 'Westminster model' Norton's viewpoint may seem rather smug and complacent. Perhaps the model worked reasonably well in the period 1945 to 1970 when British politics was dominated by the duopoly and an alleged consensus. However, since the 1960s, there is surely little ground for self congratulation about the workings of the British political system. It is of course possible to be both against Proportional Representation and yet critical of the way British democracy works. Peter Hain, a Labour Minister and author of a book attacking PR, argues that: "Nobody can deny the validity of the cries unfair, foul or antiquated increasingly levelled at the British electoral system".

Constituency level

There are distortions at constituency level; for instance, in the 2001 election about 40% of MPs were elected by less than 50% of the voters. The winning candidate in 1992 in Inverness won just 26% of the votes, 19% of the electorate. Single member constituencies do not guarantee that constituents do contact their MP, indeed surveys show a majority of voters are even unaware who their MP is.

However, the advocates of PR tend to base their arguments on the distortions produced at national level. The British system is meant to be concerned with electing constituency MPs but, in reality, at least as far as most people are concerned, general elections are about electing governments.

Unrepresentative Outcomes

What seems like a fair principle at local level, that the candidate with the most votes wins the seat, sometimes appears very unfair when votes are translated into party strengths at Westminster. There is a big problem of under-representation of certain third parties, essentially those without a strong regional base. In the 2001 general election in Britain, the Labour Party polled around 41% of the votes but won 413 seats, over 60% of the House of Commons, giving them an overall majority of 167. The clear loser in terms of proportionality was the Liberals with 17% of the votes but just 52 seats, 8% of the total. John Curtice emphasises that the system now discriminates against the Conservatives as well. In 2001 they polled about 32% of the votes but only gained 166 seats.

In the 1989 Euro-election the British Greens had polled 15%, more than the Greens in any other country in the E.U., and yet did not gain a single seat in the European Parliament. The 1994 European elections produced an equally distorted result, the Liberals got 16.7% of the votes but won just 2 seats out of a total of 84. In this election, which was not about electing a government, the unfairness of the British system was much more glaring. As a result of the 1994 European elections the Socialists were easily the biggest party in the European Parliament with 198 seats to the European People's Party's 157. The 1999 Euro elections were for the first time in Britain fought under a PR system.

The best known examples of unfairness and distortion centre on the Liberals and the Alliance. In February 1974, the Liberals were grossly under-rewarded for their votes, over 6 million almost 20% of the total but they obtained only 14 seats. Approaching 20% of the votes cast the Liberals received only 2% of the seats. no wonder their price for a deal with Heath was PR. More recently, in 1983, the Alliance polled 25.4% of the votes, a staggeringly good result for a brand new political grouping, but because of the inequities of the electoral system this resulted in only 23 seats, 3.3% of the total. The Labour Party which received just 27.6% of the votes, its worst performance as a national party, obtained 209 seats 9 times as many. The 1987, 1992, 1997 and 2001 elections produced similar distortions.

It is important to point out that not all of the smaller parties suffer from First-Past-the-Post. For example, in the February 1974 election, for just 2% of the total national vote the S.N.P. received 7 seats. In October 1974 had they managed to increase the share of the vote in Scotland from 30% to the magic threshold figure of 35%, they would have achieved truly spectacular results., approximate proportionality. The big difference between them and the Liberals, of course, is that support for the SNP is regionally concentrated.

At the 1992 election it took just 42,357 votes to elect a Tory MP, 42,876 for Labour but a staggering 304,183 for the Liberals.

A relatively small shift in the share of the votes can produce huge shifts in the distribution of seats.

The Party that Wins the Vote May Lose the Election

The obvious examples of unfairness include 1929, 1951 and February 1974, when the party which won the most votes did not win the most seats and therefore did not form the government. It is scarcely relevant to the principle of majority rule that each major party has both suffered and gained from this defect. It could perhaps be argued that in 1929 Labour had a natural ally in the Liberal Party and that therefore a minority Labour government dependent upon Liberal support was not a bad reflection of public opinion despite the fact that the Tories won more votes.

Similarly, perhaps, it could be argued that in February 1974, despite the attempted Heath-Thorpe deal (which anyway would not have produced an overall majority) the logical conclusion of the Tories' failure to get a clear mandate was a Labour minority government, abetted if not supported by the Liberals. However, the 1951 result, which provided Labour with the record number of votes for any British party until 1992 (almost 14 million, 48.8% of the votes) was surely grossly unfair and illogical. Such results cast the already dubious concept of the mandate into further disrepute.

Absence of a Real Mandate

Fair representation of voters is only one of the criteria used for judging electoral systems. In Britain the two major parties argue that the main purpose of an election is to give a party a mandate to implement its manifesto policies. Thus the Attlee governments of 1945 to 1951 had a mandate to nationalise certain industries, whereas the Conservative governments since 1979 have had an equally valid mandate to privatise. The fact that neither government had the support of a majority of voters, let alone the electorate, is not regarded as important.

The mandate theory is of relatively recent origin and full of flaws. As Denning memorably remarked 'no-one reads manifestos'. It is obvious that not all of those who voted for the party in power agree with all of its proposals. Devolution for Wales was hardly the main factor behind the Labour victory in 1997, yet Labour in the Commons dutifully voted for it and the Lords let it through because it was in the manifesto.

In October 1974 Labour won a tiny overall majority even though they were voted into power by less than 40% of voters, just 28.6% of the electorate. The obvious irony is to compare this with their losing performance in 1951. As MacLean puts it: "If talk of the mandates is to bear any relationship to voting behaviour, the Labour Opposition of 1951-1955 had a very much clearer mandate to introduce its policies than the Labour government of October 1974." The Thatcher governments, one of the most radical of the century, which was positively endorsed by just three out of ten of the electorate. Yet both parties refer to the mandate concept as though it were the last word in democratic principle. If three-party politics is here to stay, then it is increasingly likely that governments will be formed by a party winning under two-fifths of the vote. In 1997 Labour won the support of just 43% of the 72% of those entitled to vote who actually did so. In 2001, because of the low turn out, Labour won office with the support of just 25% of British adults. It does seem disturbing that a government with the support of one in four adults can introduce and implement policies whether radical or not.

Of the 16 general elections since 1945, 15 have led to single party majority government, able to claim a mandate to implement their manifesto policies. Supporters of the system claim that this vindicates Britain's electoral system and more than compensates for any perceived unfairness.

Adversary Politics

It could be argued that, until 1970, there was a strong enough correlation between votes and seats for the electoral system to have legitimacy and even in the period since 1970 the system works well for most of the parties involved.

If the Westminster Model is regarded as a desirable form of politics and if two-partyism is regarded as the norm, then the existing electoral system is doing a good job because it is providing vote's with a clear choice between two major parties.

Professor Finer believes that the present system encourages adversary politics and that this has been a major factor in Britain's economic and political decline since 1945. For Finer, P.R. would promote consensus, centrist politics in which public policy ought to develop incrementally. It is an argument in favour of the status-quo and against radicalism, either of the left or the right. It reflects Finer's personal policy prejudices and it is therefore no more or less valid than the alternative argument which favours the present system because it does not allow for radical government elected by a minority of voters.

Absence of Strong Government

One of the standard arguments in favour of the simple plurality system is that it promotes strong government. However, eight elections (out of a total of twenty-three) this century have failed to guarantee any party a working majority. The eight occasions were 1910 (twice) 1923, 1929, 1950, 1964, February 1974 and October 1974. Admittedly three of those elections - 1950, 1964 and October 1974 - did produce a tiny overall majority.

The April 1992 election produced what looked like a working majority of 21 but by 1997 through a combination of by-election defeats and MPs was another hung parliament. Three other elections produced very decisive victories but were won by coalitions - 1918, 1931, 1935. Admittedly, by 1935 the so-called National Government was in effect the Tory Party in disguise.

In over one-third of elections this century no strong government - in the sense used by Norton, a single party with a working majority - emerged. Only one election in the C20th - 1900 - produced a majority of votes for any one party.

In the pre-1945 period, particularly the 1920s, hung Parliaments were much more common because the party system was in flux. In the hung parliament of January 1924, Labour took office even though it was not even the biggest party, such is the elasticity of the British Constitution.

Perhaps it might be better to look just at the situation since 1945. After all the period 1900 to the 1930s was complicated by three-party - or, if one includes the Irish, pre-1920 - four-party politics. In the peak period of duopoly - the 1945-1970 era - hung Parliaments appeared a deviation from the norm yet five elections produced uncertain results. Again, though only one of that five - February 1974 - actually produced no overall majority at all, the other four could hardly be described as decisive, clear cut verdicts.

Italy overtook Britain economically (Il Surpasso) in the late 1980s and the frequent changes of government there do not necessarily lead to radically different policies, indeed the Christian Democrats were involved in every government from 1946 to the end of the Cold War. There have been more radical policy discontinuities in Britain since 1970 than there have in Italy or Germany.

Electoral Reform

Electoral reform can take many forms, introducing fixed term parliaments, reducing the voting age to 16 or the second ballot system as used in much of the continent or the Alternative Vote as used in Australia. AV retains single member constituencies but the voter expresses their preferences. If a candidate gets over 50% first preferences then the bottom candidate is eliminated and their second preferences redistributed and so on until someone gets a majority. The advantage would be that every MP would have got majority backing. Some left wingers such as Hain and Kellner favour the adoption of the AV system in preference to any system based on PR.

The Plant Report

An interim report was published in 1991, the full report in 1993. The committee voted by 10 to 6 against retaining the existing system. It stressed, as had Kinnock, the importance of the constituency link so it opted for a form of AV known as the Supplementary Vote but Plant distinguished between legislative assemblies such as the Commons and deliberative assembles such as the European Parliament. PR is more pressing for deliberative assemblies in that they do not form a government. Thus it should be introduced for elections to the European Parliament and for an elected upper chamber. Labour has acted over MEPs but so far there is no election for the Upper Chamber.

Proportional Representation

Most people assume electoral reform to mean PR. Too often the critics argue for or against PR as though it were a standard, uniform system with the same merits and defects. It is not, and closer analysis of the various alternatives reveals a variety of advantages and disadvantages. Thus one might be both pro-PR and pro-single-member constituencies in which case the German AMS system has attractions.

The debate about electoral systems has to move away from the clichéd dogma and unthinking reactions characteristic of too many commentators and focus closely on the precise implications of alternative approaches.

As Peter Kellner pointed out, the choice is not between good and bad systems but between systems that are imperfect in different ways. In other words, he thinks PR is not a moral issue. Hence, Kellner takes Roy Jenkins to task for concentrating on the 'eminent equity of the case' for PR. In contrast, he admires Vernon Bogdanor's honesty in admitting that STV is not a perfect system, merely the least imperfect.

It is vitally important to appreciate that PR is a principle not a system. There are endless varieties of electoral system all producing a greater or lesser degree of proportionality. Dunleavy estimates that had the UK used STV in 1992 the Tories would have won just 256 seats, under AMS they would have got 268. Liberal representation would have gone up to 102 and 116 respectively. A description of the mechanics of electoral systems is therefore necessary.

Pure Party List

The Israeli system uses the closest to pure PR, a pure party list system where the % of votes translates almost precisely into the same % of seats, with no threshold. There are no constituencies and therefore no local accountability and if one agrees with Hain that centralisation of power is to be avoided, then clearly the party list system as used in Israel is unattractive because it concentrates power in the hands of the party elite, contradicting all these notions of intra-party democracy propagated by the left since the 1970s. Most importantly like all systems based on PR it tends to produce hung parliaments.

Israel is unstable and does suffer from frequent policy changes in such fundamental areas as foreign policy. However, Israeli politics is characterised by deep cleavages and the fragmentation of parties is not just due to PR: it is due to the unique nature of the problems facing the Israeli state, problems demonstrated by the closeness of the 2002 election.

MEPs for the UK (except Northern Ireland) were previously elected by the simple plurality system but are now elected by a closed regional party list which is a modified version of the system used in Israel. The 1994 and 1999 results were as follows

1994

	Labour	Con	Lib Dem	UKIP	Green	SNP	PC
% Vote	44.3	27.8	16.8	1.0	3.2	3.2	1.1
Seats won	62	18	2	O	O	2	O
% seats	71.8	21.4	2.4	O	O	2.4	O

The clear lack of proportionality of the 1994 results is staggering

1999

	Labour	Con	Lib Dem	UKIP	Green	SNP	PC
% Vote	28.0	35.8	12.7	7.0	6.3	2.7	1.9
Seats won	29	36	10	3	2	2	2
% seats	33.3	42.9	11.9	3.6	2.4	2.4	2.4

Clearly a much more proportional result.

The Additional Member System

Those who wish to criticise the present British mechanism and yet accept that the party list system is problematic often point to Germany as an example of a stable political system. It uses the Additional Member System, a combination of first-past-the-post and PR.

German voters have two votes; one is used to elect a single MP to represent their constituency, the other is used to support a party list. MPs from the list are used to top up the party's representation, provided they surpass a threshold of 5% of the list votes or 3 MPs in the constituency section, so as to achieve an overall fair result.

There are problems with AMS; it involves two categories of MP, those who were genuinely elected and those who are there to make up the numbers, the threshold prevents pure proportionality and like all systems based on

PR it tends to produce hung parliaments. This means that proportionate representation can lead to **disproportionate power** in the hands of the smaller parties such as the FDP. In 1982 the FDP broke away from their coalition with the SDP to form a government with the CDU.

A modified version of AMS was suggested for adoption in the UK by the Hansard Society in its report on electoral reform in 1976. The Labour Party Plant Report of 1993 also favoured a modified version. AMS is used to elect the Scottish Parliament, the Welsh Assembly and the Greater London Authority.

There are 129 MSPs of which 73 represent constituencies and 53 come from the party list. Labour was the biggest party in both the 1999 and 2003 elections but on neither occasion did they win a majority.

The 1999 results were as follows

Total no of:	Constituency contests		Regional Lists		
	Share of Vote	Seats Won	Share of Votes	Seats Won	Total seats
Conservative	16%	0	15%	18	18
LibDem	14%	12	12%	5	17
Labour	39%	53	34%	3	56
SNP	29%	7	27.3%	28	35
Others	2%	1			

In 1999 Labour with 56 seats formed a coalition with the Liberals on 17. Because the Liberals were only the fourth biggest party this arrangement provoked criticisms. Again it was a case of a smaller party having disproportionate clout.

Scottish Parliament Election 2003

Party	Constituency	Region	+/- on 1999	Total
Conservative	3	15	0	18
Labour	46	4	-6	50
Lib. Dems	13	4	0	17
Scot. Nat. Party	9	18	-8	27
Greens	0	7	+6	7
Scot. Socialist Party	0	6	+5	6
Independent	2	2	+3	4

Again Labour lacks an overall majority.

The Welsh result in 1999 was as follows.

Welsh Assembly 1999

	First vote seats	%	Second vote seats	%	Total
Labour	27	9	1	39	28
Plaid Cymru	9	27	8	28	17
Conservative	1	16	8	15	9
Liberal Democrat	3	12	3	13	6

Labour governed on their own at first and then later on formed a coalition with the Liberals. In 2003 Labour scraped a technical majority of the 60 seats.

Welsh Assembly 2003

Party	Constituency	Region	+/- on 1999	Total
Labour	30	0	2	30
Plaid Cymru	5	7	-5	12
Conservative	1	10	2	11
Lib. Dems	3	3	0	6
Other	1	0	1	1

The London Mayor is elected by the supplementary vote and the GLA by AMS. The results in 2000 were as follows.

		1st vote	%	2nd vote	%	
Ken Livingstone	Independent	667,877	39.0	178,809	12.6	776,427
Steve Norris	Conservative	464,434	27.1	188,041	13.2	564,137
Frank Dobson	Labour	223,884	13.1	228,095	16.1	
Susan Kramer	Liberal Democrat	203,452	11.9	404,815	28.5	
Ram Gidoomal	CPA	42,060	2.5	56,489	4.0	
Darren Johnson	Green	38,121	2.2	192,764	13.6	
Michael Newland	BNP	3,569	2.0	45,337	3.2	
Damian Hockney	UK Ind	16,324	1.0	43,672	3.1	

Geoffrey Ben-Nathan	Pro-Motorist Small Shop	9,956	0.6	23,021	1.6
Ashwin Kumar Tanna	Independent	9,015	0.5	41,766	2.9
Geoffrey Clements	NLP	5,470	0.3	18,185	1.3
Total vote		1,714,162		1,420,994	1,340,564

Summary Result of the Greater London Assembly Election 2000

	Constituency vote	%	Seats	List vote	%	Seats
	526,707	33.2	8	481,053	29.0	1
Labour	501,296	31.6	6	502,874	30.3	3
Liberal Democrat	299,998	18.9		245,555	14.8	4
Green	162,457	10.2		183,910	11.1	3
Others	95,612	6.0		246,238	14.8	-
Total	1,586,070		14	1,659,630		11

Single Transferable Vote

Used in the Republic of Ireland, Malta and for certain elections in Northern Ireland it has the following features;

1) Multi member constituencies

2) The parties put forward the appropriate number of candidates, three each in a three member seat, five in a five member and so on

357

3) The voter can discriminate not just between parties but between candidates within a party by casting his preferences for individual candidates across the parties - that is by splitting the ticket, it is in this sense that STV is said to be a 'built in primary'

4) The 'droop quota' establishes the number of votes necessary to get elected;

$$Q = \left(\frac{\text{total votes cast}}{\text{no. of MPs} + 1} \right) +1$$

5) Surplus preferences of successful candidates are transferred and the candidates with the lowest number of votes eliminated and their preferences transferred until the requisite number get the quota.

STV would not only achieve a fairer outcome it would almost certainly increase the number of women and non-white MPs thereby making the legislature more representative and possibly heightening awareness of politics.

There are problems with STV; the constituencies are very large, a 3 member seat in the UK would involve a quarter of a million people (still half the size of the Congressional districts in the USA though), it is complicated to work out the result and the outcome might not be known for days or even weeks. The Irish election of 1989 was followed by 'wheeler dealing' on the part of the PM Charles Haughey, a process which is typical of systems using PR, governments not decided by direct election but by often closed negotiations within the political elite. The resulting government in Ireland in 1989 was made up of parties who had lost support in the election. In Northern Ireland it is used to elect the devolved assembly and the three MEPs. However if the UK were to adopt PR then it is possible it would be STV because that is the system the Liberals favour as does the Electoral Reform Society.

Should the UK Adopt PR?

One of the problems with the whole debate is that advocates on both sides use foreign examples to 'prove' their case, without taking enough account of broader differences in political culture. Those who approve of PR and regard coalition government as stable point to Germany instead of Italy or Israel. It is always difficult to make international comparisons and those who claim foreign experience as evidence ought to be treated with suspicion.

It is difficult enough comparing Britain and the USA, two countries with a similar electoral system and a shared heritage, without trying to use the Italian, German or Portuguese models as examples of what would happen if Britain was to introduce PR. For example, the success of West Germany after 1949 owed a great deal to the desire to overcome the legacy of the Nazis. Yet to listen to some of the more passionate advocates of PR, the German 'economic miracle' was due to their voting system and Britain will never escape economic decline unless it adopts PR.

Hain believes that the argument about PR is a distraction from the more pressing issue of 'opening up' British politics to promote greater participation. He argues that democracy involves a search for greater accountability of elected representatives and more decentralisation of power. Whilst not going as far as the Rousseau notion that only direct democracy is legitimate and representative democracy is a sham, Hain argues for more public involvement in the political process than a four or five yearly ballot. This is an extremely interesting argument but it does seem as though Hain is trying to deflect the issue - PR and increased participation are not necessarily mutually exclusive.

The Jenkins Report
In David Marquand's view the tragedy for progressive politics in this country is that the Labour Party has been strong enough to see off the Liberals but not strong enough to displace the Tories. He would like to see the progressive majority represented through a progressive coalition to stop the Tories dominating. The simplest way for Blair to ensure that his government lasted longer than the six years which had been the longest

any Labour administration had continuously held office was to introduce PR, that way Labour would be the dominant party in a three party system.

In 1997 the Labour manifesto promised that Labour would set up an independent commission on electoral reform and that its report would then be put to the people in a referendum. The assumption was that Labour would abandon its illogical love affair with first-past-the-post and the whole Westminster Model. The long awaited 'realignment of the left' which Blair and Jenkins had discussed may finally become a reality. The clear implication was that the referendum on electoral systems would take place before the next election.

Labour won the 1997 election by a landslide but went ahead with the independent commission under Lord Jenkins. Having look at all the options Jenkins reported in the autumn of 1998 favouring a variant of AMS known as AV plus. The constituency MPs would be elected by the Alternative Vote and would be supplemented by top up members chosen from the party list.

Jenkins claimed that had AV+ been used in 1992 it would have produced a hung Parliament whereas in 1997 it would have given Labour an overall majority of 77 instead of 179.

Labour opponents of PR such as Straw argued that the proposed system was too complex. The only major Labour figures in support were Cook and Mandelson. By December 1998 Mandelson had resigned. As Foreign Secretary, Cook was unable to make much input into the debate. By January 1999 Ashdown announced his retirement, partly because he had 'given up ' on Blair over PR. The devolution elections of May 1999 and the European elections of June 1999 were fought under PR and Labour did relatively poorly. In the Scottish Parliament they had to form a coalition with the Liberals; in Wales they formed a minority government and their number of MEPs plummeted. This strengthened the hands of the anti-PR forces within Labour who were able to point to the outcome at Westminster should PR be adopted - a coalition or minority government. At the same time Blair was influenced by the experience of his European and NATO colleagues such as Schroeder who found themselves unable to take effective decisions because they needed the support of coalition partners.

Blair would always have had to fight hard to get PR through the Cabinet and Parliament against the opposition of many Ministers, MPs and the trade unions. The clinching argument was probably the failure of the Conservatives to recover from their shattering defeat. In May 1997 it was possible to see the Labour landslide as a one off, a freak result from which the Conservatives were bound to recover as they had after landslide defeats in 1906, 1945 and 1966. Therefore Blair may yet need to work with the Liberals and to be warm towards PR. However no such Conservative recovery occurred. The Conservative performance in the 1999 European elections when they came first on a very low turn out proved to be a false dawn. Apart from a very brief period in September 2000 when the fuel protest put the Conservatives above Labour for the first time in eight years the Labour lead held. Therefore no referendum took place. The Liberals responded by withdrawing from the Committee on Constitutional reform but this hardly troubled Labour. The 2001 Labour manifesto made no reference to PR. Jenkins expressed himself disappointed in Blair but again this made little impact. Labour went on to win in 2001 by almost as big a landslide as they had in 1997. For the moment Labour have lost interest in PR but should a Conservative recovery eventually occur then perhaps Labour will rediscover an interest.

Consequences of PR

Assuming that voting patterns are not changed, then PR would lead to a minority or coalition governments. Perhaps the premise is unrealistic. Just because no party since 1935 has had a majority of votes does not preclude this from happening in the future.

However, given that a second major premise here is that multi-partyism will continue then it looks unlikely that any party will get over half of the votes which means that PR will lead to hung parliaments. Even majority governments sometimes have to abandon legislation if no party has a majority then this would become more frequent.

If PR was implemented and minority or coalition governments were to reappear, much that has been said about the decline of Parliament would need revision. Much of the power of the Prime Minister is dependent upon his or her party having a majority in the Commons. A hung parliament would undoubtedly reduce the power of the PM, as the experience of countries with PR such as Eire and Germany demonstrates: there is no way that either Aherne or Schroeder could ever be accused of concentrating power or being 'Presidential'.

Whether such a reduction in power would be a good thing or a bad thing is very much open to debate. Roy Jenkins and Professor Bogdanor would argue that hung Parliaments would produce better government because it would force a return to consensus.

The most frequently heard objection to hung Parliaments is that they produce coalition or minority governments and that these are unstable. Italy is usually cited as the best evidence of this. However, as usual with this whole debate, one can pick one country for comparison to suit one's case.

PR would affect the role of the Civil Service, in a situation of governmental instability the officials would have more influence. It would affect the Monarchy who would be drawn more into politics through having to exercise choice over the PM and over dissolution of Parliament. Most importantly it might well lead to further constitutional reform in that it would empower the Liberals who would presumably demand the enactment of a Bill of Rights and so on.

Conclusion

There is no perfect electoral system, if there were then presumably every state would adopt it. What we need to know is - what is the electoral system intended to achieve?

Put bluntly, the 'Westminster Model' works well when there are two major parties; it cannot cope with a sustained three-party system. In 1951, the duopoly polled 97% of the vote, by 1983 that figure had fallen to 70%. If three-party politics was to be a temporary phenomena then perhaps there would be a case for retaining the simple plurality electoral system, but there is no evidence to suggest a rapid return to duopoly.

Britain is now evolving towards a multi-party system. The problem is that the present electoral system distorts the consequences of multi-partyism. Minor shifts in votes can produce huge shifts in terms of seats. At the extreme, if we retain the present system and we sustain multi-partyism, then elections can become almost a lottery.

Maurice Duverger implied that electoral systems cause different party systems to emerge. Thus P.R. will create a fragmented multi-party system whereas First-Past-The-Post promotes a system dominated by two parties. McLean disagrees with this. He believes that it is not usually the electoral system but more deeply rooted factors which determine how many parties emerge. Cultural, historical, geographical factors all play a part in determining a country's political development, not just the electoral system.

Peter Mair argues that the historical record shows that multi-partyism was often a **cause** not a consequence of PR. Countries adopted it around 1919 precisely because their political alignments were already fragmented with religious, ethnic or linguistic differences. Or they adopted it to prevent a unified party of the working class from achieving power. The British case was different; firstly because, apart from Ireland, there were few serious religious or ethnic divisions; secondly because the voting system was reformed as early as 1867 long before a party of the workers appeared so no mass political threat was apparent.

The two electoral system used in Britain and America are superficially similar, in that they both employ a simple plurality mechanism, they are very different in the way they operate and the way they affect the nature of government. The American electoral system has a bearing on the way the parties have developed and the way in which politics is dominated by consensus. However, American politics is shaped more by the separation of powers and federalism than it is by its electoral mechanism. In Britain, the electoral system has had a great impact on the way, parties have developed and the way in which consensus politics has given way since 1970 to adversary politics.

Yet, in Britain too, the way politics develops owes more to other factors, such as the nature of the political cleavages, than it does to which type of electoral mechanism is in use. It is the nature of the cleavages in society which is crucial. As Pultzer argued, class was the dominant cleavage in Britain. However, this appears to be changing.

For party positions on PR see section on the Constitution

The US Electoral System

In many ways, the USA can be regarded as the home of democracy. According to David McKay, there are over half a million elective positions in the more than 80,00 governmental units of the USA ranging from local officials through to the apex of the whole system - the Presidency. There is a democratic ethos running through American life, a healthy lack of deference towards those in authority combined with respect for the positions which those people occupy. Perhaps it stems from the frontier mentality or the lack of a feudal system but there is a strong belief in accountability and the need for an open political culture, a commitment to the protection of civil liberties.

All American elections, whether for the President or the local attorney involve a two stage process, firstly the process of choosing the rival party candidates and then the contest between the parties. Dennenberg heads his chapter on elections 'Throwing the Rascals Out' - democracy implies a continuing check on those in power.

In America the government (i.e. President) is elected separately from the legislature so different criteria have to be employed when discussing the American system in comparison to that of the UK, Germany or Israel. Congressional, State Legislature, Gubernatorial and Mayoral elections all use the simple-plurality system but these elections are all essentially local and the system works reasonably well at this level, particularly now that the Republicans are campaigning effectively in the South and it is no longer a one-party region. Congressmen are certainly more concerned with the views of their constituents than they are with the wishes of the party leadership, but this is because of the frequency of elections to the House of Representatives and the independence of Senators who do not regard themselves as 'party fodder'.

The concept of the 'mandate' has little relevance to American politics where the parties do not normally even campaign on distinct party programmes. The House Republicans in 1994 did campaign on a co-ordinated platform, the 'Contract with America'. but that was an exception. The American electoral system adds to, but is not entirely responsible for, the weakness of party ties and the parochialism of Congress.

If the political culture of a nation has a big impact on the way in which power is dispersed, so does the structure of government. The USA has a federal system. Each State has its own legislature and all except one State (Nebraska) have a bicameral Assembly. Each State has a Governor who heads the executive. Some States elect their judges, whose job it is to interpret State Law and the State constitution.

Thus, simply at State level, there are numerous elective positions. Some national politicians, such as Reagan, Carter, and Clinton made their names as Governors. Following the 2002 elections there are 30 Republican Governors, 19 Democrat and one Independent. There are Republican Governors in 8 of the 10 largest states.

Within each State, there are a variety of local Government units, each having a form of elected administration. They range from conurbations, such as New York or Los Angeles, down to New England townships. Vile points out that New England experiences the form of election closest to direct democracy in its township meetings. In contrast, a city such as New York has a nationally and internationally famous mayor, formerly Rudolph Giulliani. Thus local elections play a tremendously important role in the American political system. Even Clint Eastwood is interested, he was once the Mayor of Carmel in California. However, it is the national elections which grab the headlines.

Electing the President

To understand the complex process of electing a President it is best to divide the process up into two phases; the intra-party battle for the nomination which formally begins in February and ends in the summer and the inter-party contest between the rival tickets which lasts from September to November.

Primaries and Caucuses

A direct primary is an election, by secret ballot, to decide a party nominee. They were introduced in the early 20th century. A Presidential primary, sometimes called an indirect primary, does the same thing but via delegates who go to the national party Convention pledged to a particular candidate. The number of delegates per state broadly reflects the population of the state. A primary can be open to all registered voters or closed to all but registered party supporters. About two thirds of Americans are registered. All Democratic primaries use PR.

A caucus does much the same thing as a primary but through a series of meetings, town caucus to county caucus to state caucus, rather than an election. There is open voting and as it can take hours turn out is lower; rural states such as Alaska and Wyoming often hold caucuses because the cost of mounting a primary is prohibitive.

In most states both parties will use the same method, either a caucus or more likely a primary. In 1996 42 states held primaries, 18 of them open. It is the state legislature which decides its own rules for the intra-party contest and they change from election to election whereas the presidential contest itself is fought under national rules.

The advantage of having primaries and caucuses is that it extends democracy, voters choosing not just between parties but between candidates. The disadvantages are that the system is complex, often divisive, open to media manipulation and expensive. Much time and money is spent on the intra-party battle for the nomination. In 1992 candidates were limited to spending $27 million on the nomination campaign. Much of the money is spent on TV and Radio advertising, something not permissible in Britain. Candidates have to travel the length and breadth of the nation and make their name, image and policies known from Alaska to Alabama, California to Carolina, and this costs a great deal of money.

For the 2000 election the primary and caucus season officially began in early February with the Iowa caucus and in New Hampshire in late February with the first primary, but the jockeying for the position began long before. Candidates were out raising money and making themselves known in the States which elect large numbers of delegates to the national conventions. Carter started his bid for the 1976 race as soon as the 1972 election was over. Thus we have in effect the 'permanent campaign' or what Hadley calls the 'invisible primary'.

In 1996 the Democrats had the enormous advantage of the incumbent President as their candidate. This saved them money and energy. Clinton looked statesmanlike, while Dole et al slogged it out in a complex, bruising campaign. In the Republican primaries of 1996 Forbes, Alexander and Buchanan spent millions of dollars and still failed to get nominated. The Republicans wanted to get a clear winner as early as possible so the primaries were bunched together, March 9th the New England super primary covering 9 states, 13% of all Republican delegates, March 12th Super Tuesday 6 southern states with 18% of all Republican delegates, March 19th the mid-west primaries. 77% of the 1,970 Republican delegates were chosen by March 26th making the Republican Convention a formality. The last primaries were on June 4th. However Dole spent so much money fending off these challengers that he had relatively little left with which to fight Clinton.

The Republican primaries in 2000 saw Bush locked in a bitter battle with McCain, whilst Gore saw off Bradley relatively easily. Bush had the huge advantage of money. Already by autumn 1999 he had raised so much money that potential candidates such as Elizabeth Dole were deterred. In 2004 Bush will be unlikely to face a serious challenge for the Republican nomination, unless there is some political disaster discrediting his presidency. In contrast the Democrats will have to go through the whole process again. Gore has announced that he will not seek the nomination. Hillary Clinton is very unlikely to run as she has only been in the Senate since 2000. Other leading Democrats have decided to 'sit 2004 out' as Bush is currently so popular. However much the same was said in 1991 and yet Bush senior was defeated.

As of May 2003 the leading Democrat contenders are Senator John Edwards from North Carolina who has already raised over $7 million, Senator John Kerry the Vietnam war hero from Massachusetts, Richard Gephardt the Minority Leader in the House who is blamed for losses in the 2002 elections, Senator Joe Lieberman, the former Governor of Vermont Howard Dean, Senator Bob Graham from Florida, the Reverend Al Sharpton the civil rights leader and former Senator Carol Moseley Braun. Already the interparty battle has begun with Democrtas divided over the issue of Iraq. Inevitably the field will narrow as 2004 approaches

National Party Conventions

The party conventions are held in July/August every four years to decide on the Presidential nominations. The conventions, attended by delegates from the States, may require several ballots in order to decide on their nomination, though normally the first ballot is decisive. Prior to the ballots, hard bargaining will take place between the various factions but, once selected, the whole conference wholeheartedly support their choice, they will endorse his policies and enthusiastically applaud his acceptance speech. Similarly they endorse his choice of running mate. Gore chose Lieberman, the Chair of the Democratic Leadership Conference, a moderate. Bush chose the veteran Cheney.

Apart from actually selecting the ticket, the main role of the convention is to unite the party and generate confidence in the victor. The Republican platform in 2000 'Renewing America's Purpose; Together' was heavily influenced by the ideas of 'compassionate conservatism'.

If no clear winner emerges from the primaries and caucuses then the Convention would select a nominee. This is known as a brokered convention but it has not happened since 1952 with the Democrats taking three ballots to choose Stevenson. The 1976 Republican Convention and the 1980 Democrat Convention were both close because incumbent

Presidents faced challenges from disillusioned colleagues but in both cases won them. In 1924 the Democrats took 103 ballots to choose a candidate.

In 2000 Bush achieved the necessary number of 'pledged' delegates long before the Republican Convention met in Philadelphia in early August. He knew he had the majority of the 2,066 delegates needed to secure the nomination. The Democrat Convention in mid-August in L.A. involved 4,368 delegates, the largest number ever. Again Gore knew early on that he had the necessary majority.

The Conventions bring the first phase of the process to an end. By late August 2000, both parties had formally chosen their respective tickets. It had taken months and cost tens of millions of dollars, but the real contest had not yet even begun.

The General Election Campaign

Once Bush and Gore formally received the nominations of their parties then the General Election campaign began. This is always a relatively short phase - September to November - when compared with the intra-party battle, but still over twice as long as a British election campaign. The tickets have to criss cross America again spending vast sums of money in the process.

One criticism is that the campaign is often bland and negative. Image and personality count for much more than policy platforms or manifestos. The 1988 Presidential campaign was a largely uninspiring negative affair with both candidates lacking in charisma and falling to address policy issues. It was a scare campaign designed to put voters off, rather than a positive campaign based on constructive policies. Bush was especially vacuous, avoiding any policy commitments other than the negative one of 'no new taxes'. Bush ran against Dukakis, or rather his advisers' image of Dukakis , playing upon fears of the Democrat being soft on crime, rather than running on his own programme. The concept of 'attack politics', pioneered by Bush's advisers such as Lee Attwater, reached new levels with the Willie Horton 'revolving door' advertisement.

Dukakis failed to get over a coherent message and seemed to avoid anything identified with liberalism, until October when he suddenly started boasting that he was a liberal in the Roosevelt-Truman-Kennedy tradition. By then, it was too late.

The 1992 campaign was just as 'dirty' with Clinton's campaign for the nomination plagued by sex scandals and Bush trying to attack Clinton as a womanising, dope smoking (albeit non-inhaling) 'draft dodger'. Appearing on the Larry King show in October Bush suggested that Clinton had once been the pawn of the KGB, the ploy backfired. Spending in the 1992 race reached new heights with the intervention of a billionaire third party candidate, Perot, who was prepared to spend his own money on half hour 'infomercials'.

The 1996 election saw Doles campaign attempt to contrast the war hero with the man who failed to serve his country during the Vietnam war and who allowed gays into the military. The Clinton team portrayed Dole as too old - if elected he would have been the oldest President ever to take office - and out of touch. The 2000 campaign saw Bush attack Gore as too close to special interests, especially the unions. In return Gore claimed that Bush would favour the rich, the 'top 1% of the population' and business at the expense of 'ordinary Americans'. Bush claimed that Gore was too left wing, Gore claimed that Bush would destroy social security.

The TV Debates

The supposed highlight of the campaign are the televised debates between the tickets sponsored by the League of Women Voters. The first debate was in 1960 between Kennedy and Nixon. They are now rather too contrived, lacking in the spontaneous repartee of unscripted debate. In 1992 there were two debates involving the three Presidential candidates and one involving the running mates. It was rather uninspiring, indeed the only debate which appears to have much impact on the voters was the 1960 encounter.

The League threatened to withdraw its support unless the format was changed to allow for a more genuine contest so there was a single moderator and one of the debates was a town hall style meeting as in 1992.

The Israeli election of 1996 saw an American-influenced televised debate between Netanyahu and Peres which may well have swung votes towards the challenger and in such a tight election, about 1% of the vote separated the two, which could have been crucial. The US debates in 2000 were expected to be won by Gore as he had more political experience. However, Bush came over as down to earth, a regular guy, whilst Gore came over as patronising and as someone who exaggerated his own importance, as in his claiming to have coined the term 'information superhighway' years ago. Hence they became known as the 'sighs and lies' debates. In the UK in 2001 there was talk of a televised debate between Blair and Hague with Kennedy allowed to join in. It did not happen.

The Popular Vote
The election takes place on the first Tuesday after the first Monday in November every four years - 1992, 19960, 2000, 2004 and so on. In 2000 Gore won 48.4% of the votes to Bush's 47.9%, Nader 2.7% and Buchanan 0.42%.

The Electoral College

Officially the winner of the Presidential election is not known until the Electoral College votes on December 20th. The winner is not inaugurated until January. The gap used to be longer with the President being sworn in March, but it meant a five month 'lame duck' Presidency, for example when FDR defeated Hoover in 1932.

The men who wrote the constitution were wealthy, whites who wanted to avoid two things: they wanted to avoid a monarchy and the aristocracy that went with it. They also wanted to avoid democracy because to them it meant mob rule. What they wanted was oligarchy, rule by an elite of wealthy, white males such as themselves. Therefore, as Head of State, there would be a President elected not by the people, but by an Electoral College (EC).

The President is still elected by the Electoral College. Each state has a certain number of votes in the EC. The number is equal to that state's Congressional delegation, so that in 2000 California has 2 Senators and 52 Representatives, giving it a total of 54 Congressional delegates therefore,

California has 54 EC votes. Altogether, there are now 538 EC votes, because there are 100 Senators, 435 Representatives and Washington DC is given 3 EC votes. To win the White House, a candidate needs a majority of the EC, which is a minimum of 270 votes. In 2000 Bush won 271, Gore 266 and there was one faithless elector in Washington DC. Nader voters were asked who they would have voted for had Nader not stood. By a ratio of 50:20 they would have split Gore/Bush with the rest abstaining. This would probably have given Gore Florida and therefore the Presidency.

In 1787, the members of the EC genuinely exercised choice. However, from the 1830s onwards, ordinary white men got the vote. From the 1870s, some states gave white women the vote. In 1920, the constitution was amended (19th Amendment) to guarantee white women the vote.

The 1960s saw Southern blacks actually get the right to vote which they had supposedly gained 100 years earlier. Finally in 1970, the 26th Amendment gave 18 year olds the vote. Yet, the EC survives as the formal process by which the President is elected. The EC votes are cast by real people selected by the state legislatures; they are not Senators or Representatives - in fact they change every time. Today, the EC in each state is supposed to simply rubber stamp the popular vote in that state.

Problems with the EC

The system used to elect a president is 'unfair' in several respects.

1. Because of the principle of winner-takes-all (only two states, Maine and Nebraska excepted) the Electoral College magnifies the margin of victory as in 1984 when Reagan won 59% of the popular vote, compared with Mondale's 41%, but Reagan won 525 out of the 538 votes in the Electoral College.

    In 1992 Clinton won 43% of the popular vote, but with 32 States he was able to win 370 electoral college votes to Bush's 168. Clinton won a majority of the popular vote in only 4 states. In 1996 Clinton had less than half the votes but won 376 EC votes.

2. It is possible that no one gets a majority in the EC. If this happens, it goes to the House of Representatives. Each state delegation has one

vote which is undemocratic. It has not happened since 1824, but it could do if there were three serious candidates. It almost happened in 2000.

3.   It discriminates against third party candidates. In 1992 Perot with almost a fifth of the popular vote, the best third party performance since 1912, did not win a single Electoral College vote.

In 1968 White Southern Democrats broke away from the Democrat party in protest at LBJ (Democrat) giving Civil Rights to Southern Blacks. Their candidate was the former Democrat Governor of Alabama, George Wallace, a segregationist. He got 13.5% of the popular vote, 46 EC votes, because his supporters were regionally concentrated.

4.   It is possible that the winner of the popular vote will lose in the Electoral College, indeed this happened twice in the 19th century - 1876 and 1888. Famously it happened again in 2000.

5.   There is the problem of the 'faithless elector, a member of the Electoral College who casts his vote for someone other than the winner of the popular vote in his state, they are not legally bound to follow the popular vote. This has happened in several recent elections although it did not affect the overall outcome. In 1976, someone voted for Reagan even though he was not running. In 2000 there was one such elector. Had there been two more then possibly no one would have had a majority.

6.   It is possible to be elected President by winning the popular vote in the 12 most populated states: California with 54, New York 36, Texas 33, Pennsylvania 29, Florida 25 and so on. Gore came fairly closer to achieving this in 2000.

If there are so many problems with the EC then why keep it? Because it is in the Constitution, it would require a constitutional amendment to get rid of it. The states would be unlikely to vote for such an amendment because the existence of the EC is a reminder of the federal nature of US politics. There are a number of reform proposals, such as direct election through the popular vote or a bonus of 102 (two for each state plus the District of Columbia) electoral college votes for the winner of the popular vote.

However even the distorted result in 2000 did not provoke a serious attempt to reform the system.

Low Turn Out

Perhaps US elections are so frequent, complex and expensive that in the end they alienate the citizens. Turnout in Presidential elections has fallen to around 50% from 62.8% back in 1960. Thus, in the most election-conscious nation of all, only half of those entitled to, bother to vote for perhaps the most powerful politician on Earth. An international survey of turn out in national elections put the USA 23 out of a list of 24 countries. In the 1990s the federal government tried to assist voter registration but state law sometimes hampers this. The National Voter Registration Act of 1993, commonly known as the 'motor voter' law, obliged states to offer voter registration at facilities well used by the public such as driver's license and motor vehicle offices. Voter registration did increase but turn out has not. Of course it may have dropped even further had the law not been passed.

Turn out in mid-term elections is even lower. As Curtis Gans, a Democrat pollster, put it regarding the 1986 elections in which turn out was about 36%, 'Nobody can take pride in this election. If you read the results carefully, the score would be non-voters, 64.1% ,Democrats, 18.9%, Republicans, 17%. Gore Vidal argued that the split between those who do and those who do not vote is the real two party system in the USA.

Partly, non-voting is a consequence of a registration system which is more complex than in the UK and of a mobile society, but there are more important sociological reasons. One the whole it is the poorest, the least educated, those with most to gain from voting who do not bother to do so, perhaps because they are alienated by a political process that seems to favour the rich.

Finance in American Politics

According to Professor Herbert Alexander, spending in the 1980 American elections totalled $1.203 billion, of which almost half was spent on federal elections, $275 million, for the Presidential campaign, and $239 million for congressional races. By Alexander's estimates, campaign spending increased by 759% between 1952 (when it totalled $140 million) and 1980. General prices rose by just 210%.

Apparently Reagan's 1984 campaign cost $75 million with Mondale spending marginally less. Spending in the 1992 race reached new heights with the intervention of Perot who spent over $60 million of his own money as he chose not to receive federal funding. The bunching of the 1996 primaries into a seven week campaign increased the importance of funding as the money had to be spent early to have an effect. According to Alan Grant $3 billion was spent by presidential and congressional candidates in 2000, compared with $2.2 billion in 1996. A further billion was spent in 2000 on state campaigns.

It is not just presidential races which cost huge sums of money. It is estimated that the 1994 Senatorial contest in Virgina between Chuck Robb and Oliver North cost around $30 million. Republican Congressman Michael Huffington spent vast sums trying, unsuccessfully, to get a Senate seat in California. He spent $28 million, the Democrat incumbent Diane Feinstein spent $8million. These days even House elections can be incredibly expensive, an average campaign costs a challenger approximately $200,000 but incumbents spend almost $600,000. The 2000 election saw the most expensive House race ever, in a California district where the Republican James Rogan and the Democrat Adam Schiff between them spending $10 million.

Elizabeth Drew ('Politics and Money: The New Road To Corruption', 1982) claims that money is now so important to the American political system that it threatens to pervert democracy itself. "We have allowed the basic idea of our democratic process - representative government - to slip away". Other liberal critics, for example Bob Woodward and John Kenneth Galbraith, agree with her. As Galbraith put it in his 'The New Industrial State', "the group who pays the piper calls the tune".

The liberal pressure group Common Cause was formed in 1970 specifically to improve the democratic process by, for instance, curbing the ability of 'fat cats' to donate huge sums of money to selected, usually Republican, candidates.

Major changes were introduced in the 1970s but money is more important than ever and the unintended consequence of the campaign finance reforms has been to promote the spread of Political Action Committees (PACs). By the 1990s there were over 4,000 registered with the Federal Election Commission. A PAC is an organisation formed to support particular candidates or particular policies. They are often 'offshoots' from pressure groups, such as the National Rifle Association which has formed a PAC known as the NRA Institute for Legislative Action. During their campaign against Clinton's 1994 Crime Bill the NRA spent $70 million, about 10% of it targeting Democrats who had supported the ban on assault weapons. According to Clinton (speaking in 1995) 'the NRA is the reason the Republicans control the House'.

Concern over finance pre-dated Watergate; in fact it was provoked by the spread of television in the 1950s which immediately led to a big increase in campaign spending. There are no limits on the amount of advertising which candidates can buy, and in a nation as big as America, television is a very effective way of getting a political message across. By the 1960s, various states had taken the initiative and introduced curbs on campaign finance. The first federal legislation was introduced in 1971. However, it was the illegal activities of the pro-Nixon CREEP (the Committee to Re-Elect the President) with its 'slush funds' which gave a big impetus to the reform process. The outcry caused by the Watergate revelations led to the 1974 Federal Election Reform Act.

Parts of the 1974 law were declared unconstitutional by the Supreme Court in the case of Buckley v Valeo (1975). The law was seen as infringing the First Amendment which guarantees the right of free speech and therefore the right to support particular candidates.

As a result of this legislation and the interpretation by the Court, a highly complex system now governs the financing of federal elections. Individuals can give up to $1,000 to a candidate in each primary and up to $5,000 to individual PACs. Altogether individuals are allowed to contribute up to $25,000 annually to federal elections. The PAC's can donate $5,000 to a candidate per election, but there is no restriction on the number of candidates a PAC can support and therefore there is no ceiling on their total spending. There were no limits on an individual or PACs spending in support of a particular candidate, sometimes called **soft financing**. For example the notorious Willie Horton ad was actually paid for by a PAC not, directly, by the Bush campaign. In 1996 the Democrats benefited from the TUs spending money which as 'soft money' was unregulated.

Congressional candidates can spend as much as they can raise and there are no limits to how much a candidate can spend from personal funds. Obviously, richer candidates benefit from this, hence the criticism that only wealthy people can succeed in American politics.

The 1970s legislation also introduced a system of public funding for presidential elections. Thus America, the home of free enterprise, allows public subsidy for politicians, something which has always been rejected by the major parties in Britain, despite the Houghton report of 1976. Candidates in the primaries who have attracted a certain amount of financial backing are entitled to public subsidy.

However, once a candidate accepts federal funding, then they have to adhere to an overall spending limit, set at $27 million in 1992. This indicates the scale of expenditure even at this early stage in the electoral process.

In the general election between the two rival nominees both candidates are entitled to public funding of (in 1996) over $50 million each; however, if they accept, then they are not allowed to spend anything else. The whole intricate operation is overseen by the Federal Election Commission.

It is very difficult in a free society, especially America with its emphasis on freedom of expression, to place limits or ceilings on the amount that politicians can spend in their election campaigns. It is easier, but still difficult, to regulate contributions. In Britain, there are no limits on contributions but there are strict limits on what can be spent by candidates in each constituency. Yet there are no limits at all on what the parties can spend on national advertising, which obviously benefits their candidates at local level. The thing which has prevented the escalation of campaign spending to American levels is the ban on paid advertising on television and radio. Each major party In the U.K. is allowed a certain number of party political broadcasts on television, but they cannot supplement these with commercials. Also, the fact that Britain is a much smaller nation clearly means that spending is proportionately lower, although it is growing markedly.

Congress has examined the issue every year since 1987, although no one is seriously suggesting anything as radical as banning paid advertising. In 1993 Clinton proposed a reform of campaign financing but the eventual version ran foul of Republican opposition. In 1995 Clinton and Gingrich jointly suggested a non-partisan review of the issue but little came of this initiative. The 1996 elections saw a big increase in the use of soft money. Senators McCain and Feingold repeatedly tried to get reform through but were filibustered in the Senate.

McCain made the issue the centrepiece of his campaign in 2000. He described the system as 'legalised bribery and legalised extortion'. By March 2002 McCain and Feingold had pushed the Campaign Reform Act through but they had to accept a diluted version of their original bill. It doubled the limit on 'hard money' donation. The most important reform restricts the use of soft money in attacking opponents by name in attempts to cause political damage. It restricts the coordination of soft money campaigns directly with parties or candidates.

The reform was supported by Common Cause, the Sierra Club and the business group Campaign for America. It was opposed by the NRA and the US Chambers of Commerce. Reformers were aided by the collapse of Enron and the corruption it revealed. It is the biggest change in almost 30 years but has yet to be challenged in the courts and there are already loopholes.

US Voting
In the 1992 elections the Democrats won the Presidency for only the second time in almost a quarter of a century and at the same time the Democrats held on to their control of both Houses of Congress and the majority of state positions. Just four years earlier strategists and commentators such as Kevin Phillips had talked of a Republican grip on the White House as the population shifted away from the Democrat strongholds of the North and East towards the sun-belt states of the 'New South' and the West. The

Democrats had seemed incapable of finding a candidate who would reunite the party, bring back together the tattered remnants of the New Deal Coalition by simultaneously appealing to the white South, alert to any suggestion that the Democrats favoured positive discrimination, the labor movement, suspicious of any attempt to distance the party from the unions, the blacks who accounted for an increasing proportion of the Democratic vote and the neo-liberals, the moderates gathered in the Democratic Leadership Council who blamed Jackson and the left for alienating middle class, middle of the road America.

As late as 1991 it had looked a hopeless task. Bush was bathing in the warm glow of record popularity ratings having been the President who despatched Noriega, presided over the 'Velvet Revolutions' of Eastern Europe, had ejected Saddam, from Kuwait (albeit not from Iraq) had seen the Soviet Union (America's public enemy number one for at least half a century) implode, had been able to announce that the Cold War was over and that America had won it and would henceforth be running a New World Order. So dominant did Bush look that when it came to preparing primary campaigns for 1992 leading Democrats such as Gore, the then darling of the DLC, Cuomo and Bradley decided to sit this one out. Why risk future credibility by repeating the McGovern disaster of 1972 or the Mondale collapse of 1984?

Yet Bush's popularity proved to be ephemeral. The very things that had made him popular, foreign policy success, went on to make him vulnerable as, with the Cold War over, American opinion turned towards domestic politics. Clinton's campaign, organised by James Carville, adopted the slogan **'its the economy stupid'** as an indication that this election was going to be fought on domestic issues. It was the first election since 1936 not to be dominated by foreign policy.

Why Did Bush Lose the 1992 Election?

Bush had won the 1988 election on a purely negative mandate, attacking Dukakis' liberalism and proclaiming that he would not raise taxes. He tried the first tack again in 1992 on a superficially weak target, Clinton, and yet it failed to reverse his fortunes in the way that the Willie Horton issue had done in the late summer of 1988. As for taxes, Bush had raised them in 1990 to the fury of the New Right in the party who believed that by doing so he had betrayed the Reagan legacy. Meanwhile he had to contend with the America first, moral majority Buchananite insurgency which although it had little in common with the supply sider, free trading Kemp brigade meant that Bush had a fight on his hands even to win the nomination. To cap it all the 'Perotistas' having launched a campaign and then pulled out came back again to take votes away from both candidates but almost certainly predominantly from the incumbent. Any 'anti-politics as usual' campaign must damage an incumbent President more than an Arkansas Governor and Perot won almost 19% of the popular votes, a record third party performance

Clinton won 43% of the popular vote, 32 states plus DC, a total of 370 EC votes; Bush won 38%, 18 states, 168 EC votes. As with any election leading to the defeat of an incumbent that of November 1992 was a combination of a negative reaction to those in power and the positive appeal of the challenger.

The Republicans had held the White House for 12 years, firstly under the charismatic Reagan and then under what Peele calls the 'uninspiring presidency' of Bush who was lacking in what he called 'the vision thing.' Emmet Tyrell the editor of the right wing American Spectator argued that there had been a 'Conservative crack-up' partly because the glue of the Cold War which had held things together was no longer there but mostly because of domestic failures. The US voters rejected Bush in favour of Clinton's promise of change. Even on foreign policy, Bush's favourite terrain, the survival of Saddam was evidence that the job had been unfinished. The Republicans ran a poor campaign, trying to repeat the tactics of 1988.

Clinton had chosen a fellow southern white baby-boomer as his running mate. The all southern Democrat ticket managed to win Arkansas, Tennessee, Georgia and Louisiana. They still could not take Texas, Florida, Alabama, Mississippi, the Carolinas and Virginia. There was a pronounced gender gap which may have been due to the Hillary factor as well as concern over the tough anti-abortion stance taken by Bush. Clinton-Gore clearly appealed to younger voters, they had a 15 point lead among 18-24 year olds. Perot's intervention almost certainly helped Clinton. Peele concludes that the answer to the question 'why did Bush lose?' was that it really was 'the economy, stupid!'

Clinton won the lowest share of a winning candidate since Nixon in 1968. Nixon's first victory had also been in a three party race only there the maverick, Wallace, was able to take 46 Electoral College votes because his support was regionally concentrated. The narrowness of the winning popular vote margin is arguably utterly inconsequential. The Democrats had literally scraped home in 1960 but had won the next election by a landslide; the Republicans repeated this sequence after 1968 and when Clinton won in 1992 it was little comfort to Republicans to know that he had won the positive support of under one quarter of American adults.

Edward Ashbee wrote of the great Republican crack-up as the fragmented coalition which had sustained Reagan and then less enthusiastically Bush and had promoted talk of a Republican Realignment now seemed set to disintegrate. In the post-mortem which followed defeat liberal Republicans blamed Bush for succumbing to the hard right, particularly over abortion, at the 1992 Convention. They pointed to the growing gender gap as evidence of the repellant effects of limits on choice. The Buchananites talked of a cultural war in America and the laissez faire faction blamed tax increases, surrender to affirmative action demands with the reformulated Civil Rights Act and insufficient zeal when it came to cutting spending.

However just two years later in the mid-term elections of 1994 the Republicans won control of Congress for the first time in forty years and at the same time became the dominant party at state level. There can have been fewer more rapid or more complete turnarounds.

The Significance of the November 1994 Elections

Mid-term elections such as November 1994 do not involve the President but can have huge consequences for the White House because they determine which party controls Congress. The Democrats controlled the Senate from 1954 to 1980 when several liberal Senators such as McGovern were defeated by New Right supporters, riding on Reagan's "coat tails".

Twelve new Republican Senators were elected in that year, often by very narrow margins.The Democrats regained control in 1986.

In the 1994 elections 35 Senate seats were being contested, 9 of them open because of retirement. All the open seats were won by Republicans and two incumbent Democrats lost. Republicans were then boosted by the defection of Senator Shelby from Alabama. This gave the Republicans a majority of 53 to 47. In the House they won a majority of 230 to 204 with one Independent.

To simply recite the 1994 results does not do justice to the political implications of the earthquake. It is not enough to dismiss them as a mid-term protest vote, or to focus on the low turn out. The party which controls the Executive expect to lose seats at mid-term elections, as had happened in 1990, 1986, 1982 and 1978 and turn out is often as low as 35% but they do not expect mid-term elections to so completely alter the political landscape. Even the Republicans were taken aback by the size of their victories and the status of some of the scalps they'd taken; Tom Foley, the Speaker of the House, Dan Rostenkowksi the Democrat Chairman of the House Rules Committee and the consummate deal fixer, Jim Sasser the Democrat Senator who had been tipped to become the new Senate Majority Leader.

It was just as bad at state level. Anne Richards the Governor of Texas who had given a keynote speech at the 1992 Democratic Conference, had been a success as Governor and was widely seen as a rising Democrat star, and perhaps most surprisingly of all the long time liberal Democratic Governor of New York, Mario Cuomo who had been tipped for so long as the great hope of the liberal wing of the Democratic Party.

The coat tails effect is when a President helps his party in Congressional elections; perhaps November 1994 was a case of Clinton's negative coat tails. However such elections can be deceptive as guides to the next Presidential contest. In 1986 there was a bigger than expected triumph for the Democrats but the Republican Bush still won in 1988. The turn out in the November 1994 election was very low, about 35%, and it may be unwise to read too much into it, Clinton still won in 1996.

This can all be seen at two different levels, the short term and the long term. The defeat of any incumbent, even Congressmen and Senators must be a product of two things, dissatisfaction with those in power and a willingness to believe that the opposition will do better. On the surface the 1994 results were a negative verdict on Democrat incumbents. Had the mood simply been one of anti-Washington, throwing the rascals out, the massacre of incumbents would have included Republicans but it did not. There was an anti-government mood but only directed at 'the governing party'. Clinton was a target, hence some of the Democrats attempts at distancing themselves from him. However some of those Democratic Leadership Council figures who had disagreed with him over health care on the grounds that his plan was too dirigiste were themselves defeated. It cannot have been 'the economy, stupid' as the economy was actually growing relatively well from very late 1992 onwards. Even in 1992 it was the perception of economic performance rather than the reality of it which was fatal for Bush. In 1994 the voters may well have been punishing Clinton and the Democrats for failing to deliver the change which they had promised in 1992.

Voters appeared willing to trust what had in effect been the minority party in Congress, off and on, since 1930 to do better. Exit polls show that only about one fifth of voters had actually heard of the House Republicans 'Contract With America' and as Gary Wills has shown the Contract itself was a standard product of committee compromise, anxious to avoid anything too provocative it said nothing about abortion or school prayer. The target group had been the Perot supporters and much of the emphasis had been on getting taxes, spending and the deficit down whilst reforming the political elite and making the streets safe. Policy specifics matter less than voter perception and whilst Gingrich's talk of a Republican revolution was always self-aggrandising rhetoric even Clinton was forced to accept a change in the political balance of power and already by Christmas 1994 was sounding like a Republican with talk of a tax cut for the middle class. By January 1996 Clinton was announcing that the era of big government is over and Republicans were left complaining that he sounded like Reagan.

It is easy as Gary Wills has shown to predict and then describe the collapse of Congressional Republican unity as the Dole-led Senate proved unable or unwilling to implement the revolution with the passion of King Newt's followers. Actually before long the Gingrich freshmen zealots were themselves becoming disillusioned with the stuttering performance of their leader for example over the Christmas 1995 Budget deal when Gingrich was outmanoeuvred by Clinton. Such are the necessary compromises of power when the former 'bombthrower' becomes the third in line to the President.

Similarly despite the hype about the 'Contract with America', the 1994 mid-term elections were essentially fought on local issues; there was no dominant national issue such as there had been in 1982 when the 'Reagan recession' caused a swing against the Republicans, or 1974 when the reaction to Watergate dominated the campaign.

Jeanne Kirkpatrick points out that when an American party departs from the consensus, as in 1964 and 1972, the voters 'punish' them and the party returns to the centre. In 1964 the Republican candidate Goldwater proposed a more right wing brand of Conservatism. In 1972 the Democrats chose the 'liberal' McGovern. Both of them lost heavily. In 1980, Reagan campaigned on policies very similar to those proposed by Goldwater in 1964, but by then the New Right had grown in strength and the once unfashionable free market philosophies had become the new orthodoxy. These were the only post-war Presidential elections in which there were major ideological differences between the candidates.

What is really important though is the longer term perspective and here conservatives such as Kevin Phillips and Andrew Sullivan are better guides than Democrats such as Elizabeth Drew or Gary Wills.

The 'Solid South' began to break up as early as the 1960s. White Southerners continued to vote Democrat in Congressional and State elections, but voted Republican in Presidential elections that is they 'split their ticket'. The Voting Rights Act of 1965, which finally enfranchised Southern Negroes, and the growing industrialisation of the South, part of the 'Sunbelt', did much to transform the region. By the 1970s, states such as Texas were electing Republicans to Congress, something which had not happened since the 1860s. In the 1994 mid-term elections, the majority of white Southerners voted Republican.

The defection of the White South to the Republicans since 1968 has been the biggest electoral shift in the USA in the 20th century. It helps to explain why the Republicans have won five out of the last eight presidential elections. The only time the Democrats have won since 1968 was with Carter in 1976 and Clinton in 1992 and 1996. Carter's victory can be explained by the reaction to Watergate and the fact that Carter was a White Southerner as is Clinton. 1996 saw the party retain power against a candidate. The problem is that it is extremely difficult for the Democrats to recreate the old coalition and appeal simultaneously to both ethnic minorities and the white South. The blacks and the Jews have come into conflict over 'positive discrimination'. Millions of US trade unionists, life-long supporters of the Democrats, voted for Reagan in 1980 and 1984 and to a lesser extent Bush in 1992 just as in Britain there was a shift of C2s to the Conservatives post-1979.

There was much talk in the early 1980s of a **Republican realignment**, talk of 1980 as being 1932 in reverse. In 1980, Reagan defeated the incumbent by 10 points in the popular vote. At the same time the Republicans took control of the Senate, for the first time since 1954. The Republicans held control of the Senate in 1982, despite the recession. In 1984, Reagan won an even greater landslide and the Republicans did not lose the Senate until 1986. In 1988, Bush won a decisive victory. Many people argue that Reagan dismantled the 'New Deal' comparable with Thatcher's dismantling of the consensus after 1979. Certainly US public opinion shifted to the right over recent decades.

However, by 1988, the evidence for a realignment looked unconvincing. Reagan's 1980 victory was really a rejection of Carter rather than a positive endorsement of 'Reaganism'. The Republican capture of the Senate in 1980 was an example of the 'coat tails effect' and they lost it in 1986. Reagan's re-election in 1984 was very much a personal victory. Bush's victory in 1988 might also be seen as Reagan's third victory and Bush was to survive for just one term.

Both Phillips and Sullivan remind us that the roots of the Republican realignment lie in 1968 when Nixon adopted a southern strategy to capitalise on the white South's disillusionment with the Democrats. At virtually every election since then the Republicans have made inroads into what was the Solid South. These days the white South is almost as solidly Republican as it was once solidly Democrat. In 1992 an all Southern Democrat ticket still could not take the two biggest Southern prizes (Texas and Florida) and in 1994 the Governorship of Texas went to one of Bush's sons.

The 1996 election results confirmed Clinton's extreme unpopularity with white Southern men but the more significant development is the growing racial polarity of American politics and the fact that whoever won the 1996 Presidential election would have to take cognisance of the taxpayers' rebellion first identified with the succession of Proposition 178 in California in 1978 and confirmed with Proposition 187 again in California in 1994. Voters are rejecting government solutions at the same time as they are penalising government for failing to find or implement answers to the problems. The USA is bouncing back economically and holding the challenge of the Tiger economies and deindustrialisation at bay but the success of the Buchanan forces in 1996 shows that downsizing and falling real incomes produce populist led resentment.

Epstein argues that parties are neither in revival or decline, they are simply changing. They are adapting to the post-war changes in American society, such as the spread of TV and the enormous impact that has had on politics; the improvement in educational levels resulting in a more politically literate electorate displaying partisan dealignment and less willing to vote out of 'tribal loyalty'; the process of suburbanisation which has broken up the old residential areas, the neighbourhoods where people were socialised; the growing force of new social movements such as feminism and so on. In other words, parties are shaped by the social environment in which they operate.

Although this process may have gone further in the USA, it certainly applies in Britain too. Most recent studies of voting patterns show an increase in the number of people voting 'instrumentally', out of perceived self interest rather than because that is the way they and their parents and friends have always voted.

The USA has not been immune to the same forces of suburbanisation, decline of class allegiances, changed nature of work, collapse of traditional labour movements and class and partisan dealignment which have occurred in other industrial democracies. They produce an electorate which has lost its traditional moorings and which is willing to turn to untried outsiders. Berlusconi in Italy, Perot and Buchanan (a pretend outsider in that all of his adult life has been spent 'inside the beltway') in the USA. Only this can explain the bewildering volatility which has seen the incumbent Bush go from record popularity in 1991 to defeat in 1992, the incumbent Clinton humbled within two years and yet two years later able to win again.

 What is and what should be the main function of an electoral system?

The November 2000 Presidential Election

The Presidential election of November 2000 was without doubt one of the most controversial of all time and will remain of interest to students of politics for along time to come. The Vice President, Al Gore, was the clear favourite to win at a time when the economy was still booming and the country was at peace. However, after a lacklustre campaign Gore was defeated in the Electoral College by Governor Bush, a man of limited political experience, with no apparent interest in or knowledge of foreign policy. The result was only arrived at after the intervention of the Supreme Court, in a judgment that remains very contentious. Gore thus became the first person since 1888 to lose the Presidency whilst winning the Popular Vote. To understand why Gore lost and Bush won it is necessary to look at key stages of the contest - the primaries, the general election campaign, the workings of the Electoral College and the role of the Supreme Court.

One of the reasons why Gore was assumed to be in a stronger position than Bush was that Gore had an easier primary campaign. Gore had easily defeated his rival Democrat, Bill Bradley whilst Bush had initially struggled against Senator John McCain. Gore's early triumph meant that he could conserve energy and funds for the campaign proper whilst Bush still had to concentrate on securing his party's nomination. McCain did very well in those states, which held open primaries thereby allowing

Democrats and Independents to participate in the Republican race. Once the campaign moved on to states which held closed primaries then the support of the Republican faithful, aided by his huge spending allowed Bush to win the necessary number of delegates. However the bitterness of the Republican race had left a sour taste, with McCain alienated and with Gore able to depict Bush as an 'extremist' because he had curried support from the hard line religious right.

Bush went on to prove Nixon's famous insight that the Republican nomination is won by swinging to the right but the general election campaign is won by moving back to the centre. Both candidates made what were seen as good choices of running mate. Gore chose the orthodox Jew Senator Joe Lieberman. He had been the first Democrat to break ranks and publicly criticize Clinton over the Lewinsky affair. This defused that particular legacy of the Clinton years. Bush chose former Defence Secretary Dick Cheney, someone who could compensate for Bush's lack of expertise over defence/foreign policy issues. By the time the national conventions were over in August Gore was still ahead in the polls and it was believed that the more experienced and intellectual Vice President would outperform Bush in the televised debates. In fact Gore came over as patronising and aloof and over the three debates Bush was felt to have done better. A perception was building that Bush was straight and solid and that he could be trusted more than Gore, a man who seemed to have shifted his political position too often.

One major problem for Gore was that he seemed unsure how to relate his candidacy to the Clinton years. On the one hand Gore wanted to associate him with the prosperity of the Clinton boom, the longest in American history. On the other hand he wanted to distance himself from the scandals of the administration. The results were that Clinton was rarely mentioned and was not allowed to campaign for Gore directly until very late in the day. Interestingly Democrats fighting the 20002 elections faced the same dilemma. Gore also had to contend with the candidacy of the veteran activist Ralph Nader running as a Green. Although Nader polled fewer than 3% of the votes it was enough to take crucial states away from Gore. There was a breakaway candidate of the right, Pat Buchanan running for the Reform Party, but he attracted little interest. It is a measure of how poorly Gore campaigned that he even lost in his home state - Tennessee.

Despite this Gore did win the popular vote. However it may be that this was because Republican voters in the Western states did not go out to vote once the TV networks had 'called' the election for Gore. In a sense this is irrelevant because what determines the result is the Electoral College vote not the Popular Vote. This is why Florida became so important; whoever had won the popular vote there would take all 25 of the Electoral College votes and thereby win the Whiter House. That is why all the attention switched to alleged irregularities in that state. Over a year later the media announced that had all the votes been recounted in Florida then Gore would have won. At the time attention centered on the Supreme Court, as it had to decide whether to allow manual recounting in certain counties. The Bush lawyers argued that this was a national election therefore federal Law must be paramount. This is an unusual position for Republicans who normally support states rights. The Gore lawyers argued that electoral law should be a state concern, again an unusual position for Democrats. The judges ruled by 5 to 4, the tightest decision possible, that federal law prevailed over state law on this issue.

There have of course been controversial elections before - 1824 when the House of Representatives had to decide, 1876 and 1888 when the winner of the Popular Vote lost in the Electoral College; 1948 and 1968 when there were racist breakaways from the Democratic Party and 1960 and 1976 when the Popular Vote was extremely close. However at no other election since the US had become a proper democracy had the winning' candidate 'lost' the election. There was some talk of changing the system and in particular the Electoral College. However there are major difficulties with reforming or abolishing the College. It would require a constitutional amendment and this is extremely unlikely to happen given that the College means the states play an important role in choosing the President and particularly as most of them are Republican controlled. In the event the catastrophe of September 11th swept away concern over the election result.

Direct Democracy

Referendums

A referendum is a test of public opinion. Citizens are asked their views on a particular issue. This can happen at local level as in the referendum on a directly elected Mayor for London; or at 'regional' level as in the devolution referendums in Scotland and Wales or at national level as in the 1975 referendum on whether the UK should stay in what was then called the European Community. Given that Parliament is legally sovereign then referendums cannot be binding. However it is inconceivable that Parliament could ignore the result of a referendum.

Referendums can be seen as a form of direct democracy in that the people themselves are asked their views. There had been four referendums held in the UK before 1997 - two on devolution for Scotland and Wales, one on the status of Northern Ireland and the European referendum of 1975. So far there have been four major referendums under Blair - two on devolution, one on the Good Friday Peace Agreement for Northern Ireland and the London Mayoral referendum as well as a host of minor referendums on local issues. A referendum had been promised on the Jenkins Report but it never materialised. At some point there will be a referendum on whether the pound should join the Euro.

There are various arguments in favour of referendums. They extend democracy by directly involving citizens in decision making which could be particularly important in an era of declining turn out and declining party membership. If, as Mandelson suggests, representative democracy is no longer engaging the public then direct democracy becomes necessary. They focus attention on particular issues which is not always possible in an election campaign. The 1997 election involved a whole range of issues whilst the subsequent devolution referendums were focussed on just that issue. They provide an additional mandate which could be said to be particularly important if the constitution is being reformed. Labour won the 1997 election by a landslide and the anti-devolution Conservatives lost all the seats in Scotland and Wales. Even so the devolution referendums gave Labour additional legitimacy for its policies especially for Scotland where the yes votes - 74% to a Scottish Parliament and 64% to it having tax varying powers - were so high. They help educate citizens on important issues. A referendum campaign on the Euro will address all the key aspects of the debate. They provide a channel for the expression of opinion on issues over which the main parties are united. No major party at the 1992 election opposed Maastricht so a referendum would have clarified the arguments. They help resolve issues where the main parties are internally divided as in the case of Labour and Europe in 1975.

Attlee famously described referendums as 'alien to our traditions.' There are also various arguments against. Referendums undermine representative democracy because MPs are elected to make decisions on behalf of the citizens. It would be better if those MPs made decisions on complex issues such as the Euro. They undermine the sovereignty of Parliament because Parliament would find it politically very difficult to ignore their outcome. They could be said to undermine collective responsibility as in the 1975 European referendum. They benefit the side with most resources as was obvious in the 1975 European referendum. This may have been addressed by the 2000 legislation although it will be interesting to see how this works in practice. They are manipulated by the government which holds referendums at a time and on issues of its choosing. Why was there a referendum on a Mayor for London but not on the more important issue of reforming the Lords? Why, as the Conservatives are asking, was there a referendum in Hartlepool on creating a Mayor when there will not be a national referendum on the report of the European Constitutional Commission? In 1979 almost 64% of Scots voted in the devolution referendum and of this almost 52% voted in favour. However because the yes vote was under 40% of the Scottish electorate devolution did not happen. If such a 40% rule applied to general elections it would render the current government illegitimate.

The Government broke its promise to hold a referendum on the Jenkins Report which shows that governments hold referendums when it is convenient to them. They may turn into a protest vote against an unpopular government rather than a considered view on a key issue. This is what appears to happen with by-elections, local council elections and European elections so it could easily happen with referendums. They may not generate a high turn out as in the case of the London Mayor referendum - 34% turn out - and the Welsh devolution referendums of 1997

- 50% turn out. In Wales only 50.3% of those who voted voted yes, about 25% of Welsh adults. This is a lower proportion than that favouring devolution in Scotland in 1979 and yet it was enough to see devolution introduced. This provokes questions concerning the legitimacy of Welsh devolution. They may expose the limitations of the public's knowledge of and interest in technical issues such as the Euro. If even professional economists disagree about the Euro how are ordinary voters supposed to reach a rational decision? They may also fail to give a definitive answer. The 1975 European referendum was supposed to resolve doubts about Britain's future in Europe but it failed to do so.

It could be argued that referendums used sparingly provide a useful supplement to representative democracy but used too frequently they become a threat to it.

Initiatives and Propositions
Direct democracy in the USA exists at state level rather than national level. It takes the form of propositions, initiatives and recall elections. Popular initiatives are measures that are placed on the ballot after a sufficient number of signatures have been gathered. The rules concerning initiatives vary state by state but they have increased in frequency since the 1970s. Term limits have been passed in every state that has the popular initiative and in only one without. Sometimes a reform is passed as an amendment to the state constitution, sometimes as a normal statute.

However such measures can be overturned by the courts. In the case from 2000 California Democratic Party v Jones the court struck down California's use of the blanket primary in which all voters can participate regardless of party affiliation. The Act had been passed as a result of a voter initiative.

The most famous Proposition was Proposition 13 held in California in 1978 resulting in a ceiling on taxes. Proposition 184 in California created a mandatory 25 year sentence for those convicted of a serious felony for the third time - the so-called 'three strikes and your out' rule. In 1994 Californians voted for proposition 87 denying non-emergency state benefits to illegal immigrants. In 1996 Californians supported proposition 209 ending state support for affirmative action. In the 2000 elections there were 242 propositions in 42 states. People in Alaska and Colorado voted against legalising marijuana, California and Michigan against school vouchers, Nebraska and Nevada against same sex marriages. In the 2002 elections various states again held referendums and sometimes these involved considerable numbers of people. For example in Florida two amendments, on class size reduction and on indoor smoking restrictions, each involved about five million people voting.

There are problems with such measures as there are with any form of direct democracy. For example they can be hijacked by pressure groups, they can be poorly drafted and they can work to the disadvantage of minorities. However there are also advantages such as stimulating interest in politics, helping to counter special interest and giving people a chance to make decisions.

Chapter Nine

Chapter 10
Central-Local
Relations

Introduction

As de Tocqueville said over 150 years ago 'the strengths of free peoples resides in the local community. Without such local institutions a nation may give itself free government but it has not got the spirit of liberty.' In the 20th century all states whether federal or unitary, capitalist or communist, saw a centralisation of power. We can simplify the difficult topic of centre-local relations by conceiving of three different models.

Unitary States	**Federal States**	**Confederate States**
All legal power flows from one source; in the UK - Parliament, in Israel - the Knesset	Power is shared between different tiers of government the Federal or national government and the State governments in the USA and Australia, and Lander in Germany	The regional authorities eg the Swiss Cantons hold most of the power; the central government is weak
Local authorities are legally entirely subordinate to the centre eg the GLC was abolished and the poll tax introduced by Parliament	The regional bodies have rights which are guaranteed; eg, in the US Constitution by the 10th Amendment	The 13 states that fought the War of Independence against the British formed themselves into a Confederacy through the Articles of Confederation of 1781
Devolution is compatible with a unitary system eg 1920-1972 Northern Ireland had a devolved Assembly based in Belfast known as Stormont	The Federal government deals with issues of national importance such as defence, foreign policy	The 11 Southern states which seceded in 1861 formed themselves into a Confederacy
Thus Scotland and Wales will have devolution and yet remain within a unitary UK	States sometimes claim to be federal, but in reality centralise power such as the USSR	The CIS, formed in 1991 after the break up of the USSR
	In genuinely federal systems such as the USA, Germany and Australia there is also local government, the form of which varies enormously	
	The Federal government's role in regulating local government within the USA is marginal	

A unitary state is one in which all legal power flows from one source, in which the local authorities derive their power from the central government and therefore can have their powers curtailed by the national authorities. Federalism is a system of government in which power is divided between a national or central government and regional, provincial or state governments. Generally speaking, the larger a nation is, in terms of area or population, the greater the chance of it being a federal state because this seems the best way to accommodate regional diversity. Australia, India, Canada and Brazil are cases in point. However, this is not always so, Switzerland, a small nation, has an advanced form of federalism known as a Confederation whereby the Cantons have more power than the central government. Conversely, many vast nations such as Sudan, the biggest nation in Africa, are very centralised states. A nation's history, just as much as its geography, help shape its political culture and the governmental arrangements.

Federalism is a very contentious concept, no two federal systems are identical. There are, in fact, various forms of federalism and clearly some variants differ markedly from that of the USA. The former Soviet Union was supposedly federal but it was actually one of the most centralised states on Earth. It is possible that post-Saddam Iraq will adopt a federal from. This would allow the Kurds of the north to continue to have autonomy as would the Shia dominated south and the predominantly Sunni centre.

The USA and the UK

The USA has a Federal system of government which contrasts markedly with the unitary nature of the British state. The American Constitution gives certain guarantees to the 50 states, most importantly that a state cannot be abolished without a constitutional amendment which requires the approval of two thirds of Congress and three quarters of the states. Clearly the states are never going to vote for the abolition of, say, California. In the UK local authorities are entirely subordinate to the wishes of Westminster which is itself dominated by the government of the day. For example, the Greater London Council was set up in 1963 by the then Conservative government only to be abolished in 1986 by the

Thatcher government. The Stormont Parliament in Northern Ireland set up in 1920 was abolished in 1972 when 'Direct Rule' was introduced. Following the Northern Ireland Agreement of April 1998 devolution was re-introduced.

The United States was the first major nation in the modern world to adopt federalism and it still has very important practical consequences. For instance, there is no state income tax in Connecticut, certain states such as Nevada have legalised prostitution, some states such as California allow the death penalty, some states have extremely strict restrictions on abortion, the speed limit varies from state to state and so on. Given the size of the USA (it is 3,000 miles from Los Angeles to New York, the same distance as New York to Liverpool) and the varied ethnic/racial/religious mix of its inhabitants, then it is not surprising that there is enormous regional diversity.

Federalism, which allows for a decentralisation of power, is thus an appropriate system of government for what Kennedy described as a 'nation of immigrants'. Dennenberg emphasises the parochialism of much of American politics. After all to many Americans, Washington can be a very distant place let alone Paris, London, Moscow. The American media reflect this parochialism with their concentration on local issues often to the exclusion of more important national and international problems.

The United Kingdom is, in comparison with the USA, a small nation, less than 800 miles from the northern tip of Scotland down to Cornwall, and it is still a relatively homogeneous society. The ethnic minorities are heavily concentrated in certain cities especially London, Birmingham, Liverpool, Manchester, Leicester, Leeds, Coventry and Bristol but they account for just 7% of the total population. Apart from Northern Ireland (and to a much lesser extent Glasgow and Liverpool) religion long ago ceased to provide a major political cleavage. Unlike the US, where local and regional newspapers predominate, the British press is national and also most of the regional press is owned by the national chains, such as NIC. Again unlike America, television and radio operate as national concerns although there are some regional organisations.

Although regional variations persist in the UK, especially through variety in local accents, the nation and its system of politics are effectively centralised. Perhaps only France of comparable European nations is more centralised than Britain. In the past the assumption was that Labour was the party of centralisation as it tried to iron out regional inequalities. Yet the last Conservative government centralised power further through its reforms of local authority finance, the educational system and so on. In opposition both major parties have claimed to favour decentralisation, in government they have both taken away local autonomy. Only the Liberal party can claim to have consistently supported regional self-government, devolution and decentralisation.

America has not been immune to the forces of centralisation despite the Federal system. Republican Presidents such as Nixon and Reagan have tried to slow down or even reverse this process of centralisation. Reagan was somewhat more successful than Nixon in this aim because the political climate of the 1980s favoured retrenchment. The Thatcher government tried to cut public spending by reducing the powers of local authorities, Reagan tried to do so by increasing the power and responsibilities of the states, the difference is due to the existence of federalism in the USA.

Federalism has survived in a modified form in America, indeed the federal system has perhaps been healthier since the late 1980s, the era of deregulation, tax reform and of New Federalism, than it was in the 1970s. There is talk of a revived federalism, although McKay for one is sceptical stressing that there can be no return to the limited government of the pre-1933 period. Again it is important to emphasise that centralisation of political and economic power is a world-wide 20th century phenomenon, not restricted to the USA and Western Europe. Reagan's 'the government is not the solution, it is the problem' rhetoric was never going to reverse the powerful tendencies favouring a centralisation of power. The American political culture has been heavily influenced by the decentralised nature of American society, from the 'frontier mentality' of the 19th century to the anti-Washington mood of the late C20th.

The unity and homogeneity of the United Kingdom was once regarded as a positive characteristic. However, in the 1980s and 1990s, with talk of the North-South divide, and with Scotland and Wales diverging politically from England, not to mention the chronic problem of Ulster, there was much discussion of the need for a devolution of power.

Devolution, or what used to be described as Home Rule, refers to a granting of limited autonomy to the nations, e.g. Scotland or regions such as Cornwall within the United Kingdom. It is neither novel, Northern Ireland had devolution from 1920 to 1972 when the Assembly at Stormont was abolished nor incompatible with the sovereignty of Parliament as the return of Direct Rule to Ulster in 1972 indicates. It could well be that in the C21st there will be both a decentralisation of power down to Assemblies in Scotland, Wales and Northern Ireland and a movement of power upwards to supranational bodies such as the EU.

There is currently much talk of the principle of **subsidiarity**, whereby decisions should be taken at the lowest possible level of government; in other words, if a Scottish Parliament was capable of resolving purely Scottish issues then this would combine the two desiderata of efficiency and accountability.

At the 1992 election, the Conservatives won just eleven out of 72 seats in Scotland and thereby arguably lost the vital but intangible asset of legitimacy. In these circumstances, demands for an independent Scotland - totally different to devolution - were bound to grow. At the 1997 election the Conservatives were wiped out in Scotland and Wales. In this sense, it is failure to grant devolution, not devolution itself, which is a greater threat to the union.

There is no possibility of the United Kingdom becoming an American style federal state but there is a growing demand for some local autonomy, hence the move towards directly elected Mayors. Labour have re-introduced an elected body for London in the form of the Greater London Authority working alongside a directly elected Mayor. Democratic Audit is sceptical about the degree of democracy this entails. 'The example of the London Authority which has had a highly unpopular Private Finance Initiative system for the Tube's redevelopment imposed from the centre despite its statutory responsibility for transport does not encourage any optimism about the degree of autonomy English regional government will enjoy.'

Membership of the European Union raises questions about the nature of the British state. Eurosceptics argue that their aim is to avoid the creation of a Federal European superstate. Major insisted that the 'f' word was not used in the Maastricht Treaty. However a federal system such as the USA does not actually allow for a very strong central authority, the states retain powers. If there is a likely model for the EU it is surely the Confederate system whereby the regions, or in this case nation states, have more power than the central authority. Running through the debates about the EU is the question of subsidiarity, that is to say what is the proper level of government at which to reach decisions, what is the appropriate devolution of powers.

Local Government in the UK

Introduction

Commentators such as Bernard Crick argue that the Tory governments after 1979 effectively turned local government into the servant of the centre and have robbed it of any real autonomy. This is one reason why they appeared so blase about their complete electoral collapse in local government after 1992. When the Conservatives came to office in 1979 the majority of local authorities were controlled by the Tories, by the mid-1990s they were the third party of local government. The 1992 local elections were held just four weeks after the general election and the Conservatives did extremely well, their highest share of the vote in any set of local elections since 1977, but by 1993 they were being given what Major called a 'bloody nose' and in local government were in what Clarke called a 'dreadful hole'. Subsequent local elections were even more disastrous for the Conservative Party. By 1993 they controlled only one shire council, Buckinghamshire. In the 1995 local elections the Tories lost nearly half the approximately 2,000 seats they were defending and retained control of only 8 councils. Labour now controlled 155 councils. The 1996 results were almost as bad, there were now lots of councils without a single Tory councillor. They began a minor recovery in 1997 which has continued now that Labour is in power centrally. The spring 2003 local elections saw the

Conservatives do relatively well and this eased the pressure on Smith's leadership.

The Role of Local Government

John Stewart points out the enormity of the changes in local government which have been introduced since 1979. The first two terms were dominated by the financial issue and by the abolition of seven councils. After the 1987 election the government began a radical reshaping of what remained of local government. Between 1979 and 1989 50 pieces of legislation affecting local government were put through Parliament. The changes affected its finance, structure and, above all, its role. Kingdom stresses that the new right public choice view that the frontiers of the state must be rolled back applied to local government as much as central. 'The Economist' accepts that central power has grown but believes that the drive is genuinely towards market and consumer power.

Before 1979 the councils were seen as agencies for the delivery of a series of services within its allotted scope. Their role was clear and undisputed: normally, given a job to do, the council itself did it. Its own employees ran bus services, cleaned streets, mowed parks, taught in schools, built and maintained houses etc. The third Thatcher term saw the government attempt to turn the councils **from service providers to service enablers** with service subject to more market mechanisms through compulsory competitive tendering. The push began with the Local Government Act of 1980 but intensified with the Local Government Act of 1988 which brought compulsory tendering to certain services and provided for its extension to others. The change inside councils and their workforces, facing the choice 'compete or close' has been dramatic. Work practices have tightened, manning levels have fallen. Compulsory competitive tendering is changing the entire climate of council services.

Education is the local authorities costliest single service, about 47% of all local authority expenditure is on education. The 1988 Baker Act means that councils have lost control of schools that have opted out and they have ceded control of the polytechnics, now the new universities, to the centre. A national curriculum has been imposed for the first time in British history.

Councils have lost representation on health authorities as health service trusts are established. There have been similar changes to training with the emergence of Training and Development Councils and the police, in both cases local authorities have had their role reduced.

The first, giant step was housing where the 1980 law gave council tenants the right to buy their homes. Around 1million, a fifth of the nation's stock, have been sold whilst council building was cut to virtually zero. The Housing Act of 1988 led to the setting up of Housing Associations which have taken over much of the control over local housing. Approved private-sector landlords such as Housing Associations have the right (if tenants agreed) to buy council houses, blocks or entire estates. A few councils transferred most or all of their stock to friendly Associations staffed by ex-employees.

Council rents have been forced up to the levels that would be set by the market. In 1981 'urban development corporations' were set up for London's decaying docklands and Merseyside. They can act as local planning authorities. In 1987-88 eight more were created in other cities. These UDCs are centrally financed, and their boards are centrally appointed but they are supposed to bring together private firms and local authorities. The early UDCs were fiercely opposed by the councils who had lost power to them, but most have chosen to work with the recent UDCs. In 1985 bus deregulation put private buses on the streets and required council buses to act commercially. Thus the GLC lost control of London's buses and tubes, yet another QUANGO - the London Regional Transport Board - was appointed separately to run them.

The result of all of these changes is a system where local policies and overall spending are set largely by central government; the citizen is heard more as a customer than a voter and local councils, instead of providing services, increasingly act as enablers and regulators of the services provided by others and often charged to users on near-market terms.

Is the UK now a QUANGOCRACY?

According to critics such as Stewart the government by taking control away from democratically elected politicians and giving it to Quasi

Auonomous Non-Governmental Organisations has created a **'new magistracy'**, a non-elected elite. In May 1994 Charter 88 and the Democratic Audit produced a report claiming that the true number of QUANGOs is over 5,000 and that they were responsible for about one third of all public spendng and employed about 70,000 people. Their members were predominantly white men often with links to the Tory Party.

Labour claimed that they would reform the 'quangocracy' established since 1979. The Conservatives rejected the figures and the accusations of a democratic deficit and of a patronage state. According to Waldegrave the number of QUANGOs had fallen since Thatcher came to power, from over 2,000 in 1979 to about 1,400. These do not count Executive Agencies, TECs, Health Service Trusts, opted out schools or housing associations as QUANGOs. This is one of the problems with the debate, there is no precision over the terms. Nolan's first report in May 1995 argued that all appointments to QUANGOs should be on merit and that there should be a Public Appointments Commissioner to monitor the process.

According to Democratic Audit 'Labour has made genuine moves to reinvigorate local government by promoting service quality, public consultation and partnership with the voluntary and private sectors, but Ministers continue to intervene heavily in local council affairs. It is hardly surprising that formal citizen participation as voters and candidates for election has continued to decline as a consequence.'

Their rather depressing conclusion is that 'local government in England is tightly controlled from the centre, lacking any financial independence and having suffered almost continuous reorganisation and upheaval by successive governments over 25 years. Unelected QUANGOS have supplanted local councils in many areas of governance and service delivery.'

Perhaps the introduction of proportional representation in local council elections would change things?

Devolution

What is devolution

Devolution is a process whereby a certain degree of power is handed, or devolved, downwards. In the case of the United Kingdom this involves the Westminster Parliament devolving a certain amount of power to a Parliament in Scotland and to Assemblies in Wales and Northern Ireland. The process could be taken further by establishing devolved bodies *within* England such as an Assembly for the North East or the South West of England. Devolution is emphatically not the same as independence. The Westminster Parliament has created a Scottish Parliament for the first time since 1707. However legally the Westminster Parliament remains sovereign and could abolish the Scottish Parliament. This may become increasingly unlikely as time goes on and the Scottish Parliament becomes politically entrenched. However there is a precedent. In 1920 Westminster created the Stormont Parliament for Ulster but in 1972 it was abolished. Of course Northern Ireland is in many ways untypical of the rest of British politics and the example is unlikely to be repeated.

Devolution is also not the same as federalism. In a federal system such as the USA the central government shares power with the states. The arrangements in the USA are guaranteed by the codified constitution, particularly the 10th Amendment. This means that the federal government in Washington DC could not just abolish, for example, the state of California. In a unitary state such as the UK all legal power flows from one source, the Westminster Parliament. However it could be argued that devolution is creating a quasi-federal system of government.

The Powers of the Scottish Parliament

Reserverd Powers	Areas not reserved
(not devolved)	(responsibility of the Scottish Parliament)
Common market for UK goods and services	Agriculture, fisheries and forestry
Constitution of the UK	Economic Development
Defence and national security	Education
Employment legislation	Environment
Fiscal, economic and monetary system	Health
Foreign policy, including Europe	Housing
Health (in some areas); medicine	Law and home affairs
Media and culture	Local government
Professional regulations (in certain	Research and Statistics
Protection of borders	Social work
Social Security	Training
Transport safety and regulation	Transport

Blair once stated that the Scottish Parliament would only have as much power as a parish council. At the same time the Blairites made sure that the first Minister in Wales was the Blairite Alun Michael rather than the left winger Rhodri Morgan.

What do the Main Political Parties Think About Devolution?

All the mainstream parties support devolution in Northern Ireland because it involves power sharing and that is seen as the best way forward for the peace process there. However, elsewhere devolution provokes controversy. The Liberal Democrats and the Labour Party both support devolution. They argue that it is more democratic because it gives people more control over their own affairs. In so doing it helps reduce the centralisation for which the British political system has become famous. Elective dictatorship is less likely to happen if power is decentralised. These parties also believe that devolution will produce more efficient government because local people know better than distant bureaucrats what is needed in their area. Even though the UK is not a particularly big country there are still important regional differences and what works best in one part of the country will not necessarily work well elsewhere. Most importantly the left argue that if devolution is not conceded then demands for independence will grow. Throughout the 1980s the Scots and the Welsh consistently rejected the Conservatives and yet had to subject to being governed by them. If they were not allowed some degree of autonomy then they may have turned to the separatists, the SNP and PC, who want an independent Scotland and Wales. In the meantime these nationalist parties work with devolution in the hope that it will eventually lead to independence.

The Conservatives reject all these arguments. They believe that there is no appetite for an extra layer of government which will simply lead to more bureaucracy, more spending and therefore more taxation. Turn out in elections is falling and the idea that creating new elective bodies will necessarily extend democracy and increase participation is simplistic. Far from improving efficiency it may well lead to uneven standards of provision and provoke resentment. If taxes are higher in for example Scotland than England this will impact on where people choose to live. Most importantly the Conservatives believe that devolution is unfair to England. The English comprise 85% of the population of the UK, but are the only people without a Parliament of their own. This leads to the infamous West Lothian question posed by the Labour MP for that constituency, the anti-devolution Scot Tam Dalyell. How can it be right that he can vote at Westminster on matters affecting the English but on some of those same issues he cannot vote in regards to Scotland because these matters are decided by the Scottish Parliament? The logical answer to this question is to have an English Parliament. However this would in effect mark the acceptance that the UK is federal so it is opposed by the Conservatives. Thus their argument is that devolution is dangerous and may ultimately lead to the break up of the UK.

What Has Been the Impact of Devolution?

In relation to Scotland and Wales Devolution is still only four years old and it is too soon to tell what the impact will be. The very early stages of devolution were marked by rows over interference by the Blairites who wanted to control the Scottish and Welsh Labour Parties and impose their people as leaders. The Blairites did not want Rhodri Morgan so they 'imposed' Alan Michaels. However these could be dismissed as teething troubles. Eventually Morgan did become leader and has proven to be highly competetent. There were also minor scandals over expenses, which led to the resignation of Henry McLeish as First Minister, and other issues such as the cost of the new parliament building. Again though these had little to do with devolution as such and can occur in any political system. However an interim verdict would suggest that devolution has been neither a disaster nor a complete success. The Scottish Parliament has not changed the rate of income tax as it has the power to do. It has made controversial decisions on fox hunting, on free nursing care for the elderly and on tuition fees for undergraduates but although important issues none of them is likely to convince people that devolution is going to transform British politics.

The Welsh Assembly does not have as much power as the Scottish Parliament and the Welsh have not shown anything like the same enthusiasm for devolution. However it has been argued that the Welsh Assembly as asserted itself. The Lib-Lab coalition in Wales scrapped school league tables, testing for 7 year olds, introduced free school milk and said no to foundation hospitals.

So far the English have not appeared to particularly resent the absence of devolution for England there certainly does not appear to be an irresistible demand for an English Parliament. Only English MPs sit on Select Committees dealing with specifically English affairs. Robert Hazell has argued that Westminster is developing into 'a quasi federal parliament, with an English 'parliament' nesting within it.' So far English nationalism appears confined to the red cross of England flag at football matches. However none of this should suggest that devolution is not important. In the long run it will undoubtedly alter the constitutional arrangements of the United Kingdom in ways that we cannot currently predict. The second set of devolution elections took place in May 2003. Of course like everything else the devolution elections had been overshadowed by the war with Iraq and received very little coverage. The turn out was relatively low so it may not be wise to read too much into the results. However in Wales Labour was able to scrape into power on their own whilst in Scotland it was again the biggest party but without an overall majority. There was a swing against the nationalist parties in both Scotland and Wales.

It will take time to work through the full impact of devolution and to know whether it really does extend democracy, increase efficiency and offer the best hope of preserving the union as its supporters claim. Whilst groups such as Charter 88 urge devolution, Nationalists in Scotland such as Jim Sillars, supported by the Greens, are demanding independence within the EU. In the 1970s, Tom Nairn talked of 'the break up of Britain'; perhaps that will be more likely in the twenty first century. All of this is taking place against a backdrop of an enlarged and increasingly unified EU. It will be interesting to see if the next decade sees trends towards Federalism within Europe combined with national autonomy in the UK. As Democratic Audit put it 'the Northern Ireland Secretary's decision to suspend the province's Assembly within its first 18 months shows where power ultimately lies in the event of a breakdown of the Belfast Agreement.'

Chapter Ten

The USA

Federalism and a separation of powers are the twin pillars of the 1787 Constitution even though the document itself does not mention the word federalism. Madison said that 'the Federal constitution forms a happy combination ... the great and the aggregate interests being referred to the national, and the local and particular to the state governments'. However federalism has inevitably been modified as the American Republic has developed. Federalism was the Founding Fathers' pragmatic response to the divergent demands of the original thirteen states. It represented a compromise between the Hamiltonian notion of a centralised, unitary state and the Jeffersonian concept of a confederacy where the central government would be subordinate to the states. Jefferson's **nullifaction doctrine** argued that 'whensoever the General Government assumes undelegated powers its acts are unauthoritative, void and of no force'.

The framers were very conscious of the fact that their system was an experiment and the chances of the nation remaining intact as it developed into a continental power were debatable. Now that so many nations - for example, Nigeria, Australia, Canada, Germany and Brazil - have a federal system, it is important to remember how revolutionary such an arrangement was in the eighteenth century. This was an era of unitary states and of vast empires governed from metropolitan centres in Europe. The novelty of the Philadelphia compromise lay in the autonomy and discretion which was accorded to the individual states. The Tenth Amendment, part of the Bill of Rights ratified in 1791, states that "the powers not delegated to the United States are reserved to the States respectively, or to the people".

At that time, the assumption was that the Federal government in Washington would play a rather restricted role, concerning itself with defence, a national currency and arbitration of inter-state conflicts. The states themselves would develop as "semi-sovereign nations" free for the most part of central government interference.

The Federalists

The first party system emerged as a result of disputes over the respective powers of the states and the federal government; Federalists emphasised the primacy of the central government Democratic-Republicans stressed states rights. In Article I(S.8) of the Constitution, Congress is given power to 'regulate commerce with foreign nations and among the several states' The Supreme Court under Chief Justice John Marshall (1800-1835) gave a fairly liberal interpretation to this clause in cases such as Gibbons v Ogden. It also established in Fletcher v Peck that the Federal Supreme Court could invalidate a state law and McCullogh v Maryland established the implied power of Congress to set up a Federal bank.

Dual Federalism 1835-1937

Dual federalism, sometimes known as 'layer cake federalism', existed for most of the 19th century, especially the period when Roger Taney was Chief Justice of the Supreme Court, from 1835 to 1864. It presupposed a clear division of responsibilities between the central government in Washington and the State governments, a conservative view of federal government emphasising Article 1 Section 8 and the 10th Amendment. As James Bryce put it 'two governments, covering the same ground, yet distinct and separate in their action'. Taney objected to what he saw as the usurpation by Washington, encouraged by the Marshall Court of powers that rightly belonged to the States, hence the fateful decision in the Dred Scott case of 1857 which helped provoke the Civil War.

Any lingering doubts as to the viability of federalism were dispelled by the victory of the North in the Civil War of 1861 to 1865, the greatest test the American nation has faced because what was at stake was the survival of the Union. Lincoln was prepared to tolerate slavery in the South provided the 11 rebel states renounced the Confederacy and returned to the Union. Indeed, after the end of Reconstruction in 1877, the South was allowed to introduce segregation despite the clear intention of the 14th Amendment.

With the New Deal the Federal government stepped in to provide the system of welfare and interventionist policies which the poorer, often more conservative states had opposed. The wealthier states, such as New York, under Governor Roosevelt, had already began experimenting with interventionist policies even before 1933. The New Deal meant an extension of such policies across the nation. In 1929 the Federal government had accounted for just 25% of all government spending. The Supreme Court had taken a more conservative view of the inter-state commerce clause from the mid-19th century to the 1930s and blocked attempts by Congress to regulate wages, conditions of work etc. The Schechter case saw the Court rule the NRA unconstitutional on the grounds that it interfered with intra-state commerce. After 1937 though the Court stopped blocking Federal government intervention, the turning point was NLRB v Jones and Laughlin. The era of Dual Federalism gave way to Co-operative Federalism.

Co-operative Federalism 1937-1963

Co-operative or concurrent federalism sees the states and the Federal government as part of the same governmental system and therefore expected to work together. It implies an activist view of federal government. The prime motivation was economic rather than political; states were given various forms of aid but few strings were attached, apart from categoric grants which provided for particular programmes, but states retained a great deal of discretion on how the funds were to be spent. No attempt was made to exchange federal subsidy for political influence over, for example, education policies.

Creative Federalism 1963-1969

States rights survived the great depression of the 1930s but they succumbed to the "Great Society" programme of the 1960s. Johnson's polices initiated a new phase of state-Washington relations which Johnson himself termed "creative federalism'. This time the motivation was political and the central government insisted on certain national standards, for example non-discrimination in Federal government contracts and in education and housing, upheld by the Warren Court. The Voting Rights Act of 1965 introduced Federal policing of elections to prevent intimidation.

The Inter-state Commerce Clause was significant in that it was sufficiently vague to allow for much greater Congressional regulation of the economy so that all businesses even remotely affecting 'inter-state trade' had prices, wages, insurance, transport, etc. regulated by Congress; hence 'Ollie's Burger Bar' case (Katzenbach v McLung 1964). The clause may have been consistent with nineteenth century conditions, which allowed private enterprise to operate virtually unregulated, but in a modern twentieth century economy there is far more need for central government intervention and Congressional regulation.

As MacKay points out, this form of federalism, which he describes as "redistributive centralism", survived Nixon's attempt to return powers to the states because Congress and the majority of state governments remained under the control of the Democrats.

New Federalism 1969 Onwards

The "New Federalism" as expounded by both Nixon and Reagan presupposed that the states want greater responsibilities and powers. In reality, the states are often reluctant to assume the extra financial burdens which decentralisation imposes. In the more austere economic climate that has prevailed since the 1970s, the states and the cities often need all the help they can get from Washington. Thus when New York City went bankrupt in 1975, it had to be bailed out by the Federal government. As part of Nixon's New Federalism the % of Federal grants which were categorical as opposed to block went down from 98% to 75%, i.e. there was greater freedom for states to decide how to spend the money. Revenue sharing was largely blocked by a Congress reluctant to give up financial control, only $6 billion got through. Congressional hesitancy was matched by bureaucratic and interest group opposition.

The success of Proposition 13 in California in 1978 indicated the shift in the political climate. Reagan cleverly exploited the 'anti-big government' mood to gain support for his New Federalism proposals which implied a return to a more dualist view. As with so many of Reagan's initiatives, Carter had already begun the process of giving more latitude to the states, Reagan simply took the policy much further. Between 1978 and 1988 federal grants were cut by 25%. In 1981 83 categorical grants were to be combined into 6 major types of block grant, there was to be a weakening of Federal regulations.

Reagan argued in 1981 that **'all of us need to be reminded that it was not the Federal government that created the states, it was the states that created the Federal government'**.

Executive Order 12291 of 1981 began the process of promoting cost effective federal regulations. He would have preferred (in areas such as education) to have extricated the federal government altogether, but Congress prevented this. Reagan's policy owed as much to a desire to cut the Federal deficit as it did to any notion of the proper nature of Federalism. It is of course, more acceptable politically to argue in favour of returning to the states powers and responsibilities which are rightfully theirs, than it is to admit the need to devolve the financial burden on to states, which are themselves often not in a position to shoulder it. The richer states of the South West with their broad tax-base can presumably afford to administer welfare programmes, but the depressed states of the North and Mid-West cannot take on extra commitments.

Many of Reagan's more radical plans, such as swapping the three main welfare programmes so that the states would fund Aid For Dependent Children and Foodstamps and the Federal government would fund Medicaid and the phasing out of federal grants were not implemented. At the same time the court was not supporting the states as in the Garcia judgement of 1985. Yet there have been cuts and, as Palmer and Sawhill point out Reagan's 1981 budget "Challenged many of the principles governing social policy... of growing federal responsibility for social welfare". Reagan "greatly slowed a 50 year trend towards a larger, more intrusive federal government". It is in this sense that the election of Reagan can be seen as the end of the New Deal.

The Clinton Presidency also saw a strengthening of the role of the states particularly over welfare. The welfare reform bill ended the federal government's guarantee to provide welfare to low income mothers and children which had been in effect since the New Deal. The programme was turned into a block grant to the states giving them discretion over eligibility and the level of benefits. By 1994 most Governors were Republican and they pushed for a stronger role for the states. By 1995 the National Governors Association was holding a federalism summit. When Dole became Majority Leader of the Senate in 1995 he stated 'if I have one goal for the 104th Congress it is this; that we will *dust off the Tenth Amendment and restore it to its rightful place in our Constitution.*' The Rehnquist Court has supported this move through cases such as Lopez. In 1997 the court struck down the 1993 Religious Freedom Restoration Act because it interfered with states rights. As Alan Grant puts it 'through these decisions the Supreme Court sent a signal to Congress that there are now constitutional limits in place on federal power in a way that has not been seen since the New Deal era.'

George W Bush, himself a former Governor, calls himself a 'faithful friend of federalism'. Former Wisconsin Governor Tommy Thompson who had pioneered welfare reform and Christine Whitman formerly Governor of New Jersey are in the Bush Administration. The man given responsibility for Homeland Security is former Governor Tom Ridge.

Conclusion

The USA is still a federal nation but the nature of federalism not surprisingly changes over time, as economic and political conditions alter. Federal government spending is now 67% of all government spending, there is now a federal drinking age - 21 - and the Federal government is able to set wages and working conditions for state and local employees as the Garcia case of 1985 showed. Despite the centrifugal tendencies of the post-New Deal era, the USA is decentralised to an extent unimaginable in the former "federal" USSR or in highly centralised France or United Kingdom.

Writing in 1978, the year in which Federal aid to the states reached its peak, Leon Epstein argued that American state governments remain strong and important elements in the federal system. 20 years later after the effects of Reagan's New Federalism, the states and the federal government are, according to McKay, "interdependent". The political parties remain, despite the increased centralisation of recent years, essentially state wide organisations and the Electoral College continues to give states a role in the election of the only nationally elected politician, the President. In 1993 the states and local government spent between them just over I billion dollars, almost as much as the Federal budget.

There are 82,290 forms of local government in the USA, of which 3,041 are counties, 19,076 are municipalities, 16,734 are townships and 43, 439 are school districts or special districts. It is best to remember that there are 50 policy programmes not just one. As King points out the Federal and state governments are interlinked in a variety of ways, fiscal, judicial regulatory and partisan.

Hence Grozdins argues that the layer cake description was never accurate and should be replaced by a marble cake. In reality and to the chagrin of the proponents of "states rights" there has been a long term tendency for the autonomy of the states to be eroded as American politics becomes increasingly "nationalised". This has led some commentators to believe that the USA is now Federal in name only, that it is a disguised "unitary" system. Just as the executive branch of government has developed at the expense of the legislature, so it should not be surprising that the states have had to cede authority to the central government. This may well continue under Bush because big business wants national unifdorm standards not diversity. Bush wants more control over education and in some areas his moral agenda conflicts with state autonomy. The war against terror may also work against further devolution as will a recession. It is though clearly an exaggeration to say that **'The USA is a unitary system in disguise'**.

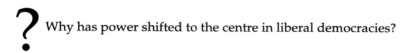 Why has power shifted to the centre in liberal democracies?

American Federalism in Practice

Powers of the States

They have their own constitution and laws interpreted by their own courts/Supreme Court

They can set their own tax levels and therefore have financial autonomy

They can block an amendment to the Constitution

The 10th Amendment guarantees their rights; the reserved powers include regulating their own commerce, running elections. Much welfare spending is the responsibility of the states, they spend almost 6 times as much as the Federal government on education

The states and local authorities employed over 15 million people in 1992

Constraints on their Powers

The Supremacy Clause of the Constitution means that Federal law and the Federal Constitution are supreme

Much of their revenue comes from Federal grants; in 1991 they amounted to $154 million, 25% of state and local authority income. Categorical grants are particularly restrictive

The Supreme Court through Judicial Review can limit their constitutional rights

The 14th Amendment has increased Federal power

The Constitution prevents the States from granting titles, making Treaties, issuing a currency

Chapter Ten

Further Reading

An introductory book such as this can only skim the surface. To probe the issues more deeply it is recommended that students look at some of the following.

On the **UK** there are of course dozens of good texts but I would particularly recommend the following;

'The Democratic Audit of the UK' The University of Essex

'The Hidden Wiring' Peter Hennessy (Gollanz, 1995)

'The Constitution in Flux' Philip Norton (Martin Robertson, 1982)

'British Politics in Focus' edited by David Roberts et al (Causeway, 1995)

On the **USA** I have made most use of

'The American Political Process' Alan Grant

'American Politics and Society' by David McKay (Blackwell, the 3rd edition 1993)

'Developments in American Politics 2' by G Peele et al (Macmillan, 1994)

On **Comparative Government** there is relatively little at the right level, two reasonably comprehensive texts are

'Modern Politics and Government' by Alan Ball (Macmillan, 1993)

'Comparative Government and Politics' by Hague, Harrop and Breslin (Macmillan, 1994)

Further Recommended Reading

There is lots of useful and accessible information to be found in *Talking Politics* published by the Politics Association, and *Politics Review* and *Modern History Review* published by Philip Allan.

At a higher level of difficulty but still well worth looking at are the following magazines.

The Economist - comes out weekly and has excellent coverage of politics in the UK and USA. Has a very 'free market' perspective.

New Statesman and Society - again a weekly but less weighty and written from a left of centre point of view.

The London Review of Books - a left of centre fortnightly.

The New York Review of Books - a fortnightly magazine which, not surprisingly is particularly good on the USA. Again a liberal perspective.

Prospect - a relatively new monthly magazine which has attracted excellent writers, mostly, but not exclusively, from a left of centre viewpoint.

To keep up to date with a rapidly changing situation it is useful to consult the annual 'Politics Pal' by Lynton Robins and Anthony Bennet's regular update on 'American Government and Politics'.

The Internet

There is a wealth of material available on the Internet and 'Grassroots', the publication of the Politics Association, provides web addresses.